PREPARING TO USE TECHNOLOGY

A Practical Guide to Curriculum Integration

SECOND EDITION

Blanche W. O'Bannon
The University of Tennessee

Kathleen Puckett
Arizona State University

PEARSON

Boston   New York   San Francisco
Mexico City   Montreal   Toronto   London   Madrid   Munich   Paris
Hong Kong   Singapore   Tokyo   Cape Town   Sydney

Acquisitions Editor: *Kelly Villella Canton*
Series Editorial Assistant: *Annalea Manalili*
Vice President, Marketing and Sales Strategies: *Emily Williams Knight*
Vice President, Director of Marketing: *Quinn Perkson*
Senior Marketing Manager: *Darcy Betts*
Production Editor: *Annette Joseph*
Editorial Production Service: *Publishers' Design and Production Services, Inc.*
Manufacturing Buyer: *Megan Cochran*
Electronic Composition: *Publishers' Design and Production Services, Inc.*
Interior Design: *Publishers' Design and Production Services, Inc.*
Cover Designer: *Elena Sidorova*

For related titles and support materials, visit our online catalog at www.pearsonhighered.com.

Between the time website information is gathered and then published, it is not unusual for some sites to have closed. Also, the transcription of URLs can result in typographical errors. The publisher would appreciate notification where these errors occur so that they may be corrected in subsequent editions.

Library of Congress Cataloging-in-Publication Data
O'Bannon, Blanche W.
   Preparing to use technology : a practical guide to curriculum integration / Blanche W. O'Bannon. — 2nd ed.
      p. cm.
   Includes bibliographical references and index.
   ISBN-13: 978-0-13-508421-2 (alk. paper)
   ISBN-10: 0-13-508421-0 (alk. paper)
1. Computer-assisted instruction—United States. 2. Internet in education—United States. 3. Educational technology—United States.
I. Puckett, Kathleen. II. Title.
   LB1028.5.O2 2010
   371.33'4 dc22   2009023699

Printed in the United States of America

10 9 8 7 6 5 4 3 2 1   B-R   13 12 11 10 09

www.pearsonhighered.com

ISBN-10: 0-13-508421-0
ISBN-13: 978-0-13-508421-2

Dedication

It is with pleasure that we dedicate the second edition of
Preparing to Use Technology to Dr. Lynn C. Cagle, Associate Dean and
Director of the Graduate School of Education in the College of Education, Health,
and Human Sciences at The University of Tennessee. His vision, leadership, and
mentoring have been instrumental in the integration of technology into teacher
education programs at The University of Tennessee.

About the Authors

Blanche W. O'Bannon is an Associate Professor of Educational Technology in the Department of Theory and Practice in Teacher Education at the University of Tennessee in Knoxville, Tennessee. Along with teaching graduate courses to practicing teachers, she serves as the Coordinator of the core technology course that is required for all students who are seeking a teaching license. Her focus, since coming to UT in 2000, has been to align the core technology course with national technology standards and develop new teachers who are capable of integrating technology into the curriculum to support instruction. You can review her vita, courses, and other resources at her web site at **www.pearsonhighered.com/obannon2e**.

Kathleen Puckett, an Associate Professor in the College of Teacher Education and Leadership at Arizona State University, has had a long and productive career in special education as a teacher, administrator, and teacher educator. Her research and writing has focused on technology applications for students with special needs. She is a co-author with William Brozo of *Supporting Content Area Literacy with Technology* (2009, Allyn & Bacon). Dr. Puckett served on the board of International Society for Technology in Education's Special Education Technology Special Interest Group (ISTE SETSIG) and was the 2009 president of the Council for Exceptional Children.

Contents

SECTION II USING RESEARCH AND COMMUNICATION TOOLS TO ENHANCE LEARNING

 The Internet   96

 Word Processing   129

SECTION III USING VISUAL LEARNING TOOLS TO ENHANCE LEARNING

Web Authoring   248

Preface

Preparing to Use Technology: A Practical Guide to Curriculum Integration, Second Edition, provides teachers with a foundation for technology practice within the real world of students, classrooms, schools, and curriculum demands. This book builds an understanding of the role of technology in teaching and learning and presents methods for using technology to enhance the curriculum. It provides a framework for prospective and practicing teachers to use as they develop technology skills for use in K–12 classrooms.

We wrote this book because of our interest in integrating technology in classroom practice. We understood the excitement and the motivation that technology provides to student learning, but were well aware of the frustrations and the fear that teachers felt when attempting to use it on a daily basis in classroom settings. We saw firsthand how simple technology adaptations could reduce barriers to learning for students with diverse academic or other special needs. Our goal was to develop a text that was concise and filled with useful classroom examples and encouragement for supporting the learning of all students. *Preparing to Use Technology* is based on our experiences over two decades as teachers, teacher educators, and avid users of technology in our teaching.

New to This Edition

This second edition updates technology tools and includes a discussion of new Web 2.0 and open source applications. Other revisions, including increased assessment coverage in Chapter 1 addressing what role technology has to play in assessment in today's classroom environment and reference to the revision of Bloom's taxonomy, are based on feedback from users of the book in university teacher preparation classes. We include new voices of exemplary teachers who tell their stories of technology joys and lessons learned as well as updated Curriculum Connections "mini-lessons" in this revised book.

Preparing to Use Technology continues to stress the development of students with 21st century technology skills that are used to create, collaborate, and communicate. The content is referenced to standards that guide our practice in teacher preparation: the newly revised National Educational Technology Standards for Teachers (NETS·T), the Interstate New Teacher Assessment and Support

Consortium (INTASC) Standards, and standards that satisfy the technology integration requirements of accreditation bodies, such as the National Council for Accreditation in Teacher Education (NCATE). In every chapter, we challenge teachers to consider the possibilities of technology use for students with special needs. Features that enhance learning and can be used for academic supports are highlighted.

We hope that aspiring general educators, special educators, teachers of English language learners, and school technology providers will use this information as a springboard for their emerging professional practice.

Special Features of This Text

- **Learning objectives and an alignment with the newly revised National Technology Standards for Teachers (NETS·T 2008)** begin each chapter.
- Each chapter begins with **Frameworks**, which highlights research findings and lays a foundation on which students can begin their study.
- Connecting to enthusiastic technology-using teachers is made possible in **Voices from the Classroom** as teachers of different grade levels and curriculum areas share their experiences and offer advice and tips for making technology work with students.
- **Curriculum Connections** provide brief synopses of curriculum-based lessons that have been implemented in K–12 classrooms. Links to additional information or to the full lesson are provided as well.
- **Adapting for Special Learners** is highlighted in each chapter and presents specific methods for using technology tools as a support for exceptional learners.
- **On the Web** provides an annotated list of popular web sites of particular importance to the chapter topic. Linking directly to these sites is made possible through the *On the Web* virtual site located at the companion site of the book at **www.pearsonhighered.com/obannon2e**.
- Each chapter of the text ends with **Hands-on Activities for Learning**, which are specific to the chapter topics and suggest activities that give learners hands-on experience in integrating technology into their curricula.

The Organization of the Book

Our book is organized into five major sections to provide a logical way to divide the learning.

Section I: Preparing to Use Technology

Chapters 1–4 introduce learners to core knowledge needed for the integration of technology and curriculum. Structures that facilitate technology integration are presented, including preparing for the challenges that exceptional learners bring to the classroom. Overviews of hardware and software tools recommended for K–12 environments are discussed, along with purchasing considerations (with an emphasis on assistive software). The section ends with a close look at professional teaching portfolios, their importance, and the advantages and disadvantages of going digital.

Section II: Using Research and Communication Tools to Enhance Learning

Chapters 5 and 6 discuss the ways that technology tools can be used to locate, evaluate, and use information. This section also addresses the means that students can use to construct, collaborate, and communicate in virtual environments. These chapters focus on using the Internet, including Web 2.0 tools, and word processing in learning environments.

Section III: Using Visual Learning Tools to Enhance Learning

Chapters 7 and 8 discuss tools that are available to facilitate the use of visual learning. Both commercial titles as well as Web-based solutions are suggested. These chapters present the versatility of using digital images in the classroom and highlight the ways that teachers can use them to implement active student learning and plan projects that align learning with curriculum standards. New Web-based tools that allow the sharing of digital images through photo sharing are presented. Other tools that facilitate and inspire student learning and creativity are addressed in the context of classroom practice. Strategies and supports for students with special needs are offered throughout.

Section IV: Using Problem-Solving Tools to Enhance Learning

Chapters 9 and 10 look at the use of databases and spreadsheets for solving authentic problems. Students are shown how to construct databases and interactive spreadsheets using familiar classroom examples and activities. Web-based tools for database and spreadsheet construction, collaboration, and problem solving are shared.

Section V: Using Multimedia Authoring Tools to Enhance Learning

Chapters 11 and 12 introduce multimedia and Web authoring tools. These chapters (favorites of our students!) explore ways to incorporate multimedia slideshows, digital stories, and podcasts. The value of these strategies are presented as well as the design of classroom web sites that can be used in professional practice.

Obviously, technology is a moving target with newer, more powerful, and smaller tools being developed and introduced to the market on a regular basis. In addition, Web-based options that provide free opportunities for students to work in collaborative virtual environments with 24/7 accessibility are expanding daily. We will continue to revise and to provide current links and updated information for instructors through our companion web site, as discussed in the next section.

Supplements

Companion Web Site

This text has a closely correlated web site developed by the authors (www .pearsonhighered.com/obannon2e) that includes the following resources for instructions and their students:

- directions for projects that can be revised by the instructor
- sample rubrics for each project that can be revised by the instructor

- artifacts created and kindly provided by preservice teachers at the University of Tennessee
- annotated resources in the On the Web section of the online guide
- slideshows that are aligned with each chapter and can be used for lectures and/or review by students that can be revised by the instructor (in PPT format)

Instructor Manual/Test Bank

This resource, containing ideas and information for instructors and a bank of test questions organized by chapter to be used for tests and quizzes, is available for download from the password-protected Instructor Resource Center (IRC) at **www.pearsonhighered.com/educator/profile/ircHomeTab.page**. There you will be able to log in or complete a one-time registration for a user name and password. If you have any questions regarding this process or the materials available online, please contact your local Pearson sales representative.

Acknowledgments

We would like to express our appreciation to the number of people who have contributed in some way to this publication. These include the doctoral students who served as instructors and took special interest in this project at the University of Tennessee: Hoda Baytiyeh, Jeff Beard, and Lila Holt; Bill Wishart, Data Coordinator for Teacher Education in CEHHS; and Dr. Judy Boser, Coordinator of Assessment and Evaluation for CEHHS.

In addition, we are grateful to the dedicated teachers and professors from across the United States who shared their experiences and lessons in Voices from the Classroom and Curriculum Connections: Dave Carroll, Deb Drew, Paul Gigliotti, Amy Graham, Melanie Hammond, Robert Kirkland, JoAnne Logan, Jennifer Lubke, Andrew McDonald, L'Jon Papillon, Valerie Pearce, Aaron Pickering, Paul Reinhart, Kevin Thomas, Anissa L. Vega, Allison Watkinson, Vicki Wells, and Lance Wilhelm. We also thank the faculty of Theory and Practice in Teacher Education at the University of Tennessee and the preservice teachers at the University of Tennessee who were so helpful in this process.

The reviewers of this book who shared our belief that this book was needed: Karen Kellison, University of Richmond; David Pratt, Purdue University; Juno Yamamoto, Slippery Rock University; and Leigh Zeitz, University of Northern Iowa.

The many companies that were willing to give permission to use their photos to acquaint teachers with the latest technology are deeply appreciated as well as the editors and designers from Allyn and Bacon, without whom this publication would not have been possible.

NETS·T for Teachers

ISTE National Educational Technology Standards (NETS·T) and Performance Indicators for Teachers

Effective teachers model and apply the National Educational Technology Standards for Students (NETS·S) as they design, implement, and assess learning experiences to engage students and improve learning; enrich professional practice; and provide positive models for students, colleagues, and the community. All teachers should meet the following standards and performance indicators. Teachers:

1. **Facilitate and Inspire Student Learning and Creativity (Chapters 5, 6, 7, 11, 12)**
   Teachers use their knowledge of subject matter, teaching and learning, and technology to facilitate experiences that advance student learning, creativity, and innovation in both face-to-face and virtual environments. Teachers:
   a. promote, support, and model creative and innovative thinking and inventiveness
   b. engage students in exploring real-world issues and solving authentic problems using digital tools and resources
   c. promote student reflection using collaborative tools to reveal and clarify students' conceptual understanding and thinking, planning, and creative processes
   d. model collaborative knowledge construction by engaging in learning with students, colleagues, and others in face-to-face and virtual environments.

2. **Design and Develop Digital-Age Learning Experiences and Assessments (Chapters 1, 4, 5, 6, 7, 8, 9, 10, 11)**
   Teachers design, develop, and evaluate authentic learning experiences and assessments incorporating contemporary tools and resources to maximize content learning in context and to develop the knowledge, skills, and attitudes identified in the NETS·S. Teachers:
   a. design or adapt relevant learning experiences that incorporate digital tools and resources to promote student learning and creativity
   b. develop technology-enriched learning environments that enable all students to pursue their individual curiosities and become active participants in setting their own educational goals, managing their own learning, and assessing their own progress
   c. customize and personalize learning activities to address students' diverse learning styles, working strategies, and abilities using digital tools and resources
   d. provide students with multiple and varied formative and summative assessments aligned with content and technology standards and use resulting data to inform learning and teaching

3. **Model Digital-Age Work and Learning (Chapters 2, 3, 5, 6, 7, 11, 12)**
   Teachers exhibit knowledge, skills, and work processes representative of an innovative professional in a global and digital society. Teachers:
   a. demonstrate fluency in technology systems and the transfer of current knowledge to new technologies and situations
   b. collaborate with students, peers, parents, and community members using digital tools and resources to support student success and innovation

   c. communicate relevant information and ideas effectively to students, parents, and peers using a variety of digital-age media and formats

   d. model and facilitate effective use of current and emerging digital tools to locate, analyze, evaluate, and use information resources to support research and learning

4. **Promote and Model Digital Citizenship and Responsibility (Chapters 3, 5, 7, 11, 12)**

Teachers understand local and global societal issues and responsibilities in an evolving digital culture and exhibit legal and ethical behavior in their professional practices. Teachers:

   a. advocate, model, and teach safe, legal, and ethical use of digital information and technology, including respect for copyright, intellectual property, and the appropriate documentation of sources

   b. address the diverse needs of all learners by using learner-centered strategies and providing equitable access to appropriate digital tools and resources

   c. promote and model digital etiquette and responsible social interactions related to the use of technology and information

   d. develop and model cultural understanding and global awareness by engaging with colleagues and students of other cultures using digital-age communication and collaboration tools

5. **Engage in Professional Growth and Leadership**   (*This text does not specifically align with NETS·T standard 5. However, the* Hands-on Activities *provided in each chapter support an emerging knowledge and skills base that preservice teachers need to participate in professional growth and leadership. Through these activities, preservice teachers explore creative applications, develop a vision of technology infusion, evaluate, and reflect on research and practice. They are encouraged to be proactive contributors to their profession and their future school and community. This knowledge and these skills will serve them well in continued professional development activities and leadership roles during the course of their professional careers.*)

Teachers continuously improve their professional practice, model lifelong learning, and exhibit leadership in their school and professional community by promoting and demonstrating the effective use of digital tools and resources. Teachers:

   a. participate in local and global learning communities to explore creative applications of technology to improve student learning

   b. exhibit leadership by demonstrating a vision of technology infusion, participating in shared decision making and community building, and developing the leadership and technology skills of others

   c. evaluate and reflect on current research and professional practice on a regular basis to make effective use of existing and emerging digital tools and resources in support of student learning

   d. contribute to the effectiveness, vitality, and self-renewal of the teaching profession and of their school and community

1 Preparing to Use Technology

LEARNER OBJECTIVES

At the completion of this chapter, learners will be able to:

- Discuss the research associated with the effective integration of technology into teaching and learning.

- Discuss the history of educational technology and its use in schools.

- Discuss the International Society for Technology in Education (ISTE), National Educational Technology Standards for students (NETS·S) and for teachers (NETS·T), and the role of the standards in technology integration.

- Describe the essential conditions identified by ISTE that are necessary conditions to effectively leverage technology for learning.

- Review a lesson plan model and discuss its role guiding the implementation of a lesson.

- Describe specific ways that the technology support staff and acceptable use policies can be used to assist teachers.

- Identify strategies used to manage learning environments during technology-enhanced activities.

- Discuss strategies for adapting technology for use with special learners.

- Discuss strategies for assessing students in formative and summative ways to inform teaching.

NETS·T ALIGNED WITH PREPARING TO USE TECHNOLOGY

2. **Design and Develop Digital-Age Learning Experiences and Assessments**

   Teachers design, develop, and evaluate authentic learning experiences and assessments incorporating contemporary tools and resources to maximize content learning in context and to develop the knowledge, skills, and attitudes identified in the NETS·S. Teachers:

   a. design or adapt relevant learning experiences that incorporate digital tools and resources to promote student learning and creativity.

   b. develop technology-enriched learning environments that enable all students to pursue their individual curiosities and become active participants in setting their own educational goals, managing their own learning, and assessing their own progress.

   c. customize and personalize learning activities to address students' diverse learning styles, working strategies and abilities using digital tools and resources.

   d. provide students with multiple and varied formative and summative assessments aligned with content and technology and use resulting data to inform learning and teaching.

Frameworks

Various tools have been used in schools to assist learning since much earlier times. In the one-room schoolhouses of the 1800s, the tools of the time were quill pens and slates. These were followed by hanging charts and models. The 1900s brought about the use of manipulatives, followed by visual displays, film, and radio. By the middle of the twentieth century, educational television made its appearance. In 1953, the first noncommercial educational TV station began operation in Houston, Texas, and in 1967 public broadcasting was established. Programmed instruction, a precursor of instructional software, first appeared in the late 1950s. Computers were used for instructional purposes by the government when training pilots in 1950; however, they were not evident in K–12 schools until the late 1970s, when the focus shifted from mainframe computers to desktop systems. Since that time, there has been a rapid progression of software and hardware development resulting in the extremely powerful systems available today. The history of computers in education since the development of the microcomputer several decades ago is summarized in Table 1.1.

Are Teachers Using Technology?

Although many assume that recent graduates of teacher education programs would have advanced experience using technology to enhance instruction, regrettably this is not the case. Most teacher preparation programs limit technology training to one required course, and many universities remain ill-equipped, with little or outdated access to technology. Further complicating the attainment of technology skills by preservice teachers is the preparation they are given. Large numbers of university faculty do not have adequate technology skills to use and model the use of technology in university classes (Panel on Educational Technology, 1997). A recent study by the National Education Association (NEA, 2008) of teachers and instructional staff reveals that slightly more than half of the teachers who participated felt that their preparation for integrating technology into instruction was adequate and less felt capable of individualizing instruction. A study of teacher education programs, commissioned by the Milken Foundation (1999), found that 70 percent of the college faculty felt that technology training was not adequate for individuals in teacher preparation programs. This study concluded that the preservice teachers who were the most comfortable with technology were the ones who used it consistently throughout their education program. However, once they got to the field, they did not feel that training was adequate. The lack of access to technology preparation is a problem in teacher inservice programs; neither has kept up with the rapid changes of information technology (Moursund & Bielefeldt, 1999). The Technology Counts State Reports (2009) reveal that while 46 states have established technology standards for teachers, merely 21 states have measures in place to assure the technology competency of teacher candidates prior into issuing the initial teaching licensure and the number drops to ten states that require technology competency for the recertification of teachers.

In 1999, to address this serious lack of preparation of new teachers to use technology to enhance instruction, the U.S. Department of Education launched the Preparing Tomorrow's Teachers to Use Technology (PT3) initiative (archived at **www.ed.gov/programs/teachtech/index.html**). More than 400 institutions that train new teachers received federal funds to change university programs systematically. These changes were not limited to teacher education programs, but included courses taken in general education training. Changes included developing existing university faculty who were capable of redesigning programs that meet the national

Table 1.1   History of Computers in Education

1970	Minicomputers are used in some schools, but very little in the delivery of instruction.
1971	Intel's first microprocessor developed; the first microcomputers (personal computers, or PCs) are developed. The floppy disk is developed to store data and is so named because of its flexibility.
1975	Apple computer donates Apple I computers to schools. Yet, some schools use mainframes and minicomputers and refuse to consider the personal computers.
1981	IBM is the first manufacturer to develop a PC; drill and practice and computer-assisted instruction (CAI) gains acceptance in schools.
1983	IBM PC clones increase; Sperry Corporation is the second manufacturer to develop a PC (actually developed by Mitsubishi in Japan); the Apple II computer finds widespread acceptance in education. Simple simulation programs are developed for personal computers.
1984	Thirty-one states use 13,000 PCs for career guidance, but there are still relatively few computers in classrooms; the Apple Macintosh computer is developed; computer-based tutorials and learning games are developed by commercial software manufacturers.
1985	Microsoft creates the Windows operating system giving PC computers' GUI interface.
1986	25 percent of high schools use PCs for college and career guidance, K–8 schools buying mostly Apple II and Macintosh computers, high schools buying mostly DOS-based clones.
1988	60 percent of all workers in the United States use computers. Laptops are developed.
1990	Multimedia PCs are developed; schools are using videodiscs; object-oriented multimedia authoring tools are in wide use. Simulations, educational databases, and other types of CAI programs are being delivered on CD-ROM disks, many with animation and sound. Textbook companies are pairing laserdisc with textbooks.
1992	Schools are using "gopher" servers to provide students with online information. Only one-fifth of computers in schools have hard drives. Only one-fifth are capable of connecting to the Internet.
1994	Digital video, virtual reality, and 3D systems capture the attention of many, but fewer multimedia PCs than basic business PCs are sold; authoring systems such as HyperCard, HyperStudio, and Authorware grow in popularity in schools; most U.S. classrooms now have at least one PC available for instructional delivery, but not all teachers have access to a computer for instructional preparation.
1995	The Internet and the World Wide Web begin to catch on at businesses and schools. Individuals begin to create web pages. Most CAI is delivered on CD-ROM disks and is growing in popularity.
1996	The Internet is widely discussed. New graphics and multimedia tools are developed for the delivery of information and instruction using the Internet; many schools are rewiring for Internet access; a few schools install Web servers and provide faculty with a way to create instructional web pages.
1997	The Internet grows rapidly and expands with new uses and new, unexpected applications. Voice recognition slowly enters the computing mainstream. Educational software grows even more popular with the introduction of much larger storage capacities on CD-ROMs.
1998	The ISTE NETS Project releases the National Technology Standards for Students (NETS·S).
2000	The ISTE NETS Project releases the National Technology Standards for Teachers (NETS·T).
2001	No Child Left Behind. The dot-com market falls and marks a turning point for the Web.
2002	The ISTE NETS Project adopts the TSSA (Technology Standards for School Administrators) as the NETS·A.
20–??	Multiple additional uses of multimedia emerge. Personal digital assistants (PDAs) offer pocket-sized access to technology. Virtual reality allows students to experience being somewhere through simulations. Videoconferencing is used frequently. The Internet includes vastly much more real-time audio and video. Web 2.0 begins to evolve.

(Continues)

Table 1.1   **History of Computers in Education**   *Continued*

2005	The National Technology Plan is released. Read more at www.ed.gov/about/offices/list/os/technology/plan/2004/site/edlite-background.html.
2006	NCES reports in a national study that classroom access of student/computer has dropped to 3.8 to 1.
2007	The NETS·S and performance indicators are revised to meet the changing needs of students. The essential conditions are revised to present the conditions that are necessary to effectively leverage technology for learning.
2008	The NETS·T and performance indicators are revised to meet the changing needs of digital age teachers. Rubrics accompany new standards to facilitate progression.
2008	Web 2.0 is growing in popularity in classrooms as ways to integrate technology in teaching and learning. Blogs, wikis, podcasts, RSS (Web) feeds, photo and video sharing, and virtual worlds are being used by digital-age teachers and students for teaching and learning. Schools are blocking access to some of these tools.
2009	The NETS·A and performance indicators are revised and launched.

Sources: "History, the History of Computers, and the History of Computers in Education" (www.csulb.edu/~murdock/histofcs.html); Shelly et al., 2004; Computer History Museum (www.computerhistory.org).

technology standards for teachers, and putting new hiring, tenure, and promotion practices into effect that (1) demand that new faculty hires have advanced technology expertise and (2) give incentives to current faculty who include technology activities in their courses. This initiative, one of the Clinton administration's initiatives for technology, funded the last round of three-year grants in 2003 and ceased to exist in 2006, despite the huge numbers of teachers, students, and university faculty who reaped its benefit and continue to need training.

The importance of integrating technology in learning was emphasized in the **No Child Left Behind Act** (P.L. 107-110). The primary goal of the section, "Enhancing Education Through Technology Act of 2001," is to improve student academic achievement through the use of technology in elementary schools and secondary schools. Additional goals are to ensure that every student is technologically literate by end of the eighth grade, and to encourage the effective integration of technology resources and systems with teacher training and curriculum development. Furthermore, the Individuals with Disabilities Education Act (IDEA, 2004) advocates improvements in the use of technology and universal design for students with disabilities (P.L. 108-446 § 611(2)(C)). However, since PT3, there is little funding that has been allocated to continue this important work.

Access to technology has improved for many students. In 2006, the NCES reported that the national average of student-computer ratio was 3.8 students per computer (with Internet access). Nevertheless, statistics indicating improving access did not necessarily mean improvement in quality of use. Many of the computers in classrooms were outdated and incapable of running current software programs, and lacked important hardware components. In 2008, the NEA, in collaboration with the American Federation of Teachers, concluded a study that found more than half of the teachers had no more than two computers in their classrooms and that number was not enough to effectively integrate technology into learning. In addition, classrooms were not the primary location of computers, especially in secondary schools.

Moursund and Bielefeldt (1999) suggest that neither university faculty nor the teachers who serve as mentor teachers model the effective use of technology for preservice teachers. Clearly, some of the more experienced teachers are not comfortable teaching with technology. This notion is echoed in the NEA study (2008) as one of the key findings. Most educators (76%) used technology for administrative tasks but fewer (32%) used technology for instructional tasks and the ones who did were the ones with less teaching experience.

Should Teachers Use Technology?

Research presents mixed reviews on the advantages of using technology in the classroom. Although the quantity of research-based studies is limited, research on the value of computer-based instruction has increased since 1990. Meta-analysis, or the analyzing of results of combined studies, offers positive conclusions in this area. The findings consistently reveal that computer-assisted instruction has benefits (Bayraktar, 2001; Christmann, Lucking, & Badgett, 1997; Fletcher-Flinn & Gravatt, 1995; Kukik & Kukik, 1991). Further, the Milken Foundation funded a study that looked at achievement scores and uses of technology. It found that scores on the National Assessment of Educational Progress (NAEP) were higher for students using specific kinds of technology at specific grade levels. Higher scores were seen with fourth graders who had received training with math learning games than those who had not. Further, higher scores were seen with eighth graders who had received training with teachers who used applications and simulations than those who had not. Finally, students who had teachers who received technology training did better than students whose teachers had no training (Schacter, 1999).

Over the past decade, public education has made tremendous strides in using technology in teaching and learning. The recent study by the NEA (2008) reports that while there is mounting evidence that reveals that teachers are more efficient with technology and students are more motivated, there remains a need for the effect on student achievement. This is echoed by other studies. Cuban (2001) reported that technology has not had the impact that was expected. He suggested the need for additional research on the degree to which teachers integrate technology into the classroom and corresponding improvement in student achievement. Furthermore, he suggests that regardless of the obvious commitment of schools to the use of technology, it appears that most teachers use computers to support their current teaching practices rather than as a tool to promote more innovative, constructivist practices. Other researchers (Clark, 1985; Healy, 1998) share this view, and suggest that the value of technology is yet to be proven, and cite the absence of long-term studies using achievement test data.

Other authors (Jonassen, Howland, Moore, & Marra, 2003) report that students do not learn from technology but rather from thinking, and that technology fosters learning when it serves in various roles. Such roles include serving as a tool for (1) supporting knowledge construction; (2) acting as an information vehicle by accessing and comparing information; (3) facilitating learning by doing; (4) use as a social medium; and (5) use as an intellectual partner.

Technology applications provide both teachers and learners with curriculum flexibility that was previously unattainable (Rose & Meyer, 2002; Male, 2003; Cullen, Richards, & Lawless-Frank, 2008). The digital format made possible by technology provides a means of content presentation that can be changed to suit the learner's needs: Text can be transformed (to speech or to Braille; customized in size, color, or background; or translated to another language) and recorded (saved for later use). Digital formats allow students choice of expression: Ideas can be expressed using voice, sound, pictures, and animation as well as with written words. Projects can be demonstrated in real time or shown asynchronously, making participation possible for those who are hospitalized, homebound, or uncomfortable expressing themselves in front of a group. Technology also offers students different ways of maintaining attention and motivation to learn. Designing lessons with digital tools increases the probability that all students will be able to participate in the learning experience (Rose, Sethuraman, & Meo, 2000).

Roblyer (2003) suggests that five elements provide a rationale for using technology in education. These include: (1) *increased motivation* evidenced by gaining student attention, increasing perceptions of control, and engaging the student; (2) *unique instructional capabilities* such as linking learners to exceptional information sources and learning tools; (3) support for *new instructional approaches* such as cooperative learning and problem solving; (4) *increased teacher productivity* by freeing up time, providing accurate information, and producing easier-to-read documents; and (5) *required skills for an information age*. This rationale is strengthened by the needs of students that are going to be successful in the 21st century.

Preparing students in the 21st century must be different than that of past decades. The world of work is changing; consequently, the skills of those who wish to succeed in it must change to meet the needs. While students are using technology in their private lives, they are doing far less in their school lives. The Partnership for 21st Century Skills (2004), a U.S. group representing education and business, reports that the United States is no longer leading the world in education. In fact, students around the world outscore U.S. students on assessment of 21st century skills. The Partnership stresses that all students must be qualified to succeed in work and life in the new global economy (p. 1). To do so, they must master 21st century skills. Further, the Partnership reports that there is a profound gap between what students need to know and what they learn in schools. They add that students will not be able to acquire these skills without having teachers who are well trained as well as supported in this kind of instruction. This group, **www.21stcenturyskills.org**, in a multiyear effort has identified six key elements of 21st century learning: (1) *core subjects*, (2) *21st century content*, (3) *learning and thinking skills*, (4) *information and communications skills*, (5) *life skills*, and (6) *21st century assessments*. Specifically, "students must be able to use information technology to learn content and skills so that they know how to think critically, use information, communicate, innovate and collaborate" (p. 13).

Is There Support for Technology Integration?

The **International Society for Technology in Education (ISTE)** is a nonprofit professional organization with international scope that focuses on improving teaching and learning through the effective integration of technology in PK–12 and teacher education. This organization provides its membership with information, networking opportunities, and guidance as they meet the challenges associated with integrating technology into schools throughout the world. There are vast resources at the ISTE web site (**www.iste.org**). The site provides links to (1) a bookstore offering publications to guide technology-using teachers; (2) a monthly journal, *Learning and Leading,* that features articles on technology integration topics and ideas; (3) a yearly conference, the National Education Computing Conference (NECC), which is attended by thousands of educators; (4) resources that share ideas about curriculum, equity, funding, policy, professional development, and technology integration; and (5) the **National Educational Technology Standards for teachers (NETS·T), students (NETS·S), and administrators (NETS·A)**. Membership in this organization is well worth the membership fee, which is reduced for all preservice teachers during their student preparation. With the membership comes immediate subscription to your choice of *Learning and Leading* or a more research-based journal for teacher educators. Travel to the ISTE site via On the Web on this text's companion web site (**www.pearsonhighered.com/obannon2e**) and experience the multitude of resources available to teachers.

ISTE National Education Technology Standards (NETS) Project

To facilitate the ability of all children to function successfully in a future that is marked by change, rapid growth of information, and new technologies, ISTE sponsors the ongoing development of National Educational Technology Standards (NETS) through the NETS Project. The project's main goal is "to enable stakeholders in PK–12 education to develop national standards for educational uses of technology that facilitates school improvement in the United States" (cnets.iste.org/nets_overview.html).

In 1998, the National Educational Technology Standards for Students (NETS·S) became the first publication of the NETS Project. Updated in 2007 (shown in Table 1.2) to meet the changing needs of today's students, these standards are to be mastered by students and should be used by teachers as guidelines to structure technology training at each grade level within their schools. In 2000, adhering to the idea that the key person in the development of student abilities is the classroom teacher, the NETS Project published the National Educational Technology Standards for Teachers (NETS·T). The NETS·T were developed to serve as a guide for new teacher education programs. These standards were revised in 2008 to meet the changing skills of teachers. Subsequent to the successes experienced by NETS·S and NETS·T, the ISTE NETS Project concluded that to bring about a systematic change, the administrators of schools must also be held accountable to standards. ISTE adopted the Technology Standards for School Administrators (TSSA) for the National Educational Technology Standards for Administrators (NETS·A) for the administrators who lead the schools. The revision to NETS·A will launch at the National Education Computing Conference (NECC) in June 2009. Our discussion does not focus on NETS·A, though teachers should be aware that these standards are available and can be found at the ISTE web site. All NETS standards (NETS·S, NETS·T, and NETS·A) are characterized by broad standards, which are further described by specific performance indicators. In the following discussion, we present the more detailed information of each.

Profiles for Technology-Literate K–12 Students

Because the six standards (shown in Table 1.2) are broad, another element of the NETS Project is the specification of **technology profiles**. Developed for specific grade ranges (K–2, 3–5, 6–8, and 9–12), the profiles identify ten performance indicators that a student should master before the completion of the top grade in the range to be considered technology literate. To accomplish this feat, school faculties must systematically work together to ensure that the **performance indicators** are mastered. The profiles for each grade range are presented in Table 1.3. The numbers that appear in parentheses refer to the NETS·S 2007 standard(s) to which the performance indicator corresponds.

National Educational Technology Standards for Teachers (NETS·T)

In June 2008, ISTE released the revised standards for teachers, NETS·T 2008. These standards are designed to guide teacher preparation programs and define the fundamental concepts, knowledge, skills, and attitudes for applying technology in educational settings. All teacher candidates seeking certification or endorsements in teacher preparation should meet these educational technology standards. It is the responsibility of faculty across the university and partner schools that serve as training sites for teacher preparation programs to provide opportunities for teacher candidates to meet these standards.

NETS·T 2008 are characterized by five standards. While there are no profiles as in the new NETS·T (profiles were in the original set), there are performance indicators listed in Table 1.4. In addition, rubrics have been developed to address progress on the performance indicators. The rubrics are developed for each performance indicator in a standard and list criteria of performance in the form of

Table 1.2   ISTE National Educational Technology Standards (NETS-S) and Performance Indicators for Students

1. **Creativity and Innovation**   Students demonstrate creative thinking, construct knowledge, and develop innovative products and processes using technology. Students:
   (a) apply existing knowledge to generate new ideas, products, or processes.
   (b) create original works as a means of personal or group expression.
   (c) use models and simulations to explore complex systems and issues.
   (d) identify trends and forecast possibilities.

2. **Communication and Collaboration**   Students use digital media and environments to communicate and work collaboratively, including at a distance, to support individual learning and contribute to the learning of others. Students:
   (a) interact, collaborate, and publish with peers, experts, or others employing a variety of digital environments and media.
   (b) communicate information and ideas effectively to multiple audiences using a variety of media and formats.
   (c) develop cultural understanding and global awareness by engaging with learners of other cultures.
   (d) contribute to project teams to produce original works or solve problems.

3. **Research and Information Fluency**   Students apply digital tools to gather, evaluate, and use information. Students:
   (a) plan strategies to guide inquiry.
   (b) locate, organize analyze, evaluate, synthesize, and ethically use information from a variety of sources and media.
   (c) evaluate and select information sources and digital tools based on the appropriateness to specific tasks.
   (d) process data and report results.

4. **Critical Thinking, Problem Solving, and Decision Making**   Students use critical thinking skills to plan and conduct research, manage projects, solve problems, and make informed decisions using appropriate digital tools and resources. Students:
   (a) identify and define authentic problems and significant questions for investigation.
   (b) plan and manage activities to develop a solution or complete a project.
   (c) collect and analyze data to identify solutions and/or make informed decisions.
   (d) Use multiple processes and diverse perspectives to explore alternative solutions.

5. **Digital Citizenship**   Students understand human, cultural, and societal issues related to technology and practice legal and ethical behavior. Students:
   (a) advocate and practice safe, legal, and responsible use of information and technology.
   (b) exhibit a positive attitude toward using technology that supports collaboration, learning, and productivity.
   (c) demonstrate personal responsibility for lifelong learning.
   (d) exhibit leadership for digital citizenship.

6. **Technology Operations and Concepts**   Students demonstrate a sound understanding of technology concepts, systems, and operations. Students:
   (a) understand and use technology systems.
   (b) select and use applications effectively and productively.
   (c) troubleshoot systems and applications.
   (d) transfer current knowledge to learning of new technologies.

Table 1.3　Profiles for Technology-Literate Students

Grades PK–2 (Ages 4–8)

The following experiences with technology and digital resources are examples of learning activities in which students might engage during PreK–grade 2 (ages 4–8):

1. Illustrate and communicate original ideas and stories using digital tools and media-rich resources. (1,2)
2. Identify, research, and collect data on an environmental issue using digital resources and propose a developmentally appropriate solution. (1,3,4)
3. Engage in learning activities with learners from multiple cultures through e-mail and other electronic means. (2,6)
4. In a collaborative work group, use a variety of technologies to produce a digital presentation or product in a curriculum area. (1,2,6)
5. Find and evaluate information related to a current or historical person or event using digital resources. (3)
6. Use simulations and graphical organizers to explore and depict patterns of growth such as the life cycles of plants and animals. (1,3,4)
7. Demonstrate safe and cooperative use of technology. (5)
8. Independently apply digital tools and resources to address a variety of tasks and problems. (4,6)
9. Communicate about technology using developmentally appropriate and accurate terminology. (6)
10. Demonstrate the ability to navigate in virtual environments such as electronic books, simulation software, and web sites. (6)

Grades 3–5 (Ages 8–11)

The following experiences with technology and digital resources are examples of learning activities in which students might engage during grades 3–5 (ages 8–11):

1. Produce a media-rich digital story about a significant local event based on first-person interviews. (1,2,3,4)
2. Use digital-imaging technology to modify or create works of art for use in a digital presentation. (1,2,6)
3. Recognize bias in digital resources while researching an environmental issue with guidance from the teacher. (3,4)
4. Select and apply digital tools to collect, organize, and analyze data to evaluate theories or test hypotheses. (3,4,6)
5. Identify and investigate a global issue and generate possible solutions using digital tools and resources. (3,4)
6. Conduct science experiments using digital instruments and measurement devices. (4,6)
7. Conceptualize, guide, and manage individual or group learning projects using digital planning tools with teacher support. (4,6)
8. Practice injury prevention by applying a variety of ergonomic strategies when using technology. (5)
9. Debate the effect of existing and emerging technologies on individuals, society, and the global community. (5,6)
10. Apply previous knowledge of digital technology operations to analyze and solve current hardware and software problems. (4,6)

Grades 6–8 (Ages 11–14)

The following experiences with technology and digital resources are examples of learning activities in which students might engage during grades 6–8 (ages 11–14):

1. Describe and illustrate a content-related concept or process using a model, simulation, or concept-mapping software. (1,2)
2. Create original animations or videos documenting school, community, or local events. (1,2,6)
3. Gather data, examine patterns, and apply information for decision making using digital tools and resources. (1,4)
4. Participate in a cooperative learning project in an online learning community. (2)
5. Evaluate digital resources to determine the credibility of the author and publisher and the timeliness and accuracy of the content. (3)
6. Employ data-collection technology such as probes, handheld devices, and geographic mapping systems to gather, view, analyze, and report results for content-related problems. (3,4,6)
7. Select and use the appropriate tools and digital resources to accomplish a variety of tasks and to solve problems. (3,4,6)

(Continues)

Table 1.3   Profiles for Technology-Literate Students *Continued*

8. Use collaborative electronic authoring tools to explore common curriculum content from multicultural perspectives with other learners. (2,3,4,5)

9. Integrate a variety of file types to create and illustrate a document or presentation. (1,6)

10. Independently develop and apply strategies for identifying and solving routine hardware and software problems. (4,6)

Grades 9–12 (Ages 14–18)

The following experiences with technology and digital resources are examples of learning activities in which students might engage during grades 9–12 (ages 14–18):

1. Design, develop, and test a digital learning game to demonstrate knowledge and skills related to curriculum content. (1,4)

2. Create and publish an online art gallery with examples and commentary that demonstrate an understanding of different historical periods, cultures, and countries. (1,2)

3. Select digital tools or resources to use for a real-world task and justify the selection based on their efficiency and effectiveness. (3,6)

4. Employ curriculum-specific simulations to practice critical-thinking processes. (1,4)

5. Identify a complex global issue, develop a systematic plan of investigation, and present innovative sustainable solutions. (1,2,3,4)

6. Analyze the capabilities and limitations of current and emerging technology resources and assess their potential to address personal, social, lifelong learning, and career needs. (4,5,6)

7. Design a web site that meets accessibility requirements. (1,5)

8. Model legal and ethical behaviors when using information and technology by properly selecting, acquiring, and citing resources. (3,5)

9. Create media-rich presentations for other students on the appropriate and ethical use of digital tools and resources. (1,5)

10. Configure and troubleshoot hardware, software, and network systems to optimize their use for learning and productivity. (4,6)

Source: Reprinted with permission by the National Educational Technology Standards for Students, Second Edition, © 2007, ISTE® (International Society for Technology in Education), www.iste.org. All rights reserved.

examples of expected behaviors for beginning, developing, proficient, and transformative levels.

Becoming a Technology-Using Teacher

Becoming a technology-using teacher is a process of a change that takes place over time, as shown in the Apple Classrooms of Tomorrow (ACOT) study. In this well-known study, Sandholtz, Ringstaff, and Dwyer (1997) identified five distinct stages through which a teacher progresses during development into a technology-using teacher. The stages are entry, adoption, adaptation, appropriation, and invention. The entry stage is frequently painful, as teachers experience the challenges of using technology in the classroom. In this stage, teachers seem to stall on small issues while ignoring the bigger ones. As teachers advance to the adoption stage, they gain confidence as they work with students and learn from past mistakes, yet meaningful integration is not always the outcome. In the adaptation stage, teachers begin to make technology work for them in the classroom and in their administrative duties. As they move to the appropriation stage, teachers begin to accept new teaching responsibilities. Finally, in the invention stage, teachers are eager to change teaching practice from the traditional methods. They share ideas freely, and begin to bring students together in groups for authentic

Table 1.4   ISTE National Technology Standards (NETS·T) and Performance Indicators for Teachers

Effective teachers model and apply the National Educational Technology Standards for Students (NETS·S) as they design, implement, and assess learning experiences to engage students and improve learning; enrich professional practice; and provide positive models for students, colleagues, and the community. All teachers should meet the following standards and performance indicators. Teachers:

1. **Facilitate and Inspire Student Learning and Creativity**   Teachers use their knowledge of subject matter, teaching and learning, and technology to facilitate experiences that advance student learning, creativity, and innovation in both face-to-face and virtual environments. Teachers:

   (a) promote, support, and model creative and innovative thinking and inventiveness.

   (b) engage students in exploring real-world issues and solving authentic problems using digital tools and resources.

   (c) promote student reflection using collaborative tools to reveal and clarify students' conceptual understanding and thinking, planning, and creative processes.

   (d) model collaborative knowledge construction by engaging in learning with students, colleagues, and others in face-to-face and virtual environments.

2. **Design and Develop Digital-Age Learning Experiences and Assessments**   Teachers design, develop, and evaluate authentic learning experiences and assessments incorporating contemporary tools and resources to maximize content learning in context and to develop the knowledge, skills, and attitudes identified in the NETS·S. Teachers:

   (a) design or adapt relevant learning experiences that incorporate digital tools and resources to promote student learning and creativity.

   (b) develop technology-enriched learning environments that enable all students to pursue their individual curiosities and become active participants in setting their own educational goals, managing their own learning, and assessing their own progress.

   (c) customize and personalize learning activities to address students' diverse learning styles, working strategies, and abilities using digital tools and resources.

   (d) provide students with multiple and varied formative and summative assessments aligned with content and technology standards and use resulting data to inform learning and teaching.

3. **Model Digital-Age Work and Learning**   Teachers exhibit knowledge, skills, and work processes representative of an innovative professional in a global and digital society. Teachers:

   (a) demonstrate fluency in technology systems and the transfer of current knowledge to new technologies and situations.

   (b) collaborate with students, peers, parents, and community members using digital tools and resources to support student success and innovation.

   (c) communicate relevant information and ideas effectively to students, parents, and peers using a variety of digital-age media and formats.

   (d) model and facilitate effective use of current and emerging digital tools to locate, analyze, evaluate, and use information resources to support research and learning.

4. **Promote and Model Digital Citizenship and Responsibility**

   Teachers understand local and global societal issues and responsibilities in an evolving digital culture and exhibit legal and ethical behavior in their professional practices. Teachers:

   (a) advocate, model, and teach safe, legal, and ethical use of digital information and technology, including respect for copyright, intellectual property, and the appropriate documentation of sources.

   (b) address the diverse needs of all learners by using learner-centered strategies and providing equitable access to appropriate digital tools and resources.

   (c) promote and model digital etiquette and responsible social interactions related to the use of technology and information.

   (d) develop and model cultural understanding and global awareness by engaging with colleagues and students of other cultures using digital-age communication and collaboration tools.

(Continues)

Table 1.4   ISTE National Technology Standards (NETS-T) and Performance Indicators for Teachers *Continued*

5. **Engage in Professional Growth and Leadership**

Teachers continuously improve their professional practice, model lifelong learning, and exhibit leadership in their school and professional community by promoting and demonstrating the effective use of digital tools and resources. Teachers:

(a) participate in local and global learning communities to explore creative applications of technology to improve student learning.

(b) exhibit leadership by demonstrating a vision of technology infusion, participating in shared decision making and community building, and developing the leadership and technology skills of others.

(c) evaluate and reflect on current research and professional practice on a regular basis to make effective use of existing and emerging digital tools and resources in support of student learning.

(d) contribute to the effectiveness, vitality, and self-renewal of the teaching profession and of their school and community.

project-based activities. Further, they use collaborative groups and inquiry-based and reflective learning.

Becker (1994) suggests that this change process is facilitated by the environment of the school setting. In a study that researched how "exemplary computer-using teachers" differ from other teachers in computer experiences and teaching habits, findings revealed that successful school settings must have four characteristics: (1) teachers are around other teachers who are using technology, (2) teachers are practicing in schools where computers are used for authentic learning situations, (3) financial support for technology at the school and district levels with professional development opportunities and support personnel, and (4) incentives such as smaller class sizes resulting in fewer students per computer. In addition, Becker discovered that exemplary computer-using teachers spent a great deal of time working with computers at school and at home, had participated in more training opportunities on computers, and had higher levels of education and more experience in teaching in their subject areas. Exemplary computer-using teachers often changed the curriculum to allow more time for computer-related activities and often gave students some choice in their learning. Collaborative teams were encouraged as well.

This research was expanded by ISTE (2002) and proposed **essential conditions** that should be in place to allow teachers to create learning environments that are conducive to powerful uses of technology. To meet the changing needs of today's students and teachers, the original conditions were revised and released in June of 2007. The thirteen conditions include a shared vision, implementation planning, consistent and adequate funding, equitable access, skilled personnel, ongoing professional learning, technical support, curriculum framework, student-centered learning, assessment and evaluation, engaged communities, support policies, and supportive external context and are explained in Table 1.5.

Basics

Teachers must make careful plans before successful implementation of any lesson. This is especially true with lessons that include technology. In this section, the discussion includes the importance of developing a lesson plan to guide the instruc-

Table 1.5   Essential Conditions: Necessary Conditions to Effectively Leverage Technology for Learning

Shared Vision	Proactive leadership in developing a shared vision for educational technology among school personnel, students, parents, and the community
Implementation Planning	A systemic plan aligned with a shared vision for school effectiveness and student learning through the infusion of ICT and digital learning resources
Consistent and Adequate Funding	Ongoing funding to support technology infrastructure, personnel, digital resources, and staff development
Equitable Access	Robust and reliable access to current and emerging technologies and digital resources, with connectivity for all students, teachers, staff, and school leaders
Skilled Personnel	Educators and support staff skilled in the use of ICT appropriate for their job responsibilities
Ongoing Professional Learning	Technology-related professional learning plans and opportunities with dedicated time to practice and share ideas
Technical Support	Consistent and reliable assistance for maintaining, renewing, and using ICT and digital resources
Curriculum Framework	Content standards and related digital curriculum resources
Student-Centered Learning	Use of ICT to facilitate engaging approaches to learning
Assessment and Evaluation	Continuous assessment, both of learning and for learning, and evaluation of the use of ICT and digital resources
Engaged Communities	Partnerships and collaboration within the community to support and fund the use of ICT and digital resources
Support Policies	Policies, financial plans, accountability measures, and incentive structures to support the use of ICT in learning and in district and school operations
Supportive External Context	Policies and initiatives at the national, regional, and local levels to support schools in the effective implementation of technology for achieving curriculum and technology (ICT) standards

Source: Reprinted with permission by the National Educational Technology Standards for Students, Second Edition, © 2007, ISTE® (International Society for Technology in Education), www.iste.org. All rights reserved.

tion. As teachers gain experience in teaching, the lesson plan may become less in-depth, although careful planning will facilitate successful implementation at any level of experience. In addition, classroom management issues should be anticipated during the lesson implementation and should be carefully considered, especially during the integration of technology as management rises to another level during instruction. Further, teachers must plan for inclusion of all learners and prepare the classroom environment for students who are considered to be "special learners." Finally, teachers must carefully plan the assessment techniques that will be used to measure if the student has reached the learning outcomes set forth in the lesson.

Preparing for Instruction by Planning

Planning for the instruction that will take place in the classroom is fundamental to effective teaching. Planning for technology-enhanced instruction is certainly no exception. Integrating technology into the curriculum would be most difficult without attention to the importance of planning.

A lesson plan serves as a guide that is followed during implementation of the lesson to provide a sense of direction for the teacher, hence building confidence. Daily or weekly plans are typically required by school administrators (Johnson, 2000).

Although new teachers typically write more elaborate plans than more experienced teachers, teachers with written plans have proven more effective (Sardo-Brown, 1988; Wolcott, 1994). Detailed planning is initially very time consuming, though studies reveal that teachers who write precise plans are better organized and fulfill instructional objectives faster (Walsh, 1992). Practicing teachers use a variety of lesson plan models. Although there is no one widely accepted format, the components offered here are generally accepted as standard in most teacher preparation programs (McBer, 2000). Lesson plans are part of a larger plan, a unit plan, for delivery of the curriculum; consequently, this discussion begins by briefly describing the relationship between a unit plan and a lesson plan.

The Unit Plan

Dividing content into units makes it manageable and understandable. **Unit plans** are composed of a series of lesson plans on related information and they are arranged across the yearly calendar. "Unit planning is the most important as well as the most time-consuming level of planning for each teacher" (Walsh, 1992, p. 178). Examples of units in history might include the Civil War or the Great Depression. A Civil War unit would consist of a series of lessons regarding segments of study pertaining to the Civil War such as the causes, the major events leading up to the war, the major battles, the major leaders, the Underground Railroad, outcomes of the war, reconstruction, and so on.

The Lesson Plan

A **lesson plan** consists of several sections that relate specific information about the lesson. A plan begins with descriptive information about the lesson, including the identification of the teacher who wrote the plan, the lesson title, the grade level(s), and subject area(s). This is followed by a brief description (overview) of the lesson and the time (periods or days) allotted for the lesson to take place. In the model that is presented in this text, the lesson goal follows the descriptive section with the curriculum standards that align with the lesson identified next. If the lesson includes the use of technology, the technology standards can be addressed in this section as well. The lesson plan continues as the teacher writes the instructional objectives, the materials and media needed for the lesson, the instructional procedures, the assessment, and adaptations for special learners.

Universal Design for Learning (UDL) (Rose & Meyer, 2002) and Differentiated Instruction (Tomlinson, 2000) are theoretical concepts that frame this description of lesson planning. UDL is a concept that encourages teachers to plan for the widest possible range of student abilities, thus increasing the probability that all students will be able to participate in the learning experience. Planning ahead for varying student abilities increases teacher effectiveness and minimizes the need for adaptations after the fact. UDL has three main principles for planning: (1) present materials in many different ways, and in multiple formats, including digital media; (2) show students examples or models of what their new learning would look like, and give them options for expressing their learning through a variety of media; and (3) attend to student interest, motivation, and engagement by offering choices of tools, adjusted levels of difficulty, and varying levels of support.

Differentiated instruction is a process for teaching students of differing abilities and interests in the same class. This model advocates adjustments in the areas of content, processes, and products based on the students' needs. Differentiating by content can be accomplished by providing for variations in readiness, interests, and learning styles or preferences of the learners. Differentiating by process involves developing a variety of activities to ensure the comprehension of the content. This may involve flexible groups and carefully selected organizational and learning strategies. Differentiating by product allows a variety of forms of expression, varying degrees of difficulty, types of coaching, scaffolding, and guidelines (Smith & Throne, 2007).

Although their origins are different, both theoretical frameworks are similar in scope. Each of the three elements of differentiated instruction—content, process, and product—supports an important UDL concept. The intent of both concepts is to maximize student learning by planning for flexible approaches to teaching and learning (Hall, Strangman, & Meyer, 2003). Technology tools can greatly assist teachers in planning lessons that accommodate the needs of most learners.

In the following paragraphs, a more in-depth description of each of these sections is provided, as well as appropriate information for each. Support and practice is provided in an online module aligned with this model, "Planning for Instruction" at **http://edtech.tennessee.edu/projects/bobannon**.

Lesson Goal　The **lesson goal** (or goals) is contained in a broad statement(s) of intent and is written in very general terms. An example might be "to increase understanding of Native American tribes." This statement may come directly from the unit plan. The lesson goal should relate to the curriculum standards and instructional objectives, a number of incremental steps to achieve the goal.

Standards Alignment: Curriculum Standards　The lesson should be aligned with **curriculum standards**. The specific standards that are expected by school districts or teacher education programs may vary, but they typically will include the state curriculum standards, the national standards (such as appropriate National Council for Teachers of Mathematics [NCTM] for a math lesson), or others that may vary from state to state. In addition, if technology is going to be used in the lesson, technology standards—specifically, NETS·S—that will be met upon completion of the lesson are identified here.

Instructional Objectives　One of the most significant and often misunderstood components of a lesson plan is the section containing the **instructional objectives**, which describe the student learning outcomes. In contrast to goals, objectives are written in very specific terms and communicate what the teacher wants the student(s) to be able to do after the lesson is completed. Instructional objectives serve two critical purposes: (1) they explain the teacher's expectation(s) to the learner, and (2) they form the basis for the evaluation. When writing instructional objectives, the teacher should identify (1) the learner, (2) the performance, (3) the conditions under which the performance will occur, and (4) the standards for which the performance will be evaluated. Smaldino, Lowther, and Russell (2008) refer to these as A (audience), B (behavior), C (condition), and D (degree of accuracy). It is important to clarify that it is common for teachers to write objectives with only the audience and behavior identified. Clearly this practice gives the learner much less information about the expectations. Following are examples of instructional objectives that contain the A, B, C, and D and communicate clearly to the reader the expectations of the teacher:

- Using mapping software as reference, the student will produce a set of directions from home to school, describing the shortest or best route in correct order.
- The student will name the eight planets in the order they appear from the sun.
- Using the text and Internet sources, the student will create a diagram that traces the passage of food from entry to exit.
- The student will correctly translate the French verb conjugations to English.
- The student will produce a word-processed document of 250 words in ten minutes with less than three errors. (This objective measures the technical skill of word processing.)
- Given a visual and written prompt, the student will write a two-page narrative that uses topic, details, and language to strongly connect with an intended audience (as defined by "voice" in the Six Traits scoring rubric).

The performance or behavior (verb) in an objective must be both observable and measurable. If it is not, a teacher cannot objectively evaluate true learning outcomes. It is impossible to evaluate whether a student knows the content, comprehends the content, or understands the content unless he or she performs a task (such as taking an objective test or performance evaluation) to indicate the level of knowledge. Therefore, terms such as *know, comprehend,* and *understand* are inappropriate to use when writing objectives. Verbs that can be measured might include, but are not limited to, one of the verbs presented in Table 1.6, which have been selected from Smaldino, Lowther, and Russell (2008).

Materials, Resources, and Technology   The materials, resources, and technology (if used) that are needed during the lesson should be listed. Such resources include (1) instructional materials such as textbooks, worksheets, and research guides; (2) technology resources such as hardware, software, and online connections; and (3) links to web sites that will be used during the lesson. When gathering instructional mate-

Table 1.6   A Selection of Measurable Verbs

add	define	organize
alphabetize	demonstrate	outline
arrange	describe	predict
analyze	diagram	prepare
build	distinguish	present
categorize	estimate	select
classify	explain	solve
compare	graph	sort
complete	identify	state
compute	illustrate	translate
construct	label	underline
contrast	name	write

Source: Smaldino, Lowther, & Russell (2008)

rials and resources, consider how technology can be used to differentiate instruction and its contribution to the UDL principle of multiple formats and presentations. As a general rule, text in digital formats gives the learner flexibility—it can be read aloud, enlarged, translated, or converted to an alternate format. Digital text can be obtained from the publisher, from web sites, or scanned electronically. Consider other materials that would provide redundant or parallel content—music, video segments, art—and also convey the concepts to be taught.

Students' Present Level of Performance and Knowledge

Identifying learners' **performance and knowledge levels** is very important to planning any type of instruction. Think about which students are working at, below, or above grade level, and consider their learning styles and interests. Which students are likely to be frustrated with the basic activities, and which students may become bored? Will the teacher have to teach basic or introductory skills prior to teaching this lesson? Will some students need additional language or vocabulary activities to activate prior knowledge or give clarity to emerging English learning? If technology is included, are the students comfortable with the hardware or software being used? How variable are the knowledge, skills, or reading levels of the students (Anderson & Krathwohl, 2001; House, Hurst, & Keeley, 1996)?

Classroom Layout and Grouping of Students

The **classroom layout** describes how the classroom is arranged and will be used during the lesson to promote learning. For example, the lesson might begin with students at their desks with the teacher addressing the entire group followed by student groups moving to tables for collaborative work or to computer centers to complete research. The grouping section identifies how students are grouped for various segments of the lesson. Strategies include whole-class introductory session followed by small-group or paired work. Flexible grouping patterns can afford teachers opportunities for differentiation of instruction. **Grouping of students** should be a dynamic process—grouping and regrouping changing with the content, project, and ongoing evaluations. In lessons designed with UDL principles, learners interact and work together as they learn new content (Hall, Strangman, & Meyer, 2003).

Instructional Procedures

The **instructional procedures** section is the heart of the lesson plan and describes the teacher's and students' actions during implementation. The lesson begins with the lesson set, followed by step-by-step techniques and activities, and ends with the lesson closure.

The **lesson set** (often called *anticipatory set*) is the introduction to the lesson and involves getting the students motivated for the learning. The set should establish and provide the relation to previous learning and life experiences. To accommodate a variety of learners, this may involve activating background knowledge lessons using multiple formats—talking, multimedia, video, or objects as props. The lesson set is also used to express the importance of this learning, and communicates the procedures that will be used during the lesson. The **techniques and activities** follow the set and include a step-by-step list of the activities in the lesson. Techniques and activities include presentation, modeling of the concept, and guided practice by the students. To increase the probability of success of this lesson for all learners, these strategies should follow UDL principles: present information in multiple ways, allow students to express themselves in multiple ways, and have multiple ways for the students to be engaged.

The **lesson closure** is the method that is used to bring the lesson to a close, and should include a summation of the learning and how the learning will relate to future learning. Students should be actively involved during the closure, so consider a variety of ways that they may participate in a review of what they have learned.

TECH TIP

If information from the Web is needed for student research, the teacher should locate, evaluate, and bookmark appropriate sites that the students will need to avoid wasting valuable research time. This is easier if the teacher maintains a web site that can present the sites for ease of access for students.

TECH TIP

Student comfort with the technology (hardware or software) is paramount to their success in using technology as a tool for learning.

The general concept here is to use procedures and strategies that place students into active learning roles, described by ISTE (2007) as *emerging learning landscape*. Plans that integrate technology promote students' active learning. Research shows that traditional learning environments, those that place the students in passive roles and include instructional strategies such as lecture or teacher-directed discussions, no longer provide students with the skills needed to be successful in the workplace. Table 1.7 provides a continuum of these environments from traditional to emerging along several dimensions (ISTE, 2007). Notice the potential that technology affords when incorporating these new strategies—students are actively engaged in collaborating with peers, and exploring, inquiring, and evaluating their learning. Computer tools and Web-based applications make it possible for the teacher to differentiate by content and by process according to the variance in the class.

Supplemental Activities Supplemental activities include enrichment activities that extend the learning or activities that the teacher can use to reteach, if necessary. Supplemental activities can provide the necessary teaching redundancy that accommodates diverse learners; look for other ways for the teacher or the students to say it, show it, model it, or express it using a different format.

Table 1.7   Transforming Learning Environments with Technology

Traditional Environments Landscape	Emerging Learning
Teacher-directed, memory-focused instruction	Student-centered, performance-focused learning
Lockstep, prescribed-path progression	Flexible progression with multipath options
Limited media, single-sense stimulation	Media-rich, multisensory stimulation
Knowledge from limited, authoritative sources	Learner-constructed knowledge from multiple information sources and experiences
Isolated work on invented exercises	Collaborative work on authentic, real-world projects
Mastery of fixed content and specified processes	Student engagement in definition, design, and management of projects
Factual, literal thinking for competence	Creative thinking for innovation and original solutions
In-school expertise, content, and activities	Global expertise, information, and learning experiences
Stand-alone communication and information tools	Converging information and communication systems
Traditional literacy and communication skills	Digital illiteracies and communication skills
Primary focus on school and local community	Expanded focus including digital global citizenship
Isolated assessment of learning	Integrated for learning

Source: Reprinted with permission by the National Educational Technology Standards for Students, Second Edition, © 2007, ISTE® (International Society for Technology in Education), www.iste.org. All rights reserved.

Adaptations for Special Learners   In this section of the plan, adaptations for special learners—students who are English language learners (ELLs), or students who struggle academically—are outlined. This section is also used to explain how adaptations from students' Individualized Education Plans (IEP) will be implemented. Adaptations are further classified into two categories: accommodations and modifications.

An **accommodation** is a change in the way a student accesses material, or a change in the way a student expresses what is known, without involving a change in the content or achievement expectations of what is learned. Accommodations can be a support or a service and are generally provided in three areas: alternate acquisition modes, content enhancement, and alternative response modes (Nolet & McLaughlin, 2005).

Alternate acquisition modes provide a different format for input, or studying, the content. For example, translation support (digital bilingual dictionaries, or handheld scanners) is an alternate acquisition accommodation for ELLs. Screen reading or magnification software may be required for students who have visual impairments. For students who have difficulty with reading, an accommodation using alternate acquisition would be to offer the text in a digital format, and allow the student to listen to the text read aloud using text-to-speech software. For students who are deaf and use the services of an interpreter, a room arrangement whereby the student can see the faces of all who are speaking, and a copy of lesson plans and notes provided ahead of time for the student and the interpreter, is an alternate acquisition accommodation.

Content enhancements are strategies that help students identify, organize, comprehend, and remember information. Content enhancements include supports such as advance organizers, concept maps, templates, and peer learning groups. For example, a content enhancement strategy for students who have difficulty with written expression is to make an electronic template available to provide structure for a report or a paper. A similar example is to teach the use of a concept map (paper and pencil or an electronic version) as a note-taking strategy. Extra practice sessions, tutoring, and learning strategy instruction are other examples of content enhancement strategies.

Alternative response modes attempt to reduce the barriers to expression created by language difficulties or disabilities. Examples include allowing alternate forms of student reporting (such as a multimedia presentation instead of a written description). Students with cognitive delays may need more time to complete an assignment. Teaching assistants may serve as "scribes," writing the students' verbatim responses. Students with language barriers may be encouraged to diagram or develop an illustration that demonstrates their learning.

A **modification** reflects changes in the subject matter or the expected performance level of the student. Common modifications include reducing the amount of work required, reducing the difficulty level of the content, teaching different content, or attending to individualized curriculum goals that are standards based but loosely connected to the lesson. Modifications are usually developed by the student's IEP team, and are usually considered when accommodations are not sufficient to reduce barriers to learning.

Assessment/Evaluation   The assessment section outlines the plan for *evaluating the learning outcomes and the methods used to assess the students' mastery of the lesson objectives.* **Informal methods** are conducted during the lesson implementation and include teacher monitoring of students and questioning for understanding. These methods are used to cue the teacher to the level of student understanding so that adjustments to the lesson can be made. **Formal methods** of evaluation are methods for assessing levels of learning and performance and a grade is given. The assess-

> **TECH TIP**
>
> Both PC and Mac systems provide ways to adapt the system software to promote accessibility. (See Chapter 3, Figure 3.6, page 74.)

ment/evaluation section affords yet another opportunity to consider alternate and multiple ways for students to express what they have learned—strategies supported by the UDL and differentiated instruction models. More details regarding assessment of technology literacy follow in the next session.

Preparing for Assessment

Assessment of technology literacy of K–12 students has become an important aspect of the K–12 classroom with the inception of NCLB and the revised NETS·S. Although typical teacher preparation programs have a stand-alone course on assessment and evaluation, we present a brief overview of assessment concepts and practices that may be applied as you proceed through this text.

Educational assessments are usually used for either formative or summative purposes, depending on the type of decisions being made by the teacher. **Formative assessment**, implemented during an instructional unit, provides information on student progress as their mastery develops so that the teacher may make adjustments to the instruction and ultimately improve student learning. Feedback of this nature may be generated from informal assessments such as observation and class discussion, as well as more formal methods such as quizzes and homework. In contrast, **summative assessment** is utilized at the end of a unit, semester, or year to provide culminating feedback for the purposes of making a final decision, such as pass/fail, promotion/retention, or assigning a grade. Common summative methods include formal assessments such as tests, performances, demonstrations, and projects.

Assessment methods can also be categorized as alternative or traditional. *Traditional assessment* methods are typically tests and quizzes, which utilize items that only have one correct response. Traditional methods are easy to grade but often are limited to measuring basic knowledge and understanding of content. *Alternative assessment* methods include portfolios, performances, demonstrations, products, open-ended responses (i.e., essays, theme papers, short answers), and encourage higher-level skills such as application, analysis, and evaluation of content. This type of assessment will often utilize some scoring instrument such as a rubric or a checklist in an attempt to decrease the subjectivity of grading such outcomes. Even so, the grading of alternative assessments can be time consuming and more difficult.

When developing an assessment plan for measuring student technology literacy, you are encouraged to utilize both traditional and alternative assessment methods in order to create a more accurate picture of student ability. However, since the nature of technology focuses on the application of tools to generate a process or product, the utilization of alternative assessment methods are typically more appropriate. Consequently, being able to develop a variety of scoring instruments to evaluate technology outcomes is an important skill for K–12 teachers.

Two types of scoring instruments are commonly used in assessing student technology literacy: checklists and rubrics. A *checklist* is a list of behaviors, skills, or characteristics that are easily observed so that the teacher may indicate whether each skill has been demonstrated. Checklists are most appropriate for complex tasks that can be broken down into a series of specific skills. Figure 1.1 presents a checklist used to assess the development of a spreadsheet.

A *rubric* is a more developed scoring guide that specifies various levels of performance criteria and can be especially helpful in evaluating specific technology knowledge, skills, and abilities among students. Depending on the degree of specificity and levels, an assessment rubric may be categorized as holistic or analytic. A *holistic rubric* presents levels of criteria for scoring the overall process or product as a whole. Figure 1.2 presents a holistic rubric for evaluating web page

FIGURE 1.1 Checklist for Evaluating the Development of a Spreadsheet

Skill	Yes	No
Enter data and column/row headings		
Format text (type, style, size, alignment)		
Adjust column width		
Create formulas for mean and sum		
Format numbers (out two decimal places)		
Create appropriate bar chart		
Save and transmit file		

Source: Courtesy of Rachel Vannatta, 2008

FIGURE 1.2 Holistic Rubric for Evaluating Web Page Design

Level	Description
5	Four or more pages created, one of which is a title page. Navigation is clear between pages and to other resources; all links work. Layout is consistent, enhances content. Formatting extends Level 4 by including at least two of the following: images as hyperlinks, lists, tables, color or background image, frames, image map.
4	Three pages are created with clearly labeled sections and easy navigation; all links work. Layout uses headings and styles and is consistent across pages. Formatting extends Level 3 by including images and hyperlinks to related material.
3	Two pages are created with navigation between pages (or one page is created with links to other resources). Layout uses headings for sections to create a hierarchy; may be inconsistently applied. Formatting uses headings, titles, and at least two types of tags (preformatted text, alignment, styles, lines, lists).
2	One page is created that has a title bar and heading. Text is divided into paragraphs with headings.
1	Only one page is created. Layout is unorganized. Formatting does not utilize HTML tags. Text is not organized into paragraphs.

design. Notice that criteria and attributes of the task are broadly described across several levels.

In contrast, an *analytic rubric* breaks down the criteria into components or attributes of the task so that the teacher will then sum the component score to determine a total score. An analytic rubric is much more common in assessing student technology-based projects since it allows for specificity in guiding the task/product itself as well as providing detailed feedback to the student. Figure 1.3 presents an analytic rubric for evaluating a multimedia project. Notice that the

FIGURE 1.3   Analytic Rubric Evaluating a Multimedia Project

	Beginner: 1 point	Novice: 2 Points	Intermediate: 3 points	Expert: 4 points	Total
Topic/Content	Includes little essential information and one or two facts	Includes some essential information with few citations and few facts.	Includes essential information with most sources properly cited. Includes enough elaboration to give readers an understanding of the topic.	Covers topic completely and in depth. Includes properly cited sources and complete information. Encourages readers to know more.	
Technical Requirements (to be filled in by teacher)	Includes _____ cards or less, few graphics from outside sources, few animations and advanced features.	Includes _____ cards or less, fewer than 3 graphics from outside sources, fewer than 3 animations and few advanced features, such as video, 3-D, or sound.	Includes at least _____ cards, at least 3 graphics from outside sources, at least 3 animations and some advanced features, such as video.	Includes at least _____ cards, 5 or more graphics from outside sources, 5 or more animations and several advanced features, such as video.	
Mechanics	Includes more than 5 grammatical errors, misspellings, punctuation errors, etc.	Includes 3–4 grammatical errors, misspellings, punctuation errors, etc.	Includes 2–3 grammatical errors, misspellings, punctuation errors, etc.	Grammar, spelling, punctuation, capitalization are correct. No errors in the text.	
Cooperative Group Work	Cannot work with others in most situations. Cannot share decisions or responsibilities.	Works with others, but has difficulty sharing decisions and responsibilities.	Works well with others. Takes part in most decisions and contributes fair share to group.	Works well with others. Assumes a clear role and related responsibilities. Motivates others to do their best.	
Oral Presentation Skills	Great difficulty communicating ideas. Poor voice projection. Little preparation or incomplete work.	Some difficulty communicating ideas, due to voice projection, lack of preparation, or incomplete work	Communicates ideas with proper voice projection. Adequate preparation and delivery.	Communicates ideas with enthusiasm, proper voice projection, appropriate language, and clear delivery.	

Scale: 18–20 = Expert   15–17 = Intermediate   Total Points
10–14 = Novice   6–9 = Beginner

Source: Developed by Caroline McCullen, Instructional Technologist. Copyright © SAS Institute Inc., Cary, NC, USA, All Rights Reserved. Used with permission.

author of this rubric has identified five components of criteria (topic/content, technical requirements, mechanics, cooperative group work, oral presentation skills) across four levels of achievement (beginner, novice, intermediate, and expert).

Now that you know a little more about scoring guides, you are ready to learn about "how" to create an effective scoring instrument. Development of any effective scoring instrument for a technology performance should apply the following steps.

1. Determine the purpose of the assessment. The purpose should be aligned with the instructional objectives and student outcomes.
2. Identify an authentic and meaningful context for the performance.
3. Identify the skills that students should demonstrate in the performance task.
4. Specify the criteria, observable indicators, and attributes that should be demonstrated in the task. To keep this process manageable, only identify indicators for key skills and outcomes.
5. Determine the appropriate type of scoring guide to be used: checklist, holistic rubric, or analytic rubric.
6. Brainstorm characteristics that describe each criteria/indicator/attribute for various levels.
7. Organize descriptions into a scoring guide:
   • Checklist. List specific skills and criteria (observed or not observed).
   • Holistic rubric. Write narrative descriptions for four to five levels of achievement. Be sure to integrate all attributes within each level narrative.
   • Analytic rubric. Write brief narratives for each attribute across three to four levels. You may want to group criteria and attributes into common components.
8. Create or select exemplary student responses. This will help you determine if your scoring instrument is appropriate and will guide students in understanding how the task will be assessed.
9. Revise the task as necessary.

You can see that the development of a scoring instrument really requires careful thought about the entire performance task and the instruction leading up to it. An appropriate scoring instrument is crucial to implementing an effective and meaningful performance assessment. Although the development and implementation process of such requires a great deal of reflection, planning, and organization, an effective scoring guide can create a rewarding learning experience for students.

Finally, technology-related assessments are not only limited to alternative assessments, but *traditional assessments,* such as quizzes and tests, may also be utilized to evaluate specific knowledge and skills. This type of assessment typically involves the use of *objective test items,* which require students to identify a single correct response. Common item formats include: true/false, multiple choice, and matching. Since technology literacy often involves the demonstration of specific skills through the development and creation of a specific product or task, objective test items have several limitations. First, they are best used to assess what students know about basic technology application and concepts, since objective test items are less effective at evaluating higher-order thinking skills. Second, the process of achieving a task using technology may be conducted through multiple paths and/or steps; therefore, it is difficult for objective test items to confirm a student's performance of a specific task. Last, effective objective test items are difficult to develop. Consequently, if you decide to utilize objective items in your assessment plans, we recommend reading an educational assessment textbook, which presents the steps for developing objective test items. In addition, you may want to utilize items from a commercially developed item test bank. Such items

FIGURE 1.4   Sample Eighth-Grade Test Items

1. Commonly used output devices are called:
   - Microphones
   - Printers
   - Keyboards
2. Copying copyrighted software and giving it to others for free is:
   - Not a big concern for software companies
   - A criminal act
   - Always allowed
3. Which of the following activities would be best accomplished using a word processor?
   - Prepare a report and have a classmate edit it using Track Changes
   - Use formulas to solve mathematical equations and word problems
   - Generate a graph about students' favorite books

Source: Learning Point Associates. Available at: www.techpt.org/assessments.php. Copyright © Learning Point Associates. All rights reserved. Reprinted with permission.

are often aligned with the NETS·S benchmarks. Figure 1.4 presents example test items for the eighth-grade benchmark. Technology-based assessments are also available so that students complete the test on the computer and can respond to more interactive and performance items. Many states and school districts have started utilizing objective test items as part of their assessment program for technology literacy.

Preparing for Special Learners

Teachers must prepare for classrooms with children from a variety of backgrounds and challenges—those who live in poverty as well as in affluence; from differing language and cultural backgrounds; and with varying physical abilities, gifts, cognitive abilities, and emotional needs.

Learning challenges affect memory and language, as well as academic performance in reading, spelling, or math. Children with behavior challenges may have difficulty with attention and activity demands of the classroom, and may also exhibit aggressive or withdrawn behaviors. Cultural differences affect children's motivation, work styles, pattern of eye contact, physical contact, and response to persons in authority. Economic differences affect issues of health and safety, as well as opportunities for access to technology and to books that are critical to literacy development. These students come to school with a variety of labels. Teacher training literature refers to such diverse learners using terms such as students with disabilities, English language learners, students at risk for academic failure, and children who live in poverty. No matter the terms that are used to identify them, these students are challenging teachers to think differently about the process of teaching and learning. Using technology throughout classroom practice is a key component in accommodating this diversity.

Students with disabilities now have legislative safeguards that protect their right to participate in the general education curriculum and to obtain services to help them achieve to the best of their abilities. This legislation supports the use of **assistive technology (AT)** devices and services when needed to achieve learning goals. An AT device is defined as "any item, piece of equipment, or product system," excluding a surgically implanted device, "whether acquired commercially off the shelf, modified, or customized, that is used to increase, maintain, or improve functional capabilities of individuals with disabilities" (IDEA 2004, P.L. 108-446 § 602(1)(B)). AT services are any services that assist the student in the selection, acquisition, or use of these devices. AT services include evaluating a student's needs in the customary environment (which includes the classroom) and providing training or technical assistance to the student and professionals in the use of AT devices. These definitions of AT can refer to a broad range of software, hardware, and services that may or may not be designed specifically with individuals with disabilities in mind. Many of the software and hardware suggestions offered in this text can be used in an instructional manner for *all* students, or in an assistive manner to improve performance of students with disabilities.

IDEA 2004 regulations state that AT must be considered for every student with an IEP. The procedures that IEP teams are to use in this process, however, are unspecified. As a result, many teams make a careful consideration of AT for students with obvious physical barriers (such as limited use of the hands, or inability to see clearly), but not necessarily for students with milder disabilities or learning difficulties. Among the reasons for this discrepancy is that many teachers are simply unaware of the powerful assistance that technology can offer in compensating for learning difficulties. A second reason is related to the procedures used by IEP teams in considering technology. There are too many students with high-incidence disabilities for whom individually prescribed devices and software purchase would be feasible. Ironically, it is this group of students—those who may need a different presentation or support for expressing what they have learned—that technology use can most often greatly assist. Moreover, much of the general-use software, when used in an assistive manner, would greatly aid their learning needs.

In order to meet the challenges of these learners, researchers are beginning to advocate a more open access to technology for all learners. Edyburn (2000) recommends that all teachers have readily available access to a broad range of technology tools that support individual learning styles, instead of assigning AT devices and software to specific students. The Consortium for School Networking (**www.CoSN.org**) has developed a leadership initiative that seeks to expand the use of assistive and accessible technologies by combining the expertise of instructional technology and AT communities. This initiative encourages the use of accessible technologies on a systemwide basis. Its mission is to embed accessibility functions in all current instructional applications and to foster their use in K–12 environments. Language in IDEA further encourages using technology that supports a wide range of learners without requiring AT (Mittler & Heiman, 2005). The primary message from these and other sources is that technology is becoming more accessible, and a formal distinction between assistive and instructional application is not always useful. The researchers continue to encourage teachers to use technology with all learners, to adapt existing software when needed, and to use assistive devices and software when necessary for computer access.

In the sections on adaptations that follow throughout this text, we take the perspective of using readily available applications, broadly applied to multiple classroom situations, as a means of including students with special needs in general curriculum activities. This perspective on technology use is supported by concepts of UDL and differentiated instruction, which were introduced earlier when discussing instructional planning. We hope to show that much of this technology is also easy to learn and use.

More specialized technology—hardware devices and software—can also be part of an AT plan for students who experience significant barriers to computer access, such as mobility challenges or low vision. The detailed information necessary for implementing many of these systems, however, is beyond the scope of this text. Teachers will most likely need to consult members of the IEP team who are providing AT services. Teachers who use technology regularly can become valuable assets to the IEP team as they consider the need for AT for these students.

We encourage teachers to use technology as often as possible, in a wide variety of applications, and with all students. Become proactive. Learn how the applications presented here can be used to access new learning. Observe student performance and success in using technology, and advocate for needed hardware, software, and services for classroom use.

Preparing to Manage the Classroom

Managing the classroom during technology integration is key to providing students with the best possible experience while using technology. In order to provide positive experiences for students, *the teacher should be comfortable with the technology and the process* that is being implemented and should plan carefully for critical issues that may affect the experience, including the equipment use and placement, available support during implementation, established norms for student behavior during technology use, and assessment of student performance during technology use. In addition, many studies conclude that *students must be comfortable with the technology tool being used* (such as the hardware or software program being used) so that it will not limit the success of the learning. Teachers should realize that comfort levels are not reached without continued use—for children as well as for teachers.

In this discussion, management considerations for technology integration have been divided into three broad themes that parallel research: (1) managing equipment access and layout, (2) managing time, and (3) managing student behavior.

Managing Equipment Access and Layout

Teachers should take a technology inventory when preparing to use technology: What access to technology do students have in order to complete assignments? Where and how many computers are available for student use: in the classroom, in computer lab(s), in the school library, or at home? Do mobile labs provide checkout access to individual students? What are the best ways to use technology with a limited number of computers in the classroom? How should the classroom be arranged for optimal computer use?

A computer in the classroom can serve many purposes: to present information to students in large groups; as a teacher workstation for creating instructional materials, recording grades, and generating reports; as a learning center for students where they can work alone or in small groups.

Many times, the introduction of a computer or several computers into the classroom environment changes the dynamics in the classroom. Access to computer-based technologies encourages the use of strategies like project-based learning and inquiry learning rather than direct instruction. These changes can be dramatic. The use of technology can challenge the relationship between teachers and students, because technology helps learners gain control of their own learning. Technology provides access to information that was once available only under the control of teachers.

Equipment Layout   The layout (way computers are arranged in the classroom) can encourage positive experience as well as extend the life of equipment. Computers should be placed where students have ample space for project work. Chairs should be grouped around the computer workstation. If possible, additional desks can be placed close by to expand the work area.

Computers should be arranged in various locations around the classroom, away from the main traffic flow in the room, close to electrical outlets and avoiding the glare coming from windows. The arrangement should also create the least distraction for students who are not working with the technology. Any food and drinks should be prohibited in the computer workstation areas. Not only will this prevent friendly visits from the ant population, but it will also prevent equipment from being ruined by spills. See that all cords and electrical outlets are in good working order. Use duct tape to secure electrical cords to the floor to avoid tripping hazards.

If All Else Fails   Have Plan B (an emergency plan) when equipment fails. Such failures may be caused by network failures or equipment crashes. The network that provides access to the Internet may become unavailable without warning, and the failure may last momentarily or throughout the entire lesson period and/or day. Electrical failures and equipment failures can make it impossible for students to complete their tasks; consequently, it is important for teachers to always have a backup activity available.

Equipment Equity   Be sure that all students have equal access to the equipment. This is not only a consideration for activities occurring at school but also at home. The *Digital Divide* is defined as the gap between people with access to digital and information technology and those without this access. This is a great concern for teachers who are using technology in the classroom. The students who do not have access at home must have every opportunity to complete work at school and be advised as to other options offered in the community. This could be accomplished by offering access to computers before classes, after classes, or allowing these students to be among the first to access school computers in the classroom. Students without access should be made aware of other options such as teaming with a friend who does have access at home or going to the library. The Divide widens in the schools with differing levels of computer access. The best location for computers is in the classroom with the teacher and students. However, many teachers must reserve labs or mobile carts that are shared by many making the integration of technology more difficult. However, achieving equipment equity in the classroom can be accomplished by a rotation schedule and can even be monitored by classmates. Sign-in sheets ensure that all of the students have access. This is particularly important when students do not have home access. Collaborative groups are common practice and are most helpful if managed properly. Monitor student group interactions to facilitate equity and individual domination of the equipment during work time.

Cooperate with other teachers to share equipment in nearby classrooms when not in use. This cooperation can expand the time your students have to use computers and allow access to peripheral equipment that you might not have in your own classroom.

Make sure that students fully appreciate the importance of saving their work. Encourage students to save work frequently and to create backup copies of their projects on removable storage devices such as USB drives.

As much as possible, select software that is compatible with both Mac and Windows operating systems to reduce student and parent frustration. The operating system used at school may not match what a student uses at home. Find out what systems the students have at home and accommodate them by making the documents accessible from the Web for download for both platforms. In addition, online tools such as Google Docs provide space where documents can be uploaded and worked on, eliminating compatibility issues.

Open source software can economically supplement school-owned software. However, it is important to be sure that this software is compatible with the school network. Contact the school's technology support staff before installing these applications on school computers. Students can download open source software at home, thus promoting students' accessibility to what is used at school.

Managing Time

Managing time when involving students with technology is critical. With a limited number of computers available and limited time to use these computers, students should clearly understand the expectations of the assignment before going to a workstation. In addition, students should understand that much of the work for a project can be completed away from the computer as they plan for the project. Students can print out some materials from the Internet and use these hard copies in the planning stages while working at their desks or in the library.

Prerequisite Skills   Teachers should assist this process by making sure that students have the required skills before going to the computer. Research has suggested that much time is wasted because students lack knowledge of the software. Teachers should tell students what to bring to the workstation with them—such as books, notebooks, and/or pencils—so that time will not be wasted going back to desks for needed items. In addition, web sites that are to be used for research should be previously bookmarked on each computer to save time in searching for them. Templates for projects can be created so that students do not have to start from scratch. Rubrics or checklists should be developed that explain what tasks the student is held accountable for.

If students are working in groups, make sure that at least one student in each group has good computer skills. These students can assist students with lower skill levels. Additionally, each student should be assigned a specific role in the group such as being the one who controls the mouse. This role assignment scheme can be rotated. Teachers should create a schedule for time spent at workstations in classrooms with limited computer access to ensure that all students have equal access to computers.

Managing Student Behavior

Teachers can face challenges when students are working in groups and working on different tasks. Such an environment can produce opportunities for students to become distracted from the original task.

Teachers should be familiar with the school's acceptable use policy (AUP). Such a document details *appropriate behavior* and the *consequences* for breaking school rules. Both parents and students should understand this policy information. Teachers should communicate expectations as well as penalties and enforce policy. Students can assist with the creation of some of the class policies that are not covered in the AUP. Ideally, students will take ownership of these rules and will encourage each other to comply. Post these rules in a prominent area near the computers.

Avoid situations in which students have to stand in line and wait to use a computer. This situation encourages students to talk and create disturbances for other students. Develop a rotation plan that prevents this problem. Have students use headphones to limit noisy distractions when using the Internet or software. A calm environment will encourage calm behavior.

Near the computer, keep a notebook that contains a place to record computer use. Have students sign in each time they use a computer and record when they were using the computer. This creates a sense of responsibility for what happens on and to the computer during that time.

It is helpful to have additional supervision and support as technology is implemented. Teacher assistants, teacher interns, parents, or the technology coordinator can provide this support.

Support Provided by Technology Coordinators

The **technology coordinator** plays a key role in assisting teachers with the integration of technology in the classroom and should be able to provide needed support to new teachers in various ways. Some of the most common ways that tech coordinators support the teaching staff are: (1) *providing assistance to the new teacher* in defining the school's and school district's vision of technology, (2) *explaining the acceptable use policy* (AUP) as well as other policies that guide students with Internet use, (3) providing *professional development opportunities* for teachers, and (4) *providing technical guidance* for software and hardware purchases as well as desktop support to all users. Frazier and Bailey (2005) explain that the technology coordinator must be a person who is multiskilled. They also point out that tech coordinators must have management and budgeting skills to complete hardware and software acquisition, technical skills to provide maintenance and technical support, and be able to present a successful faculty development program. And if technology integration occurs, the tech coordinator must be there to work with teachers and students and model effective use. In Voices from the Classroom, Lance Wilhelm, PhD—a former classroom teacher, technology coordinator, and now Director of Technology for Ames, Iowa, community schools—shares his thoughts about available support for technology integration.

Voices *from the* Classroom

The Technology Coordinator
Lance Wilhelm, PhD

Dr. Lance Wilhelm was a K–12 teacher for 11 years and is in his 16th year as a district-level technology director. He received his doctorate in Curriculum and Instructional Technology from Iowa State University, and also served as an assistant professor in the College of Teacher Education and Leadership at Arizona State University. He is currently the Director of Technology for the Ames (Iowa) Community Schools. We asked him to share his experiences in the use and integration of technology and the support that is offered for teachers.

Even though technology is playing an ever-growing role in society, many teachers do not integrate technology into their classrooms because of a number of barriers they encounter—not enough time, not enough equipment, not enough technical support, and so on. As a long-time advocate of the effectiveness of educational technology, I encourage you to look *past* any barriers you encounter, and use the resources you have to make technology a regular part of the fabric of your students' learning. The

key word in the phrase "technology integration" is *integration*. Make your students' experiences with technology meaningful by tying them to your content area and, ideally, to the real world. Please *don't* treat technology as a "special," where you drop your students off at the lab and pick them up half an hour later. Instead, use technology in ways that add value to what your students are studying. Used appropriately, technology can engage your students by addressing their multiple intelligences. Used efficiently, technology can also "free up" students to focus on higher-level thinking. For example, a spreadsheet can do the drudgework—the calculations—and your students can do the "what if " thinking that is enabled through the use of this tool. One of the best examples of technology integration that I ever saw was done in a small-town school district in eastern Iowa. The students in an elementary grade created a CD that illustrated the history of their town. As I listened to the teachers and the technology coordinator describe the project (and the technology-related lessons they learned the hard way), it was clear that technology

(Continues)

was the *catalyst* for this project. They were doing something new, so they could think outside the box. And while this project did use cutting-edge technologies, it also used established technologies such as the video camera, the tape recorder, and the telephone. And what really excited the students as much as using technology was their *interaction with the real world.* They used the phone to set up interviews with *real people,* and then they recorded these interviews. When they were finished, they wrote thank-you notes to real people, and invited them to come see the digital movies they created. A real audience—beyond the classroom teacher—is a powerful motivator. As I mentioned, there can be significant barriers to technology integration. In order to overcome any barriers you encounter, take advantage of a key resource available in most K–12 school districts: a team of technology integration experts. These team members might include your district's technology coordinator, your building's media specialist, your department chair, or one of the many "early adopters" among the teachers in your district. Ask around—there *is* help available. These teams vary in composition and size from district to district, and in small districts, it might be a team of one, but technology will have some level of support in your district. You just need to know who to email (or call, if your email isn't working!). I've included here some examples of how the team in your district might assist you. For example, while surfing the Web at home, you find a great site that you want to use with your class. However, when you come to school, your browser says that it can't find that site. A likely possibility is that the site is blocked by your school's filtering system, and your technology coordinator can tell you how you can request to unblock that site. Your district undoubtedly has an acceptable use policy that governs the use of the Internet, and it is important that all district students and employees are familiar with this policy. At times you will come across some software that will potentially help your students learn. Keep in mind that it's important that you know and follow the process set up by your district. I'll share a short story that illustrates how good intentions can go awry. There may be agencies that provide valuable services to the school districts. Oftentimes, these specialists have access to innovative software that can benefit special needs students, and they like to pilot this software, if they can find a willing teacher. During my service as the technology coordinator, a "willing teacher" allowed the installation of new and innovative software, which resulted in the computer crashing during the installation process. The mortified teacher, whose "entire life was on that com-

puter," called me in a panic. After some time, we were able to restore her files and get the computer back to normal. While I did this, I reminded the teacher of what she should have done, which was to turn in a request to have the software installed, and why most districts, in order to keep computers virus-free and easy to troubleshoot, control how software is installed. By following the procedure, we could have answered several questions prior to installation. Did the agency have a license that allowed this software to be installed on our computers? Could this program be installed without any adverse effect on the other software? If so, then the request would be granted, and the software would have been properly installed. Here's another example: You want to know if there is some software available that can model a complex concept with which your students always struggle. However, you don't want to look through the pile of catalogs on your desk, and you don't feel confident that ten minutes of searching with a search engine will give you the answer. This is a great opportunity to consult your technology team—they will be more than happy to identify some possibilities and give you the pros and cons of each. Most likely, there will be someone on the team who will help you learn the new program, and offer suggestions on how to incorporate it into your students' learning. Some districts employ technology integration specialists who will co-teach your class as you integrate a given technology for the first time. One time, in my role as technology coordinator, I helped a social studies teacher use a program that simulated the presidential election process. The first year he used it, I caught a couple of the classes with him, and it was great fun. Believe it or not, many people in administrative roles used to be teachers, and they love to get back into the classroom now and then! In sum, take advantage of the resources provided by your technology team. Most technology coordinators are very friendly folks who want you to use technology extensively. Admittedly, some are more controlling and offer little support to teachers and students with integration, but those people are the exception, rather than the rule. Keep in mind that even the friendly people have rules and procedures that need to be followed. As you work closely with your team, you'll see that these rules usually are in place for good reasons, and they seldom represent insurmountable barriers. You will find the experience of integrating technology challenging and frustrating at times, but ultimately rewarding. You will gain a new perspective on teaching, and your students will become more engaged in their learning.

CURRICULUM CONNECTIONS

GRADE LEVEL: 12
CONTENT AREA/TOPIC: American Government

Short Description of Lesson

In this lesson, student groups use Web sources to research current U.S. Supreme Court justices to determine personal biographical data, professional experience, important cases the justice has ruled on, and other interesting facts. Each group develops their research conclusions into a multimedia slideshow and presents it to the class.

Time Allotted for the Lesson

4 blocks (90 minutes per block)
2 blocks for research/creation of PowerPoint
   presentation
2 blocks for presentations

Instructional Objective(s)

After research of a Supreme Court justice, assigned by the teacher, the student will be able to:

1. Identify and analyze the judicial philosophy of the justice.
2. Identify and analyze major cases in which the justice has taken part.
3. Present biographical and professional data about the justice.
4. Present interesting facts about the justice.

Tennessee State Learning Accomplishments to Be Addressed and Assessed

4.5 Understand the role of the U.S. legal system.
6.4 Understand how the philosophies or liberalism and conservatism correlate to the two major American political parties.
6.6 Understand the role of individual leaders who have affected policies, case laws, and legislation.

National Education Technology Standards for Students (NETS·S) to Be Addressed and Assessed

2. Communication and Collaboration
   b. Communicate information and ideas effectively to multiple audiences using a variety of media and formats.
3. Research and Information Fluency
   b. Locate, organize, analyze, evaluate, synthesize, and ethically use information from a variety of sources and media.

Classroom Layout

- Classroom time will be conducted in a computer lab and the classroom. The computer lab will offer a computer for each person to have access for research and creation of the slideshow. Each computer will have the sites bookmarked for easy access by the students.
- The classroom will be used for presentations. Students will have access to a computer with PowerPoint, a screen, and LCD projector for presentations.

Materials and Resources

1. Microsoft PowerPoint or other slideshow software
2. LCD Projector
3. Browser software with all the following web sites bookmarked:
   Findlaw, www.findlaw.com
   Google, www.google.com
   Oyez: US Supreme Court Multimedia, www. oyez.com
   United States Supreme Court, www.supreme courtus.gov
   The USCC+ Database of US Supreme Court Opinions, www.usscplus.com
   Wikipedia, www.wikipedia.com

Prerequisite Technology Skills

1. Basic computer skills including the use of a keyboard and mouse.
2. The ability to use Web-based resources to gather information.
3. Basic use of Microsoft PowerPoint software.

Student's Present Level of Performance and Knowledge

1. All students should have basic research skills learned through the eleventh grade.
2. All students should have an eleventh-grade reading level.
3. At least one student per group should have experience using Microsoft PowerPoint.

(Continues)

CURRICULUM CONNECTIONS *Continued*

Instructional Activities

Set *The introductory question, "What information do you know about the Supreme Court Justices?" The teacher will then present a sample PowerPoint presentation on a former Supreme Court Justice. This presentation will serve as a model for the students to follow when developing their own presentations.*

Techniques and Activities:

1. Prior to the lesson, the teacher gives each student a questionnaire asking them about their individual ability relating to PowerPoint as well as their preference of Supreme Court Justices.
2. The teacher will assign students to a group based on their experience level using MS PowerPoint and Supreme Court Justice preference.
3. The teacher distributes the project requirements and scoring rubric and explains the student expectations.
4. Students begin to gather information on their justice by using the textbook and Internet resources.
5. Students finish collecting information and begin creating their PowerPoint presentation.
6. The teacher will meet with each student individually to discuss progress, provide feedback and suggestions, and to check for understanding.
7. Students will finish their PowerPoint presentation.
8. Each student group presents research in a ten-minute presentation to the class.
9. Students will entertain questions from the class concerning their justice.
10. Students will turn in a copy of their PowerPoint presentation to the teacher for assessment.

Closure *The teacher will close the lesson with a discussion/recap of Supreme Court justices and their roles in the federal judiciary system.*

Extensions and Remediation Activities

Students who do not participate due to absences will be required to write a four- to five-page research paper on their assigned justice. The paper will be in Microsoft Word format with one-inch margins, twelve point Times New Roman font, and double-spaced.

Student Products

Each group will create a PowerPoint presentation pertaining to their assigned Justice. If the student is absent and does not participate with his or her group during the actual presentation, he or she will be required to submit a four- to five-page research paper on their assigned Justice.

Adaptations for Diverse Learners

Students can be paired depending on learning ability.

Evaluation

Students will be graded on their presentation using a scoring rubric. The scoring rubric will measure a student's ability to meet each of the instructional objectives, including identifying and analyzing judicial philosophies and major Supreme Court cases, presentation of biographical and professional data along with interesting facts, and presentation of material to the class.

Lesson Supplements Available at Companion Web Site

1. Sample PowerPoint presentation used by teacher during set.
2. Requirements for project.
3. Scoring rubric.

On the Web

This section includes only a snapshot of web sites that the authors recommend for viewing. To access live links and a larger and continuously updated collection of sites, go to the companion web site at **www.pearsonhighered.com/obannon2e**.

Managing the Classroom during Technology Implementation

Managing Computer Use: Challenges and Solutions
www.intel.com/education/newtotech/managing.htm
Intel shares information about managing classrooms during computer use at this site. Common challenges faced by teachers such as how to keep students on task and productive, getting each member of collaborative tech group to participate, and dealing with the digital divide are a few of the topics discussed.

Popular Educational Indexes

Blue Web'n
www.kn.pacbell.com/wired/bluewebn/#table
This online searchable library, sponsored by AT&T, is a great place to find lesson plans and a host of other resources.

Discovery Education
http://school.discoveryeducation.com
Sponsored by Discovery Communications, this great site offers links on topics in science, natural history, and geography. The site also features the well-known *Kathy Schrock's Guide for Educators*, a clip art galley, worksheets to go, homework helpers and a Puzzlemaker.

Education World
www.education-world.com/index.shtml
Education World provides a searchable database for educational resources. Additionally, the site offers original lesson plans, practical information for educators, information on how to integrate technology in the classroom, articles written by education experts, web site reviews, daily features, and more. *Techtorials* are weekly step-by-step instructions on using various aspects of technology including emerging technologies.

Kathy Schrock's Guide for Educators
http://school.discoveryeducation.com/schrockguide/edles.html
This index is a rich resource for teachers. Schrock, a former technology coordinator, keeps this site updated regularly and provides links to a vast amount of information for teachers.

PBS Teachers
www.pbs.org/teachers
The Public Broadcasting Service (PBS) provides a large collection of standard-based resources for the arts, health and fitness, math, reading and language arts, science and technology, and social studies, as well as a section for early childhood learners. A featured resource is online professional development on assessment and evaluation.

Planning for Instruction, Lesson Plans, Objectives, and Assessment

Planning for Instruction
http://edtech.tennessee.edu/projects/bobannon
This online module developed by Blanche O'Bannon assists preservice teachers in developing lesson plans. Information about *why plan*, *unit plans*, *lesson plans*, *instructional objectives*, *writing objectives*, *classifying objectives* (revised Bloom's taxonomy), and *instructional methods* are included. There is an interactive practice provided for writing objectives.

Special Learners

Center for Applied Special Technology (CAST)
www.cast.org
At this site, CAST provides abundant information regarding Universal Design for Learning (UDL). CAST, a nonprofit educational research and development organization, works to create opportunities for all students, particularly those with disabilities, through using technology to make education more flexible and accessible. The book, *Teaching Every Student in the Digital Age*, which outlines the process of UDL, is available online at this site.

Assistive Technology Training Online (ATTO)
http://atto.buffalo.edu
ATTO offers information on assistive technology (AT) applications that assist students with disabilities in elementary classrooms. This award-winning site, funded by the U.S. Department of Education Office of Special Education and Rehabilitation Services, provides basic information on AT use, information on AT decision making, and new tutorials about how to use AT hardware and software. The site includes links to other resources and organizations.

Standards-Based Sites

National Education Standards for Teachers (NETS·T) and Students (NETS·S)
www.iste.org/AM/Template.cfm?Section=NETS
NETS·T (2008) provide teachers and teacher preparation institutions with standards, performance indicators, and rubrics for teachers. The online site does not provide the rubrics but they can be purchased from the NETS Resource Library found at this page. NETS·S (2007) provide teachers with student standards, profiles, and performance indicators.

Key Terms

No Child Left Behind Act (4)

International Society for Technology in Education (ISTE) (6)

National Educational Technology Standards for Students (NETS·S) (6)

National Educational Technology Standards for Teachers (NETS·T) (6)

National Educational Technology Standards for Administrators (NETS·A) (6)

Technology profiles (7)

Performance indicators (7)

ISTE essential conditions (12)

Unit plan (14)

Lesson plan (14)

Lesson goal (15)

Curriculum standards (15)

Instructional objectives (15)

Performance and knowledge levels (17)

Classroom layout (17)

Grouping of students (17)

Instructional procedures (17)

Lesson set (17)

Techniques and activities (17)

Lesson closure (17)

Traditional learning environments versus new learning environments (18)

Accommodation (19)

Modification (19)

Informal methods (19)

Formal methods (19)

Formative assessment (20)

Summative assessment (20)

Assistive technology (AT) (24)

Technology coordinator (29)

Hands-on Activities for Learning

1. Visit the On the Web companion site (**www.pearson highered.com/obannon2e**) and review the sites available.

2. Visit the ISTE web site, www.iste.org, and examine the many resources provided, including the listing of current web sites, books, or periodicals that relate to educational technology provided to teachers by this organization.

3. Observe two or three K–12 classrooms that have at least one computer. Draw a sketch of the classroom. Interview the teacher. Ask how the computer(s) are used as a part of the curriculum. Ask about policies and procedures for computer use. Request a copy of the school's acceptable use policy for review.

4. Research the technology support available in a school district in your local area. Interview a technology coordinator or a teacher to find out what support is available to teachers.

2 Hardware Basics

LEARNER OBJECTIVES

At the completion of this chapter, learners will be able to:

- Identify a computer system and its components.
- Explain the relationship between the sectors of the central processing unit (CPU) and the flow of information during processing.
- Identify the purpose of input, output, and storage devices and give examples of those that are typically used in educational settings.
- Identify the role of software.
- Discuss major considerations for purchasing a computer for home or classroom use.
- Identify methods for adapting and using computer systems with special learners.

NETS-T ALIGNED WITH HARDWARE BASICS

3. **Model Digital-Age Work and Learning**

   Teachers exhibit knowledge, skills, and work processes representative of an innovative professional in a global and digital society. Teachers:

   a. demonstrate fluency in technology systems and the transfer of current knowledge to new technologies and situations.

   b. collaborate with students, peers, parents, and community members using digital tools and resources to support student success and innovation.

   c. communicate relevant information and ideas effectively to students, parents, and peers using a variety of digital-age media and formats.

   d. model and facilitate effective use of current and emerging digital tools to locate, analyze, evaluate, and use information resources to support research and learning.

Frameworks

Computers provide unique learning opportunities for students in classrooms where teachers realize the potential and need for their use. Technology integration is dependent on having access to the physical components, as well as a teacher who is capable of facilitating learning using these components. As discussed in Chapter 1, the ISTE essential conditions that must be in place for successful integration to take place include **equitable access**. This condition states that "robust and reliable access to current and emerging technologies and digital resources, with connectivity for all students, teachers, staff, and school leaders" is necessary to effectively leverage technology for learning (ISTE, 2007, p. 3).

Access options to technology in PK–12 schools vary from school to school across the nation, with typical classroom access being provided by one or more options including: (1) one or more stand-alone computers, (2) computer learning centers where a single computer is available for students to visit in collaborative groups, (3) a computer workstation consisting of several computers connected to a scanner and printer, (4) a centrally located school computer lab consisting of 25–30 single networked computers, or (5) mobile technology options available for checkout. The mobile technology options vary as well, and are usually either mobile labs (typically with 15–20 laptop computers) or mobile workstations frequently referred to as COWs (computers on wheels). COWs may include a desktop or laptop computer and usually include a printer, as well as a CD player. Mobile technology labs give additional access to teachers. Because many classrooms share these labs, a teacher must carefully schedule time to have access to the mobile lab when needed. Even with dedicated planning, this option does not always fit into the curriculum. In addition, school libraries typically offer a few computers for student access during study periods. The National Center for Education Statistics (NCES) concluded from a study completed in 2005 that the nationwide average student/computer ratio was 4.4:1. A more recent study conducted by the National Education Association (NEA) in conjunction with American Federation of Teachers (2008) reports student/computer ratio dropped slightly in the last few years to a ratio of 3.8:1. Although this ratio may seem sufficient, a visit to many classrooms reveals great disparity in equitable access because many computers are outdated and lack the ability to run new software programs.

Basics

Discussion in this section is intended to facilitate a fundamental understanding of computer systems and other hardware that is available for technology integration. It is important for readers to be mindful, throughout the discussion, that hardware is continuously under development and manufacturers are continuously working to provide more powerful, smaller, and more affordable options for school settings. Teachers and their students should have a basic knowledge of a computer system, as well as the multiple devices available to input, output, and store information to realize the full potential of the computer. In addition, teachers should understand the power that these tools offer to teaching and learning. Although schools' technology budgets may be limited, there are many grant options for teachers to pursue in order to bring more access into their classrooms. Review the grant sources listed at On the Web: Hardware at the companion site (**www.pearsonhighered.com/obannon2e**).

Computer System

A **computer system** refers to the computer and other support devices (called *peripheral devices*) that work as a team to (1) receive information (or data) as the user inputs it, (2) process that information per the directions that the user defines, and (3) output the information in a usable format. The processing of the information takes place in the **central processing unit (CPU)**, often referred to as the processor.

The CPU, located inside the computer body in the form of computer chips, is composed of three units (or sectors) that work together: the control unit, the arithmetic logic unit (ALU), and the memory unit. The **control unit** retrieves the instructions and sends command signals to the rest of the computer system to tell them what to do. The **arithmetic logic unit**, or ALU, is the sector of the CPU that performs the mathematical calculations that are required in many data processing programs. The **memory unit** allows storage of information, is internal to the computer, and is divided into two types of memory: RAM (random access memory) and ROM (read-only memory).

RAM is temporary memory that is designed to hold new data and is available only while the computer is turned on. The information held in RAM is lost when the computer suffers a power surge or a computer crash, or is turned off. Consequently, it is very important to save work frequently on the hard disk or external memory device. The amount of RAM is an important consideration during the purchase of a computer, because it determines the type of software programs that can be used as well as the number of programs the computer can successfully run at the same time. The general rule is to get as much RAM as you can afford. For teachers and classrooms using basic computing, with standard desktop applications and the Internet, 512 RAM may be fine. However, if the user is going to include working with graphics, the Web, or games, more RAM is needed or the computer will be sluggish. The power of the operating systems also dictates the amount of RAM needed. The latest version of OS at this writing is Apple OS 10.5.6 Leopard, which needs 512 MB of RAM. Windows XP works well at 512 yet to get the same performance from Vista, 1 GB is needed. Teachers must be aware that the amount of RAM needed depends on the types of programs that the computer is going to run and the type of work that is going to be done on the computer. RAM can be expanded in computers relatively cheaply if needed. **ROM** is permanent internal memory inside the system, is inaccessible by the user, and is used to store the instructions that are installed or programmed at the manufacturer. Figure 2.1 identifies the sectors of the CPU and the way the data moves through the processing functions.

Memory Explained in Bits and Bytes

A computer system works with a **binary coding system** called **ASCII** (pronounced *ASK-ee*, standing for American Standard Code for Information Interchange) code, made up of a series of zeros and ones. A binary character (a zero or one) is referred to as a **bit** and is the smallest unit of binary information. Eight bits make a **byte**, which can represent one alphabetic (A, B, C) or one numeric (1, 2, 3) character of information. A unique combination of zeros and ones represent each letter of the alphabet. For instance the eight-bit, or one-byte, binary code 01000001 represents the alphabetic character "A" and the code that represents the character for small "a" is 01100001. Generally measured in **kilobytes**, **megabytes**, and **gigabytes**, computer memory is measured in the amount of information that it can hold. Table 2.1 explains terms used to describe the power of the

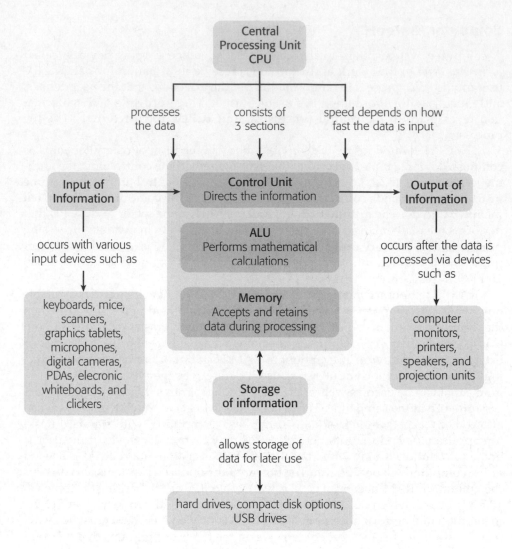

FIGURE 2.1   Central Processing Unit (CPU)

size of memory and storage devices. **Terabyte** storage options are becoming a reality for hard drives.

Processor Speed

The speed of the processor is also important and conveys how fast data can be moved in and out of the memory. The **processor speed** is expressed in **megahertz** (MHz), which equals one million cycles per second or **gigahertz** (GHz), which equals one billion cycles per second. The higher the number listed, the faster the speed that the data moves in and out of memory. A typical entry-level computer at the printing of this book might have a 2 GHz processor and a top-level computer might have in excess of a 4 GHz processor. The **cache** (pronounced *cash*) provides a temporary storage area that provides a quick access to information. The processor uses a cache as does browser software. The cache prevents the computer from having to access memory again from the CPU. When working on the Web, the browser cache allows access to data that has previously been downloaded.

Table 2.1   Memory Conversions

Bit = a single binary number: a zero or one

Byte = 8 bits; the binary code for one character of data. 01000001 = A; 01100001 = a

Kilobyte (K/KB) = 1,024 bytes = 1 K or approximately 1,024 keyboard characters of information

Megabyte (M/MB) = 1,024 kilobytes = 1 MB or approximately a million keyboard characters of information

Gigabyte (G/GB) = 1,024 megabytes = 1 GB or approximately a billion keyboard characters of information

Terabyte (T/TB) = 1024 gigabytes = 1 TB or approximately a trillion keyboard characters of information

Input, Output, and Storage Devices

A computer system must have **peripheral devices** to: (1) input the information, (2) output the information into a form that is easily read by the user, or (3) store the information for later use. In addition to the common input, output, and storage devices with which most readers are familiar, there are also a variety of additional, less common options that should be examined—and the number of these is growing daily. A desktop computer system that is appropriate for school environments is pictured in Figure 2.2. Figure 2.3 shows a recent laptop option available at the printing of this book. These small and colorful laptops have keyboards for input, flat-screen monitors, and a variety of connection ports for many peripheral devices, as well as the latest and fastest removable storage devices. These tools bring power to the classroom for students to learn 21st century skills as they communicate, collaborate, and construct knowledge.

FIGURE 2.2 Desktop Computer System with Standard Input (keyboard and mouse), Output (monitor), and Storage Drives
Courtesy of Dell Inc. All Rights Reserved.

Input Devices

Input devices allow the input of data into the computer. Examples include keyboards, mice, scanners, graphic tablets, microphones, digital cameras (still and video), Web cameras, electronic whiteboards, PDAs, "clickers," and cell phones. The next pages discuss each of these, as well as the pros and cons of using some of them in the classroom. In the Adapting for Special Learners section of the chapter, devices that are helpful for special learners are discussed.

   Keyboards and **mice** are the most familiar input devices. Keyboards, similar to typewriter keyboards, offer the input of alphabetic and numeric information, as well as additional operational and input keys. Although there are variations of keyboards and mice, most are quite similar in function. The **touch pads** and **trackballs** that serve as the mouse on some laptop computers can take some time to master, and some teachers may prefer to purchase a traditional mouse that can be connected through a port on the computer. Another mouse option is the **wireless/cordless mouse**. Although cords do not hamper these devices, they require batteries, may have restricted movement, and must be used with a computer that is equipped to receive the signal. A **mouse pad** allows good movement of the mouse—and comes in many trendy designs. Other input options include game devices such as **joysticks** that come in a variety of designs.

FIGURE 2.3 Laptop Computer System with Standard Input (keyboard and touch pad), Output (monitor), and Storage Drives
Courtesy of Dell Inc. All Rights Reserved.

FIGURE 2.4 Flatbed Scanner

Photo provided courtesy of Hewlett-Packard Company

FIGURE 2.5 Graphics Tablet

Photo courtesy of Wacom Technology Corp.

FIGURE 2.6 Headphones and Microphone

A **scanner** is an input device that is connected to the computer through a port connection, and that allows the conversion of a printed page (which is a type of analog data) of text or graphics to digital format. There are several types of scanners available; the most common are flatbed or sheet-fed scanners. In addition, some scanners can scan slides, and some are used primarily for commercial jobs. Scanners and their value to teaching and learning are discussed at length in Chapter 7. To allow the scanning process to take place, the computer must have specialized software loaded. Typically, entry-level software comes with the scanner, though it usually has limited features. Converting text is performed by **optical character recognition (OCR)** software. Graphics can be scanned; interesting images can be achieved by scanning various types or patterns of cloth or even foil. Scanners have become quite inexpensive and are most useful in the classroom. A flatbed scanner is pictured in Figure 2.4.

A **graphics tablet** is also connected to the computer through a port connection. The teacher or student draws on the electronic tablet with a stylus to transfer the image to the computer. A stylus is a pen-shaped tool that is designed to press on the tablet surface with no resulting damage. Artists or people in similar professions usually are the major market for graphic tablets; however, they are also used in the classroom, primarily by art teachers. Figure 2.5 shows an example of a graphics tablet.

Audio can be input into the computer with the use of a **microphone**. Some computers have built-in microphones, and others require use of an external microphone. External microphones must be plugged into a connective port on the back of the computer before using. The port is connected to a **sound card**, which allows the input of sound into the computer. Sound, while most beneficial in many instructional situations, can be distracting in the classroom. Teachers should consider the use of **headphones** when individual students are using multimedia programs that include sound. In addition, if a person is talking into the microphone, a quiet room is needed so that background noise will not be captured. Figure 2.6 shows a set of headphones and a microphone.

Video can be input into the computer with the use of digital cameras, video cameras, or Web cams. **Digital cameras** are cameras that are capable of inputting data into a computer instead of onto film, and are common tools in teaching and learning across grade levels. Digital cameras are quite similar in use to traditional cameras, with basically the same parts, yet they have many advantages, including immediate access to pictures, the ability to select only the best pictures and delete the others, and the ability to store the pictures easily in digital format for inclusion in electronic materials. There are various cables and ports for connecting cameras to the computer for transfer of the pictures, depending on the model of camera used. Some also offer removable storage devices such as memory cards and memory sticks, and some of the latest models can transfer photos via a wireless connection. Various camera categories are marketed to consumers, with differing power and features available. Figure 2.7 presents a point and shoot digital camera.

Digital video cameras can record video that can be input into the computer with specialized software and cables. Last, another camera that is useful in the classroom is a **Web cam**, pictured in Figure 2.8, a tiny camera that sits on (or is part of) the computer and feeds video directly into the computer. Typically used for video conferencing, these cameras can also take photos of anything at which they are pointed. Specifics are discussed in detail in Chapter 7, along with how teachers are successfully adapting their curriculums to include these tools.

Another method of input that has become quite popular in recent years is **pen input**, more commonly known as a **personal digital assistant (PDA)**, as seen in Figure 2.9. These small, portable tools allow the user to input handwritten notes on a small screen using a special pen or a tiny keyboard. These notes can be downloaded (synchronized) into a computer for later use. PDAs have multiple uses for teachers and students. There is a wide range of sophistication with these devices. The lower-end models are designed for personal information management, and include such things as an address book, calendar, and task list. More sophisticated models also offer access to software applications such as word processing or spreadsheets, and some offer access to email and the Web, with the use of an Internet service provider (ISP). PDAs have multiple uses for teachers, such as noting grades, appointments, student behavior, classroom activities, and student information. Some models include built-in keyboards or foldable keyboards that can be attached and used to input data easily. There are various sizes, shapes, and types of PDAs available, and their capabilities have changed quite significantly over the last several years. As with other hardware, teachers should consider the purpose of the PDA as well as its compatibility with the computer system that is being used. Refer to the On the Web section of this chapter for resources with information about using PDAs for instruction, and Voices from the Classroom—Mobilizing My Students, which describes using this technology to incorporate real-world examples of challenging projects. Curriculum connections can be made in math, science, English, social studies, and other content with these portable devices using specialized software.

Tablet computers are complete computer systems in a slate format. There are a variety of models available, in two formats: a slate design without a keyboard and a traditional laptop that converts to a slate. When working in slate mode, the user can make notes using a stylus or digital pen on a touch screen as shown in Figure 2.10. These notes can be stored and transferred for later use.

Interactive whiteboards are becoming quite common in today's classrooms. These boards (shown in Figure 2.11) serve the same purpose as a traditional blackboard, yet they offer outstanding functionality, serving as dry-erase and interactive whiteboards. When this board is connected to a computer, the sensitive screen captures everything written or drawn on its surface, which can later be transferred to the computer and printed. One option for using these boards during instruction could be that students would no longer be required to take notes. They can listen and collaborate and later download the notes taken by this technology by email or from the Internet. To watch an interactive whiteboard by SMART Technologies in action in a classroom, go to **www.smarttech.com**. There is a section at that site

FIGURE 2.7 Digital Camera
Used by permission of Sony Electronics Inc.

FIGURE 2.8 Web Cam
©2008 Logitech. All rights reserved. Image used with permission from Logitech.

FIGURE 2.9 Personal Digital Assistant, or PDA
Used by permission of Palm, Inc.

FIGURE 2.10 Tablet Computer

FIGURE 2.11 SMART Board
Used by permission of SMART Technologies, Inc. Copyright 2001–2008 SMART Technologies, ULC.

Voices *from the* CLASSROOM

Mobilizing My Students
JoAnne Logan, PhD

JoAnne Logan, a native of Boston, Massachusetts, is a happy transplant to the University of Tennessee in Knoxville. She has been teaching college classes in climatology, geographic information systems, and environmental science since 1987. Currently she is director of the undergraduate program in Environmental Sciences and co-director of the Southern Appalachian Science and Engineering Fair. She has enjoyed being on the "bleeding edge" of instructional technology in her classes, including multimedia, course management systems, mobile computing, Global Positioning Systems, tablet PCs, and PDAs. We asked JoAnne to enlighten us about some of the new computer technologies used in teaching environmental science.

What could be more challenging than keeping students' interest during a 2½-hour computer lab? This was a dilemma I faced in teaching an introductory undergraduate college class in a computer-mapping program called geographic information systems (GIS). Most students are juniors and seniors in agriculture and natural resources. Generally, the students sit in front of desktop computers, learning the "bells and whistles" of the software. Although I try to make the sessions more interesting by including real-world examples and challenging projects, it's not always easy to keep their interest as the semester wanes. The innovative Technology Center (ITC) at the University of Tennessee sponsors a wireless initiative that includes Toshiba® personal digital assistants (PDAs) with wireless cards, Global Positioning System receivers (GPS), Pocket PC®, and the Mobile GIS program ArcPad (ESRI, Redlands, CA). I was able to secure 10 PDAs to use in a class of 20, grouping the students in teams of 2. As part of the wireless project, ITC set up a WiFi transmitter at the UT Botanical Trial Garden, several acres that provide an excellent "playground" for Mobile GIS. They also provided a one-hour training session on the use of the PDAs during the first lab period. The students spent a total of two lab periods in the garden—mapping the garden plots and structures, linking the maps to the garden database, and uploading the data in real time via the wireless to the server in the computer lab. This exercise is very typical of the Mobile GIS applications conducted on the job in many fields especially Utilities. Forestry, and Environmental Management in the future. I would like my students to employ Mobile GIS to complete an inventory of buildings and trees on campus, with images and updated information for each.

During the project, we experimented with some other PDA applications such as Skype, which acts much like a "walkie-talkie system" over the wireless. The students were able to chat about their mapping progress to each other. This helped them to better organize their mapping strategy and avoid redundancies in data collection. I also tried a Wireless Pocket PC-based Classroom Response System that functions much like a "clicker." Questions needed to be assembled ahead of time and not "on-the-fly," which was somewhat inconvenient. Newer versions of software have improved features. Many classroom instructors use PDAs to remotely control their PowerPoint presentations. Overall, using the PDAs to help mobilize my GIS students, get them out in field, and expose them to a real-world application, was a positive experience for both the students and me. PDAs have so much potential, especially on a wireless campus.

They also have great possibilities in K–12 schools that lack wireless Internet connectivity. There are many reference programs such as a dictionary, thesaurus, calculator, book reader, metronome, health monitor, astronomical guide, spell checker, math flash cards, grammar, foreign language, and encyclopedia; mapping programs; programs to simulate musical instruments; sketching programs; image viewers; word processing; etc. Many of these programs are available as shareware at minimal cost. It is also possible to add peripherals such as a collapsible keyboard and display device, greatly enhancing the functionality of the PDA.

for educators that presents teacher-created videos on YouTube and TeacherTube channels. To watch classroom applications with Activboard by Promethean go to **www.prometheanworld.com/us/**. While this technology is not cheap, the possibilities that interactive whiteboards offer to the classroom facilitates student-centered, performance-focused learning. There are various opportunities for grant awards for K–12 at the Smarter Kids Foundation (**www.smarterkids.org/k12/index.asp**). International collaborative learning opportunities await teachers of students who are five to 12 years old, as explained under Imaginations at **www.smarterkids.org/imaginations/index.asp**. This is a must-see site for teachers interested in teaching about the various cultures around our globe. An option for turning any whiteboard into an interactive whiteboard is mimioBoard by Virtual Link, available at **www.mimio.com**. Read about mimioGrants available for K–12 teachers at **www.mimio.com/solutions/education/funding/mimiogrant/index.php**. The following two Voices from the Classroom in this chapter share the experiences of teachers who use interactive whiteboards in their schools.

A **classroom response system** or **"clicker"** is a handheld device that resembles a TV remote that allows students to respond to questions posed by the instructor. These responses are wirelessly sent to the instructor and shown in real time or stored for later viewing. Although this technology is not new, educators have seen the possibility with these devices of getting more reliable answers to awkward questions that might go unanswered. Clickers allow students to give instant feedback and allow the instructor to get a feel for the depth of understanding of the information. Commonly used in university classrooms, some of the interactive whiteboards now include clickers with purchase. Discover more about teaching ideas with this technology in On the Web: Hardware located at the companion site.

Output Devices

Output devices produce the data after it has been processed in hard copy (paper for permanent media) or soft copy (displayed on the screen or nonpermanent means). Categories of output include text documents, graphics, or multimedia. Output devices, commonly found in classrooms, yet not all-inclusive, include computer monitors, printers, speakers, projection units, document cameras, interactive whiteboards, and portable media players. These devices are discussed in the next sections.

Computer Monitors   **Computer monitors**, also called **screens** or **displays**, are the most common output device. They display information on the screen, where it can be edited and sent to the printer. Today's monitors are available with various features with which teachers should be familiar in order to make informed decisions regarding purchases for the home, the classroom, and even the school labs, if technical support is limited. Such decisions may result in saving money, and—most important—getting the most out of your budget! Monitors are usually a separate purchase from the processor, and are available in varying sizes, viewable areas, and resolutions. Monitors use either **CRT** (**cathode ray tube**) or **LCD** (**liquid crystal display**) technology, and the choice between the two affects price, viewing area, space on the desktop, and crispness of the output.

When considering monitor size, teachers should understand the difference in the size and the area that is actually available for viewing information. Monitors have become quite large in recent years, with the most common sizes for desktop models at 15", 17", 19", and 21". Laptop screens are smaller, generally 12", 15", or 17". But what exactly do these dimensions represent when making a purchasing decision and what size do teachers need for teaching and learning purposes? **Monitor size** is measured diagonally from corner to corner. A difference exists between CRT and LCD screens. A CRT screen is measured including the casing surrounding the screen, whereas an LCD monitor is measured inside the casing. Consequently, a 17" LCD screen will provide a larger viewable area of the screen contents than a 17" CRT monitor. In addition, a flat-screen monitor takes up less room on the desktop (also known as having a "smaller footprint"). There is little

Voices *from the* Classroom

On the Cutting Edge: One Classroom — The World
L'Jon Papillon

L' Jon Papillon, a classroom teacher for 30 years, has taught in rural, suburban, and inner city schools. For more than twenty years, she has been on the cutting edge of technology in the classroom, beginning with a "21st Century Classroom" award from Knox County Schools and the Tennessee Department of Education. One of the first kindergarten teachers in the state to receive this award, she used the funding to purchase computers and peripheral equipment for her kindergarten classroom. She has taught parents, teachers, administrators, and students from kindergarten through fifth grade to become more technologically adept. Moving ever forward, she was the first in her inner city school to attain a "SMART Board" for classroom use. "Technology is the tool of the future, starting today," she tells her students. "Let's get started!" She has served on the Technology Team in two different schools, and has bought computers for her classroom when local funding was unavailable. Currently employed as a Talented and Gifted teacher for third- through fifth-grade students in three different schools, she continues to embrace the wonder and excitement technology brings to everyday lessons in whatever forms available for use.

Learning to use new technology such as interactive whiteboards is not so much about steps and procedures as it is about putting into practice a child-like attitude. Give a child a PlayStation or a Wii, and the instruction booklet's plastic protective cover is never breached. Yet, within moments, a game is up and running, and excitement builds as a new door is opened or a new strategy learned. So it goes with interactive whiteboards in the classroom.

Every subject provides teachers and students with an opportunity to learn from a wide variety of venues.

Whether it is the definition of a word, animal pictures stamped on a "page," a customized graphic organizer, or an interactive analog clock, lessons become bigger than life, more readily accessible, present-day current, and ultimately more successful than any overhead or chart of yesteryear's classrooms. Second- through fifth-grade students in my reading class were participating in a novel study in which the main character "collected houses," listing the location, price, and "fascinating details" about each house in her "dream book." The students were bewildered, thinking she may have "listened to the news," or "heard it on the radio," but clearly, they had no idea how a person could look for, or determine the cost of, a house in different parts of the world.

The curiosity of that moment began a practical, life-based unit of study on housing types and materials, interest rates, square footage, and unique abbreviations in real estate advertisements. A student-generated list of countries and interesting areas of the United States prompted a student "Recorder" to select the keyboard option on the "SMART Board," and enter class-suggested geographical locations. Literally, "Google Earth" brought a world of houses into our inner-city classroom.

The vast data bank of the "SMART Board Teacher Tools" provided the class with the necessary graphics for individual/team job charts. The large screen increased visibility of the search, allowing me to "talk" the students through the process of finding and setting up another chart for job assignments. Every student benefited from the exercise in unique ways. By watching the data bank search, student awareness of the numerous graphics increased, and many were able to use the data bank as the year progressed and need arose. One student remarked in science class

difference in cost between the 15" and 17" models, but prices begin rising rapidly thereafter.

Resolution defines the clarity of the image that is seen on the computer screen. Monitor resolution is measured in pixels. A **pixel** is a single colored square on the screen. When pixels are joined, the image can be viewed. Resolution is measured horizontally and vertically. Therefore, if the resolution of a screen is 800 × 600, there are 800 columns of pixels horizontally and 600 rows of pixels vertically. The screen size may dictate the resolution. Most new monitors have adjustable resolution so the user can adjust to accommodate the needs of software.

Voices *from the* Classroom *Continued*

one day, "Ms. Papillon, I saw a blank food chain in the SMART Board bank!"

Although the big moments are wonderful to experience, everyday use of an interactive whiteboard increases awareness of student expectations, and often becomes a motivational tool for mundane activities. As students arrive, a problem-solving activity on one page can precede the daily schedule, followed by pages containing vocabulary words, student reminders, or challenges for the day. My students looked for the display of the "Big Idea" or lesson focus every day. Short film clips from Discovery Education often set the stage for an upcoming lesson, or as a backdrop for review.

A study of mythology led first to looking up images of the different gods and goddesses, but resulted in a larger study. The class researched maps from different sources, identified ancient world boundaries and land divisions, and discussed subsequent historical changes. These activities prompted a comparison of the classroom student atlases, maps, and various globes against current time online information. Teachable moments are everpresent with an interactive whiteboard!

Social Studies DVDs, played through the computer onto the screen, allowed numerous "teachable moments" because I could pause the video and ask students to label time zones and landforms on the screen with different colored markers. The "camera" tool kept a visual record of each study. Saving these "records" in a desktop folder gave the students a resource for printable pages to use in their reports and presentations.

Instead of textbook skill/concept review, the images could be reviewed as needed, and more often than not, were navigated by the students. Used as an assessment tool, students recalled necessary information with greater success than paper/pencil tests.

As I became increasingly familiar with the incredible potential of the SMART Board, I made templates for each class and each subject. The Essential Question, "Big Idea," daily schedule, morning math problem, and vocabulary warm-up formed one template. For math class, I created different templates based on the area of study. For example, pages for a measurement unit had tools, grouped by category, to be displayed and used in an instant. Elapsed time, always difficult for students to do, was easier to understand using an interactive clock with moveable hands because it could be duplicated as many times as needed.

For most elementary students, the SMART Board provides access to the world through pictures, language, music, and activities. Lessons on most every subject are available for classroom use. Skills-based games often provide a learning center during differentiated instruction. When students use an interactive whiteboard, their spontaneity results in higher-order questioning. By allowing the teacher to observe students' thought processes in action, they can be corrected, guided, and provided positive feedback on the spot. The class, as a whole, are engaged and interested, reducing off-task behaviors and increasing learning.

Using an interactive whiteboard requires planning and a willingness to search for the "best" tools available. All technology demands flexibility, and the whiteboard is no exception. When the calibration of the board gets off and my writing ends up in a different place than intended, the students invariably laugh. As I join their laughter, I recognize another teachable moment arising. While I stop and calibrate the board with the marker, we talk about calibration, and by the time we are back into the original lesson, they know what *calibrate* means and can use it themselves. The possibilities for learning with an interactive whiteboard are endless, the excitement visible, and the impact as vast as the world itself.

Printers   A **printer** outputs the data after it has been processed in what is called a **hard copy,** or a readable, permanent copy. As with monitors, printers differ in resolution and the higher the resolution, the crisper the picture. With printers, the resolution is measured in **dots per inch (dpi)**. Text or graphics are printed in a series of dots. The higher the dots per inch, the more distinct the text, graphics, and color will appear. Printers use different print technology methods and come in a variety of speed, quality, and price.

Currently, printing options are primarily ink jet printing and laser printing. Impact or dot matrix printers may still be found in some schools, although it is quite

FIGURE 2.12 Printers
(Ink Jet and Laser)
Photos provided courtesy of
Hewlett-Packard Company
and Dell Inc.

FIGURE 2.13 Speakers

FIGURE 2.14 Data
Projector
Courtesy of Dell, Inc.

outdated. In impact printing, the characters are formed when the letters strike the paper. These printers use ribbons, similar to typewriters. **Ink jet printers** (Figure 2.12, top) produce characters by squirting minute amounts of ink on the page. Ink jet printers use printer cartridges and can print in black and color. Although these printers can be purchased very inexpensively today, the cartridges must be replaced on a regular basis, which can get somewhat expensive for the teacher's meager budget. Over time, having an ink jet printer for the classroom can be very expensive. Copies from ink jet printers are of good quality, although the printed pages will run if allowed to get wet. **Laser printers** (Figure 2.12, bottom) produce the highest quality output. Once cost-prohibitive for individual classrooms, the prices of laser printers, both those that can produce only black text and those that produce colored text, have dropped dramatically. Teachers should be aware that while the hardware is affordable, there is still an expense related to maintaining the ink supply. Laser printers affix the toner to the surface of the paper using a laser beam. The printers use toner cartridges that are expensive to buy, but that produce a large number of copies. Color laser printers have recently decreased in price; even so, these printers are not typically purchased for single-classroom use. One of the largest expenses incurred in color laser printers are the four-ink toner cartridges that are required.

Each of the printers in this discussion is capable of making **transparencies**, thin sheets of transparent plastic, for use with overhead projectors, although teachers should be mindful that each printer category has a specific type of transparency medium designed for it. If the wrong transparency is used, results can include a bad product—or even a melted product. For example, a transparency used in an ink jet printer will not withstand the heat generated by a laser printer. Further, the transparencies that are designed for use in a laser printer are more expensive, and teachers would certainly not want to waste money by using an expensive option unnecessarily. In summary, there are several criteria on which to base printer purchasing decisions. These include the number of copies that are needed per month, the print speed (how many pages per minute that can be printed), the resolution (higher resolution produces sharper images), cost of operation (prices of consumables), ability to network—to workstations connected to the network—availability of consumables, and size of the paper tray. Some of these decisions would differ if the printer were going to be used in the classroom, the school office, or the library.

Speakers Some **speakers** are built into the computer or monitor, and others are external to the computer (see Figure 2.13) and must be plugged into ports at the back of the computer. Speakers vary in capability. If a teacher needs to play sound to the entire class, it is quite important to know the power of the speakers on hand. Some speakers are meant only for a single user working at a station. These speakers, at maximum volume, would not provide the volume needed for a whole class. The need for more volume can be supplied when connecting the computer to a projection system, such as a data projector or a television. However, it is important to note that although basic computer speakers may not have enough volume for a large class, they are still loud enough to be distracting in the classroom. Therefore the use of headphones (as mentioned earlier) is needed when individual students are working with software programs that output sound. Headphones are plugged into headphone ports in the computer.

Projectors **Data projection units** combine a liquid crystal display (LCD) unit with a light source (see Figure 2.14). A rarity in classrooms in the past because of cost, projection units bring many advantages to the modern classroom over connection to a television. The resolution and brightness vary among projectors, as does the price. The brightness of the projector is measured in **lumens**. It is important to buy a projector with enough lumens that projection can take place in a room with full light. Turning off the lights makes note taking difficult for students, and prevents a deaf or hard-of-hearing child from seeing an interpreter. Determining the number of lumens necessary will depend on the lighting in your classroom and can be assessed by the technology support team. The image quality increases as the projector resolution increases. The resolution should be compatible with the computer and other devices that will be used with it, such as a DVD player, an interactive whiteboard, or a stand-alone document camera (discussed in the next section).

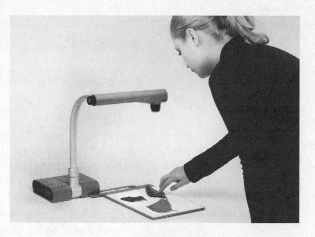

A major consideration with a projector is the price of the replacement bulbs, which are very expensive, the cost being based on the number of lumens available. A typical replacement bulb costs about $300. Some bulbs are even more expensive and all bulbs are somewhat fragile. Careless use, including exposing it to extreme temperatures, turning the projector off before the bulb cools, or a sudden jolt, can result in the bulb needing early replacement.

Some projection units are portable because of their small size and weight. As the weight decreases, the price increases. If the teacher travels from school to school, or if the projector is a shared resource for several classrooms, these portable options may be worth the extra money; however, if travel is unnecessary, a larger and cheaper one might be a better choice. As with all purchases, consideration should be given to making sure the projector has the capabilities needed by the teacher.

Additional features that are usually found on data projectors include built-in speakers and a remote control. Some projectors are equipped with document cameras, which allow the projection of opaque objects (see the next section for more information). Even though these models are quite costly, they serve many needs of the classroom teacher.

Document Cameras   Some data projection units are equipped with **document cameras** and some document cameras are stand-alone, as the one pictured in Figure 2.15. These cameras are one of the most versatile presentation tools around; they display slides, transparencies, text, documents, 3D objects, and microscopic objects. The more expensive models have lights on each side that allow objects to be illuminated and projected onto the screen via the projection system in the room. There are a number of companies that design models. New, more affordable models are now available for the classroom. This is a great tool for teachers to project opaque objects just by making a change in the settings on the projector.

Portable Media Players   **Portable media players** are portable devices that store and play audio such as music or podcasts and/or audio and video. The most popular of the audio video players, also referred to as MP3 players, is the iPod by Apple Computer. Apple has increased the number of models available of this nifty tool, first released in 2001. The current models include the iPod Classic (internal hard drive), the iPod Touch (touchscreen), the iPod Shuffle (audio only), the Nano (video capable). These players can serve as storage options with the capacity varying by model. These players are affordable options for the classroom and bring new opportunities to teaching and learning.

Storage Devices
Storage devices allow storage of data for later use. Storage devices include internal storage options and external storage options. It is quite important to check the

Voices *from the* Classroom

iPower in a Third-Grade Classroom
James Andrew McDonald

After receiving an MS in Human Ecology from The University of Tennessee and an Early Childhood teaching license, Andrew McDonald moved to Bangkok, Thailand, to pursue teaching in international schools. For the next three years he taught at two international schools. During that period, he spent much of his time working with students on issues that are also found in the United States: fluency, accent, and vocabulary. Thus, he began a four-year experiment of how to use iPods to develop non-threatening, realistic training of how children hear, and speak, and eliminate fears of public speaking. We asked Andrew to share his story.

In my classroom on the other side of the world, I encountered students who had heavy Asian accents when they spoke English and they were generally far behind their native English speaking counterparts in reading. I decided to experiment with an iPod to see if I could improve their ability to read. I recorded myself reading English assessments. Three times a day, I had the slowest readers listen to the iPod and read at the same speed as my recording. I assessed their ability to read on Monday and again on Friday after reading the passage with the recording. The improvement in their reading speed was significant, but the progress went far beyond just fluency. Their reading tone and articulation matched the rise, fall, and accent of my voice much more closely than before. (*Teacher Note:* You can differentiate easily by increasing your reading speed for more competent readers.) Students who were afraid of speaking in front of the class used my computer to record themselves and then listened to their recording on the iPod. This worked! Students became used to hearing themselves and became able to critique their reading after hearing the recording.

There are many time savers that greatly increase my effectiveness as a teacher by incorporating the iPod into my teaching. I record myself reading the words for a spelling test and then I give the iPod to a student who has difficulty hearing or keeping up with the rest of the class. The student(s) can repeat the test several times in order to hear the words and I can continue teaching. The student is learning the words and is not embarrassed in front of the other students.

Currently, I am teaching in Oak Ridge, Tennessee, with students who have the same needs as those in my previous international schools. To facilitate my students' success, I established an "iPod-based listening station" with five headphones. The beauty of the iPod is that I can record any number of books, on my MacBook, that I want the group to practice reading. I can read the book once and copy and paste it on the computer as many times as I want the children to read it. I usually put together several readings to make a 15-minute program and the children sit and read while I work with Guided Reading Groups. I only have to start the iPod and leave and there is no changing of CDs or tapes or going back and forth between groups. This wonderful center/station is like having another teacher in the room. (*Teacher Note:* I record different levels of books for different students. I record one book at a time and save in a folder. Then I drag and drop different stories until I have the 15 minutes. Instant differentiation!)

After the reading, I frequently add a vocabulary exercise. I place a stack of note cards with vocabulary words at the listening center and record directions. As the children spread out the cards and listen as I read a definition, they point to the correct word. They correct themselves with other peers as I read the correct word. The exercise is recorded and saved for next year! And I do not have to physically be there for this to occur.

My plans for this school year have increased the potential of this device. I have created slideshows for my students in Social Studies and Science that contain discussion questions and multimedia content. By purchasing a program I can convert the slideshows to be able to be viewed on my video iPod and the children can now view a lesson on their own free time. I am considering letting children who are falling behind check out the iPod to take home. I am also trying to get a grant that allows the purchase a set of iPod Nano's to allow children to take the iPods home.

As with every strategy, there are challenges. Children have to be technologically savvy or they must be taught to use the equipment. This can be time-consuming, depending on the student's age and economic status. An iPod is pretty indestructible and no one is allowed to move it from the station. Developing the different activities does not require a lot of time on my part and I see only good from having iPower in my classroom!

compatibility of the computer and the storage devices being used as well as the pros and cons of each device type.

Internal storage is offered within the computer by way of a computer hard disk drive, or hard drive. A **hard disk drive** holds large amounts of information and is significant in the purchasing decision of a new computer system. Hard disk drives hold data on circular disks called platters. The hard disk can vary in memory size and is referred to as the C drive on a Windows machine and as the HD on a Mac system.

External hard disk drives (see Figure 2.16) can be connected to the computer through cables; these allow large quantities of data to be moved from one physical location to another. That ability is quite important to busy teachers who need to work on various machines at school, at home, and during professional development. External hard drives offer large amounts of storage space at affordable prices for technology-using teachers who want the portability. There are a variety of additional removable storage options that fit a range of needs, including the versatile USB drive, compact disc (CD), and digital video disc (DVD). Additionally, there are others specific to cameras that are discussed in Chapter 7. Each is briefly discussed next.

Floppy and zip disks, once commonly used, are considered obsolete; new computers are no longer equipped with the drives necessary for use of these. These have been replaced with USB drives. **USB drives**, also called pen, flash, or jump drives, were introduced in 2002, and provide great flexibility in mobile storage devices (see Figure 2.17). These small devices are plugged into USB (Universal Serial Bus—see the next section for more information) ports in the back, front, or side of the computer or back of the keyboard, are not platform-specific (Windows or Mac), and new models hold from 512 MB to 16 GB of information. The price rises as the storage capacity enlarges, though prices have fallen dramatically. These great little storage options are affordable for teachers and students, as long as their computers are equipped with USB ports, which are common on recent models. Because of their small physical size, they can be easily misplaced or lost. As with all external storage, backing up files to a second location is a necessity. No important data should be kept on only one type of storage, and everything should be backed up.

There are a variety of **compact disc options** (CD-ROMs, CD-R, CD-RW) as pictured in Figure 2.18, and each has unique qualities though physically they appear the same. **CD-ROMs** (compact disc—read-only memory) are removable and hold approximately 650 MB of information. CD-ROMs are equivalent to about 400 floppy disks. Users cannot add new information to CD-ROMs; they are readable only.

The **CD-R** (compact disc—recordable) allows the user to record data once for storage purposes; after information is recorded it cannot be edited. However, a CD-R can be recorded in multiple sessions. CD-Rs will hold approximately 650–700 MB of information and are useful for storing large projects such as student portfolios. In order to create (or "burn") CD-Rs, a computer must be equipped with a CD-R–burning drive and CD-R–burning software, and the user must have some blank CD-R discs. Blank CD-Rs are continually decreasing in price and can be purchased in packs of 10 to 100. Typically, the more purchased, the cheaper the price per CD-R.

Yet another option, a **CD-RW** (compact disc—rewritable), also allows the recording of data, but also allows the user to edit the information after disc creation. The storage capacity is identical to regular CD-ROMs and CD-Rs. In order to create and edit CD-RWs, the user must have a computer with a CD-RW drive, specialized burning software, and CD-RW discs. The drawback of using this option is that computers must have special drives in order to read the discs, so if the user transports the disc to another computer that is without these capabilities,

FIGURE 2.16 External Hard Drive
LaCie Rugged Hard Disk designed by Neil Poulton, used with permission

FIGURE 2.17 USB Drive
Used with permission of SanDisk

FIGURE 2.18 Removable Storage Options

TECH TIP

How to care for CDs:
- store vertically in covers
- hold by edges
- store in cool and dry areas
- do not store in direct sunlight
- label with felt tip, water-based markers

it is useless. Blank CD-RWs are more expensive initially than CD-Rs, but allow much more flexibility if the teacher has the appropriate hardware and reason to use high-volume storage; plus, they are reusable.

Another disc-type media is the **DVD-ROM** (digital versatile disc—read-only memory). The major advantage of a DVD is the large storage capacity. A DVD looks like any other disc; however, it can store data on both sides of the disc, as opposed to the one-sided capability of the CD-ROM. A DVD can store approximately 4.7 GB of information. Some special double-sided DVDs can even hold 17 GB of information if both sides and both layers are used. In addition to DVD-ROMs, a DVD-ROM drive can read CD-ROMS, CD-Rs, CD-RWs, and music CDs, making the drive far more versatile than CD-only drives. This media brings tremendous advantage to classrooms through the quality of video that can be presented using DVD technology.

The newest of the disc technologies is the **Blu-ray disc**, called such because a blue laser is used to read or write on this disc. Having the same appearance as the other discs that we have discussed, Blu-ray discs store significantly more than DVD formats and are used for high definition video and audio in consumer electronics, personal computer, recording media, video games, and music companies.

There are a variety of removable storage options for other digital devices including digital cameras, digital music players, digital voice recorders, and other devices that store digital information. These are presented in Chapter 7.

Connecting to the Computer

In order for any device (printer, scanner, network connection, and so on) to communicate with a computer system, it must be connected to the computer. This connection is made through an opening called a **port**. The ports are generally located on the back of the desktop or laptop computer although newer computer models may offer some ports on the sides or front. Usually a variety of ports, each specific to a particular type of device, is provided, including parallel, USB, Ethernet, Firewire, and audio and video ports.

Parallel ports were developed by IBM and used to connect a computer to a printer. Although parallel ports are still found on some printers, they are being replaced by Universal Serial Bus (USB) ports. **USB ports** provide an easy, universal way to connect an array of devices and provide faster transfer of information to printers, scanners, digital cameras, storage drives, modems, speakers, and other devices. These ports offer "hot plugging" (the ability to connect and disconnect devices without turning the computer off). All USB plugs are not created equal. There are three types of USB connection: fast transfer of data (1.1), faster transfer of data (2.0), and fastest transfer of data (3.0). The newest standard (3.0) is reported to be ten times as fast as 2.0. Sometimes, you might have more USB devices than you do available USB ports—in this case, a **USB hub** can provide additional ports, as seen in Figure 2.19. An **Ethernet port** is used for high-speed connection to the Internet or another network, such as an intranet, or internal network. **Firewire** (also called **IEEE 1394**) **ports** provide a very fast connection to transfer large amounts of data quickly. New computer models have Firewire ports, which (for instance) provide a connection between a camcorder and the computer for transfer of video data. If the transfer of digital video is a planned part of the curriculum, Firewire or USB 2.0 or 3.0 connections are necessary.

Considerations for Purchasing a Computer System

When buying a computer for home or classroom use, the first consideration should be determining what the computer will be expected to do. For example,

FIGURE 2.19 USB Hub
Courtesy of Belkin
Corporation

consider the types of tasks (word processing, browsing the Internet, calculating budgets, or designing high-end graphics and video) that the computer will be used for most of the time. In addition, if the computer is a home computer, to be used by multiple users with assorted skill levels and needs, an assessment will give more information. In turn, the same considerations should hold for a computer to be used in the school setting. Each of these evaluations will make a difference in the power of the computer that you purchase. In addition, the available budget dictates much of the final decision. The processor speed, hard drive size, and RAM are additional key considerations.

The available budget must be kept in mind, although teachers should note that some features (such as screen size) may differ little in cost and it is worth doing some research. Although the budget will somewhat influence whether a desktop or laptop may be purchased, there are other very important items to keep in mind when selecting a computer, including what is included with the base price, such as an extended warranty, technical support, or software. For example, is the support and maintenance available locally, or does the computer have to be mailed out of town? An important issue with a laptop purchase is typical battery life and cost of a battery replacement. Sometimes, the price quoted for a desktop computer does not include a monitor, keyboard, or mouse, which might have to be purchased separately.

As mentioned earlier, the processor speed dictates how quickly information is processed in the CPU. A good policy to follow is to get as fast a processor as the budget will allow. Technology is a moving target and what is considered lightning-quick today might seem quite slow in a year or less. The larger the hard drive, the more information and applications can be stored. The size of the RAM dictates how many programs can successfully run at the same time. A related consideration is whether more RAM can be added later, and how much space for RAM expansion is available.

As you will remember from earlier in this discussion, pricing does not cover the monitor unless the computer is a laptop, in which case the computer will have an LCD monitor and the size should be based on main purpose of the computer, the amount of travel involved, and the available budget. If price is no object, keep in mind that flat LCD screens are the most expensive; nevertheless, these take up less room and provide more viewable area and a clearer picture.

Another important decision you have to make when buying a new computer is whether to get a CD-ROM drive, a CD-burner, or a DVD-burning drive (sometimes called a Super Drive). This decision is also related to the purpose of the computer, as well as the users who are going to be working with it. Teachers should also keep in mind that technology is progressing at a very fast pace, and with each increase in capability, the price goes up. Buy the best you can afford now. You could wait forever, because the changes are constant. Having the ability to burn CDs makes it easier to back up, store, and transport classroom information. In addition, many textbooks are packaged with CD-ROMs.

Internet Connections

Consideration must be given to connecting to the Internet. How you will connect to the Internet will determine the digital modem that is used. There are three major types of digital modems that are commonly used: ISDN, DSL, and Cable. ISDN and DSL use phone lines to connect while Cable uses a cable line.

Computer Case

If the computer is a laptop, a computer case is not optional; providing a protective travel environment for the hardware is essential. Because there are a variety of cases available, the nature, frequency, and mode of travel that is demanded in daily personal and work life must be considered. If, for example, if you must walk long distances with your laptop computer, cabling, external storage, teaching papers, and books, perhaps a case on wheels would be appropriate. If there is a need to keep hands free during the trip, the best case could be a backpack style. Other case choices include soft or hard cover, dividers and pockets for storage drives and cabling, handles, shoulder straps, and wheels.

The Need for Software

In order to function, a computer must have software that tells the computer what to do. **System software** is a part of each computer system. Typically seen in schools are the Windows operating system, and the Mac OS, which is used on Apple computers. The latest system software as mentioned earlier is Vista for Windows users and OS 10.5.6 (Leopard) for Mac users. Both computer systems use a graphical user interface (GUI), pronounced "gooey." A GUI means that these computers have menus and icons that represent commands and programs, making point-and-click navigation with a mouse quite easy. Both computer systems are found in schools, making it necessary for teachers to feel comfortable on each.

Application software allows the computer to carry out specific functions, such as word processing, creation of databases and spreadsheets, and so on. In education, we have a category of software referred to as **instructional software**, which presents content in tutorial, simulation, instructional game, problem solving, and drill-and-practice forms. In addition, **assistive technology (AT)** includes devices for special needs students, such as readers, special keyboards, and so on. In addition to commercially available software, open source software offers new options for teachers and their students. There is more in-depth information on application software, including open source alternatives, in Chapter 3.

Adapting for Special Learners

Given appropriate hardware arrangements, almost all students with disabilities can access technology. Most individuals can view the monitor display and use the mouse and keyboard for input, but alternative access is available for individuals who have motor impairments, are blind or have cognitive challenges and need simpler choices. Hardware adaptations focus on devices that allow alternative access to the functions of the computer. Because hardware is continually improving, the discussion here is general enough for the near future. Specific recommendations for hardware items will depend on the individual needs of the student. Our perspective on hardware adaptation is similar to that described earlier—to design a learning environment that can appropriately accommodate all individuals (The Alliance for Technology Access, ATA, 2004). The following hardware additions can be used to remove barriers that some students experience when accessing computers.

Monitor Adaptations

Computer-screen magnifiers, anti-glare filters, and monitor mounts enhance or alter the display or position of a standard monitor. These monitor adaptations are useful for students with limited vision or photosensitivity issues.

Students who need low-level magnification to see the screen may benefit from a computer **screen magnifier**. These devices fit over the computer monitor and magnify the images that appear on the screen.

Anti-glare filters are clear screens that fit over a computer monitor to reduce glare from overhead lights and large windows. They also improve the contrast on the monitor and reduce screen flicker. These filters can improve visual access for students who are sensitive to bright light or who work in areas of glare. The reduction in monitor flickering may also reduce symptoms of physical stress for students with seizure disorders or who are prone to migraines.

Monitor mounts allow the placement of the monitor in the most easily seen position. These devices are useful for students of different heights or for those in a prone or other nonstandard position.

If a student is blind (has complete loss of vision), the monitor display may be used with **speech output software**, which audibly speaks screen content and commands. These software applications are further discussed in the next chapter. However, when speech output is either impractical (as in the case of someone who is also deaf or hard of hearing) or undesirable (as in the case of one who prefers to read Braille than listen to audio, or finds a voice display annoying), a hardware device called a **refreshable Braille display** is an alternative. This device presents a line of text from the screen in Braille format by raising pinpoints under a membrane. The pinpoints are cleared when the next line of text is displayed.

Keyboard Adaptations

Arm and wrist supports stabilize the placement of the arms, wrists, and hands. They also are used to avoid pain and fatigue when using the keyboard or mouse. Supports may be mounted to a table or chair. Wrist rests may be attached to the keyboard. Students with mobility impairments may find these supports useful. The use of these supports is also increasing among adults with repetitive stress disorders.

Alternate keyboards offer input options in size, layout, and complexity. Keyboards that have larger keys, high-contrast colors, or are color coded by function (typing fingers, or vowels, consonants, and controls) may be easier to use for students with vision or dexterity barriers. Miniature keyboards, by contrast, are much smaller than standard keyboards and allow someone with a limited range of motion to access all the keys. Programmable keyboards can be customized so that letters, numbers, words, pictures, or phrases can be entered by pressing areas on a membrane board.

Keyboards can be made more accessible by using keyboard additions such as keyguards, moisture guards, and alternative labels. **Keyguards** are hard plastic covers with holes for each key. They prevent someone with an unsteady finger or someone who uses a pointing device from striking unwanted keys. **Moisture guards** are thin sheets of plastic that protect keyboards from spills and any unwanted liquids. **Alternative labels** are taped or glued to tops of frequently used keys on the standard keyboard. They can be a different color to add visual clarity, or have raised letters to provide tactile feedback to someone using the keys.

Students who cannot use their hands to access the keyboard may be able to use a pointing or typing aid, an **adjustable wand** or **stick**, to strike keys. These devices are most commonly worn on the head, held in the mouth, attached to the chin, or held in the hand. All can be used with standard, alternate, or modified keyboards.

Touch screens have become commonly used in grocery self-checkouts and ATMs. Touch screens are also available for computers in the form of a device that is either placed on the monitor or built into it. Touch screens allow direct selection or operation by touching the appropriate area of the screen. They are also useful for young children and those with cognitive disabilities. Interactive whiteboards function as much larger touch screens and can be used to encourage interaction and engagement in small-group settings.

Switches can be used as an alternative to the keyboard. Switches come in various sizes, shapes, and colors. They are usually activated by one or two movements, such as pulling or squeezing, sipping or puffing, blinking, or pressing. Enough switch options have been developed that a switch could be placed anywhere—near the hands, in the mouth, or attached to any controllable area of the body, such as near the eyes to be activated by a blink. Connecting the switch to the computer usually requires an additional piece of hardware, called a *switch interface,* and specialized software to interpret the operation of the switch. Switches are used with software programs that employ onscreen scanning. With onscreen scanning, the computer prompts the user by highlighting in sequence (either by sound, visual cue, or both) the letter, number, or picture choices available. When the prompt hovers on the desired keyboard or mouse function, the user activates the switch. Several software programs have built-in onscreen scanning options to allow switch use; others require additional software.

Electronic pointing devices allow the user to control the cursor using ultrasound, an infrared beam, eye movements, nerve signals, or even brain waves. Electronic pointing devices will operate most computer programs and environmental controls. They require that the user have good head control, eye control, or that the user learn to control the device through nerve signals or brain waves. Depending on the skills of the user and the type of device selected, computer commands can be accessed in a variety of ways. Some allow the user to control the cursor by head motions; others allow control of the computer with eye movement. The user may pause or dwell on a key to activate it, or perform an action such as an eye blink, to make a selection.

Mouse Adaptations

For students who have difficulty using a standard mouse, alternatives (some mentioned previously) include alternate keyboards, touch screens, and switches, which can be set up to substitute for the movement and click of a standard mouse. Two other mouse alternatives are joysticks and trackballs.

Joysticks are a common mouse alternative, because they are similar to what other students would use to control computer games, minimizing the effects of feeling "different" for children with physical disabilities. Newer joysticks can be plugged into the USB port and may or may not require additional software for mouse emulation, or control of the cursor on the screen. Joysticks are available within a variety of price ranges and with a variety of features. Joysticks that feature direct control allow movements in all directions (360°) and respond to the distance and speed with which the user moves the stick. These are the same movement patterns as those used with joystick-controlled power wheelchairs; hence the student could use familiar muscle movements for both. Joysticks can also be controlled by other body parts, such as the chin.

A *trackball* looks like an upside-down mouse, with a movable ball on top of a stationary base. The ball can be rotated with a pointing device, a single finger, the thumb, the hand, or even a foot. Trackballs are typically lower-cost, simple-to-use mouse alternatives.

Peripherals

Computer technology offers accessible alternatives to regular printed materials for students with disabilities. The most common alternative is **printed text translated into digitized text,** which can then be converted to auditory or tactile formats.

The process for converting printed text to digitized text begins with a scanner equipped with OCR software (mentioned earlier). Once a digital copy of the text is obtained, it is "read" by one of a variety of software programs. Examples of these software programs can be found in Chapter 3. The selection can then be saved in a digital format, which can then be manipulated by any word processor. Another option is to convert the text into an audio file (usually MP3 or WAV format), which can be played on a portable device.

Blind students who read Braille can use a translator and embosser. A **Braille translator** is a software product that converts text, either obtained by scanning or produced by a word processor, into Braille. The user can then print this translated text using a piece of hardware called a Braille embosser.

Headphones and microphones were mentioned earlier in this chapter as standard equipment on many computers. Headphones are essential for listening to any voice output, such as a screen reader, without distracting others in a lab or classroom setting. Microphones are the input device in speech-recognition software systems (see Chapter 3). If the student must use speech recognition as the primary method of accessing word processing or computer controls, a microphone and headset combination that can be adjusted for a consistent placement near the mouth will render a more accurate transcription of speech. For occasional use, or for demonstration purposes, the built-in microphone on many computer models or a stand microphone will give adequate, if not especially accurate, results. Check for microphone compatibility with the software vendor prior to purchase.

PDAs are becoming a viable access option for some students with special needs because of their ease of use and relatively low cost. The options available for PDAs are growing commercial selections of electronic audiobooks. Other applications—such as calendars, word processing, spreadsheet, concept mapping, dictionary, and language translation programs—can be purchased for the PDA. This technology may be more readily available than more expensive classroom machines, making access to computer technology more of a reality in schools with budgetary challenges (Walser, 2004).

The **PAC Mate** (Freedom Scientific, **www.freedomscientific.com**) is a PDA designed for blind or low-vision users. The traditional PDA stylus and screen is replaced by a choice of keyboards (Speech only, Perkins, QWERTY, or Braille) and JAWS screen reading technology. The units are preinstalled with Microsoft Office, Internet Explorer, and Media Player. Add-ons include a bar code reader for product identification, Daisy players for electronic books, GPS software, Braille display, and a face-to face package that enables deaf-blind individuals to communicate with a sighted person via a wireless (Bluetooth) interface.

Classroom Sound Field Amplification Systems

Many school districts are installing classroom amplification systems in newly constructed schools. These systems have obvious benefits for students with hearing barriers, but are also useful for students who are acquiring a new language, making it possible to attend to natural speech and intonation. Other alternatives include portable amplification stations and assistive listening systems designed for students who are hard of hearing.

Learning to Use Adaptive Hardware

The array of assistive devices mentioned here varies from those that are quite simple (such as a screen filter or trackball) to the very complex (such as electronic pointing devices), and this brief discussion may leave some beginning teachers feeling intimidated or overwhelmed at the thought of learning all this new technology. By way of reassurance, it is quite unlikely that students in any one inclusive classroom would use all of the hardware mentioned here. Teachers and students can expect to have training and support, especially when learning more complex hardware. Furthermore, the responsibility for recommending and using AT devices is shared by the support structure of special education services in the school and the district. Classroom teachers and special educators who are members of the IEP team must consider the need for AT devices and services for every student with disabilities. AT services include an assessment to determine which devices are appropriate, given the classroom setting and the curriculum that is being taught. These services extend to training and support for students, parents, and teachers. Classroom teachers should become familiar with the school-based procedures for accessing these services. Many districts have adopted the SETT framework (Zabala, 1995) as an organizational tool for determining which devices and software applications are needed. This framework allows the IEP team to consider the abilities of the student, the classroom environment, the academic tasks, and technology tools before recommending a specific product.

The greatest assistance that a classroom teacher can render in this process is to become a collaborative partner in the IEP team process (Male, 2003). For most classroom teachers, this involves becoming familiar with the general categories and features of assistive hardware devices, observing student performance when

CURRICULUM CONNECTIONS

Computers Inside and Out: Outer Hardware

CONTENT AREA/TOPIC: Computer Connections: Inside and Out

GRADE LEVELS: 2–5   **NETS·S:** 6

Description:

Kaboose presents a series of 10 online lessons on Computer Connections: Inside and Out, developed by Carol Welch, that are free to use for nonprofit purposes. "Outer Hardware" is the first of the series and presents basic information that identifies the parts of a computer system, common input, and output and storage devices. All lessons have cover-related topics.

Preparation:

Teachers download the available worksheets and answer keys that are provided free at the web site, and may be copied for students.

Active participation:

Depending on the age of the students, the information may be delivered in large groups, in cooperative-learning groups, or at computer centers. This information could be used as supplementary information to accompany a demonstration or as the basis for a research project.

Variations:

These lessons provide a great tool to work with students who are learning the basics of computer systems and hardware.

Source: Kaboose, Inc. http://parenting.kaboose.com/education-and-learning/learning-resources/brain-computer-lesson.html. By Carol Welch.

using technology, keeping the IEP team informed of successes and concerns, and advocating for technology use. Be aware that not all students needing assistive technology have access to it (Edyburn, 2003). Some students have not been given full consideration by their school-based teams. Other students are limited by a general lack of knowledge of AT on the part of their teachers and other professionals. With an awareness of the existence of these devices, classroom teachers can help to advocate for technology access for students whose potential may have been overlooked.

Common Vendors for Adaptive Hardware

The adaptive hardware described in this chapter can be further researched by visiting the vendors listed on the companion web site for this chapter. Although the list is not exhaustive, it is a representative sample of vendors that offer the products in the discussion. Additional information and company overviews may be found at the vendor's link of the Alliance for Technology Access web site (**www.ataccess.org/hub**).

The Office of Special Education and Rehabilitative Services of the U.S. Department of Education maintains a comprehensive listing of AT products and noncommercial prototypes and designs. This AT information center, Abledata (**www.abledata.com**), contains a database that lists device descriptions, features, price, and contact information for manufacturers and distributors of 30,000 AT items.

Voices *from the* Classroom

Increase Classroom Access through Writing Grants
Valerie Pearce

Valerie is a preschool special education teacher who serves as part-time technology coordinator and mentor for her colleagues. Always interested in technology and its use as a classroom resource and a teaching tool, Valerie constantly seeks grant opportunities to increase access in her practice. We asked her to share her experiences with a Mimio (www.mimio.com) awarded to her through a grant.

I have recently discovered a piece of technology that allows me to reinforce a variety of skills with my students in a whole new way. I was fortunate to receive a Mimio as a result of a grant effort from a winning essay that I wrote. This piece of technology attaches to any whiteboard and displays the images written on the whiteboard through the computer.

One exciting aspect to using the Mimio is increased communication with parents regarding their child's work and current level of functioning. All of the work drawn on the Mimio can be saved on the computer and added to any document for varying uses. I have even taken student drawings and made an Intellipics program and overlay so the children can use their own drawings on the computer. It is very easy to make a hard copy of their work to take home to their parents.

I am always amazed that different computer hardware may be designed for a specific purpose but can easily be adapted to serve many different needs. The Mimio was designed as an office assistant. We use it to strengthen fine motor skills, encourage creative representation, reinforce visual motor skills, and much more. We have printed the children's drawings and made buttons of their pictures for parents to wear. The only limit to the technology is your own creativity. I'm sure there are many pieces of technology that can support and enhance any learning environment. The challenging part is discovering what they are and how they can be obtained. Visit the On the Web at the companion web site (**www.pearsonhighered.com/obannon2e**) to see this technology tool in action.

On the Web

This section includes only a snapshot of web sites that the authors recommend for viewing. To access live links and a larger and continuously updated collection of sites, go to the companion web site at **www.pearsonhighered.com/ obannon2e.**

Computer Basics and Tutorials

The following sites offer basic information, lessons, and tutorials about computer basics.

How Stuff Works

http://computer.howstuffworks.com

This searchable site is rich of information and is a leading resource for explanations about how computers work. The site includes but is not limited to information about hardware, software, security, peripherals, and the Internet. Check out the Computer Channel that provides information about how Twitter, and social networks including LinkedIn, and Facebook, works.

Sandy's Classroom Tutorials

www.compukiss.com/tutorials/index.php

This site, developed by Sandy Berger and powered by CompuKISS, offers helpful tutorials about computer basics, care and maintenance, email, hardware, the Internet, troubleshooting, and so much more. Read about Sandy's background and roam around this very informative and useful site.

Input Devices: Digital Cameras, Scanners, and Reviews

Digicamhelp

www.digicamhelp.com

This guide for digital camera beginners and beyond originally started by an educator to help her less technical friends, has since transformed into pages that present information on digital cameras and photography. This information-rich site connects the reader to a buying guide, features, accessories, taking pictures, working with images and more.

Nuance: Scanner Guide for First Time Users

www.nuance.com/scannerguide/firsttimeusers/

Nuance Communications (formerly Scansoft) offers a scanner guide of basic information for first time users of scanners or to refresh one's memory.

Portable Audio (and Video) Devices

http://store.apple.com/us/browse/home/shop_ipod/ family/ipod_shuffle?mco=MTE2NTQ

Apple offers various models of iPods. The iPod shuffle plays music, podcasts, and audiobooks. These nifty little audio players have a 1 GB capacity and prices begin around $50. The iPod nano plays music, podcasts, audiobooks as well as video from movies, TV shows, and videos. There are more models that are more expensive with greater capabilities.

Web Cams

www.besttechie.net/2008/01/03/picking-the-best-webcam/ Web cams allow video conferencing. The little camera perches on your computer and streams video across your network. You can see a video at this site. The Web cam that Jeff Weis-

bein recommends is from Logitech (logitech.com) and the cost is approximately $130.

Input/Output Devices: Electronic Whiteboards

Mimio

www.mimio.com

A Mimio bar converts any whiteboard to an interactive electronic whiteboard for the P-12 environment and converts the classroom into a vibrant teaching and learning space. At this site, you will find many support activities and lessons, plus more information about Mimio products.

Promethean

www.promethianworld.com

Promethean markets the Activeboard, an interactive whiteboard, found in many of today's classrooms. The Activeboard+2 has a projector mounted to the board making installation a breeze. This site offers an interactive video and more.

SMART Technologies

http://smarttech.com

This company markets the well-known SMART Board that is commonly found in business and educational training settings. See these interactive whiteboards in action as you watch the online video. A special section for educators allows teachers to browse the resources available. SMART offers the all-in-one board that brings together the interactive whiteboard and the projector to offer more flexibility in the classroom.

Storage Devices: Drives and Removable Storage Options

Iomega

http://go.iomega.com/home?p=4760

The Iomega site shares information about external hard drives (external and portable) with huge storage capacities, as well as CD-RW/DVD players and much more. An online store is available as well as store locators at this site.

Kingston Technology

www.kingston.com

Kingston Technology offers memory for multiple manufacturers and devices at this site from a drop-down list. It is possible to search by memory type, model name, or part numbers that are system specific. There is also a selection of storage choices including USB drives, photo/video storage solutions, mobile solutions, and media readers.

Lacie

www.lacie.com/us/index.htm

Lacie offers its well-known hard drives and DVD burners as well as other accessories and displays. Check out this site for the latest in storage and backup possibilities.

SanDisk

www.sandisk.com

This site advises consumers about storage for digital cameras, digital video cameras, and portable storage devices, reader/ writers, adaptors, and MP3 players. Research this site to see what this company offers and where these products are found.

Key Terms

Equitable access (36)
Access options (36)
Computer system (37)
Central processing unit (CPU) (37)
Control unit (37)
Arithmetic logic unit (ALU) (37)
Memory unit (37)
RAM (37)
ROM (37)
Binary coding system (ASCII) (37)
Bit (37)
Byte (37)
Kilobyte (37)
Megabyte (37)
Gigabyte (37)
Terabyte (38)
Processor speed (38)
Megahertz (38)
Gigahertz (38)
Cache (38)
Peripheral device (39)
Input device (39)
Keyboard (39)
Mouse (39)
Touch pad (39)
Trackball (39)
Wireless/cordless mouse (39)
Mouse pad (39)
Joystick (39)
Scanner (40)
Optical character recognition (OCR) (40)
Graphics tablet (40)
Audio (40)
Microphone (40)

Sound card (40)
Headphones (40)
Video (40)
Digital camera (40)
Digital video camera (40)
Web cam (40)
Pen input (40)
Personal digital assistant (PDA) (40)
Tablet computer (41)
Interactive whiteboard (41)
Classroom response system ("clicker") (43)
Computer monitor (screen, display) (43)
Cathode ray tube (CRT) (43)
Liquid crystal display (LCD) (43)
Monitor size (43)
Resolution (44)
Pixel (44)
Printer (45)
Hard copy (45)
Dots per inch (dpi) (45)
Ink jet printer (46)
Laser printer (46)
Transparency (46)
Speakers (46)
Data projection units (46)
Lumens (46)
Document camera (47)
Portable media player (47)
Storage devices (47)
Internal storage (49)
Hard disk drive (49)
External hard disk drive (49)
USB drive (49)

Compact disc options (CD-ROM, CD-R, CD-RW) (49)
Digital versatile disc—read only memory (DVD-ROM) (50)
Blu-ray disc (50)
Port (50)
Parallel port (50)
USB port (50)
USB hub (50)
Ethernet port (50)
Firewire (IEEE 1394) port (50)
System software (52)
Application software (52)
Instructional software (52)
Assistive technology (AT) (52)
Screen magnifier (52)
Anti-glare filter (53)
Monitor mount (53)
Speech output software (53)
Refreshable Braille display (53)
Arm and wrist supports (53)
Alternate keyboards (53)
Keyguard (53)
Moisture guard (53)
Alternative labels (53)
Adjustable wand or stick (53)
Touch screen (53)
Switches (54)
Electronic pointing devices (54)
Printed text translated into digitized text (54)
Braille translator (55)
PAC Mate (55)

Hands-on Activities for Learning

1. Visit the On the Web companion site (**www.pearson highered.com/obannon2e**) and review the sites available.
2. Write a reflection in your technology blog about hardware that is available in a school that has the target population that you will be teaching.
3. Interview a practicing teacher to discover what access to technology is available at the school where he or she teaches. In your research, cover the teacher's classroom, the computer lab, the library/media center, the mobile multiple laptop cart(s), and any COWs (computers on wheels). Of these, mention how many have Internet connections and similar features.

4. Complete Web research to discover how electronic whiteboards can be used in the K–12 classroom.
5. Complete Web research to find grant opportunities for teachers that allow the acquisition of equipment.
6. Go to the Alliance for Technology Access web site and access the online book Computer Resources for People with Disabilities (**www.ataccess.org/resources/atabook/s00/s00-01.html**). Visit Part II, the technology toolbox, and review the "ask yourself" charts. Explore one or two specific sets of charts, with a particular student's abilities in mind.

Chapter 3

Software Basics

LEARNER OBJECTIVES

At the completion of this chapter, learners will be able to:

- Discuss the characteristics and functions of operating system, application, Internet, and assistive software.
- Describe the purpose of instructional software categories including drill and practice, instructional games, tutorials, simulations, problem solving, reference, and integrated learning systems (ILS).
- Discuss open-source software, its advantages and common titles used in schools.
- Evaluate instructional software programs using research-based criteria.
- Use teacher utility software programs including grade programs and task generators.
- Explore the accessibility options for students with disabilities that are available in operating system software.
- Discuss features of assistive "access" software, including text to speech, word prediction, scan and read, speech recognition, magnification, screen reader, and dedicated assistive software.

NETS·T 2008 ALIGNED WITH SOFTWARE BASICS

3. **Model Digital-Age Work and Learning**

Teachers exhibit knowledge, skills, and work processes representative of an innovative professional in a global and digital society. Teachers:

a. demonstrate fluency in technology systems and the transfer of current knowledge to new technologies and situations.

b. collaborate with students, peers, parents, and community members using digital tools and resources to support student success and innovation.

c. communicate relevant information and ideas effectively to students, parents, and peers using a variety of digital-age media and formats.

d. model and facilitate effective use of current and emerging digital tools to locate, analyze, evaluate, and use information resources to support research and learning.

4. **Promote and Model Digital Citizenship and Responsibility**

Teachers understand local and global societal issues and responsibilities in an evolving digital culture and exhibit legal and ethical behavior in their professional practices. Teachers:

a. advocate, model, and teach safe, legal, and ethical use of digital information and technology, including respect for copyright, intellectual property, and the appropriate documentation of sources.

Frameworks

The hardware components of a computer system are the physical components, and these, alone, are not capable of performing tasks. In order to work, the hardware must be directed to do so by the control unit in the CPU. Specific instructions must flow to the control unit in order for it to direct the hardware to perform tasks. These instructions come from **software programs**. A software program is "a series of instructions designed to cause the [computer] system to perform a logical sequence of steps that will produce the desired result" (Lockard & Abrams, 2003, p. 33).

There are various categories of software programs that all computer users must make use of to complete basic tasks. These include operating system software, application software, and Internet software. In addition, there are specialized categories of software commonly used in educational environments. These are instructional software, teacher utility software, and assistive software. In this chapter, a synopsis of each broad category of software is made to provide basic understanding of each. Special emphasis is placed on the use of instructional software and the criteria that guide teacher evaluation of software titles for use in teaching and learning. Finally, discussions of assistive software reveal how this specialized category can make learning environments more accessible for students with diverse needs.

Basics

Knowing certain information about software is fundamental to working successfully with technology in the classroom. Many times, acquisition of software in the school setting is a task of the technology coordinator or director at the district level. Budgets for software purchases are generally quite limited and purchasing decisions may be a result of the *ease of support and maintenance,* and *conformity of software* for professional development activities. Therefore, some school districts conform to a "toolkit" approach: established choices or inflexible selections in software packages across all of the schools within the school district. The same holds true for purchases at university campuses with software updates being reliant on the numbers of students needing access to particular software. Nonetheless, teachers may be able to influence these purchases, for instance, by writing grants for their teaching site, as well as making better-informed decisions for home use. General considerations must be taken into account when making purchases for your school site, classroom, and home computer.

Considerations for Purchasing Software

Software must be compatible with the computer system(s) that the teacher and students use in the school environment. In addition, the software documentation, pricing, and licensing must be considered. Is there documentation, such as an instructional manual, that is included with the software? Is the price within the budget allocation for technology provided at the school? Can the license that is within the budget provide the amount of access that is needed? In addition, in order to be effective in planning instruction that includes technology, teachers must understand the various types of software that are available, the function, and feasibility for the school environment. Is this a high-priority software title? Should the full versions be purchased or would a program already bundled with the computer be acceptable? Are open source titles a possibility? The following discussion provides some answers to questions that must be carefully thought out before purchase.

Compatibility

A major consideration when securing software is that the hardware and software can communicate; they must be compatible. Buying a new software program does little good if a computer system is not capable of running it. The hardware specifications that must be checked for **compatibility** with the software are the (1) operating system, (2) speed of the CPU, (3) amount of available RAM memory, (4) capability of the monitor, and (5) space required on the hard drive to house the program. The required specifications are typically written on the side of the box in which the software is packaged.

Software is written specifically for Windows, Macintosh, or Linux operating systems. Today, many software programs can be installed on all or a mixture of operating systems. Although the latest versions of operating systems (Windows Vista and Mac OS X) have many advanced features, they have limited support for software programs written for former versions. This presents a real challenge for schools that have limited budget allocations for new software. It is most important that teachers check the operating system available and the version of the operating system that is required for the software being purchased.

The software will require a minimum speed of processor to run as intended, as well as a certain recommended amount of RAM. If that amount of RAM is not available, the software will not run properly. It is important to ensure that there is enough space on the hard drive to accommodate the new software. Finally, some software will require specific capabilities of the monitor (e.g., resolution) for optimal performance.

Documentation

It is important that **documentation** is included with the software package that is purchased. Manuals, either printed, on a CD, or online, will provide much valuable information about the software. Electronic documentation is often quick to navigate. Educational versions of instructional software usually include manuals containing lesson ideas. In some instances, there will even be worksheets included. These can be tremendous time-savers for teachers.

Price

Another consideration for software purchase is **price**. Software may be purchased as single programs or, in some instances, in bundles of more than one program. Software is bundled by manufacturers (1) to provide the consumer with a lower price when buying several full programs, or (2) to provide several different options for consumers who need access to various tools yet not a complete set of all features. **Application suites** are a group of programs that are sold as a package to solve common problems; the most common application suites are office suites. **Microsoft Office Suite** (MS Office, office.microsoft.com) and **Apple**'s productivity suite, **iWork** (www.apple.com/iwork) are examples of application suites; each containing three programs (word processor, spreadsheet, and slideshow) that can be purchased for a lower price when buying the set.

Integrated software packages combine a variety of more basic versions of software versus the full programs, into one package. In a typical integrated package, there is a **word processing tool**, a **database tool**, a **spreadsheet tool**, a **graphics tool** for drawing and painting, and a **slideshow tool.** Integrated software packages are much cheaper and provide access to an array of tools. An example of an office suite is Microsoft Works.

Licensing

When software is purchased, a license is issued. **Licensing** can be issued for a single user, for multiple users, or an entire school site. In school settings, it is cheaper to buy multiple user licenses or site licenses.

Single-user licenses for software may be loaded and used on only one computer. Some software programs can be purchased under a *multiple-user license,* meaning that the software may be installed on the number of computers that the license permits. Examples include lab packs allowing for five or ten installations. Site licenses can also be purchased for most commonly used software programs. A *site license* generally allows unlimited use of the software across the network, or some of these might limit the number of computers on which the software can be installed.

It is very important for teachers to keep in mind the type of license that the school has provided for the software on the computers in their classrooms and do not pirate software! Copying or installing software without a license ("pirating" software) is illegal and can result in huge fines for the teacher or the school district.

The **free open source software (FOSS)** movement has created a market of software that is very attractive for schools. Open source software is developed by a group of programmers who, in turn, offer it for download to willing users at no charge. The major difference in open source and proprietary (commercial) software is the ownership of the software. **Proprietary software**, such as Apple or Microsoft programs, grants a license to a user but the company reserves all rights to the software. Therefore, if a user puts the software on more machines than they have licenses for, copyright is broken. An **open source software license** allows the transfer of the license to the end user. The end user can adapt the software as needed (if they have the skill set to do so) as well as distribute, as they like. Thus, equipping a computer lab, a mobile cart, or a classroom with current versions is not only easy but fits the budget! A productivity suite that is open source is Open Office (www.openoffice.org). Read the Voices in the Classroom section in this chapter by Aaron Pickering as he shares his experience with open source solutions for his classroom.

Types of Software

In Chapter 2, the importance of software was introduced. Computers and their peripheral devices, such as cameras and scanners, require software in order to communicate and work. Software is needed to operate the computer system as well as specialized software for every task completed on that computer. In this discussion, the fundamental software categories and their characteristics, including operating system software, application software, Internet software, instructional software, and assistive software, are presented. In the chapters that follow, we discuss how specific software categories can be used in teaching and learning.

Operating System Software

Operating system software is the master control software system that serves as a foundation for application software programs. In other words, it controls and interacts with the hardware components and the other software that are being used. The operating system is included with the computer and is loaded by the manufacturer. A backup copy, usually on CD or DVD, of this software is bundled with the computer. Keep it in a safe place! Examples of operating system software include **Microsoft Windows**, **Mac OS X**, and **Linux**. The most popular of these are Microsoft Windows (on PCs) and Mac OS X (on Apple computers); nonetheless, there is a growing market for Linux. The newest version for Windows-based

Voices *from the* Classroom

My Open Source Classroom
Aaron Pickering

Aaron Pickering has taught social studies at Oak Ridge High School in Oak Ridge, Tennessee, for seven years. He earned his Specialist in Education degree in Instructional Technology from the University of Tennessee in 2008. Aaron's research investigated the effectiveness of online course management systems and open source software in high schools. We asked Aaron to introduce Open Source Software and share how he uses it in his classroom.

As teachers implement technology in their classrooms they are faced with difficult choices. Hardware and software are expensive and few schools have adequate funds to support their technology needs. Even when a school purchases software, students are not always able to purchase the same software for their home computers. Open Source Software (OSS) offers a solution to these problems.

OSS is free. Unlike commercial software, there are no expensive licensing fees. If a school has a large number of computers this can save thousands of dollars. OSS is created and maintained by a community of software developers. Like community-generated web sites such as Wikipedia, Open Source projects make use of the collective creative and editorial efforts of thousands of program-

mers who produce high-quality products. Further, open source projects are generally developed for all three of the major desktop operating systems: Microsoft Windows, Apple Mac OS X, and Linux.

The greatest benefit of using Open Source Software in your classroom is having access to software that you might not otherwise be able to afford. In my classroom we use OpenOffice.org (**www.openoffice.org**) as an office suite alternative to Microsoft Office, the GNU Image Manipulation Program (GIMP) (**www.gimp.org**) as an image-editing alternative to Adobe Photoshop, and Audacity (**http://audacity.sourceforge.net/download**) as an audio editing alternative to Sony Sound Forge. I also use an online course management system called Moodle (**http://moodle.org**) as a free alternative to the Blackboard Academic Suite. These programs give my students access to the same tools that they will use at universities and as professionals at no cost to my school.

Students are placed in a difficult position when schools use expensive commercial software. If the students wish to use the same software at home, they must spend hundreds of dollars to obtain a legal copy of the program on their home computer. Unfortunately, students often turn to software piracy so that they may work at home. By using OSS,

machines is Windows Vista and the newest system for Apple systems is Mac OS X 10.5 Leopard. The current names might change, with each new version bringing in more features. Figure 3.1 displays the three most common operating systems that are available.

In 1984, Apple successfully marketed the Macintosh, which sported a **graphic user interface** (or **GUI**, pronounced *gooey*) that allows icons (small graphics) to represent the tools for the system and uses a mouse to move about. Microsoft Windows evolved into a similar visual interface making it much easier to use than the former command-driven system (DOS). Today, the Windows operating system has a larger sharehold, although many schools use only Macs or a mix of the two, making it important for teachers in preparation to be familiar with both systems found in PK–12 settings. Although teachers may feel somewhat reluctant to learn both systems, if their training and comfort level is primarily on one or the other system, there are many similarities between the two and having knowledge of both is a good self-marketing tool for new teachers.

UNIX was originally designed for mainframe computers, very large, expensive machines used to store huge quantities of information, and is the basis for Mac OS X. Linux (pronounced *linn-uks*) is a free desktop version of UNIX that

Voices *from the* Classroom *Continued*

rny students are able to install the same tools that they use at school on their home computers freely and legally.

If your school computers or your students' home computers are outdated, Open Source Software can bring life back into older hardware. Commercial software frequently push the limits of the latest hardware. These bloated programs are inefficient and impractical for schools. Open Source Software strives for efficiency and will run on older computers. If your school relies on a hodgepodge of older donated computers, it is possible to standardize these computers by installing the same Open Source applications on all of the computers. I have taken very old computers and turned them into reasonably quick Internet browsing and word processing stations by installing Xubuntu (pronounced *zou-boun-tou*) (**www.xubuntu .org**), a lean version of the Linux operating system, rather than outdated versions of Windows and Mac OS. In addition to saving money on software, by using OSS, I get more life out of existing hardware!

OSS is particularly useful for school and system-wide information technology services. Although you may not realize it, the majority of web sites that you visit are running on Open Source Software. The Open Source Web server Apache running on Linux is the most popular Web server on the Internet. Giants such as Google rely on the same software that is freely available to schools. Wikipedia relies on the Open Source MediaWiki. Countless blogs use

the robust and free blogging program WordPress. Moodle offers an Open Source version of the course management functionality and Web 2.0 tools universities and corporations use to enhance instruction and offer distance learning. All of these Web-based Open Source programs can be installed and run freely on most any computer that can act as a server in your school.

When I use Open Source Software in my classroom, I open doors for my students. They have access to professional-level tools that most schools cannot afford. My students are able to work and learn at home without violating copyright laws or spending their scarce funds on expensive commercial software. My students learn to adapt to new software and broaden their experience beyond a small set of commonly used commercial software. In my opinion, training students to use specific versions of commercial software is ineffective. By the time they graduate, the version of the software they learned is already outdated. With Open Source Software, my students always have access to the latest version. They learn how to use a wide variety of software tools and are better able to adapt to a constantly evolving workplace.

If you do not have unlimited resources to spend on your technology needs, you should consider Open Source Software. You can learn more about Open Source Software and browse a list of useful programs for educators at **www.aaronpickering.com/opensource/**.

runs on a number of hardware platforms. It is very popular among computer scientists, but has little visibility so far in schools.

Application Software

Computers need additional software to perform specific tasks. Such software programs fall into the category of **application software** and these programs perform

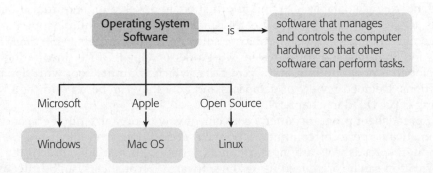

FIGURE 3.1 Operating System Software

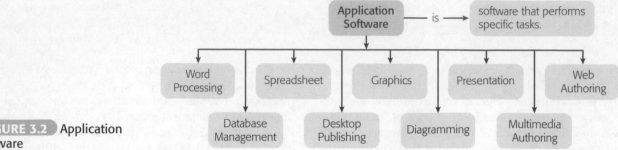

FIGURE 3.2 Application
Software

unique tasks such as word processing, database management, and spreadsheet calculations (see Figure 3.2). As mentioned earlier, application software can be purchased as a single unit, as a bundle of related programs in one package, or open source solutions can be downloaded from the Web. Additionally, there are Web-based packages such as Zoho (**www.zoho.com**) and Thinkfree (**www.thinkfree .com**) that offer Web access to selected application software. In the following paragraphs, each software category is briefly described and includes general ways that it is used in teaching and learning. In-depth explanations of each are presented in subsequent chapters.

Word processing programs are likely the most important applications used by students and teachers. No longer limited to simple typing, some word processing programs now provide sophisticated features that allow the creation of professional-looking documents once only available in high-end **desktop publishing programs**. Although word processing is typically associated with report writing, there are endless ways to incorporate its power in the classroom. Some ideas include creating alphabet books, keeping daily journals, creating newsletters, writing collaborative stories and reports, outlining, and creating reports with tables and graphs. A host of word processing programs are available but well-known examples include Word (MS), WordPerfect X4 (WordPerfect), Pages (Apple), and Writer (Open Office). There are also word processing applications in Google, Zoho, and Thinkfree that allow Web-based access for students and teachers. An in-depth look at word processing and its use in the K–12 setting is provided in Chapter 6.

Database programs allow teachers and students to record, organize, and manage information in related categories, and to retrieve, manipulate, and display this information in various forms. Databases can be used with elementary, secondary, or post-secondary students. Teachers can use databases to organize student information, compile bibliographies of relevant books and articles, make a record of available equipment and materials, and keep archives of lesson plans. Students can use databases to find information, to develop higher-order thinking skills, to solve problems, and to create original databases on multiple topics to use as resources. Familiar titles of database software include Access (MS), FileMaker Pro, and the database functions in MS Works or Open Office. Inspiration has developed a new application, Inspire Data, which is a nifty tool with database functions. Detailed review of databases and how they can be used in the PK–12 setting is provided in Chapter 9.

Spreadsheet programs offer a convenient way to organize numbers, and can automatically perform computations, such as addition, averaging, and so on. Although spreadsheets are most commonly used with numbers, practically any information can be organized using the software. Spreadsheets can be effectively integrated into many different curriculum areas in ways that excite students and enhance their learning. Spreadsheets can also assist teachers with grade books, lesson plans, rubrics, classroom inventories, club budgets, and charting students' growth and development. Students can creatively display data using charts on the spreadsheets in addition to sorting and manipulating data, thereby using higher-order thinking skills. Well-known spreadsheet titles include Excel (MS), Numbers (Apple), Quattro Pro (WordPerfect), and Calc (Open Office). There are also spreadsheet applications in Zoho and Thinkfree that allow Web-based access for students and teachers. A comprehensive review of spreadsheets and their use in the PK–12 setting is provided in Chapter 10.

Graphics software is a broad term that relates to several categories of software programs with quite different functions. Within this category, the authors have included programs that are used to *develop or edit graphics* such as drawing and painting programs and those that are used to *alter or enhance graphics*. **Draw programs** create digital images in the form of shapes called *vector graphics*, which are composed of lines and curved segments. Such programs use tools to create geometric shapes such as lines, circles, squares, and polygons that can be moved, resized, altered, or adjusted. Each element is treated as an object and can be moved in front of or in back of another. Vector graphics can be resized easily with no distortion. Drawing programs that are common in the PK–12 environment are *Kid Pix Studio Deluxe* by Broderbund, *Kid Works Deluxe* by Knowledge Adventure, and *SuperPrint Deluxe* by Tom Snyder Productions at Scholastic.

Paint programs are used to create or "paint" pictures by using tools that mimic traditional paint tools such as brushes, spray cans, and paint buckets. The image is created through the "painting" of pixels, which are small squares located on the screen. Images created by this method are referred to bit maps or raster graphics. *Bit maps* graphics are common file formats and are more difficult to resize without distortion. Paint programs that are common in the PK–12 environment are usually integrated into packages. There are also paint functions in *Kid Pix Studio Deluxe* by Broderbund, *Kid Works Deluxe* by Knowledge Adventure, and *SuperPrint Deluxe* by Tom Snyder Productions at Scholastic.

Finally, some application programs have a graphics feature included, such as a clipart or photo library or draw tools that can be used within the program. More about graphics and their uses in the K–12 setting is provided in Chapter 7.

Diagrams, maps, and webs are popular in K–12 classrooms and can be used by teachers and students across all subject areas. This category of software allows students to visually represent the structure of information and its relationship using hierarchical diagrams. The most popular techniques include concept mapping, idea mapping, webbing, and storyboarding. Popular software titles include *Inspiration* and *Kidspiration* by Inspiration Software. A thorough look at **visual learning tools** and their value in the PK–12 setting is provided in Chapter 8.

Multimedia programs allow the development of multimedia content with text, graphics, audio, and video. A popular category of software capable of producing multimedia is slideshow or presentation software. This software allows the development of dynamic content for the classroom and is generally used to accompany oral presentations and reports. Typically, slideshows consist of a linear presentation of information (sequential presentation), but recent software versions allow the design of nonlinear structures giving the ability to navigate through them in a random fashion, creating a viable tool for nonlinear tutorials or remedial presentations for students. Slideshow software is user-friendly and can be used with elementary, secondary, or postsecondary students. Presentation software programs are available from a variety of companies, but an old favorite is *PowerPoint (Microsoft)*. Apple offers *Keynote,* a slideshow tool reportedly rival to PowerPoint. Corel WordPerfect Office contains *Presentations X3* for Windows users. Integrated packages, such as *MS Works,* offer slideshow options, as does *Kid*

Pix Studio Deluxe by Broderbund/Riverdeep; and *HyperStudio* by Roger Wagner/ Software MacKiev. Web-based free solutions such as Google, Zoho, and Thinkfree provide anytime, anywhere access to facilitate collaboration and sharing with colleagues who are at a distance. These can be made public or easily embedded in blogs or a web site.

Audio and video creation and editing software is included in this group. iPods are capable of playing several audio formats including MP3; some Nanos (video capable) can play MPEG and QuickTime video formats. Apple iMovie and Windows Movie Maker are easy to use titles for video creation and editing and are often used for digital stories. An in-depth look at multimedia software and its use in the PK–12 setting is provided in Chapter 11.

Web-authoring programs (Web editors) allow the development of a web page or site that can be posted on a server for others to view. Most editors are quite easy; however, a newer method of Web-authoring takes place with Web-based programs that manage the content and take all of the technical expertise away. These easy-to-use and free programs allow teachers and students to put their time into developing the content rather than thinking about the code. Google Sites is a Web-based application within Google that allows the development of pages by students and teachers. Blogs and wikis can be used for designing web pages, too. Web page editors as well as content-managed online software offer a visual, word processing–like, familiar interface to create the web page. More about Web authoring is presented in Chapter 12.

Internet Software

Software is required for the various uses of the Internet (see Figure 3.3). The most basic Internet software includes Web browsers and email. **Browser software** allows the access and navigation of the information on the Web. Text, images, audio, and video are retrievable through browser programs, which are free to download for Windows, Apple OS, and other operating systems. Navigating the Web is done by clicking on highlighted (hyperlinked) words and graphics. Electronic mail, or **email**, allows individuals to exchange messages. To read and write email, a specialized mail program or a program offered through a browser must be used. Most email programs are free; a few must be paid for.

Media players provide the ability to hear and see audio and video files. These software programs are also referred to as **plug-ins**. Plug-ins help a browser per-

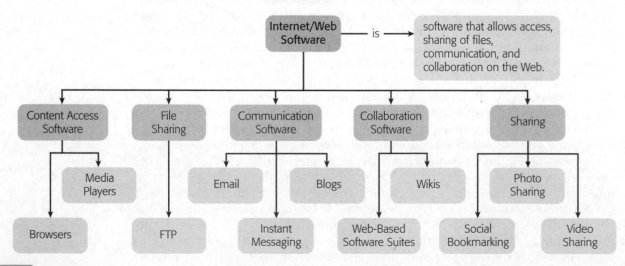

FIGURE 3.3 Internet/ Web Software

form specific functions such as viewing video or certain graphic files. The most popular titles include Windows Media Player, RealPlayer, and QuickTime. Adobe Flash Player and Adobe Shockwave Player are needed to be able to view many of interactive sites found on the Web and Adobe Reader is needed to view PDF (Portable Document Format) documents. PDF files provide a wonderful way to transfer documents over the Internet and keep the original formatting. Most Web authors will provide links to specific web sites to download the players for the types of documents found at their web sites. All players and readers are free downloads and the links can be found in the On the Web section of this chapter and at the companion web site.

File transfer protocol or **FTP software** is used to transfer files over a network. If a computer is connected to the Internet, the user can use one of a host of FTP software programs, such as WS-FTP (Windows) or Fetch (Mac), to upload or download files. In addition, some Web editing software such as Dreamweaver has a FTP capability built into the program. FTP downloads can also be performed with a Web browser. For example, when the user is downloading software from a web site to a local machine, the browser's FTP ability is being used.

There is a new group of Web 2.0 software that is discussed in Chapter 5 and throughout the book where appropriate. These new tools are Web-based and allow teachers and students to communicate, collaborate, and share information. These new software applications include blogs, wikis, social bookmarks, and more.

Instructional (Educational) Software

Instructional software is not meant to replace teachers, but rather to enhance or remediate the teaching and learning process. Such programs are designed to assist student instruction in various content areas and on various reading and grade levels. Instructional software can also be used to supplement IEP goals and objectives for students with disabilities. Instructional software (see Figure 3.4) is often categorized by its purpose, though in recent years many titles have become a blend of categories. For the purpose of this discussion, the common categories of drill and practice, instructional games, tutorials, simulations, problem solving, and reference software are reviewed. In addition, Integrated Learning Systems (ILS) are discussed. It is important to note that access to the Web in schools has decreased

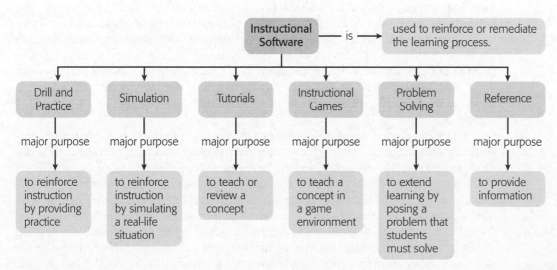

FIGURE 3.4 Instructional Software

the number of titles available from software companies. Many titles are offered online through subscriptions. We can expect this to increase in the years to come.

Drill-and-practice programs provide exercises that students complete and get immediate feedback on the accuracy of their answers. Some are designed with varying levels of difficulty. Favorable characteristics should include: (1) user control of the presentation rate of information, and (2) immediate feedback. Such programs, often referred to as "drill and kill" programs, have often been criticized, but may be used in the place of a worksheet when practice is needed for a test. Drill-and-practice programs are typically developed for math. One example, *Ultimate Math Invaders* (EdAlive), offers space attack math to drill number facts.

Simulation programs provide a computerized model of a real-life situation. Simulation is considered to be one of the more powerful instructional software categories; however, its effectiveness depends on how well it fits into the curriculum. Such programs are divided into several categories based on their purpose, including: (1) physical simulations, (2) procedural simulations, and (3) situational simulations. Simulations are a good choice in the classroom, because they can: (1) speed up or slow down a process that occurs in real life, (2) place the student in an active role, (3) provide a safe alternative to reality, (4) allow the student to participate in events that would not be possible otherwise, (5) provide a cheaper and more controllable method of instruction, and (6) allow for repetition. Although experts agree that real-life experience is better, simulations can be used in place of lab experiences, role playing, and field trips. Simulation software is often found in but not limited to science. Well-known programs include *Operation Frog Deluxe* (Tom Snyder) and *CrossCountry Photo Safari* (Ingenuity Works) as well as the newly revised *Oregon Trail* (Riverdeep).

Tutorial programs are designed to teach concepts. The instruction should be complete, so that it stands alone without help from the teacher. Favorable characteristics of tutorials include: (1) interactivity, (2) user control of the presentation rate of information, (3) adequate coverage of content, and (4) adequate feedback. Tutorials may be used for review of concepts or as an alternative teaching strategy. Some excellent online tutorials are provided for application software, such as MS Word. A long-time favorite tutorial program is *Mavis Beacon Teaches Typing* (Broderbund).

Instructional games are designed to teach concepts in a game environment. They are highly motivating to students and should be included with other instructional activities, not used exclusively for instruction. Instructional games may take various forms; however, all include game rules, elements of competition, and creative formats. Favorable characteristics of instructional games include: (1) elements of adventure, (2) levels of complexity matched to student ability, (3) adequate feedback for correct answers, and (4) a lack of violence. Games may be used to replace worksheets, to encourage collaboration, and to reward. Well-known titles include the Math Blaster series and Reading Blaster series from Knowledge Adventure.

There is no clear definition of software that fits into the category of **problem-solving software**. Sherman (1988) says that problem-solving software includes three elements: (1) a recognized goal, (2) a process, and (3) mental activity to reach a solution. Roblyer (2003) claims that two categories of problem-solving software exist, one specific to teaching content-area skills and one free of content skills with focus on recalling facts, dissecting a problem into steps, or predicting outcomes. Teachers must evaluate software to determine whether the desired problem-solving skills that they want their students to master can be developed through use of the software. After confirming that the software is adequate, the teacher must provide sufficient time for student interaction with the software, vary the amount of direction and assistance, promote a reflective learning environment through open discussion, and promote collaboration by having students work in pairs or teams. Well-known examples include *Oregon Trail,* which is also a simulation.

Reference software programs include encyclopedias, dictionaries, thesauri, or collections on specific topics. These are offered in multimedia formats on CD or DVD and sometimes offer an attractive alternative to a visit to the library. One example, *Merriam-Webster's Visual Dictionary* (Innovative Knowledge) offers full-color definitions for more than 20,000 words.

Integrated Learning Systems (ILS)

Integrated learning systems (ILS) has existed since the 1970s even though its features have changed. This software product is housed on a computer network or the Internet, and offers various instructional methods, including drill and practice, tutorial, simulation, problem solving, and tool software, plus a student management feature that keeps records of individual student achievement. Further, ILS includes: (1) instructional objectives for each lesson, (2) lessons aligned with curriculum standards, and (3) lessons that span grade levels. There are pros and cons about the use of ILS. These systems are highly interactive and provide feedback on student progress. Most of the negatives arise from the expense of the software and the way that teachers allow such systems to drive the curriculum and replace instruction. Roblyer (2003) suggests that the power of ILS systems can be best experienced when they are used as a supplement to other teaching methods. Uses include remediation, the introduction of information to students, and the fostering of constructivist applications through student use of features such as electronic encyclopedias, word processing tools, and so on. Reading and math are typically the topics of choice. Two well-known systems are *Plato Learning* (**www.plato.com**) and *Accelerated Reader* (**www.renlearn.com/ar/**).

Teacher Utility Software Tools

A number of software programs are designed to assist teachers with daily tasks such as grade keeping and generation of tests, puzzles, or rubrics. Sometimes referred to as **teacher utility programs,** these may organize and analyze information or simply create more attractive documents quickly by using built-in templates. These tools can offer the teacher improved productivity, accuracy, and appearance. See Figure 3.5 for the different uses of teacher utility software.

Grade Programs   There are software programs designed specifically to assist the teacher with grade keeping. Student names, attendance, assignments, and scores can be entered and analyzed by these **grading programs** quite easily. In addition, some titles offer seating charts and the ability to make notes on student behaviors. Some well-known titles include *Easy Grade Pro* by Edline, *Micrograde* by Chariot (**www.chariot.com/micrograde**) and Pearson has added MyGradeBook, a Web-based gradebook that replaces Misty City's well-known *GradeMachine*.

Task Generators   Teachers use **task generator software** to produce worksheets, tests, IEPs, puzzles, and rubrics. Using these generators is preferable to using a word processor, because they are set up with templates and make the task quite easy and quick. Visit the companion web site (On the Web: Software) to access direct links to a variety of task generators.

Test generators allow the teacher to input the questions, and then the software creates the test. The teacher does not have to worry about formatting issues and the software can quickly produce different versions of the same test upon

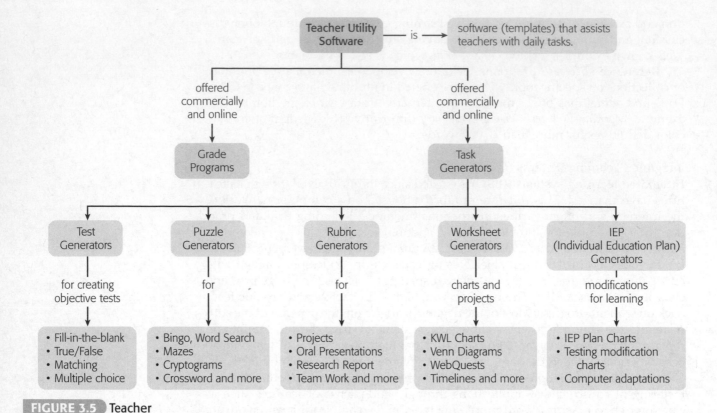

FIGURE 3.5 Teacher
Utility Software

request. Common features include: (1) the ability to create various forms of objective tests such as fill-in-the-blank, true/false, matching, and multiple choice; (2) random generation of questions; and (3) answer keys.

Learning is fun with the use of puzzles that are developed by the teacher using **puzzle generators**. There are ten types of puzzles that teachers can create using the tools offered at Discovery School's Puzzlemaker (**http://puzzlemaker .discoveryeducation.com**). Teachers can create mazes, word searches, criss-cross, number blocks, math squares, double puzzles, cryptograms, letter tiles, and fallen phrases puzzles with information from the curriculum in their classrooms. Essential Tools by Tom Snyder (**www.tomsnyder.com/products/product.asp? SKU=ESSCLA**) offers the ability to create puzzles and other materials similar to the ones mentioned previously. Other puzzle generators can be found by contacting an educational software company.

Rubrics can be generated quickly, easily, and at no charge by using a **rubric generator,** like Rubistar (**http://rubistar.4teachers.org/index.php**). Rubistar is an online tool that offers templates for oral projects, math, multimedia projects, research and writing, reading, art, work skills, science, and music.

IEP generators allow the teacher to create Individual Education Plans (IEPs) for students with disabilities. Students with disabilities are required to have an IEP that serves as a blueprint for instructional activities. Reporting procedures developed by school districts to meet the requirements of special education legislation, however, can be overwhelming for teachers. Software programs for IEP development offer solutions to this paperwork burden. IEP management programs are typically database programs with a template structure that can be customized to meet state and local school requirements for IEP formats and reports. The software is easy to use and has prompts for required components for the plan. IEP generators are available as standalone versions for classroom computers or as Web-based versions that connect with district record databases.

Evaluating Instructional Software

Software has improved greatly over the early days of computer-assisted instruction and teachers can be fairly sure that there will be relatively few technical difficulties, yet, how does a teacher know that a certain title will reinforce concepts that are being stressed in the classroom? It is not always a good idea to rely on descriptions written by software manufacturers. There is no way to determine whether the software matches what the teacher is trying to accomplish in the curriculum without a hands-on review of the software.

Teachers should (1) identify the objectives that the lesson/activity should meet, (2) locate suitable titles, and (3) complete a hands-on review. As with all instructional situations, the target population should be considered. Is the software appropriate for the age, skill, and reading level of the learners? What technological skills and time are required to use the software? Is the software pedagogically sound and does it meet the objectives set forth in the curriculum?

There are many checklists for hands-on reviews; however, the teacher should keep in mind that there are certain general qualities that should be used to determine the appropriateness of a software title. The software evaluation guide designed by the authors is aligned with research and is provided as a PDF document at the student materials section of the companion web site. The first section is descriptive and identifies the title, publisher, grade level(s), subject area(s), and associated costs of the available licensing. Computer system requirements including the platforms, RAM, and hard drive space, and peripherals are covered in the next section; and instructional modes are in the third section. The reviewer is asked to give an overview of the software and evaluates the documentation and support available. This is followed by evaluation of the appropriateness of the software for the targeted audience, design of the program, the content, and the assessment and feedback.

Adapting for Special Learners

Much of the application and instructional software introduced earlier can be used in an assistive manner by students with disabilities. Some students, however, need more specialized features to accomplish cognitive or physical tasks that would otherwise be difficult or impossible for them. This section introduces **assistive technology (AT) software** that is most commonly used for learners with mild or moderate disabilities. These software programs are typically found in classrooms, are easy to use, and are of value for accessing the general curriculum.

Assistive Software

As explained in Chapter 1, an AT device is broadly defined as any item used to improve the learning of an individual with disabilities. Assistive software refers to a wide range of products. This software may or may not have been designed specifically for individuals with disabilities. Assistive software includes operating system software—options, adjustments, or adaptations for accessing operating system, application, and instructional software. Other programs, called *access software*, must be purchased as separate programs. Figure 3.6 depicts the organization of this discussion.

Operating System Software

All computers have accessibility options and adjustments included with the operating system software. Use of these adjustments may be all that is needed for a

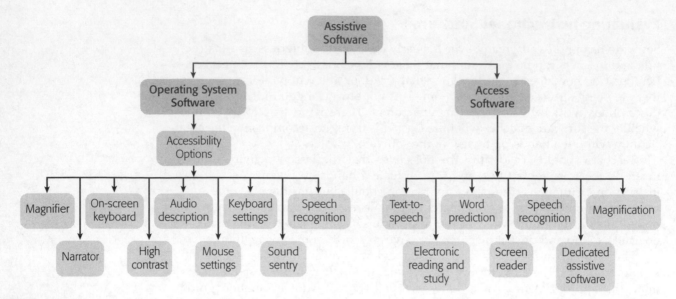

FIGURE 3.6 Assistive
Software in the Operating
Systems and Access
Software

student to access the screen or the keyboard. They can also be helpful for a student who is temporarily disabled because of accident or injury. Once these adjustments are made, applying all settings to the logon desktop will save them without changing the default settings for others. The settings can also be applied as defaults on an individual computer.

Accessibility options are usually pre-installed on the computer at the time of purchase. If this software has not been installed, it can be found on the installation CD. Occasionally, local technical support personnel may restrict access to or disable these settings. These settings should be available to any individual who needs them; contact the technology coordinator or the network administrator and request the access to these options.

On Windows Vista operating systems, the accessibility options are located in the control panel's *ease of access* folder. In XP and earlier versions, these features are located in two places, the accessibilities options of the control panel, and the accessories, found in the start>programs location. On Mac OS X machines, the accessibility options are set in System Preferences, in the Universal Access panel.

Accessibility Options

The *magnifier* makes items on the screen appear larger. This feature opens a window over the screen that can be sized and set to magnify for 2 to 16 times the original. The magnifying window can be set to follow the mouse cursor, keyboard commands (Tab or arrow) or text editing, to see what is being typed. A little experimenting will determine how useful this feature can be for an individual user. The magnifier is a useful feature for students with visual impairments who are working on "public" machines that may not have more permanent screen magnification features installed.

The *narrator* is a basic screen reader. Narrator reads aloud the text in any part of the desktop selected. Settings and keystrokes allow the user to control what the narrator reads. The current version will "echo user's keystrokes" as they are being typed in addition to reading events on the screen. Narrator also has voice controls for changing its speed, volume, and pitch. While the feature is intended to be used for access to most computers, students who are blind or experience print disabilities may need a more full-featured commercial screen reading program. Experimenting with narrator allows the teacher and student to determine its adequacy on a temporary or more permanent basis.

The *on-screen keyboard* can be particularly useful for students with mild learning disabilities who get lost when changing visual planes, that is, when gazing between paper, keyboard, and computer screen. Students with severe mobility barriers, however, will need a dedicated software program that works more conveniently with on-screen scanning and switch access programs.

High contrast allows adjustments for viewing the display in black on white or in white on black. An array of other high-contrast settings is also available here.

Audio description is a relatively new feature that allows the user to set the computer to describe the happening in videos by hearing an audio description. This feature is only available for videos in which the authors have provided this documentation, and can only be accessed when this feature is turned on.

The user may adjust the cursor settings to reduce distraction and increase visibility. In the Ease of Access Center, cursor thickness settings are located in the selection, "Make the computer easier to see." Cursor blink rate settings are located in the selection, "Make the keyboard easier to use." Ideal individual preferences can be determined through experimentation with these settings.

The *mouse settings* allow the user to maneuver the cursor with the numeric keypad on the keyboard instead of using the mouse. This setting is useful for individuals who are able to strike keys, but have limited lateral movement in the hands (needed to move the mouse). Other mouse options allow the user to customize features such as click speed and right- or left-handed configurations.

Other keyboard settings are *sticky, filter,* and *toggle.* Sticky keys make it possible to use the shift, control, or alternative keys with shortcuts by pressing one key at a time instead of having to hold them down. This setting makes one-handed typing possible. Filter keys adjust the acceptance rate of keystrokes and ignore repeated strokes. Students with motor control difficulties, such as those caused by cerebral palsy, may find this adjustment beneficial. Options within this setting include "bounce," if you want repeated keystrokes to be ignored until a certain amount of time has passed, or "repeat keys and slow keys" if you want the computer to ignore brief keystrokes according to the time limits you set. Experimentation with the user will help determine which setting is most useful. Toggle key settings produce a sound to warn the user whenever a lock key is pressed (cap lock, num lock, or scroll lock). This setting may be useful for an individual with visual impairments.

Sound sentry adds a visual notice whenever the computer produces a sound. Sound sentry flashes the caption bar, window, or desktop when a sound is produced, and the option to show sounds displays captions for the sound. These settings are useful for students with hearing impairments or for students who need visual reminders along with sounds.

Speech recognition is a new systems feature in Windows Vista that gives users the opportunity to run the computer by voice rather than mouse and keyboard. The feature can be used with other software options, such as dictating documents and emails in Office or other applications, using voice commands to start and switch between applications, and to control the operating system.

Access Software

Access software does not come with the operating system software and must be purchased separately. This software is used to access general education curriculum tasks, increasing the learner's cognitive skills and productivity. Access software includes features such as text-to-speech, word prediction, scan and read, speech recognition, magnification, and screen reading. It also includes dedicated software designed to work with specific hardware and software combinations.

Text-to-Speech (TTS)

Text-to-speech word processors allow auditory feedback of text in a variety of formats: as each letter, word, or sentence is typed or as a "read all" option. Those that are most adaptable for classroom use highlight the word and sentence as it is read, increasing the visual prompt for the student. Spelling, dictionary, and thesaurus support can also be read aloud. Auditory settings can be adapted in speed, inflection, accent, and choice of voice. Examples of text-to-speech word processors commonly used in classrooms are *Intellitalk, Write: Outloud*, and *Read & Write GOLD*. Newer versions of MS Word (2003 and later) have text-to-speech capabilities, but without highlighting or other advanced features.

Other text-to-speech options include *Simple Text*, available on Macintosh OS versions 7.5 and higher and *VoiceOver*, available on Mac OS versions X and higher. Microsoft Office (2003 and later versions) has a "speak text" feature accessible within the speech tools. In both of these low-cost options, the text is not highlighted as it is read, and access to the controls is not as convenient as it is in a text-to-speech program designed specifically for that purpose.

Word Prediction

Originally intended for users with physical disabilities, **word prediction programs** are recommended for students with difficulties in transcription, severe spelling problems, and fine motor problems (MacArthur, 1998). This feature offers choices for prediction, after one or two keystrokes, based on grammatical structure and syntax. (Contrast this feature with *word completion,* which is used in text messaging and other programs and is based on the frequency of word usage.) Most word prediction programs work with or include TTS to read the intended choices. Most word prediction programs work in conjunction with a word processor. *Co:Writer* (Don Johnston, Inc.) allows the writer to select an appropriate dictionary, based on ability level, for word prediction. As writing ability increases, the user may choose a dictionary with more word choices. *Read & Write GOLD* (Texthelp Systems Inc.) works with a standard word processor and provides word prediction as one of its multiple features. Word choices are displayed in a suggestion box, which can be repositioned on the screen. Other programs with word prediction features include *Kurzweil 3000* (Kurzweil Educational Systems) and the integrated programs of IntelliTools' Classroom Suite. Factors to consider when choosing a word prediction program include its ease of use for the student, the sophistication level of the vocabulary it is possible to predict, and the ability to add additional words.

Electronic Reading and Study Programs

Not every student can use the printed version of a textbook. Some read slowly, others have difficulty recognizing words in print, and others have low vision. Auditory versions can make the text accessible. Teachers already use adaptive strategies such as reading partners or tape-recorded passages, and technology offers options that make access to text even more independent for the learner. **Electronic reading and study programs** work with a scanner to convert books and other print media to digital text using **optical character recognition (OCR) software**. Once digitized, the text can be highlighted as it is read by the software, saved as a text or word processing file, or converted to MP3 format for audio playback on a portable device. A variety of such software products are available, offering varying levels of ease, instructional support, and cost.

Kurzweil 3000 has a highly accurate OCR feature. It discerns between pictures and text effortlessly, requiring little adjustment from the user. It also offers an array of literacy supports. Dictionary, thesaurus, and translation capacities are available options for any digitized word. Text can be highlighted and then extracted from the body of the work and displayed on a split screen, keeping the original text displayed on the same visual plane. Text notes can be placed anywhere on the screen or attached as footnotes, enabling teachers to devise questions, activities, and other reading strategies. *Kurzweil 3000* is available for both the Macintosh and Windows platforms. The professional version converts print-based text to a digital format, and reads unlocked files in the PDF format. The less-expensive read-only (learn station) is appropriate for student workstations once the text has been converted to a format that can be read by the program.

Read & Write GOLD operates as a support to other office products (Word, Excel, PowerPoint). This program is available for both the Macintosh and Windows platforms and is moderately priced. It also reads PDF files.

The IDEA requires textbook publishers to provide instructional materials in a standard electronic format (NIMAS) to students with print disabilities, thus by-passing the need to scan, or convert many texts from print-based to digital format. In most districts, these requirements will be implemented as new text adoptions are scheduled. A number of products read these files in addition to providing study support. *ReadOutLoud* (Don Johnston, Inc., **www.donjohnston.com**) will read electronic books in the NIMAS format. WYNN (Freedom Scientific Inc., **www .freedomscientific.com**) is popular among individuals who are blind.

Product selection should be based on the needs of the individual for a specific academic task, the availability of electronic files or the quality of the optical character recognition software, ease of use, and an analysis of cost and features. Expect to see improvements in features and operation with each upgraded version of these software programs.

Teachers may experiment with the process of converting text to a standard computer file by using the OCR software that comes with most scanners. Most OCR programs will give a plausible, but not fully accurate, transcription from print to digitized text. Someone (usually the teacher) must then read through the resulting file and correct the inaccuracies (such as "%" for "s"). The resulting file can then be pasted into a text reading program. The Internet also provides a number of sites with freeware and shareware programs that have text reading features, some of which work quite well in temporary situations. While OCR software can be used in this manner when access to specialized software is limited, students who rely on electronic text on a consistent basis will need a software program with higher accuracy.

Speech Recognition

Speech recognition programs use an individual's voice for dictation or for executing computer commands. These programs use adaptable recognition models that accommodate the unique characteristics of a speaker, such as accents or particular speech patterns, and can recognize speech that is spoken in a natural cadence, without the need to slow down the speech or emphasize individual words. Users create an individual voice profile by reading designated passages into program files. The accuracy of this profile improves with use, as the software refines its recognition capacity by updating misrecognitions. These programs hold promise for students with special learning needs who are willing to spend the time and effort necessary to learn dictation, editing, and voice command strategies. They work best when used in a quiet location with a high-quality microphone (preferably a headset microphone with a consistent placement near the mouth). Examples of speech recognition software are *Dragon NaturallySpeaking* (Windows), *Via Voice* (Mac), and *MacSpeak* (Mac) (Nuance Communications, Inc., **www.nuance.com**).

An emerging use of speech recognition technology has implications for students who are deaf, hearing impaired, or who experience other communication access needs. The program *iCommunicator* (PPR Inc.) translates speech to text and sign language in real time. American Sign Language (ASL) signs in English word order (subject+verb+object) appear on the computer screen along with text of the words that are being spoken. Prerequisites for using this software include strong literacy skills and basic computer skills in a Windows environment. *Dragon NaturallySpeaking* is the speech and voice recognition "engine" used with this software, and the speaker must establish a speech and voice recognition file prior to initial use. Currently, the software is available only for the Windows platform and requires careful evaluation of the user's skills and needs to determine whether the application is viable. The *iCommunicator* may also increase access to certain communication settings, such as lectures, for other students who have difficulty understanding auditory material.

Microsoft Office (version 1997–2003) has a speech recognition feature that is accessed through the Tools menu. Although not as accurate as the more specialized voice recognition programs, it has an adequate level of accuracy and may be a viable option for students who prefer to write using dictation, or others who are experiencing repetitive stress injuries. As mentioned before, this feature is also included in the systems software of Windows Vista, making it accessible to other software applications. Microsoft Office (version 2007 and above) access speech recognition features through Windows Vista system software.

Magnification

Control panel or accessibility **magnification features** that are available on most operating systems may serve students with mild disabilities or may be adequate for short-term use. Students with severe visual impairments, however, may need a magnification software program that operates in a more convenient or user-friendly manner. One such example is *MAGic* from Freedom Scientific. *MAGic* combines magnification features with screen reading, a feature explained in the next section.

Screen Readers

Although the narrator program available on all computers may be a useful adjustment for some, students with very limited vision or who are blind need a more convenient program. *JAWS*, a **screen reader** from Freedom Scientific, is designed for users to access computer controls and any screen content in a consistent manner. *JAWS* reads text, dialog boxes, and commands aloud, and will also output to Braille paper printers or refreshable Braille displays (a tactile screen that can be erased). Other screen reading options are available for students with print disabilities who use sight and mouse movements to access computer controls. Information on other technology vendors offering screen reading software can be found on the Alliance for Technology Access web site (**www.ataccess.org**).

Dedicated Assistive Software

Students with more severe physical or cognitive disabilities may need dedicated software, combinations of software and hardware designed to work together for specific purposes. For example, a student whose physical limitations prevent the use of mouse, keyboard, or voice will need an alternative input arrangement. This student may need to use a single action, such as an eye blink, or a sip and puff from a specialized straw, to control the computer. This form of software is designed to provide onscreen scanning, or a controlled movement over potential choices, and to respond to the selections made by the user's switch actions. A thorough review of dedicated software is beyond the scope of this text, but teachers interested in this technology may begin their research efforts by consulting the Alliance for Technology Access web site (**www.ataccess.org**) for further information. Students who are using these devices and their teachers should receive AT services to assist in training and troubleshooting. Teachers should keep the student's IEP team informed of progress and concerns when using this technology.

CURRICULUM CONNECTIONS

Abuelita y Yo: Just Grandma and Me

CONTENT AREA/TOPIC: Foreign Language, Language Arts, Reading
GRADE LEVELS: 1, 2   **NETS·S:** 4

Description: In this lesson, students use an interactive storybook to practice Spanish as they analyze the story, plot, and characters. The interactive storybook, by Mercer Mayer, provides the setting for activities that allow young students to distinguish the order of events, improve reading comprehension, and practice the target language.

Teacher Preparation: Teachers (1) develop story cards to represent the major sections of the plot for students to use in sequencing activities, (2) create questions for comprehension based on the story, and (3) identify ecosystems that are in the story and use associated words as the key words to learn in the target language.

Active Participation:

1. Students experience the story in small groups. After the students are familiar with the story, they should identify the plot and characters (with the assistance of the teacher).
2. Students use the sequence cards to order the story and practice retelling the story. If they are unsure of the sequence, they can go back to revisit the story.
3. The teacher asks the students comprehension questions in the target language.
4. Finally, the ecosystems are analyzed and graphically represented on a diagram and show similarities and differences found in the city and at the seaside.

Assessment: Evaluation of learning includes the responses by the students to oral, written, and visual measures. Small groups are a good way to promote collaboration.

Variations: This activity could be completed with any multimedia story that students are reading and can be used to construct learning.

Software: Available for older systems as well as XP and Vista (**www.kidsclick .com/descrip/justme_grandma.htm**).

Source: Adaptation of the original lesson *Abuelita y Yo: Just Grandma and Me,* created by Nila Jacobson, from Nebraska. The adaptation is found in *Learning Connections, Learning and Leading with Technology 33*(2), p. 34. Original source: Jacobson, N. (2000). *Abuelita y Yo: Just Grandma and Me.* National Education Technology Standards for Students: Connecting Curriculum and Technology, ISTE, pp. 78–79.

Voices *from the* Classroom

Software Equalizes My Classroom
Valerie Pearce

Valerie has taught special education preschool for more than 10 years. She has always been interested in technology and uses it as a classroom resource as well as a teaching tool. She has three computers in her classroom for student use and one teacher workstation. We interviewed Valerie to discover her thoughts on the use of technology with children with disabilities.

The children in my class are between the ages of three and five. All of the children have some type of disability that qualifies them for special education based on the state standards. The disabilities vary greatly, as well as their developmental levels. The greatest challenge I face is developing lessons that meet both their individual developmental and chronological age levels. I find that I can often meet their needs through the use of technology.

The children in my class learn best when they use both visual and auditory modalities. I usually display images from the computer through a large television screen when introducing new material. This enables us to discuss the images as a large group. I am always trying to find new ways to engage my students and find technology to be an excellent way to keep young children motivated and interested. I recently introduced the song "Five Little Pumpkins." Due to the visual nature of my students, I needed to find a way to visualize the rhyme so they could integrate the language more readily. I decided to create a lesson using the Intellitools software. I created a program using *IntelliPics,* telling each part of the rhyme. I then created an overlay to go with the program. I printed the overlay and used an adaptive keyboard so all of the children in my class could actively participate in the lesson.

Showing the program through the television, the children used the overlay to choose individual pictures that corresponded with the rhyme. I used the overlay in many ways. I asked them specific questions that they would have to find the answers to on the overlay. I had them sequence the story by choosing the pictures in order, and I let them use free exploration to listen to the story independently. I was so excited to see how quickly the children learned the rhyme and how excited they were to use the *Intellikeys* and share their knowledge. The children also learned how to take turns and work in small groups. Even my nonverbal children could answer simple questions by using the large keyboard with the overlay and feel successful. I want the children to be as independent as possible and be able to use technology without having to rely on others. I have since made several other overlays to use with other *IntelliPics* programs to learn rhymes, songs, and vocabulary. I have also scanned books and made overlays so the children can "read" a book by themselves using the computer and an adaptive overlay.

I learned an extremely valuable lesson: There is no limit to what you can do with technology. I really struggled when I first started trying to find different programs to use with very young children that would meet their needs. After many trials and errors, I discovered that with persistence and a little bit of time, technology can enhance the learning of all children, regardless of ability and developmental level.

A Final Word on Assistive Software

A number of software developers are creating instructional software with built-in accessibility features. These advances in software design continue to make general-use software programs accessible for students with special needs. The important concept for teachers to understand is that software is a tool to support instructional goals. It can also increase the probability that all students will be able to participate in the learning experience, reduce the need for elaborate adaptations and modifications of material after the fact, and promote the inclusion of all students (Rose & Meyer, 2002).

On the Web

The 21st century has been characterized by an immense decrease in the availability of software vendors, largely due to increased access to the Internet and the development of Web-based options that offer many advantages. Many smaller companies that were well known in the field of education have been purchased by larger companies such as Riverdeep Interactive, Sunburst Technology, and Scholastic, Inc. This section includes only a snapshot of web sites that the authors recommend for viewing. To access live links and a larger and continuously updated collection of sites, go to the companion web site at **www.pearsonhighered.com/ obannon2e.**

Assistive Software Companies

Don Johnston
www.donjohnston.com
Don Johnston Incorporated provides a full array of software products for literacy instruction. Write:Outloud, Co:Writer, and Draft:Builder are among the more popular school-based products found at this searchable site. Information about products, downloads, newsletters and support is available.

Intellitools
www.intellitools.com
Intellitools provides an array of products that are can be used by students with disabilities and in general education classrooms. The Classroom Suite 4 combines tools for building reading, writing, and math skills.

Kurzweil Educational Systems
www.kurzweiledu.com
Kurzweil 3000 is a reading, study skills and writing software program that is used with struggling students, ELL students and students with special needs. Information regarding Kurzweil 1000, used by people who are blind, is also available at this site. Locate information regarding products and services, customer support, resources and downloads. The ability to order online is available as well as locating a reseller.

Mayer Johnson
www.mayer-johnson.com
Mayer Johnson offers Boardmaker, a symbol-based software program used to develop communication boards and other systems for students with special needs. Links are provided to other software products, communication devices, educational books, and training aids.

Educational Software Publishers

Knowledge Adventure
www.knowledgeadventure.com
Knowledge Adventure, a leader in developing, publishing, and distributing the well-known Blaster series (Math Blaster, Reading Blaster, JumpStart Learning Systems), offers information about their products. Visit this interactive site to experience the software.

PLATO Learning
www.plato.com/index.asp
PLATO Learning is a provider of personalized instruction and standards-driven assessment. It is developed to sustain continuous academic improvement from kindergarten to adult learning. Their solutions provide supplements to class instruction and are presented with multimedia content and real-world situations, as well as active learning situations.

Sunburst Technology
http://store.sunburst.com
Sunburst Technologies offers over 500 software titles for the K–12 market. The well-known brand names include Knowledge Adventure, famous for the well-known Blaster series (Math Blaster, etc). This site offers curriculum correlations as well as an opportunity to order a catalog.

Grade Programs (Web-based)

Grade Connect
www.gradeconnect.com/front/
This online tool functions as a course management system with pages for announcements, assignments, a calendar, annotated links to web sites, a custom gradebook and even a database to manage the assignment of textbooks. Accounts are free for teacher and students and make communication a breeze.

EasyGrade Pro
www.edline.com/solutions/gradebook_and_classroom_ management/easy_grade_pro.html
This Web edition by Edline and Orbis software allows 24/7 access for teachers, students, and parents. Easy Grade Pro 4.0, is available for Windows 2000, XP and Vista, and Mac OS 10.2+.

Engrade
www.engrade.com
This online classroom community offers free Web-based tools for educators. Engrade provides an online assignment calendar, gradebook, and attendance book that is private, secure and easy to use. View a demo of this tool and sign up to keep students and parents informed.

Task Generators

Puzzlemaker
http://puzzlemaker.discoveryeducation.com
Discovery Education presents Puzzlemaker, a puzzle generation tool for teachers, students, and parents. Word search, crossword, mazes, math puzzles, and much more can be easily created using word lists.

Rubistar
http://rubistar.4teachers.org/index.php
Rubistar, a free tool, assists teachers in rubric development for project-based learning activities. At this site, templates are

provided for teachers who want assistance with rubric development for oral projects, multimedia, math, research and writing, reading, art, work skills, science, music, and art.

Personal Education Plan Generator

www.teach-nology.com/web_tools/materials/goals/

Created by a teacher, this personal education plan generator is offered at Teach-nology and is defined as a "cross between a behavior contract and an IEP." This form offers to identify the goals, objectives, responsibilities, products, and how the success will be evaluated along with dates for meetings.

Hot Potatoes

http://hotpot.uvic.ca/

Hot Potatoes by Half-Baked Software offers a suite of six applications that create various types of interactive quizzes. This software is free of charge for nonprofit educational institutions that make their sites available on the Web. Learn about the newest versions for Windows, Mac OS X, and Linux. Check it out!

Key Terms

Software program (61)
Compatibility (62)
Documentation (62)
Price (62)
Application suite (62)
Microsoft Office Suite (62)
iWork (Apple) (62)
Integrated software package (62)
Word processing tool (62)
Database tool (62)
Spreadsheet tool (62)
Graphics tool (62)
Slideshow tool (62)
Licensing (63)
Free open source software (FOSS) (63)
Proprietary software (63)
Open source software license (63)
Operating system software (63)
Microsoft Windows (63)
Mac OS X (63)
Linux (63)
Graphic user interface (GUI) (64)

UNIX (64)
Application software (65)
Word processing program (66)
Desktop publishing program (66)
Database program (66)
Spreadsheet program (66)
Graphics software (67)
Draw program (67)
Paint program (67)
Visual learning tools (67)
Multimedia program (67)
Web-authoring program (68)
Browser software (68)
Email (68)
Media player (68)
Plug-in (68)
FTP software (69)
Instructional software (69)
Drill-and-practice program (70)
Simulation program (70)
Tutorial program (70)
Instructional game (70)

Problem-solving software (70)
Reference software program (71)
Integrated learning system (ILS) (71)
Teacher utility program (71)
Grading program (71)
Task generator software (71)
Test generator (71)
Puzzle generator (72)
Rubric generator (72)
IEP generator (72)
Assistive technology (AT) software (73)
Text-to-speech word processors (76)
Word prediction programs (76)
Electronic reading and study programs (76)
Optical character recognition (OCR) software (76)
Speech recognition programs (77)
Magnification features (78)
Screen reader (78)

Hands-on Activities for Learning

1. Visit the On the Web companion site (www.pearson highered.com/obannon2e) and review the sites available.
2. Using the evaluation instrument provided, review and evaluate two instructional software titles. In addition, write an overview of the software to acquaint your peers with the product.
3. In a collaborative group with peers, examine educational software that is classified as tutorial, simulation, instructional game, problem solving, and reference software.
4. Use a task generator (puzzle generator) at Discovery School's Puzzlemaker at puzzlemaker.discoveryeducation

.com to create a puzzle with a list of key terms from a text used in the curriculum of the student audience that you will be teaching.
5. Use a grading program (download a trial version, keeping your system requirements in mind) from the list of grade programs in the On the Web section. Use a dummy set of grades for ten students to see how this software works.
6. Examine the accessibility options in the operating system software of a computer to which you have access, and improve accessibility for learners who need assistance.

LEARNER OBJECTIVES

At the completion of this chapter, learners will be able to:

- Discuss research related to the effective use of digital portfolios in learning.
- Use basic terminology associated with portfolios.
- Distinguish the difference between working portfolios, assessment portfolios, and showcase portfolios, and the purposes of each type of portfolio.
- Describe the advantages and disadvantages of developing digital portfolios.
- Describe the supporting documentation that is included in a digital portfolio.
- Describe the types of artifacts that should be included in a portfolio.
- Collect supporting portfolio documentation and artifacts and convert them to digital format.
- Describe alternative assessment portfolios and discuss the advantages of using digital versions to document the progress of students with significant disabilities.

NETS·T ALIGNED WITH PORTFOLIOS

2. **Design and Develop Digital-Age Learning Experiences and Assessments**

   Teachers design, develop, and evaluate authentic learning experiences and assessments incorporating contemporary tools and resources to maximize content learning in context and to develop the knowledge, skills, and attitudes identified in the NETS·S. Teachers:

   a. design or adapt relevant learning experiences that incorporate digital tools and resources to promote student learning and creativity.

   b. develop technology-enriched learning environments that enable all students to pursue their individual curiosities and become active participants in setting their own educational goals, managing their own learning, and assessing their own progress.

   c. customize and personalize learning activities to address students' diverse learning styles, working strategies, and abilities using digital tools and resources.

   d. provide students with multiple and varied formative and summative assessments aligned with content and technology standards and use resulting data to inform learning and teaching.

Frameworks

A **portfolio** is an organized collection of artifacts or individual, tangible products that verify an individual's professional growth. Kilbane and Milman (2003, p. 4) define portfolios as "a goal-driven, organized collection of artifacts that demonstrate a person's expansion of knowledge and skills over time." Portfolios serve as forms of alternative assessment that link curriculum and assessment (Bitter & Pierson, 2002). Used for authentic types of assessment, portfolios provide a record of growth over a period of time, thus enabling the developer to compare personal progress against the standards of quality in their profession.

Portfolios are growing in popularity for practicing teachers and their students and are becoming a requirement for preservice teachers. Many teacher education programs are starting to adopt portfolios to monitor and evaluate teacher candidates (Barry & Shannon, 1997; Guillaume & Yopp, 1995; Rakow, 1999). Most frequently used are **standards-based portfolios**, which focus on performance standards for teachers and are based on the belief that high standards of student achievement can be accomplished if teachers have the knowledge and skills necessary to prepare students to meet the standards.

Three professional associations concerned with teacher quality have increased the push for standards in teacher preparation programs. These associations—the National Board for Professional Teaching Standards (NBPTS), the Interstate New Teacher Assessment and Support Consortium (INTASC), and the National Council for the Accreditation of Teacher Education (NCATE)—have agreed on standards of quality for teacher performance. NBPTS and INTASC were formed in 1987; each looks at a different stage of the teacher's professional life. NBPTS (**www.nbpts.org**) is composed of classroom teachers, administrators, and other educational professionals, whose mission is advancing the quality of teaching by setting rigorous standards for practicing teachers. INTASC is a consortium of state education agencies and representatives from the teaching profession, including practicing teachers, teacher educators, school leaders, and state agency staff, whose mission is to reform assessment techniques for initial licensing, and develop accountability for compatible educational policy among states for teacher preparation programs (**www.ccsso .org/projects/Interstate_New_Teacher_Assessment_and_Support_Consortium**). Finally, NCATE (**www.ncate.org**) is an accreditation agency for colleges and schools of education that prepare new teachers. A fourth professional association, the International Society for Technology in Education (ISTE; **www.iste.org**) has developed the National Educational Technology Standards for Teachers (NETS·T), which provide performance indicators and rubrics to measure the teacher's performance at various levels of their development, as discussed earlier in this book.

There is no nationally agreed-upon requirement for teacher candidates. The individual teacher preparation program, of which the preservice teacher is a candidate for licensure, identifies the standards that each graduate must accomplish. The requirements range from the INTASC standards set for beginning teachers to state-mandated content standards and content standards of professional organizations. Additionally, teacher candidates from NCATE-accredited teacher education programs are required to meet those standards as well as the ISTE NETS·T standards. Although each association has developed different standards, a close inspection reveals that there is much overlap.

Basics

When teachers, teacher educators, authors, and others speak of a portfolio, they may be talking about quite different types of collections, despite using the same terminology; this situation can be quite confusing. There are different types of portfolios consisting of quite different types of collections that differ in content, organization, and presentation of materials and that are targeted to different audiences. During a teacher preparation program, preservice teachers may come across different kinds of portfolios and use portfolios quite differently with their future students. The portfolio types that we discuss are working portfolios, assessment portfolios, and showcase portfolios. These categories may have different names in other references or in practice; therefore, the authors caution new teachers to think about the purpose of the portfolio rather than focusing exclusively on the names. Most will fall into the three categories mentioned, even if they are called something else.

Working portfolios contain large collections of a preservice teacher's work over time. Constantino and De Lorenzo (2008, p. 3) identify a working portfolio as "a vehicle for documenting growth and development toward performance standards and teacher education program requirements." Components may include unit plans, lesson plans, photographs, multimedia presentations, videotapes, and other materials created over the preparation period. Historically, portfolios were print-based and stored in files, boxes, and/or notebooks. Cumbersome to transport, print-based portfolios are a thing of the past and have been replaced with digital portfolios that are stored on hard drives, CDs and DVDs, USB drives, or Web servers.

The assessment of the collection happens during the preparation program, with mandates as to the specific artifacts that must be a part of the assessment record. So actually the **assessment portfolio** is an outgrowth of the contents saved over time from the working portfolio. **Showcase portfolios** present the preservice teacher's best work and are composed of a subset of the working portfolio contents. The artifacts are chosen carefully after reflecting on the representative category, such as a standard, that the artifact represents. These portfolios are generally used for employment purposes upon graduation. Figure 4.1 shows facts about portfolios and their uses.

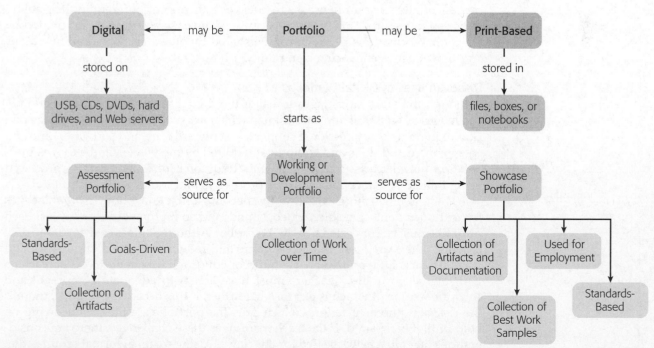

FIGURE 4.1 Portfolio Types and Characteristics

After securing a teaching position, the new teacher can modify the portfolio to become a professional teaching portfolio that will include a variety of materials and artifacts from the teaching practice. Kilbane and Milman (2003) suggest that new components might include various examples of teaching substantiated by examples of student work. The Voices from the Classroom section in this chapter features a teacher who developed her portfolio during her preparation period and continues to make changes as her practice develops.

More about Digital Delivery

Digital portfolios, sometimes called cyber portfolios, electronic portfolios, e-portfolios, or Web folios, contain the same type of artifacts as their older (traditional) cousins; yet, because they are digital in nature, these provide several advantages over paper ones—particularly portability. There are other advantages as well as disadvantages, discussed in the following sections.

Advantages of Digital Portfolios

Lieberman and Reuter (1997) conclude "the electronically enhanced portfolio augments the traditional print portfolio with electronic materials that can strengthen particular portfolio components." Kilbane and Milman (2003) list six advantages of going digital: accessibility, portability, creativity, technology, self-confidence, and community. Because of the ease of reproduction, the digital portfolio becomes accessible to greater numbers of people at the same time. This is particularly true of Web-based portfolios. Obviously, portfolios in digital format are much easier to transport, because of the nature of the storage media: USB drives, CDs/DVDs, external hard drives, or the Web. The creativity of the teacher is enhanced, as artifacts are presented in linear and nonlinear formats that allow many opportunities for creative presentation of information. In addition, teachers become much more comfortable with multimedia or Web environments because of the time that is spent during the creation process. The creation of a digital portfolio is a great way for teachers to highlight their ability to use technology, while including artifacts that provide evidence of the integration of technology and the curriculum. The process builds self-confidence, as teachers become more confident in their ability to use software programs. Finally, because of the easy access that is provided by the digital format, the portfolio can be shared by other teachers, administrators, and parents, thus enhancing community.

Disadvantages of Digital Portfolios

Although there are advantages to using the digital medium, there are certainly challenges as well. Kilbane and Milman (2003) list six challenges: knowledge and skill requirements, professional support, cost of hardware and software, time and energy, increased skills and equipment required by the viewer, and a digital presentation that detracts from the content. Traditional portfolios can be produced using limited software such as word processors and multimedia, but digital versions require much more expertise. Teachers must first know how to organize files for text documents, graphics, video, sound, and so on to avoid losing files. Each print file must be converted to a digital format. Although this is easy for some documents, others are more time consuming and require advanced knowledge and skills. There is little professional support or education in schools to assist teachers with digital portfolios. Teachers must have access to adequate equipment and software—some of which is expensive. Further, if this access is available, there is the risk of equipment failure, which puts the portfolio's editing or viewing on hold until it is repaired. If the teacher survives these challenges, there are considerations that must be addressed for the viewer. Using a digital format requires that the viewer have the skill and equipment necessary to view the documents. No skill is involved in viewing a traditional portfolio; the digital portfolio presentation requires more technical ability. Finally, there is the chance that the presentation will overshadow the content. Viewers may get so distracted by the technology that they fail to notice the accomplishments of the teacher.

Components of the Portfolio

Portfolios, whether traditional print or digital, consist of elements that can be put into two categories: supporting documentation and artifacts. Supporting documentation communicates information about the teacher or the organization of the portfolio. The artifacts are the elements that are critical to demonstrating professional knowledge. In addition, the teacher's educational philosophy should be included as well as reflections. Each artifact is discussed in the following paragraphs.

Supporting Documentation

Supporting documentation examples include a table of contents, personal information, credits, and permission statements. A table of contents is most important to the organization of the portfolio to assist the reader in locating the information. In a digital portfolio, the table of contents provides links for the reader to various sections in the portfolio. Personal information might include what the teacher does outside of the profession, such as hobbies and so on. Caution should be used as to how much information is shared, for privacy. Credits would acknowledge anyone who significantly contributed to the completion of the portfolio, such as the technology coordinator. If work from students is included, a permission statement should be included. Such a statement would generally say something like "I have received permission to use the student work in this portfolio." The statement would of course have to be accompanied by written permission slips, signed by parents or guardians, and kept on permanent file.

Artifacts

An **artifact** is tangible evidence of successful achievement of necessary knowledge and skills and the ability to apply understandings to complex tasks (Campbell, Melenyzer, Nettles, & Wyman, 2000). Tangible evidence might include a resume, a transcript, and educational philosophy statements, unit plans, lesson plans, or action videos of performance. Kilbane and Milman (2003) offer suggestions for digital portfolios and break the types of professional artifacts into the following five categories: education and experience; theory and beliefs; curriculum, planning, and management; student assessment; and communication. Each is listed in Table 4.1, with suggestions for acceptable elements. Specific categories will be determined by the teacher preparation program in which the teacher is a participant, but we believe that these categories present a well-balanced guide.

Educational Philosophy

An **educational philosophy statement** is an important element of a teaching portfolio. Kilbane and Milman (2003, p. 49) define the educational philosophy statement as "a description of your beliefs about teaching and learning." Some typical topics are the teacher's ideas on the goal or purpose of education, the role of the teacher in the educational process, the role of the student in education, and the role of parents in the educational process. Reasons should be given for each philosophy. Some of the things that a teacher of the 21st century might include are views on the integration of technology, diversity issues, management techniques, use of collaborative learning, and student-centered learning. During the initial

Table 4.1 Professional Artifact Categories with Typical Elements

Education and Experience	Theory and Beliefs	Curriculum, Planning, and Management
Professional resume	Educational philosophy	Unit plans and/or units
Transcripts	Long- and short-term goals	Lesson plans
Awards or honors	Professional development plan	Student work samples
Letters of recommendation	Reflective statements	Videos documenting teaching
Technology Endorsements or Certificates		Classroom management plan
Special skills (such as technology skills)		Classroom policies and rules
Workshops or other training outside the degree		Classroom web site
Observations by others, such as the mentor teacher or principal		
Teaching evaluations/Checklist		

Student Assessment	Communication	
Rubrics	Letters to parents or students	
Student portfolios	Parent-teacher conferences	
Individual education plans (IEP)	Newsletters	
	Classroom blog	
	Classroom web site with curriculum links	

Source: Kilbane & Milman (2003), p. 56.

stages of the teacher preparation program, this philosophical statement may be fairly short. As experience with teaching and learning increase, this philosophical statement may become more elaborate. If you have not written an educational philosophy statement yet, you should begin crafting one. If you currently have one, you may want to fine-tune it as you progress through the program. The final statement should be approximately 300–400 words.

Reflection

"A digital teaching portfolio without reflection is merely a multimedia presentation, a fancy electronic resume, or a digital scrapbook" (Barrett, 2000). Reflection is important to the learning process and should occur throughout the portfolio. **Reflection** is the process of examining one's professional practice within the rationale of principles that have guided the work. During the reflective process, long-held beliefs or knowledge may be questioned, and goals for change in professional practice established (Dewey, 1933). The ability to reflect on professional practice is a required element of most teacher preparation programs.

The following steps are recommended for developing portfolio reflections:

1. Obtain a list of the professional standards or goals developed for the teacher education program being completed.
2. Write a general reflective statement describing progress toward achieving each standard.
3. Select artifacts that represent the achievement of each standard.
4. Write reflective statements for each artifact, elaborating on why it was selected and its meaning and value in the portfolio. Questions that could be answered in this reflection include: (a) How does this artifact demonstrate competence for the particular standard(s) referenced? (b) What was learned as a result of creating or implementing the activities generated by this artifact? and (c) What changes could be made, or what, if the activity is repeated, could be done differently?
5. From the reflections and feedback, set learning goals for the future.

Source: Barrett (2000)

Digital Commandments

Kilbane and Milman (2003) present what they refer to as the *Digital Teaching Portfolio Commandments*, which offer good advice for organizing and saving work. All teachers who have worked with technology for very long will recall, with grimaces, the importance of these. The time spent on organization of the digital files will be repaid over and over. We have adapted the explanations to include our experiences.

1. *When in doubt, don't throw it out.* Although there may be doubt about whether a file will be included as an artifact in the final assessment or showcase portfolio, keep it filed safely away! A better example documenting growth or meeting a particular standard may not come along, or one that is doubtful may look better as time passes. The file can always be ditched after reviewing all possible artifacts—the one that is gone may be the one that best meets the guideline.
2. *Do it digitally.* Storing files in digital format rather than as paper copy offers many advantages. Not only do digital files take up less physical space, but quality is also preserved for many years. It is a good idea to always keep files that are easily viewed on the Web, as it is increasingly becoming the viewing medium of choice. Converting files from word processing, database, spreadsheet, and concept map programs to PDF format preserves the original formatting. Files can then be uploaded to the Web or linked to a slideshow or another presentation method. Save images as JPEG or GIF files, as they are the two formats that are readily accepted by the Web and recognized by all browsers. Audio and video files should be converted to files that are compatible with Web viewing as well.
3. *Be organized, not frustrated.* There cannot be enough said about proper organization of files. Organization will enhance sanity when trying to locate important documents and making decisions about which artifacts will be used in the portfolio. Keep in mind that although some artifacts are well chosen for an assessment portfolio, they may not be ideal for an employer to see. Folder organization should match the sections of the portfolio. For instance, consider the five major topics of the portfolio mentioned earlier: *education and experience; theory and beliefs; curriculum, planning, and management; student assessment;* and *communication.* In the education and experience file, store digital copies of a professional resume, personal transcripts, letters of reference, classroom observations, observations from the mentor teacher or principal,

descriptions of workshops, other training, and so on. If there are multiple artifacts, a final decision can be made later regarding which to include.

4. *Log it or lose it.*   Keeping up with information at the beginning of collection is quite easy, but a year or so down the road, locating specific documents is often difficult. This task becomes impossible without the file organization discussed in the previous step; however, even with file organization, it is easy to lose documents that are not easily identified. Kilbane and Milman (2003) suggest that all documents, photos, videos, and the like should be logged. This process can be done in a database program such as MS Access, Filemaker Pro, an open source selection, or by hand. Obviously, the database is easier to view at a glance when the artifacts grow in number. Suggested data fields include file name, date, artifact, description, and location. In addition, if a signed permission is needed, begin the arduous task of getting the permission as soon as you know it's needed. Waiting until they are mandated may mean losing the use of the artifact.

5. *If it is nice, save it thrice.*   Always keep a backup! Or better yet, keep several. Backups are copies of your work. Digital backups can be made easily by saving to a USB drive, the hard drive, a CD/DVD, or a Web server. Each time the work changes, update the backups as well. Although following that rule seems easy enough, saving a new copy doesn't necessarily mean that you can find it easily from among your multiple copies. It is a good idea to decide where new work will be stored, such as on a USB drive that you use only for work in progress. Then save a copy of all work to the backup media. Working in various locations can become confusing, and you can easily get mixed up about what's current and what is not. New versions should always be labeled with descriptive labels—one method is numbering each version. The key to numbering the versions is to be consistent! Don't confuse yourself.

6. *Be careful, not sorry!*   Pay heed to legal and security concerns. As mentioned previously, one of the advantages of digital portfolios is easy access to the information for different audiences. However, this easy access brings security issues as well. Because your information is so easily accessible, think carefully about the personal information that you are willing to share. Never share information such as your Social Security number, and use caution when sharing your home address and phone number. Such information can be shared at the appropriate time, more privately, with the proper personnel. It is possible to protect privacy by authorizing access by password entry only. Use secure passwords that include a mix of letters, numbers, and other punctuation known only to you and those you give it to.

7. *Give credit where credit is due.*   Teachers and students should always be cautious with copyrighted materials. Many teachers and students think that copyright law is not applicable to them because they're using materials for educational purposes. This is a myth. Although there are some fair use policies for teachers and students, none of them apply to publishing on the Web. Once the portfolio is Web-based, and more access is provided to the materials, it becomes a serious offense to use copyrighted materials without permission. If some artifacts include the work of other authors, identify the co-authors. Photographs of students should be included only with the written permission of their parents. In addition, caution should be used when sharing specifics about students that might be identifiable. Copyright is discussed further in Chapter 7.

8. *Protect the privacy of your students and colleagues.*   Use extreme caution when using the work of students. Never use the full names of students, even if permission has been granted. This rule is often misunderstood and confused with fair use policies. Privacy and safety issues are of paramount concern when the portfolio resides on the Web.

9. *Create and stick to a timeline.*   When a new teacher enters a teacher education program, expectations for the portfolio will be explained. These will differ with four-year and five-year teacher education programs, and the alternative licensure programs, because of the nature of the length and type of each program. Once the expectations are clearly understood, the collection of artifacts that meet expectations should begin. Development will be a time-consuming process, so don't put it off until the last semester of work. Most teacher education programs expect or require specific artifacts from each course. Many teachers in preparation will be required to use online formats designed by commercial companies (which also service the accounts throughout the teacher education experience); others will use portfolio templates on CDs, and others will be required to design their own portfolios using a software program such as MS PowerPoint. The timeline is essential in order to keep on task and end up with a product that speaks well of your abilities.

Source: Adapted from Kilbane & Milman (2003), pp. 96–104.

Portfolios are an assessment tool used by teacher education programs, as well as an assessment tool that you may choose to use in your classroom with your students; however, they can also work wonders by getting you the job that you want at the school of your choice. The Voices from the Classroom section shares an inspiring story of how a teacher began her portfolio during her preparation period and continues to make it work to showcase her work.

Adapting for Special Learners

Portfolios are also used to show the progress of students who are not able to participate in state-level assessment systems even with special accommodations. These portfolios are part of an alternative assessment system, aligned with state content standards, for a small number of students with severe to profound disabilities (1% or less of the total student population of the district). The alternative assessment portfolio is a yearlong collection of evidence of performance, including student work, teacher observations, charts, checklists, pictures, video clips, interviews, and notes from peers. Approximately half of the states use portfolio assessment of learning for displaying alternative assessment evidence; others have procedures to gather similar indicators, reporting results in checklist formats (Thompson & Thurlow, 2003). Each state has developed a set of templates to guide the collection of the data and has specified scoring systems to document student progress. Specific state policies may be obtained by consulting the respective state department of education web sites, or from the National Center on Educational Outcomes, an organization that examines state policies and practices regarding alternative assessment.

Special education teachers may use a variety of digital tools to construct an alternative assessment portfolio (Denham & Lahm, 2001; Byrnes, 2004). Although most of the literature describes the portfolio in terms of a paper-based product, teachers can create an electronic assessment portfolio using a format similar to that described in this chapter. An electronic version offers advantages described earlier: It can be shared with the student, parents, and administrators (accessibility and community), it is lightweight and easily stored (portability), and it offers teachers and students considerable latitude in capturing the growth and progress of the student (creativity).

Alternative assessment systems are required by both IDEA and NCLB legislation for students with significant disabilities as a means of documenting access to and progress in the general education curriculum. Most state guidelines in this area clearly focus on assessment of learning, but allow the teacher considerable

Voices *from the* Classroom

The Benefits of My Digital Teaching Portfolio

Anissa L. Vega

Anissa L. Vega graduated with an MS in Education from the University of Tennessee in May 2002. Although her content specialty is math, she was offered and accepted a position as the Instructional Technology Specialist at a private PK–6 school and has continued in that position since her graduation. We asked her to share her thoughts on the importance and benefits of teacher e-portfolios as well as the lessons learned.

When I was completing my teacher education program in 2002, I was lucky enough to be introduced to the idea of an electronic teaching portfolio through a PT3 grant, Project ImPACT (Implementing Partnerships Across the Curriculum with Technology) at the University of Tennessee. Since I had enjoyed teaching with technology during my yearlong teacher internship, many of my student work samples, pictures, and lesson plans were already in electronic formats. Instead of cutting and gluing pages of a three-inch binder together, I decided to attempt creating an electronic portfolio. This portfolio was my first attempt and was certainly a challenging learning experience; however, the benefits I received from that time investment have paid for it over and over again.

One of the most exciting functions of my electronic portfolio was providing momentum to my job hunt. I was excited about the possibility of teaching in a location other than my hometown, but was unsure about how I would manage interviewing out of state. My electronic portfolio turned out to be a time- and cost-efficient way to get schools around the country to become familiar with me and my expertise. At first, I mailed my portfolio on a CD with my resume to several school systems in which I was interested. Later, I decided to post my resume and portfolio on the Web, which allowed me to show it to principals directly at no cost. By the time I was ready to accept a position, I had four solid job offers on the East Coast, in Princeton, Washington DC, Atlanta, and Charlotte! With the experience of creating my own professional portfolio behind me, I've become very comfortable and proficient at creating electronic portfolios. Now, I have extended this practice into my daily work. I have worked with sixth-grade students as they develop individual learning portfolios to showcase their best work and some of their favorite learning experiences at Trinity School. In addition, as an instructional technology specialist, I assist other teachers in the development of their own professional portfolios. These portfolios have been used for recertification purposes, personal growth, and continued learning.

As in most schools, I have a yearly performance review with my supervisor. I feel very comfortable before these reviews, as I know I will have no trouble expressing my accomplishments to her through my portfolio. This method helps me to be sure that my review is not dependent on her memory or mine, and it is less subjective, making my yearly review more indicative of my actual performance during the school year. In addition, because the electronic portfolio formats I use allow for reflection, my supervisor and I have been able to quickly identify my strengths and weaknesses and any professional growth I have experienced over the past year. I have learned that it is difficult for any parent, coworker, supervisor, or principal to argue with evidence and reflection presented in a portfolio—most people will not even try.

As with all things, there were lessons learned that I want to share. It is not easy to maintain a portfolio of any kind, electronic or binder-held. I found that I was overly ambitious in the beginning. First, I tried to develop my portfolio in Adobe Dreamweaver, an application that I was not very familiar with at the time. This decision wasted a lot of my time and energy. Initially, I used programs with which I was very familiar, such as Adobe Acrobat, Microsoft Word and PowerPoint, and Netscape Composer. Today, I find that the free Google products such as Google Pages or Google Sites have not only free hosting, but the user interface is exceptionally simple with several components that allow for easy customization. Second, when creating my first portfolio, I had to rely on my memory in order to find artifacts to include. That approach led to a lot of revisions that also wasted time. Now, I just keep an electronic folder on my computer in which I save copies of potential artifacts as I create them. Third, in the beginning I tried to include too much in one portfolio. This mistake is common—the sixth graders and teachers who I work with also have had trouble overcoming it. I learned that it is important, for the purpose of both my time and the time of any person viewing my portfolio, to keep it simple. Be sure to pick only your best works and samples. Depending on the portfolio's purpose, I suggest including only a few lesson plans and one or two accompanying student samples. Then put your extra effort toward describing your experi-

Voices *from the* Classroom *Continued*

ences and thoughts in your reflections. Creating my electronic portfolio was absolutely the best investment of time I ever put into my teaching career. Even today, six years after the development of my first portfolio draft, this

dynamic personal resource continues to evolve and change with the available technologies all the while it showcases my own professional evolution. Now, to decide how I will incorporate this piece into my portfolio!

flexibility in presenting the assessment results. Using digital portfolios to display this evidence can ease the paperwork burden for special education teachers. Within the e-portfolio process, assessment for learning can be achieved by involving the student in decisions regarding content and reflection, perhaps through audio clips or other means of indicating participation. These strategies, which are easiest to accomplish in an electronic format, should serve to increase motivation and a sense of accomplishment for the students.

CURRICULUM CONNECTIONS

Teachers of grades K–12 are beginning to use digital portfolios, or e-portfolios, in the classroom as a means of authentic assessment. Teachers can also facilitate the creation of digital portfolios for their students. Teachers might consider the creation of a template to guide the student collection with a similar format. It is important to keep in mind the amount of information and the time period that the portfolio should cover before development begins.

Student e-portfolios, like the professional portfolios discussed earlier, can be classified as working or showcase. But the underlying purpose of student e-portfolios needs to be acknowledged as well. According to Barrett (2005), student portfolios are used for two general purposes: assessment *of* learning and assessment *for* learning. Assessment of learning is used to document the attainment of standards, or to offer evidence that compares the learning with grade-level expectations. Assessment for learning documents the learning process as it unfolds. It is designed to provide the type of feedback that supports reflection and improvement. In assessment of learning, the portfolio is a formal product, which may be submitted to an administrator as documentation of learning. When used in this manner, portfolios provide evidence that the student really does have the skills and the knowledge indicated by grades and test scores. In assessment for learning, the portfolio is owned, developed, and reflected on by the learner. It helps to build metacognitive skills, engage the student in the learning process, and is intrinsically motivating. Researchers have documented the validity of both purposes of e-portfolios, and it is often possible to combine these purposes in one portfolio system. However, e-portfolios that are used for assessment purposes only and that are not also student centered are generally disliked by teachers and students.

On the Web

This section includes only a snapshot of web sites that the authors recommend for viewing. To access live links and a larger and continuously updated collection of sites, go to the companion web site at **www.pearsonhighered.com/obannon2e.**

Commercial Portfolio Products Used in Teacher Preparation Programs

LiveText

https://college.livetext.com/college/index.html

LiveText provides comprehensive online services in colleges and universities for portfolio development. This growing network is used by many institutions. Read all about this Web-based accreditation management system at this site.

TaskStream

www.taskstream.com/pub/

Faculty can manage and distribute course materials, review student work, track student progress, create portfolio templates and assess students' portfolios online, develop curriculum, reference state and national standards, and prepare assessment rubrics using this tool. The reporting tools aggregate and disaggregate data for accreditation support.

Electronic Portfolios

Creating e-Portfolios with Web 2.0 Tools

http://electronicportfolios.org/web20portfolios.html

Dr. Helen Barrett, well-known expert on the development of electronic portfolios, presents ideas for creating portfolios with Web 2.0 tools with how-to's and samples.

Electronic Portfolios in the K–12 Classroom

www.educationworld.com/a_tech/tech/tech111.shtml

Education World presents an interactive article with access to advice from experts, guidelines for developing a digital portfolio program, tools for growth, and multiple links to resources for teachers.

Helen Barrett: electronicportfolios.org

http://electronicportfolios.com/

Travel to Dr. Barrett's professional page with much information regarding electronic portfolios with more information about communications, resources, frequently asked questions, and digital storytelling.

Teaching Portfolios

http://gallery.carnegiefoundation.org

Visit the great examples provided by the Carnegie Foundation.

Rubrics

Teacher Helpers: Assessment & Rubric Information

http://school.discoveryeducation.com/schrockguide/assess.html

Kathy Schrock and Discovery School offer this huge rubric collection. You'll find web page rubrics, subject-specific rubrics, multimedia rubrics, and rubric generators. A great resource for teachers who use performance-based assessment.

Rubrics for Assessment

www.uwstout.edu/soe/profdev/rubrics.shtml

The University of Wisconsin–Stout presents rubrics for cooperative learning, slideshows, podcasts, web page and e-portfolios, video and multimedia projects, writing, games, simulations, and more. What a great resource!

Rubistar

http://rubistar.4teachers.org/index.php

Rubistar, a free tool, assists teachers in rubric development for project-based learning activities. At this site, templates are provided for teachers who want assistance with rubric development for oral projects, multimedia, math, research and writing, reading, art, work skills, science, music, and art.

Key Terms

Portfolio (84)
Standards-based portfolio (84)
Working portfolio (85)
Assessment portfolio (85)

Showcase portfolio (85)
Digital portfolio (86)
Supporting documentation (87)

Artifacts (87)
Educational philosophy statement (87)
Reflection (88)

Hands-on Activities for Learning

1. Visit the On the Web companion web site (**www.pearson highered.com/obannon2e**) and review the sites available.

2. Depending on the teacher preparation program of which you are a student, e-portfolios have already been addressed by the time you're involved in the technology class. Determine how the skills built in this class can be used to develop additional artifacts for your teaching portfolio.

3. Write or revise your educational philosophy, a statement that reflects your philosophy about teaching and learning and how it will frame your future career.

4. Develop a professional resume that can be used for your first job interview. The resume should address your job objective, education and certification, experience in education, additional experience, awards, special skills, and community service. Download a template for your professional resume from this chapter of the companion web site. Complete the resume and post it at your blog, your web site, or your professional e-portfolio.

5. Set up a folder for your portfolio documentation. Within that folder, create subfolders that will hold documentation for your education and experience; theory and beliefs; curriculum, planning, and management; student assessment; and communication. (This list may differ depending on the teacher preparation program requirements.) Begin filing artifacts for these areas. Digitize paper documents for later insertion into your portfolio.

The Internet

LEARNER OBJECTIVES

At the completion of this chapter, learners will be able to:

- Define Internet-related terms.
- Explain the difference between the Internet and the Web.
- Identify the services available on the Web.
- Explain the options for connecting to the Internet and the advantages and disadvantages of each option.
- Use search tools for information-gathering on the Web.
- Apply knowledge of "netiquette," ethics, and safety on the Web.
- Evaluate educational web sites.
- Identify Web 2.0 tools and ways that such tools can be used in the classroom.
- Review lessons that integrate the use of the Internet to enhance the curriculum.
- Plan and develop a student-centered inquiry-based lesson that uses the Internet as a tool for learning.
- Identify methods for adapting and using computer systems with special learners.

NETS·T ALIGNED WITH THE INTERNET

1. **Facilitate and Inspire Student Learning and Creativity**

   Teachers use their knowledge of subject matter, teaching and learning, and technology to facilitate experiences that advance student learning, creativity, and innovation in both face-to-face and virtual environments. Teachers:

   a. promote, support, and model creative and innovative thinking and inventiveness.

   b. engage students in exploring real-world issues and solving authentic problems using digital tools and resources.

   c. promote student reflection using collaborative tools to reveal and clarify students' conceptual understanding and thinking, planning, and creative processes.

   d. model collaborative knowledge construction by engaging in learning with students, colleagues, and others in face-to-face and virtual environments.

2. **Design and Develop Digital-Age Learning Experiences and Assessments**

   Teachers design, develop, and evaluate authentic learning experiences and assessments incorporating contemporary tools and resources to maximize content learning in context and to develop the knowledge, skills, and attitudes identified in the NETS·S. Teachers:

   a. design or adapt relevant learning experiences that incorporate digital tools and resources to promote student learning and creativity.

   b. develop technology-enriched learning environments that enable all students to pursue their individual curiosities and become active participants in setting their own educational goals, managing their own learning, and assessing their own progress.

   c. customize and personalize learning activities to address students' diverse learning styles, working strategies, and abilities using digital tools and resources.

d. provide students with multiple and varied formative and summative assessments aligned with content and technology standards and use resulting data to inform learning and teaching.

3. **Model Digital-Age Work and Learning**

Teachers exhibit knowledge, skills, and work processes representative of an innovative professional in a global and digital society. Teachers:

a. demonstrate fluency in technology systems and the transfer of current knowledge to new technologies and situations.

b. collaborate with students, peers, parents, and community members using digital tools and resources to support student success and innovation.

c. communicate relevant information and ideas effectively to students, parents, and peers using a variety of digital-age media and formats.

d. model and facilitate effective use of current and emerging digital tools to locate, analyze, evaluate, and use information resources to support research and learning.

4. **Promote and Model Digital Citizenship and Responsibility**

Teachers understand local and global societal issues and responsibilities in an evolving digital culture and exhibit legal and ethical behavior in their professional practices. Teachers:

a. advocate, model, and teach safe, legal, and ethical use of digital information and technology, including respect for copyright, intellectual property, and the appropriate documentation of sources.

b. address the diverse needs of all learners by using learner-centered strategies and providing equitable access to appropriate digital tools and resources.

c. promote and model digital etiquette and responsible social interactions related to the use of technology and information.

d. develop and model cultural understanding and global awareness by engaging with colleagues and students of other cultures using digital-age communication and collaboration tools.

Frameworks

The Internet is considered one of the great achievements of the twentieth century. The beginnings of this extraordinary network started in 1958 with the establishment of the Advanced Research Projects Agency (ARPA), whose mission was to provide state-of-the-art technology for the country's defense system. The first computer network was established in 1969 and was called the ARPANET. The 50 most significant moments in Internet history shares the highlights from the beginning through the present. This interesting display of Internet facts is created by CNET UK and found at **http://crave.cnet.co.uk/software/0,39029471, 49299033-1,00.htm**.

The Internet consists of many computers around the world that are linked to each other. When a computer is connected to the Internet, communication with others that are also connected can take place. The size of the Internet is massive and growing daily. In June 2008, Internet World Stats (**www.internetworldstats .com**) reported that the number of Internet users worldwide had exceeded 1.4 billion and that more than 248 million of those users reside in the United States and Canada (Internet World Stats, 2008). In fact, Nielsen (June 2008) reports that 72.5 percent of the U.S. population is using the Internet (**www.internetworldstats .com/am/us.htm**).

Is this type of usage typical in our schools? During the past decade, educators have witnessed exponential growth of Internet access in public schools. A longitudinal study by Kleiner and Farris (2002) reported that in 1994 only 3 percent of public schools reported Internet access in instructional rooms (which were defined as classrooms, computer and other labs, library/media centers, and other rooms that are used for instructional purposes). By 2005, 94 percent of public schools reported Internet access in instructional rooms (Wells & Lewis, 2006). Access in instructional rooms varied somewhat by location with ranges from 88 to 98 percent. All public schools (100%) have some form of access to the Internet, either in instructional or other areas as compared to 35 percent in 1994. Further, the ratio of student/computer with Internet access has dropped to 3.8 to 1.

The speeds of Internet connections have steadily improved as well. In 1997, 74 percent of all schools that were connected to the Internet had a dial-up connection (Heaviside, Riggins, & Farris, 1997). By 2003, 95 percent of all schools with Internet connections were using broadband connections (Parsad & Jones, 2005) and by 2005, 97 percent used broadband (Wells & Lewis, 2006). Further, 45 percent of schools reported having wireless connections in 2005. The percentage of schools with wireless connections, using broadband wireless, ranges from 92 to 99 percent. Wireless connections were found in 15 percent of instructional rooms in 2005. Dial-up and broadband are explained later in this chapter, in the Choose Your Connection section.

Wells and Lewis (2006) report that 99 percent of schools employ various methods to control study access to inappropriate materials on the Internet. Almost all (99%) used blocking or filtering software. Further, 96% reported teacher monitoring and 79% reported signed contracts were required of students and parents. This study stated that professional development on how to use the Internet in the curriculum was offered in 83 percent of the schools, yet was not mandatory; therefore, the participation by teachers varied greatly.

Ways that the Internet was used in schools varied as well with 89 percent reporting that the Internet was used to provide data to inform instructional planning, 87 percent reported using the Internet for assessment results to inform individualized learning and 87 percent reported that it provided digital content from digital museums and libraries. Additional uses reported were online professional development and providing access to students for online distance learning (Wells & Lewis, 2006).

Basics

The Internet provides teachers with many opportunities for increased productivity, efficiency, and personal and professional knowledge. Teachers can use the Internet during lesson preparation, research and development, communication, and Web authoring. The vast information available on the Internet constitutes a powerful resource for teachers as they prepare lesson materials and locate information resources to guide their work or the work of their students. There are online libraries of lesson plans, many of which have been evaluated for excellence, such as those found at the Awesome Library (**www.awesomelibrary.org**) or the ever-popular guide from Kathy Schrock (**http://school.discoveryeducation.com/ schrockguide**). In addition, as discussed in Chapter 3, many tools that generate tests, puzzles, worksheets, and rubrics are available online in user-friendly template format, such as those found at Discovery School (**http://puzzlemaker .discoveryeducation.com**) and Rubistar (**http://rubistar.4teachers.org/index.php**). Professional development resources, such as online tutorials, are plentiful, and afford teachers the opportunity for access to information and activities at times and places of their choosing.

Communication is greatly enhanced by the Internet, which allows teachers and students to communicate in a variety of ways, including email, discussion

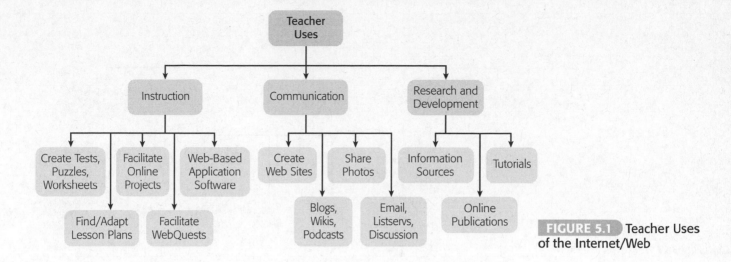

FIGURE 5.1 Teacher Uses of the Internet/Web

forums, listservs, newsgroups, and real-time communication (chat), blogs, wikis, and podcasts and share different kinds of information with social bookmarks, photo sharing, and video showcasing. The most common of these communication options is electronic mail, or email, which teachers routinely use to communicate with other teachers, parents, and students. The newest tools that promise to change the way that teachers and students interact are the Web 2.0 tools. Finally, teachers may plan, design, and publish web sites, using various tools, to share information about classroom activities and provide links to information and curriculum sources. Figure 5.1 shows common uses of the Internet for teachers. (Diagrams in this chapter represent common uses of tools and are not meant to be all-inclusive.)

When teachers promote the use of the Internet during instruction, they increase students' access to information as students participate in research and communication projects, problem-based learning activities, tutorials, and virtual field trips. A popular use of the Internet includes the use of information search, collection, and analysis to assist learning tasks. Searching can be very time-consuming and offers abundant opportunities for students to quickly stray off task. Consequently, it is wise for teachers to perform search activities and bookmark sites needed for the lesson prior to the activity.

Internet projects can be divided into categories that include communication, information collection and analysis, and problem solving. Communication exchanges can be made from student to student, group to group, and student to mentor. Various communication exchange activities allow students global access to others. Communication approaches include ePALS, generally referred to as keypals or cyberpals; this tool allows students to communicate with students from other schools, states, and countries. The ePals Classroom Exchange (**www.epals.com**) is an international provider of collaborative opportunities for cross-cultural learning. The Internet provides many opportunities for problem-based learning activities as students use the Internet to participate in real-time projects, collaborative projects, simulations, and WebQuests. The Center for Innovation in Engineering and Science Education (CIESE) provides access to several real-time science projects (**www.k12science.org/realtimeproj.html**). Students work with project data to actively construct their learning. Students may use the Internet as a tutor for learning software techniques, as well as to travel to various places in the world on virtual field trips. The newest way to use the Internet is to use the

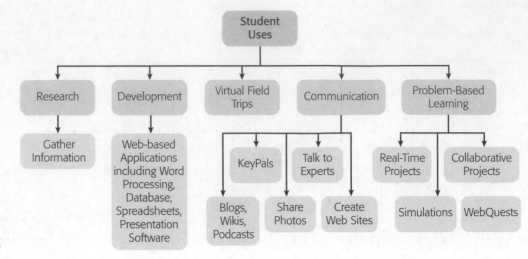

FIGURE 5.2 Student
Uses of the Internet/Web

Web 2.0 tools to construct knowledge and build literacy skills. Web 2.0 is discussed later in this chapter. See Figure 5.2 for common student uses of the Internet.

Internet Capabilities

In order to successfully integrate the Internet and its services into learning activities in the PK–12 classroom, teachers need to know how to connect, navigate, search, and use the services on the Web. Teachers also need to practice good manners, ethics, and safety, and to convey these practices to their students. In addition, teachers and students should understand how to evaluate Internet sources in order to extract reliable and current information. Obviously, the amount of information that can be comprehended by young children will dictate the depth of information shared. Teachers should be able to use Web 2.0 tools and teach their students to use these tools to collaborate and share information and construct knowledge. Primary and elementary school teachers can use the NETS·S standards to guide their instruction. In the following pages, we introduce each of these topics.

Connecting to the Net

To gain access to the services and information on the Internet, a computer connection must be established. There are four basic requirements to having access to the Internet, including: (1) a computer, (2) a connection, (3) an Internet Service Provider (ISP), and (4) software. Although any computer may be an option for connection, most schools use computers running Windows or Mac OS and some schools run Linux systems. Be aware that the different models of computers may vary somewhat in the way they are set up, and that newer models have the necessary features for Internet access built in.

To establish a connection with the Internet, contact an **Internet Service Provider (ISP)**, which offers Internet and email services for a fee. This company will also provide software and directions for configuring the computer to make the connection. Not all providers offer identical services. Some will provide faster service at a lower price. In addition, some include extra services such as multiple email accounts, enticing start-up plans, antivirus software, referral fees, free installation, no contract, and great technical support. "Do your homework" in order to make an informed decision. Computer users residing in the local area may offer recommendations on personal experiences with ISPs and the services provided by these companies.

Browser software allows the computer to display text, graphics, and links on a web page. Browsers contain other helpful features, such as the ability to bookmark favorite web sites and download documents and software. Familiar browsers include Microsoft Internet Explorer (IE) for (Windows users only), Firefox (for Windows and Mac users), and Safari (for Mac OS X users only).

Choose Your Connection

Your decision about the type of connection should take into account the location of the computer, personal preferences, and availability of services. Current options include broadband connections: DSL, digital cable, or satellite technology, in some places, a wireless connection. These connections vary in speed as well as the price of the service. The speed of a network connection is identified as the bandwidth and is measured in kilobits (1,000 bits) per second (kbps) and megabits (1 million bits) per second (mbps). This explains how many bits of information can travel through the connection.

Broadband Connection

When connecting to the Internet, speed is a major concern. Broadband connections, as stated previously, include DSL, digital cable, digital satellite, and broadband wireless. Each option is described in the following subsections. Important considerations include availability, ease of installation, and the speed of the connection.

DSL (digital subscriber line) connections transmit digital data over regular phone lines and deliver typical download speeds for Web viewing or receiving files from 500 kbps up to 1 or 2 mbps. Upload time (sending files) is somewhat slower. Besides speed, advantages include a signal that does not interfere with phone conversations and a connection that stays on. The downside is that this service is not available in all areas, especially in some rural locations. The price of this service varies, depending on other subscribed phone services and local competition.

Digital cable provides the fastest broadband connections. Digital cable transmits information through cable lines with typical speeds between 1 mbps and 2 mbps. Digital cable is a continuous connection, like DSL. Equipment includes the installation of a cable line and a cable modem, rented or purchased through the providing company. The price of the service varies in part depending on the competition in the area. Disadvantages include that the service is often offered jointly with a subscription to cable TV and many times neighborhoods are sharing the bandwidth provided making the available service slower during peak usage.

Satellite Internet offers broadband access alternatives for rural Internet users whose location is not served by DSL or digital cable providers. Satellite Internet is much faster than a dial-up connection, but for residential users, it may be slower than cable and DSL. Trees, dense clouds, heavy rains, and user traffic can affect the reception of the Internet signal. Download and upload speeds are much higher for commercial users, the result of a more powerful (and expensive) satellite dish.

A **wireless connection**, also known as *fixed wireless*, is available for residential use in some geographic areas. Fixed wireless uses microwave technology to transfer data between a radio transmission tower and a rooftop antenna, called a transceiver, installed by the consumer. Cables from the transceiver to a modem complete the connection. Many universities and K–12 schools use commercial versions of this technology. Students may access the Internet in any building or classroom served by this technology, using appropriately equipped laptops. Fixed wireless connection speed is in the broadband range, with download speeds ranging from 500 kbps to 1.5 mbps, and upload speeds of approximately 256 kbps.

This is not to be confused with **wireless fidelity (WiFi)** networking, which offers public access in locations such as a hotel airport or coffeeshop.

In summary, the type of connection determines how quickly information can be downloaded to and uploaded from the desktop. The authors recommend that teachers get the fastest connection that is within their budget as well as investigate the connection that their students have at home.

Navigating the Web

The Internet is composed of different services, the largest and most interesting of which is the **World Wide Web (WWW)**, or simply the **Web**. The simplest component of the Web is a web page, a document that resides on a server, which is a powerful computer that hosts web files, each identified by a unique address known as the **Uniform Resource Locator (URL)**, which must be used to access the page. A group of common pages is referred to as a **web site** with the entry page known as the **home page**. Web pages are written in a special language called **HTML** (HyperText Markup Language), which specifies how the page looks and acts. Pages are viewed through specialized software called *browser software.* In order to travel from page to page, the user clicks on a **hyperlink** (typically text or an image/button) that connects to the new location/information. The information on the Web is presented in multimedia format with text, graphics, audio, and video. Multimedia files, though bringing interest to the site, are often very large and take extra time to access and download (or transfer) to the desktop. Often, additional software programs called **plug-ins** are needed to access some of the multimedia files. Plug-ins, usually free, can be downloaded from the manufacturer's web site and provide read-only access or viewing capability to popular multimedia formats. For example, Flash, found at **www.adobe.com**, is animation software that is used to create interactive multimedia files (such as interactive games or animated birthday cards). The free download available at this site is player software that enables access to animations created using Flash without the necessity of purchasing the full-featured program.

The URL is the address of a web page or file. It typically begins with http://, a prefix that signals the browser that a web page follows. Following the prefix, most addresses will continue with www. The part of the address following the first period and before the first slash is referred to as the *domain name.* A domain name is unique. Top-level domain names include familiar .edu, .com, and .gov, and identify specific types of users. **Domain names** must be registered with the Internet Network Registration Center (InterNIC) and cannot be assigned to more than one university, school, business, or person. If the site is a large one, it will be divided into smaller sections called *directories.* Each section is divided by a slash: /. To see a specific page, a user types the URL into the address box in the browser software. Pressing the enter key or return key on the keyboard or clicking a button on the browser enables navigation to the desired page.

Typing in URLs must be completed with precise accuracy or the reader will not reach the site. If one space, one extra dot, or one incorrect letter is entered, the result will be a failure to connect. Although there are a number of reasons that a user might not see the desired web page (the address is outdated, has moved, or the computer where the file is stored is temporarily not functioning), much of the time, it is because the URL has been improperly entered. Because gaining access to a web site may be frustrating, it is wise for teachers of students of all ages to complete early research and to bookmark pertinent sites. Refer to Figure 5.3 to identify the parts of a URL including the protocol, the host computer name, the second-level domain, the top-level domain, the directory name, and the file name.

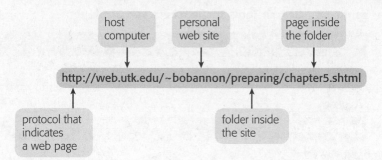

host computer

personal web site

page inside the folder

http://web.utk.edu/~bobannon/preparing/chapter5.shtml

protocol that indicates a web page

folder inside the site

FIGURE 5.3 Structure of a URL

Hyperlinks provide an easy way to jump to other pages on the Web without having to type in the URL. Hyperlinks are visually apparent to the reader because they are typically a different color than regular text and are underlined to alert the reader to the purpose. The standard colors for links are blue for an unvisited link and purple for a visited link.

If a user wants to revisit a site later, the site can be bookmarked in the browser software to provide easy and quick access on a return visit. The process for adding a bookmark differs slightly by browser. For example, in Internet Explorer, the command is Favorites/Add; for Safari, the command is Bookmark/Add Bookmark, and for Firefox, the command is Bookmarks/Bookmark this page. Bookmarks can be organized into folders and grouped by content, for example. They can also be exported to a file, which could be saved to disk, placed on a computer network, or emailed to another user. This feature is useful for setting up specific sites to be visited when using multiple computers, such as in a classroom. An easier method of bookmarking web pages is using social bookmarks that are Web-based, thus access is provided from any computer. Social bookmarking is discussed later in this chapter.

The **cache** is the space that the computer designates on its hard drive to temporarily store previously viewed web pages. Because cached pages reside on the computer, there is no download time involved on a return visit and they are quick to pull up. The larger the cache size, the more pages the browser can retain to view again without downloading. The size of the cache depends on the size of the hard drive. Assigning 1 GB to the cache on a 10 GB hard drive is appropriate. Keep in mind that the cache takes up space, and there may be a time when the pages that are being pulled from cache are not the most current. Because previously viewed web pages are stored in the cache, they may be returned to using the History or Go button on the browser menu bar. This feature gives a history of the sites visited, and can serve to reduce the time-consuming and confusing nature of some navigation sessions.

Searching the Web

Currently, hundreds of tools are available to search the vast amount of information on the Web. These tools are categorized as search engines, subject directories, and meta-search engines. Teachers and students need a basic understanding of the features of each in order to select the tool best suited for their search. NoodleTools (**www.noodletools.com**) offers assistance on determining what information is needed and the tool that will best suit that need. This resource may be accessed at **www.noodletools.com/debbie/literacies/information/5locate/adviceengine .html**. The discussion that follows lists tools used primarily by older students and adults. Search tools designed for younger children can be found in Table 5.1 and in the On the Web section at the end of the chapter.

Table 5.1   Search Tools for Teachers and Students

Search Engines	
Google	www.google.com
Yahoo! Search	http://search.yahoo.com
Ask.com	www.ask.com
Subject Directories	
Librarians' Index	www.lii.org
Google Directory	www.google.com/dirhp
Yahoo! Directory	http://dir.yahoo.com
Meta-Search Engines	
Clusty	http://clusty.com
Dogpile	www.dogpile.com
Search Tools for Kids	
Ask for Kids	www.askkids.com
KidsClick	www.kidsclick.org
Yahoo.KIDS	http://kids.yahoo.com

A **search engine** is a program that searches the Web for information using software programs called *spiders* or *robots.* When the most results or the most current results are desired, using a search engine is the best choice. About one-fifth of the information on the Internet is catalogued by search engines. Examples include Alta Vista (**www.altavista.com**), Google (**www.google.com**), and HotBot (**www.hotbot.com**). Search engines do not offer subject directories. Furthermore, the selection process is automated; there is no human selection, or individual who chooses or verifies the appropriate sites.

Subject directories are similar to phone books. They list web sites by categories, which are further linked to subcategories. Subject directories sites are selected by humans. The sites are handpicked and offer the best-organized results. Examples of subject directories include About.com (**www.about.com**) and Yahoo! (**www.yahoo.com**).

A third category of search tools is **meta-search engines**, which search several indexes at one time. The keyword is submitted and supplies a number of hits. Examples of meta-search engines include Metacrawler (**www.metacrawler.com**), Dogpile (**www.dogpile.com**), and Mamma (**www.mamma.com**).

The best practice for teachers—as well as students—is to know the search tool and its capabilities. Many times, computer users simply pull up a search tool without fully knowing its capabilities, thus preventing full use. All search tools will not offer identical features. In this discussion, we present typical features for basic knowledge.

Terms that are commonly used when searching the Internet include *query, hit, Boolean operators, wildcards,* and *modifiers.* A **query** is a request for information, which explains as clearly as possible the information for which the user is looking. Queries are constructed from **keywords** and are entered into a search box on the site. The search is completed and the results are brought forth, each of which is called a **hit**. Many times, a query results in thousands of hits, or very few, making it necessary to narrow or expand the original search.

Boolean operators are parameters (restrictions) that assist in searching in a more precise way. These logical operators are "or", "not", and "and". "Or" broadens the search where "not" and "and" narrow the search. Boolean logic is a form of algebra, in which all values are either true or false. This logic is used in math and computer science and was named after a nineteenth-century mathematician George Boole. An example used to narrow a search using these operators is: "Cows not Dairy" or "Dogs not Terriers."

A **wildcard** is the asterisk character (*) and is used as a wildcard to match any form of the word; therefore, the term *butter** would include *butterfly, buttermilk,* and *buttercup.* Wildcards can expand a search and can return unpredictable results. Using a wildcard is called *truncation.* Some search tools automatically perform this operation.

Modifiers are symbols that require the search engine to complete a specific function. Modifiers include +, –, and " ". Use a plus sign (+) to make sure a search includes both names, such as George + Strait. Results would pull up pages on the singer and other folks or towns by this name. By entering only George, the results would include Washington, Bernard Shaw, or Jones. Use a dash (–) when you want to make sure that something is omitted, such as George–Washington. Use quotation marks (" ") when you want an exact phrase, such as "George Washington."

There are safe sites and search tools that are designed for students under 12 years. Table 5.1 lists three such tools.

Steps for conducting a basic search are:

1. Determine what information is needed and what keywords are best suited for the query.
2. Determine which family of search tools (search engine, search directory, or meta-search engine) is best suited for the search.
3. Construct the query. Research the advanced search options of the tool (Boolean operators, wildcards, and modifiers) and use these as needed to expand or restrict the number of hits returned.
4. Perform the search.
5. Evaluate the matches and keep the most beneficial pages to gather needed information.

Information/Communication Services on the Net

A number of information/communication services are available on the Internet, each with different functions for providing information to students and teachers. The most common services include email, discussion forums, listservs, real-time communication, file transfer protocol (FTP), and the World Wide Web (WWW). The Web 2.0 tools (blogs, wikis, podcasts, photo sharing, and video sharing) have added a number of new ways to communicate and share information on the Internet. Communicating using one of these tools provides either asynchronous or synchronous communication. **Asynchronous communication** occurs at random times; all participants do not have to be at a computer at the same time. Email is an example of asynchronous communication. The users can comment at any time and others react to their comments when they wish. **Synchronous communication** occurs with all participants at one time. Chats (also known as *instant messaging,* or *IM*) are an example of synchronous communication.

Discussion forums are found on web sites that are designed to facilitate information exchange. Their structure holds messages, articles, and comments. The reader may read ongoing discussions or enter into the discussion.

Email programs allow the user to send messages and attach files over the Internet using personal addresses. An email address consists of a username, followed by @, followed by the domain name or the server that holds the individual's account. The domain name may also include several domains (as is the case with most K–12 schools). The address concludes with a top-level domain category, expressed as the same two- or three-letter extension that is used in Web addresses. These extensions, and their respective top-level global domain categories, are listed in Table 5.2. For email addresses outside the United States, a country code is added as the final extension.

Web-based email providers, such as MSN Hotmail and Yahoo!Mail, enable the user to access email from any browser, with no special software required and are very beneficial. Google offers Gmail, a free Web mail service. Gmail offers huge storage capabilities to users, plus instant messaging, and *no* pop-ups or large banner ads. The advantages of having this type of email account is that it is more private than the messages sent through a school or business computer. Spam, which is unsolicited and unwelcome "junk" email, usually a form of advertising, is a nuisance. If an email address is not protected by anti-spam or filtering software, spam can easily clog mailboxes, taking up valuable memory and requiring time to examine and remove.

A **listserv** is a communication program that delivers discussion through an email account. A listserv, commonly called a list, allows ongoing email discussions between individuals who have a common interest. Messages sent via lists are typically announcements, questions, and replies from subscribers. Lists may be **moderated**, which means that the information is reviewed before it is posted, or open, where the information is not reviewed. In order to get messages from a list, an individual must **subscribe** to the list. The procedure to subscribe is usually completed by sending an email message and inserting something like the follow-

Table 5.2   Domain Categories

Global Top-Level Internet Domain Suffixes for U.S. Organizations	
Business	.biz
Commercial	.com
Cooperatives	.coop
Education	.edu
Government	.gov
Individuals, by Name	.name
Information	.info
Internet Communication Services	.tel
Museums	.museum
Mobile Devices	.mobi
Network	.net
Organization	.org
U.S. Military	.mil

ing command in the document area: subscribe (listserv name) (your first name) (your last name). Some lists offered on the Web can be subscribed to using an email address. If you are subscribing to a list using email, the method is a little different than signing up on the Web. An example would be:

subscribe EDTECH Jane Doe

A list will provide (via a web site initial email) directions or methods of subscribing and how to unsubscribe if desired. Some lists are very busy and can bog the user's mailbox down with many daily messages. It may be wise to silently watch (called *lurking*) for a while to get a feel for the information flow on the list before participating.

Instant messaging is a common method of real-time communication. A synchronous delivery of conversation takes place as people "talk" online using software that displays messages as they are written. People can also converse in online chat rooms accessed by chat programs. **Chat room** conversations resemble instant messaging, but they are public sites that generally anyone can enter and begin a conversation. **Course management systems (CMS)** used by universities, such as BlackBoard or Web CT, offer chat features that are limited to the people enrolled in the course. Although CMS chat rooms are useful tools that allow students to communicate at a distance, most become bogged down when used by more than a group of five in synchronous chat.

File transfer protocol (FTP) transports files between computers on the Internet. Common uses include uploading and downloading files. FTP is used to upload files to servers—including displaying the posting of personal web pages—and is now a feature included in some Web editors, such as Dreamweaver. Various FTP software programs are made for Mac and Windows platforms.

Although all the information services available on the Internet increase the ability to communicate, the greatest resource for information is the Web. The World Wide Web is the collection of web pages, constituting the information you see using a Web browser. This information may be presented in the form of text, graphics, audio, and video. Some of the audio and video will need assistance from browser plug-ins (see Chapter 3).

Web 2.0 Tools

The Partnership for 21st Century Skills (2004) explains that while students use Web 2.0 tools in their personal lives, they are not given the opportunities to use the same tools in their classrooms. By Web 2.0, we are talking about the "participatory web" where student use tools that are Web-based and collaborative applications. Soloman and Schrum (2007) declare that using Web 2.0 tools can have a profound effect on learning because these tools promote creativity, collaboration, and communication. This ever-increasing collection of tools is free and Web-based, giving students 24/7 accessibility as long as they have an Internet connection and browser software. Soloman and Schrum describe the differences in the old Web and the new Web or what they term Web 1.0 and Web 2.0 in Table 5.3.

Learning that takes place when using Web 2.0 tools is grounded in constructivism; the learner constructs new information based on past and current knowledge. In this theory of learning, students are building on what they know; adding to their pool of information. Web-based tools support this type of learning. In addition, project-based learning, a constructivist approach, allows students to use inquiry methods to further their knowledge regarding specific real-world and relevant problems. Problem-based learning is student centered and places the

Table 5.3 Comparison of Old and New Ways of Working

Web 1.0	Web 2.0
Application-based	Web-based
Isolated	Collaborative
Offline	Online
Licensed or purchased	Free
Single creator	Multiple collaborators
Proprietary code	Open source
Copyrighted content	Shared content

Source: G. Soloman & L. Schrum (2007)

student in charge of his learning. Web-based tools promote project-based learning as students are able to collaborate as teams in some tools.

Web 2.0 tools are an ever-growing collection of tools, the most familiar being blogs, wikis, and podcasts. In the next paragraphs, we briefly discuss several of these tools and how they can be used in K–12 classrooms.

Blogs

The most widely accepted Web 2.0 applications are web logs, commonly referred to as *blogs* (Richardson, 2006). Blogs allow individuals (bloggers) to share ideas, reflections on daily work or experiences, and resources with a Web audience who may respond with comments. A blog can be reflective in nature like the examples that are shared in Figure 5.4. These blogs are stories of the journey that two pre-service teachers are making in the core technology course in their teacher training.

A **blog** is a web page that contains text, images, and links. The entries are called *posts*. The blogs that are shared here were created in Blogger and designed using templates offered by the program. As you see, the blog entries are posted in reverse order and provide links to previous entries. Teachers can create classroom blogs to communicate with parents and others about class activities. Students can join in and add posts to the classroom blog as well.

Some well-known blog software used in education include Blogger (www .blogger.com), WordPress (http://wordpress.org), and Edublog (http://edublogs .org) for teachers and students.

Wikis

The Read/Write application, **wikis**, originally created by Ward Cunningham in 1995 but used relatively sparingly in the past in education, allow individuals (members) to create, edit, and link web pages as well as incorporate sounds, movies, and pictures into a website. Wikis provide a means of asynchronous communication and collaboration to members of a wiki community, while providing an easy method for teachers and students to collaborate through a Web browser. Wikis permit individuals to read, post, modify, and delete information. The most well-known wiki is Wikipedia (http://en.wikipedia.org/wiki/Main_Page), a collaborative online encyclopedia that has "become a clearinghouse of information based on the work of thousands of amateur researchers" (Richardson, 2006). Currently, over 2.8 million articles reside in the English-language version of Wikipedia (accessed April 2009 at http://en.wikipedia.org/wiki/Wikipedia:Size_of_Wikipedia) and the number is growing at a staggering rate. Soloman and Schrum (2007) report that Wikipedia "includes more up-to-date entries that the Encyclopedia Britannica" (p. 58).

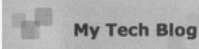

My Tech Blog

🗓 Friday, October 3, 2008

Picture This!

This week we learned all about digital images and how they can be used in the classroom. It was fun experimenting with the many different ways to upload and save images. I've been familiar with uploading images and using a digital camera for a while, but since we use Macs in the lab I am always learning something new about the Mac.

Wednesday was a really fun day in class! We got to go on a digital scavenger hunt around campus. It was awesome getting out of the classroom and doing an assignment that could be used in the classroom. It is a great way to incorporate digital images into the classroom and a great way to get students to observe and discover things around them that they might not have ever noticed before. Along with doing this project, I really enjoyed seeing what other groups took pictures of as well. I definitely feel more comfortable about using digital images in the classroom!

↳ Posted by Kathleen at 1:40 PM

📰 **Blog Archive**

▼ 2008 (6)
  ▼ October (2)
    Making Movies!
    Picture This!
  ▶ September (4)

 technology
stephanie

ON MY WAY TO BE A TECHNOLOGY GURU

monday, october 6, 2008

Jumping for Joy about Digital Images

Goodness! I have learned a wealth of knowledge in the past couple of days in IT class. We have been working with digital images and how we can use them to enhance the learning environment in our classrooms. We worked on a digital

blog archive

▼ 2008 (5)
  ▼ October (2)
    Camp Soh Cah Toa
    Jumping for Joy
    about Digital
    Images
  ▶ September (3)

about me

 Stephanie A. Hales

View my complete profile

FIGURE 5.4 Examples of Blogs (Reprinted with permission.)

Voices *from the* Classroom

The Teacher/Learner and Web 2.0
Jennifer Lubke

Jennifer was a high school language arts teacher for 11 years before taking an extended leave to start a family. During her absence from the classroom, she completed a master's degree in Instructional Technology at the University of Tennessee. As a graduate student, Jennifer experienced the power of Web-based technologies and social-participatory media for self-directed learning. She explains how she used social bookmarking, RSS, blogs, and virtual learning communities to create her own personal learning network.

Teachers have long relied on time-intensive, cost-prohibitive, trainings, workshops, and conferences to stay current in their content areas and versed in the latest instructional strategies. But Web 2.0 is changing the face of teacher professional development. The new Web tools empower us to build *personal learning networks* (PLNs) that extend and enrich the traditional, face-to-face professional development model. My PLN helped contextualize my graduate school studies and connected me with educators from around the globe who share my interests, passions, and educational philosophy. I encourage you to develop your own PLN. At some point in your career, you will inevitably encounter feelings of isolation and frustration due to the normal time pressures, limited resources, and geographical boundaries associated with classroom teaching, but you can always count on your PLN to deliver free, just-in-time learning from an innovative and collaborative global community!

Web-based bookmarking, or *social bookmarking,* is an easy and fun way to jump-start a PLN. Social bookmarking sites, such as delicious, have many advantages over browser-based bookmarks. First, you can access your favorite sites from any computer. Second, a variety of user features allow you to annotate, save, and categorize your resources using special keywords called *tags.* Third, if you select the "share" option, your bookmarks are searchable and viewable by other members in the bookmarking community, making it easy to connect and collaborate with users who share your interests. At any time, I can click on one of my tags, such as "poetry" or "multimedia" or "censorship," and browse through the latest sites that other delicious users have located and saved.

RSS is another way to develop your PLN. RSS (*real simple syndication* or *rich site summary*) delivers new content directly to you as it is generated at your favorite blogs, wikis, social networks, and news services. RSS is a huge timesaver for teachers who want to monitor a variety of sites on a daily basis; all new content is collected in one place so you never miss an update or breaking development. You can even use RSS to track specific delicious tags!

To get started with RSS, choose an aggregator (software that checks for new content at specified web sites and at user-determined intervals to retrieve new information) such as Bloglines or Google Reader. Begin with just a few feed subscriptions and practice adding, deleting, and re-adding feeds as your needs and interests change. I grew my list of RSS feeds by scanning the blogrolls of some of my favorite educational bloggers. (A *blogroll* is simply a list of a blogger's favorite blogs.) Now, when I log into my aggregator, it's like opening a personalized, optimized journal of blog posts, articles, and links related to the issues and content I care most deeply about. This daily practice keeps me apprised of important themes, questions, and debates in my specific content area as well as the general field of education.

Like social bookmarking, RSS enables the teacher/learner to dip into the shared knowledge base of the virtual

Educators are concerned, however, because Wikipedia allows open editing; students *must* be cautioned to use care when evaluating information as accurate and appropriate. Quite a number of wikis are currently available on the Web; the safety associated with their use, if public, is questionable. While many wikis offer the option of freely joining the collaboration, which opens the door for destructive practice, wikis can be configured to be private. Obviously, different software provides various features as well as security, of utmost consideration when using this tool with K–12 students. Three commonly used wikis in education are Peanut Butter Works (formerly PBwiki) (**http://pbworks.com**), Wikispaces (**www.wikispaces .com**), and Wetpaint (**www.wetpaint.com/category/Education**). Each are fully Web

Voices *from the* **Classroom** *Continued*

learning community. To get the most out of this essential Web 2.0 tool, you must make it a priority to manage information as it flows in and out of your network. Try integrating your RSS routine with your daily email routine. Just as reading email is essential to managing a professional and personal life, the daily discipline of sorting and filtering RSS feeds is crucial to developing your PLN. *Filtering* is the practice of scanning content to determine if it is usable to you at that very moment. If it is not, delete it. Also, it is not enough just to consume content. Just as with email, you must occasionally respond. Start commenting on others' blogs whenever and wherever appropriate. As soon as you do so, you will have officially joined the global conversation!

After a few weeks of reading others' blogs, you will probably get the itch to start your own. Such was the case for me. I chose Blogger, one of the oldest sites, and was up and running with a functional and attractive blog within 30 minutes. It was one of the most transformative moments in my journey as a teacher/learner. Yet, my plunge into the world of blogs has not been completely devoid of questions. What blogs lack in technical complexity, they make up for in the kinds of practical and pedagogical concerns they raise for the teacher/learner. Questions worth considering include: Should I blog under an assumed identity or just be myself? What is my school's policy regarding teacher blogs? How can I merge my blog successfully into my classroom practice without compromising my authority and professional standing?

These are important questions, but don't let them deter you from experimenting with blogs. My blog is a place for me to flex my writing muscles. I use my blog to test new ideas and to invite response and feedback from readers. It is a great way to add interactivity and sociability to my formal learning experiences, and the added layer of transparency and accountability ensures that I concretize my thinking before I publish it.

Blogs are great for creating and contributing content within a learning community, but they are not necessarily the best way to stimulate conversation. To really enter into a two-way conversation with other teachers/learners, it is important to add a social network to your PLN. MySpace and Facebook are perhaps the most famous examples of social networks, with millions of users, but a number of small, specialized networks exist for individuals with specific backgrounds and areas of interest. A social network greatly expands your PLN because, unlike blogs, these communities offer a built-in audience. When you post a question or observation to a high-traffic discussion board or forum, you are more likely to receive prompt feedback than if you were to post it in your blog. Conversations flow through discussion threads that closely resemble synchronous dialog. Some threads remain active for days and even weeks. I joined Classroom 2.0 (**www.classroom20 .com/**), an international network for teachers of all subjects and grade levels. Since joining the community, I have engaged in a number of interesting discussion threads with topics ranging from "nature deficit disorder" to video games. I have conversed with individuals as close as Iowa and as far away as Australia.

As you embark on your teaching career, you will doubtless have access to a wealth of workshops, lectures, videos, books, and even traditional web sites and online courses. It is tempting to settle for these comfortable and familiar professional development formats. And, as incidents of abuse and excesses within online environments continually make local and national headlines, it is even more tempting to just opt out altogether for fear that your ventures in virtual learning might somehow compromise your professionalism. A certain degree of risk taking and responsibility is required of the teacher/learner who experiments with all that Web 2.0 has to offer, but I think the unprecedented levels of affordability, accessibility, sociability, and usability afforded by a PLN more than make up for it.

hosted so there is nothing to install. PBworks reports to have more classroom wikis than the others and offers public or private spaces. Wikispaces offers public wikis for free and private and ad-free spaces for a monthly fee. Wetpaint is free, ad-free, and easy to use. Site templates at Wetpaint make building the sites easy and teachers can control who sees as well as contributes to the site.

Wikis can be used in various ways in a classroom because they are easy to use and provide immediate information to members. Further, they offer the added advantage of allowing individuals to focus on the information rather than the technical aspect of the tool. Perhaps the most common pedagogical use of wikis is supporting writing instruction (Lamb, 2004). Collaborative writing projects are a key use of these tools. In addition, Mader (2008) cites curriculum development, project development, peer review, group authoring, tracking group projects, data collection, and class/instructor reviews. Duffy and Bruns (2006) suggest that wikis can be used to publish course documents, build annotated bibliographies, and even be used as a presentation tool. Figure 5.5 is an example of a wiki community of preservice teachers seeking elementary licensure in the core technology course in their teacher training, who are building a collection of Web resources that they can use with future students.

Podcasts

Individuals (podcasters) use **podcasts** to create and distribute multimedia to an audience who can access/listen to audio (voice and music) files through an Internet connection or mobile device. Podcasts, so named by combining Apple's iPod and broadcast, provide an abundance of opportunities for teachers and students as they create digital audio on various topics.

The Education Podcast Network (**http://epnweb.org**) offers student and class podcasts as well as subject-specific podcasts for review (see Figure 5.6). In addition, many professional organizations are using podcasts to share keynote speeches, provide news updates or interviews with people, and more. The term, *podcasts,* is used when referring to the content as well as the delivery. They can be used to sup-

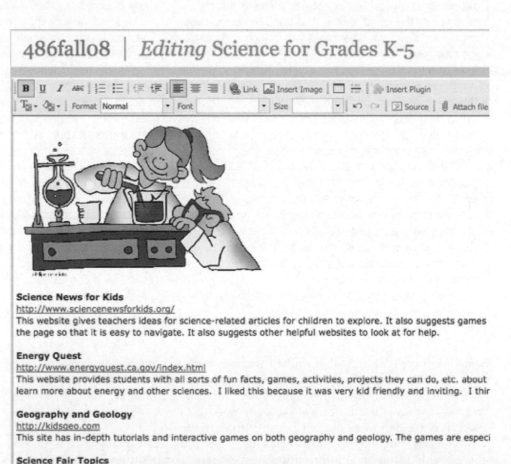

FIGURE 5.5 Using a Wiki to Create a Collection of Web Resources
(Reprinted with permission.)

FIGURE 5.6 EPN, the Educational Podcast Network, an effort to provide a place for podcasts for elementary, middle school, and secondary classrooms as well as subject-specific podcasts. (Reprinted with permission.)

port the curriculum in many ways for 21st century learning. See Chapter 11, Multimedia Tools, for podcasting tools as well as steps to creating a podcast.

Other Tools for Schools

There are other Web 2.0 tools that are helpful to teachers and students that share various types of information. Since they are Web-based, they provide immediate access from any computer. These tools include social bookmarks, photo sharing, and video sharing. Each are discussed in the following paragraphs and well-known services are provided.

Social Bookmarking

Social bookmarking is a Web service that provides the user with Web access to bookmarks that have been collected and assigned "tags" to describe them for their classification. The bookmarks organize themselves and collections emerge. Rather than saving "favorites" in a browser, the user saves the bookmarks on the Web. The advantage of such a service is that you are never without your bookmarks as long as you have a Internet connection. Well-known services are Delicious (**http://delicious.com**) (Figure 5.7) and diigo (**www.diigo.com**).

Photo Sharing

A well-known photo sharing and management tool is Flickr (**www.flickr.com**), which allows the posting of photos in an online account where others can view them in albums or slideshows. Tags and notes can be added to the photos and visitors can make comments. The photos on Flickr are in the Creative Commons licensing, therefore, they may be shared by anyone. Some ways to use such tools in the classroom would be documentation of field trips as well as digital scavenger hunts. Another service is Picasa from Google (**picasaweb.google.com/home?hl=en&tab=wq**). A third photo sharing service is Shutterfly (**www.shutterfly.com**). This site will create prints that can be picked up at Target. Other products, such as posters and calendars, can be ordered from your photo collections.

Video Sharing   TeacherTube (**www.teachertube.com**), similar to YouTube, was launched in 2007 to provide an online community to share instructional videos. Teachers can post videos at the site that are designed for student viewing, providing a rich resource that can be reviewed over and over. Once a community member, you can upload, tag, link to, and share videos as well as upload support files to attach to the videos, such as notes, lesson plans, activity sheets, or anything else that is desired. Further, community members can browse the videos that are posted at TeacherTube.

Practicing Netiquette, Ethics, and Safety on the Web

Netiquette is similar to etiquette—except that it is employed on the Internet. In other words, netiquette is being courteous to others while using the Web and its communication tools. This is also important when using Web 2.0 tools. More information can be found at the On the Web section of the companion web site. Flaming and shouting are two discourteous online practices. The term *flaming* refers to personal attacks on other users or posting offensive remarks in email or on online discussions. *Shouting* is the use of ALL CAPITAL LETTERS in online correspondence.

Ethics on the Web involves the appropriate and responsible use of the Internet by students, teachers, and staff. Ethics on the Web should be detailed in the guidelines set forth in the district's acceptable use policy (AUP) to be developed in conjunction with a technology plan. This policy outlines specific behaviors for the acceptable use of the Internet. Such ethics should be modeled for students of all ages by their teachers.

Well-designed AUPs focus on the responsible use of computer networks, including the Internet, and the accessing and transmitting of information in K–12 classrooms. Acceptable use policies should always include these minimum components: (1) a description of the instructional philosophy to be supported by Internet access in schools; (2) a statement reminding users that Internet access and the use of computer networks are privileges; (3) a statement on the educational uses and advantages of the Internet in the school; (4) a list of the responsibilities of teachers, students, and parents for using the Internet; (5) the standards governing behavior while using the Internet, with a clear description of what constitutes acceptable and unacceptable uses of the Internet; (6) a description of the consequences of violating the AUP; (7) a disclaimer absolving the school, under specific circumstances, from responsibility; (8) signature lines for teachers, students, and parents indicating their understanding of and intent to abide by the policies set forth in the document. The Northwest Regional Educational Laboratory (**www .netc.org/planning/planning/aup.php**) offers information and links to samples of acceptable use policies.

Copyright

The discussion of copyright law in the Chapter 1 presents the basic copyright information that teachers should know and practice. Access to information on the Internet is free; however, if the information is to be to reproduced and distributed, approval from the author must be obtained. This rule includes images, video clips, and sound downloaded from the Internet. Information regarding copyright laws are found at the U.S. Copyright Office online at **www.copyright.gov**, and the copyright web site at **www.benedict.com/Info/Info.aspx** offers much information on the basics of copyright, fair use guidelines, and more useful information. Fair use laws allow teachers to use materials for educational purposes and circumstances in which they do not make money. However, that guideline can be misleading, as it tends to give teachers the mistaken impression that as long as it is not for gain monetarily or for use in the classroom, they are not breaking any laws.

Plagiarism

Plagiarism is found in various situations. There is the obvious culprit who turns in another author's complete work exactly as it appears elsewhere. People who do this are usually turning the spotlight on themselves, as most papers that are stolen are quite good and often the offender has a history of lower-quality work. A second type of offense is using exact language from another source without using quotations or citing the source. Another wrongdoing is using a sole resource with the language rearranged a bit differently but basically as the same work. Examples of plagiarism, with a quiz to test your understanding of these three offenses, are provided by the School of Education at Indiana University Bloomington (**www .indiana.edu/~tedfrick/plagiarism**).

Access to the vast information on the Internet promotes the ease of plagiarism in the information age. Due to the vastness of the Web, it is most difficult to distinguish unethical behaviors that at one time might have been quite obvious. Of major concern are the many "papermills" available for students to quickly access and purchase completed essays on many topics. This problem is not found at one grade level more than another. Many students are confused, as are teachers, regarding what is public domain and what is actually copying someone else's intellectual property. Plagiarism.org (**www.plagiarism.org**) and Turnitin (**www .turnitin.com**) have committed to help students understand the differences while they develop needed writing skills. There are many resources at these sites for both teachers *and* students.

Safety on the Web

Online safety is essential when students are using the Internet, whether at school or at home. Because Web content is basically unregulated, it is impossible to eliminate unacceptable sites, although they can be blocked. **Blocking** sites is performed by filtering software programs.

One of the key ways to protect students is to have computers equipped with software programs called **filtering programs**, which can be used in schools or on home computers to control access to offensive web sites. Well-known titles include Cyber Patrol (**www.cyberpatrol.com**) and Net Nanny (**www.netnanny.com**).

Although such programs may do an adequate job and are mandated by some states in schools and libraries, they are not perfect. Many filtering programs search sites for previously determined unacceptable words or phrases. This method occasionally allows an unwanted site to slip through or a perfectly acceptable site to be filtered out. In addition, they create a false security for teachers. There should always be teacher supervision when students are using the Internet, and students should be aware of expectations for acceptable use. Many schools and school systems have designed acceptable use policies that outline expectations for students using the Internet. Teachers should bookmark acceptable sites for students to use for research purposes.

Safety for Your Computer

Not only should precautions be taken to provide safety to students and their teachers on the Internet, but precautions must also be taken for their computers. **Malware**, short for malicious software, is developed for the purpose of doing damage to computer files. These unwanted programs create serious havoc in home or classroom computers. The most common forms of malware include computer viruses, worms, Trojan horses, macro-viruses, and spyware, described in this section.

Computer viruses are man-made programs that invade a computer, hide there, reproduce, and cause major difficulties. Viruses attach to other programs that act as their host and run secretly when the host program runs. As the host program runs, the virus can reproduce and attach itself to other programs. Most viruses spread through email, usually through attachments, but some are embedded within the message itself. Email viruses are spread through the use of email and can spread to everyone listed in the address book.

Worms are small pieces of software that reproduce by using the network (email) yet do not need a host file to spread.

Trojan horses are not considered viruses because they do not reproduce, but these can still do much damage. This sort of program appears to have one purpose, such as a game, but actually does damage, such as erasing the hard drive, when run.

Macro-viruses are little programs that attack MS Word or Excel documents. If these nasty viruses are allowed to invade, be ready for files to be deleted and not recordable. The best way to protect from macro-viruses is to not enable macros when opening documents unless you know why there would be a need for a macro. Macro viruses travel with email attachments in Word and Excel File.

Spyware, one of the more recent developments to avoid, is a computer program that lives in your computer without your knowledge, usually piggybacking in with another file that you install intentionally (such as freeware). This invisible little "Peeping Tom" collects information about you and sends that information back to the person responsible for putting it there. There are some shareware programs that can be run on your computer that bring spyware to the surface for destruction. A way to diminish the transfer of spyware is to use extreme caution when downloading software that is not from a reliable source. Free software may result in a high price for the computer user! Do not install file-sharing software to share music.

All computers should be equipped with **antivirus software**. Some of the popular manufacturers include McAfee, Norton, Trend Micro, and Symantec.

Antivirus software must be updated regularly, because viruses change as writers design new ways to infect computers. It is a good idea to upgrade antivirus software by downloading updates weekly (or more often). Some companies automate this procedure for the user.

Firewalls are programs that perform tests on incoming information to prevent other harmful programs from entering the computer. A firewall acts like a filter for the information trying to enter your computer through the Internet. Firewalls deter spam and some viruses, but it is wise to always protect your computer with antivirus software.

Privacy

A very important consideration is the privacy of the students and teacher. No information about students should be posted on class web sites unless written parental permission is given. Even if permission is obtained, no specific personal information such as pictures, names, addresses, or phone numbers should be listed. School districts normally address privacy issues in the acceptable use policy guidelines. The privacy issue is certainly a concern for all individuals, because the Internet allows much easier access to personal information.

Cookies are small text files that a web site stores on your computer. For instance, a first visit to a site may ask for a name or a registration. The information is then often stored on a "cookie" on the hard drive. Upon return to that site, the site looks at the cookie file to retrieve your name and personalizes the message to you by saying "Welcome back, Jane Doe!" Has this happened to you lately? This technology gives a warm and fuzzy personal touch, and if used without fraudulent intentions, the use of cookies is not a bad thing. However, cookies can record credit card numbers and personal information about you that you enter at a web site. In this way, they could be a privacy threat.

One of the relatively new but growing scams is phishing—and it is on the rise. **Phishing** is the fraudulent practice of sending emails disguised to appear to be sent from a legitimate business such as a bank, credit card company, or retailer, and requesting that the user update their personal information. Phishing is used for purposes of identity theft, as well as access to financial documents. Do not update information of this nature on the Web. See **www.antiphishing.org** for more information.

Evaluating Web Sources

Sometimes information on the Web is offensive and/or incorrect. Therefore, it is necessary for teachers and students to evaluate sources to determine their value. A number of evaluation tools or checklists have been developed; however, most agree that the reliability of an Internet source can be determined by identifying five elements, including: (1) the author, (2) the publishing body, (3) a lack of bias, (4) the accuracy, and (5) the currency or timeliness of the information. Very important today is the accessibility of the web site.

The **identity of the author** is perhaps most important in evaluating web sites. Is the author identified? Is the author an expert in the field? Is the author associated with a university or organization? Establish the author's qualifications before using the information contained in the web site. Keep in mind that anyone can publish on the Web.

The **publishing body** is the group that is ultimately responsible for the information found on a site. Usually the information has gone through some measure of standards. Is the publishing body one that is familiar? Is the publishing body recognized as a leader on the topic? Does the document reside on a server that is not a personal home computer? This information can usually be established by looking at the domain name to determine if it is a government agency (.gov), an educational institution (.edu), and so on.

The author often has a point of view, rather than being completely neutral on a subject; reviewers should determine whether there is **objectivity or lack of bias** in the message. Is the author a member of a political or philosophical group? Is the message obviously written by someone with extremist views?

Accuracy of information is vital to using the information. Usually reputable web pages link to additional resources that can document facts and have a bibliography listed that shows that the information comes from research rather than opinion.

The **currency of the information** should be determined. How current is the page? A creation or revision date should be located. Caution should be used with pages that have not been written or revised within the last year. How time-sensitive is the information? Most authors update dates on the pages even if they have not changed the information to let a reader know that they have looked at the information. A lot of information resides on the Web that is sorely out of date. If no creation or revision date is provided, one should beware.

In addition, if the site is found to be reliable, other considerations should be reviewed. As with software, the design of the site must be considered. Is it easy to find and navigate? Is it appealing to the audience that you need to target? Are the graphics distracting, or do they take a long time to load? Is the site accessible to all?

In addition to hands-on evaluation, some sites offer indexes of screened sites for teachers and students. A powerful site, mentioned in Chapter 1, developed by a technology coordinator and continually growing, is Kathy Schrock's Guide for Educators (**school.discoveryeducation.com/schrockguide**). This index, sponsored by Discovery School, offers a large index on many topics, and each site has been screened.

A web site evaluation instrument developed by the authors and aligned with research can be found in student materials at the companion site: On the Web, Internet. This PDF file can be downloaded and used to evaluate web sites (see Figure 5.8 as a preview).

Adapting for Special Learners

All students can be included in the excitement of Web-based learning. Most adaptations for students with special needs center on tools and techniques that increase personal and independent use of the Web.

The first thing to consider is the general accessibility of the web site in question. An accessible web site is designed according to guidelines that make the pages usable for everyone (for instance, see the Web Accessibility initiative at **www.w3.org/wai**). Accessible sites provide text equivalents for visual and audio information, and a logical, consistent design in all pages. These features make the site usable for individuals with physical, perceptual, hearing, or vision barriers who must use mouse alternatives, different browsers, or screen readers in order to navigate without assistance. One way to determine whether a site is accessible is to look for the "Bobby Approved" logo at the end of each page. This logo means that the site has been tested using specialized software that checks for accessibility. IBM currently owns the rights to the Bobby accessibility software and includes it as a test in the Rational Policy Tester Accessibility Edition. This software may be used to certify sites for accessibility compliance.

Evaluating Web Sites for Reliability and Usability

Name of Site _____ URL _____

Contact Information of Author: _____ Phone: _____ email: _____

Special Requirements Needed to Access Information at the Site:

Browser Specific(s)

Plug-ins Needed to Access: ☐ Flash Player ☐ PDF Reader ☐ Real Player ☐ Other

Primary Purpose of Site: *Check the primary purpose of the site.*

☐ Interactive Simulation ☐ Primary Source ☐ Reference ☐ Tutorial

☐ Teacher Utility ☐ WebQuest ☐ Other: _____ [Please identify]

Overview of site: *Give an overview of the site and include how it could be used by K–12 students for learning.*

Directions: The criteria found in the sections that follow should be apparent in web sites that are used for educational purposes. Sites should be reliable, accurate, current, presented with no apparent bias and follow good design principles for accessibility. Review the site and indicate, with a Y for yes or N for no that the criterion is met by the site.

Author: *Based on your review, discuss the reliability of the author.*

_____ The author of the site is identified.
_____ The author's qualifications suggest that he/she is an authority on the subject.
_____ The author is affiliated with a university or professional organization that is considered reputable.
_____ Contact information for the author is provided such as a phone number or email address.

Comments:

Publishing Body: *Based on your review, discuss the reliability of the publishing body.*

_____ The publishing body is identified for the site.
_____ The publishing body is considered a leader on this topic.
_____ You know the publishing body.
_____ The page(s) reside on an official web site rather than a personal website.

Comments:

Bias of information: *Based on your review, discuss any bias that is apparent in the information at the site.*

_____ The information appears to be an advertisement, political or philosophical in nature.
_____ The site conveys an objective point of view.

Comments:

Accuracy of information: *Based on your review, discuss the accuracy of the information at the site.*

_____ The information at the site is factual and is documented with references to support its accuracy.
_____ The site is free of spelling and grammar errors.

Comments:

Currency of information: *Based on your review, discuss how current the information appears to be at the site.*

_____ The date that the site was originally created is identified.
_____ The date that the site was last revised is identified.
_____ The site has been revised within the last year to keep the information current.
_____ The site appears to be complete and is free of sections that are identified as "under construction".
_____ The links at the site are active; no dead links or "404" messages.

Comments:

Design of Interface: *Based on your review, discuss the design and usability of the site.*

_____ The interface is uncluttered and appealing to the targeted audience.
_____ The text is easy to read on the screen (typeface, size, color, contrast with background)
_____ The graphics are related to the text and enhance the information presented in the text.
_____ The graphics and/or animation found at the site are not distracting to the reader.
_____ The audio (if present) enhances the learning and is easily accessible to the reader.
_____ The navigation scheme is easy to use.
_____ The navigation is consistent throughout the site.
_____ The site can be seen on the monitor screen without horizontal scrolling.

Comments:

Accessibility: *Based on your review, discuss the accessibility of the site.*

_____ The site is free to access (no membership fee is associated with access to the site).
_____ All graphics found at the site have alternative text (alt tags) to assist special learners with screen readers.
_____ All graphics load quickly on a computer with less than a hi-speed connection.

Comments:

Recommendation: ☐ Highly recommend ☐ Recommend with reservations ☐ Do not recommend
Based on your evaluation, justify your overall recommendation for use in a K–12 classroom:

FIGURE 5.8 Web Site Evaluation Form (sample; full-size version on companion web site)

Voices *from the* Classroom

The Internet: Enhances Communication and Student Learning
Dave Carroll

Dave Carroll, a native of Roanoke, Virginia, has been teaching high school science courses (earth science and meteorology) for 23 years. Regarded for his excellence as a science teacher, Dave received the Governor's Award for Technology in Virginia in 2005. We asked him to share the ways that he uses the Internet with his students to enhance communication and student learning. Of special interest is a unique use of technology in a real-life time-intensive field-based course that allows a live link in May of each year.

The Internet expands the classroom not only to students but also parents and community members, which can be a very important link in the community. I have used the unique features of the Web to augment contact outside of the classroom in three ways.

First, the typical email contact with students and parents can provide a nonthreatening method of communication with the home. I find that students often email questions to me after hours simply because it is a comfortable medium for them, and parents find electronic communication to be nonconfrontational and appreciate the ability to contact a teacher at their convenience.

Second, I conduct online "help sessions" either scheduled at routine times or the night before a major test. I place time limits on the sessions (which often go on long after the posted deadline), and on some nights have fielded as many as a hundred questions from students reviewing material. The help sessions often take on a life of their own, with students answering each other's questions, which is exactly the learning atmosphere I am striving to attain.

Third, use of the Internet in unique ways can help bridge the information gap between what is happening in our schools and the community as a whole. Each year, I take a group of students on a two-week storm-chasing adventure as part of the meteorology course that I teach. The students who stay back at school act as our "lab support" and help with forecasting, as they typically have the superior Internet connection. The student chase team calls back each class period to get the latest weather model and real-time data, and via speakerphone the entire class becomes involved in the analysis, with the chase team on the road conversing with students half a continent away. On the road, the student chase teams also have wireless Internet access to evaluate weather conditions, and with the help of the students in class, a "target area" for severe/tornadic storms is established.

Another unique aspect of using the Web is in a combination of Internet, amateur radio, and GPS resources. Combining the various technologies, we provide students, parents, and the community back home a way of tracking the chase team over the Web. Using a system known as APRS (automatic position reporting system), everyone back home can track our location in real time (updated every 60 seconds) via a web site on the Internet, and overlay maps and even weather radar to see where the group is located around storms. Utilizing these technologies can make a truly positive impact on the community's impression of the school.

Over time we have expanded the community-school interaction on yet another level: using local media to provide coverage for the students, parents, and local community while we are on the road. Using the local broadcast media's Internet pages, they post video of the trip while it is in progress, and the online edition of the local newspaper updates a blog and provides still photos and video clips for the community for the duration of the trip. Utilizing this many outlets to reach students may seem like a lot of work, but in reality often all it takes is a simple phone call (or e-mail!). Local media outlets are often searching for school-related human interest stories, and from my experience are very willing to jump on board.

Read more about the previous trips at the Storm Chase Archive at **www.icsrc.org/ICSRC/TILT/Weatherline/chasearchive.htm** or read testimonials and find more interesting information at **www.icsrc.org/ICSRC/TILT/Weatherline/stormchase.htm**. Archived local media link: **http://blogs.roanoke.com/weatherjournal/storm_chasing/**.

Voices *from the* Classroom

The Internet: An Effective Teaching Tool
Deb Drew

Deb Drew teaches English in a suburban high school in Ohio with a student population of approximately 1,400 in grades 9 through 12. She received a Masters of Education in Classroom Technology several years ago and strives to use technology in her classroom as much as possible. Most teachers at her school have a laptop computer that they use in their classrooms. There may be one additional computer for student use in each classroom. This limited access makes the computer labs essential. The school has two stationary labs, and two mobile laptop labs each with 25 computers, available to reserve for the 90 teachers on staff. We asked Deb to share the ways that she uses the Internet/Web to enhance instruction.

I have found the Internet to be an effective teaching tool. Computers motivate most students, and the Internet offers a vast array of information that is available with the click of a mouse. One of my goals is to make real-life connections to the information that my students learn. Sometimes students think that English literature or novels have no relevance to their lives. The Internet's vast resources enable students to take the literature and tie it to the present day. Thus, their education becomes more effective and "real." Students tend to retain more when they do Web research, compared to only reading and discussing class material. I want students to think critically as much as they can, and Internet activities can encourage this process.

I have also found the Internet to be a great way to facilitate collaborative learning. At the end of a unit on a novel, I've used the Internet to extend learning with WebQuests or Internet Scavenger Hunts, allowing students to work in groups to accomplish tasks. Both strategies allow students to work together to access new information, while also drawing on what they already know. By putting information and their heads together, students can synthesize the information into new ideas and conclusions.

A lesson that I have learned is that although it is wonderful to have so much information available on the Internet at the students' fingertips, it can also be a hindrance. I have seen students spend an entire period in the computer lab trying to find just one tidbit of relevant information. To alleviate this problem, I make their tasks as focused as possible, and I encourage them to use a Web-filtering tool that our school subscribes to called WebPath Express. With a username and password, students can access this from home or from school through our high school media center web site. This tool filters Web content by grade level, and educators review all sites to verify them for accuracy, authenticity, and educational value.

At times, I complete the research first, and give students a list of web sites where I know they will find information that is of value. Because our school has limited computer access, every minute that students are on the Internet is valuable. By providing web sites and web site filters to the students, I can ensure that they spend their time learning and problem solving rather than searching for information. Another advantage to using the Internet is that it is available at any time from any place. If students don't finish what they need to do in class, they can finish researching on their own time. Overall, I have found that students like computers and the Internet. The Internet is a way to spark student interest in ways that traditional classroom approaches may not. Most importantly, teachers must keep in mind that using the Web is merely a means to the end, not the end in itself.

Students with vision, hearing, cognitive, and economic barriers to Internet access may need further tools or techniques. Solutions for bypassing these barriers are offered by the Alliance for Technology Access (ATA) and summarized here. Further information can be obtained at their web site, **www.ataccess.org/ resources/webaccess.html**.

Vision Barriers

Obtaining information from the Web requires a student to read text and view images. For students with low vision, the text may be too small; the contrast between the page, the type, and the graphics may be indiscernible; or the page may not be viewable at all. A simple solution is to adjust the browser settings for personal preferences. Text can be viewed in a variety of sizes, fonts, and colors. Background colors can be set to provide higher contrast between text, background, and graphics. The browser can also be set so that images are not loaded, making the use of screen reading software, which will read text-based descriptions, or tags, more efficient or less confusing.

Some students require magnification beyond the screen adjustments available in the browser. A number of screen magnification programs enlarge print, and can be used in conjunction with the Internet. Most magnification programs are platform-specific; that is, are developed for use with either Windows or Macintosh machines. A discussion of screen magnification and specific vendors is also included in Chapter 3. For some students with visual barriers, screen reading software is a more efficient or a necessary strategy for obtaining text-based information from the Internet. These programs are also reviewed in Chapter 3.

Hearing Barriers

When evaluating the suitability of web sites for classroom use with students who have hearing barriers, use sites that provide captions for sound in animations and video. Settings to turn on closed captioning are found in the system preferences or the application preferences for media players such as Quick Time. Most media authors are working to incorporate principles of Web accessibility into their design, which includes providing text captions for spoken dialog. The setting, *text captions for spoken dialog when available,* is an accessibility feature of Windows Vista and above. When either closed captioning or text captions are not provided by the media author, teachers will need to plan for other forms of assistance (transcription or interpretation) in order for students who are deaf or hearing-impaired to access the information in uncaptioned sounds.

Cognitive Barriers

Students with learning or cognitive barriers benefit from images, animation, sound, and video clips. These visuals can provide explanation of a concept that is not understandable in print, or can serve as memory aids for the concept presented. When reading ability presents a barrier to understanding the information, a screen or text reader, such as those recommended for students with visual barriers, may be useful. Macintosh users of OS X and later versions have access to VoiceOver, a built-in screen reading system. Narrator will work as a screen reader in Windows Vista and above. With earlier operating systems, the Web-based text may be pasted into Web-based text-to-speech programs.

Some web sites offer information with a choice of complexity and reading levels. For example, NASA's StarChild (http://starchild.gsfc.nasa.gov) offers explanations of principles of the solar system in two reading and cognitive levels and with the option of multiple languages.

Another strategy that may bypass learning or cognitive barriers is reducing the volume of the text. Students may copy and paste selected sections into Microsoft Word, and then execute the Auto Summary command. This tool reduces the number of words and sentences to a certain percentage of the original text. Finally, some students may have cognitive barriers that prevent them from finding selected web sites. If a student has difficulty accessing bookmarked or "favorites" sites that have been preselected by the teacher, other software programs can be used to launch these sites. For example, both MS PowerPoint and Inspiration have features that accept hyperlinks. A file could be created in either of these programs, establishing appropriate links that are embedded and intuitively accessed by the student.

Economic Barriers

Many students and teachers work in schools and live in homes with older computer equipment, slow Internet connections, or both. Turning off the image downloading in the browser settings can greatly increase access speed, and in some cases can make a difference in whether the page can be loaded at all. Most of the images can then be loaded at will by clicking (Macintosh) or right-clicking (Windows) the picture tag in question. The practicality of this solution is diminished, however, for sites that do not "tag" or provide a text-based description of the picture, or for sites where the navigation is unintuitive.

Physical Barriers

Students with physical barriers can still access the Internet. Adaptations are available for any form of computer input. Mouse alternatives include items such as trackballs or switches for almost any part of the body to emulate clicking. Keyboard alternatives include onscreen keyboards operated by touch or by gazing, programmable or miniature keyboards, and voice recognition. These basic hardware adaptations are discussed in Chapter 2.

CURRICULUM CONNECTIONS

The Cinderella Project (An ePALS Project)

OUR WORLD'S WATER (ePALS PROJECT)

CONTENT AREA/TOPIC: Science, Language Arts, Writing

GRADE LEVELS: 2–7   **NETS·S:** 2, 3, 4

Description: In this project, students research the worlds' water problems. The focus is on how their personal use of water affects aquatic ecosystems in their communities. Students participate in email exchanges with students from a partner school to explore global importance of water with particular focus on the communities of the ePals.

Teacher preparation: Teachers review the project at **http://content.epals.com/projects/info.aspx?DivID=Water_overview**). Teachers should secure a partner from another country from the Connect with Classroom Page. Teachers determine whether this will be a group project or one done between individual students. Teachers partner and collaborate to determine which activities will be completed using the Project elements on the web site. Bookmark the ePALS site Water Project.

Active participation: Students research the essential questions from this project: What is water? What is the water cycle? Why is water important? What problems does the world face with its water supply? Students complete project activities.

Source: ePals.com Global Exchange. Retrieved April 30, 2009, from **www.epals.com/projects/info.aspx?DivID=Water_overview**.

Note: This is one of many projects found EPals. Please review other projects at the site.

CURRICULUM CONNECTIONS *Continued*

Ask an Expert

CONTENT AREA/TOPIC: Science
GRADE LEVEL: 3   **NETS·S:** 2, 3, 6

Description: In this activity, students contact "experts" for answers to their science questions at the Center for Innovation in Engineering and Science Education site at **www.k12science.org/askanexpert. html.** This site provides hundreds of volunteer experts in fields of science ranging from astronauts to zookeepers.

Teacher preparation: Teachers should explore this site to discover the science categories that fit with the science topics that their class is studying. A new category at this site is Animals, a topic studied in elementary grades. Teachers will explore the process required for students to ask questions and plan a training session to explain the important of etiquette when using the site.

Active participation: Students should think of a question that they are unable to find in their research and that goes along with class study. Find the expert that matches the question. Link to the expert's site and follow directions for submitting a question. Teacher guidance should be used.

Variations: There are a number of Ask the Expert sites many of which are in science. Some of the project sites have an Ask the Expert section.

Source: CIESE: Curriculum: Ask an Expert Site. Retrieved April 30, 2009, from **www.k12science.org/askanexpert.html**.

Planet WebQuest

CONTENT AREA/TOPIC: Science, Language Arts
GRADE LEVEL: 3   **NETS·S:** 1, 2, 3

Description: This top-rated WebQuest allows students to collect data about a planet. A data sheet guides student research. Students present findings as they write a virtual postcard about their planet.

Teacher preparation: Teacher should go to the Planet WebQuest site and print out directions for creating a Crew Patch, each of the data collection pages, and the draft postcard sheet for students to use. Teacher should examine the Space Links, Space Books, and the Evaluation Rubric provided by the authors. Teacher should divide students into groups of three (depending on student numbers) to research an assigned planet from the links in the WebQuest. Bookmark the Planet WebQuest at **http://webquest.org/index-2007a .html.**

Active participation: Students read the mission that has been given to them. Students create a Crew Patch according to the template provided. Students click on their assigned planets to access information on the data sheets. After collecting the data, students compose a rough draft of a cyber-postcard that tells facts about the planet and their adventures. Finally, students share the virtual postcards with other crews from other missions from Mission Control.

Variations: Students could write blogs rather than postcards.

Source: Gunning, R., & Thomson, W. (2007). Planet WebQuest. Retrieved October 7, 2008, from **http://webquest.org/index-2007a .html**

CURRICULUM CONNECTIONS *Continued*

The Diary of Anne Frank Blog

CONTENT AREA/TOPIC: Literature

GRADE LEVELS: 6–7   **NETS·S:** 2, 4, 6

Description: Students read the same book. In this lesson, the book is *The Diary of Anne Frank.* The students meet in literature circles and take on different roles to discuss and debate events and ideas from the book.

Teacher preparation: Choose a book for students to read. Determine the roles that students will play. Assign the roles to students. Facilitate the lesson.

Active participation: After reading the book, the students meet in literature circles in which they take on different roles to discuss and debate events and ideas

from different perspectives. Students write blog articles. In this lesson, the teacher posts the student blogs.

Variations: This lesson could easily be varied to use a wiki for students to share their posts. In addition, in a wiki, they could respond to their peer's posts with thoughts or questions.

Source: http://thediaryofannefrank.blogspot.com; Lenva Shearing, Bucklands Beach Intermediate School, New Zealand. Accessed October 5, 2008.

Book Review Podcasting

CONTENT AREA/TOPIC: Language Arts, Writing, Research Skills, Technology Skills

GRADE LEVELS: K–8   **NETS·S:** 1, 2, 3, 6

Description: This project, "Brookline Book Review Podcasting Project," involves the Instructional Technology Specialist, Elizabeth Davis, the librarian, teachers, and students working together, to create a database of book reviews that students can use to find a good book to read.

Teacher preparation: The tech coordinator, librarian, or teacher prepares the introduction of the concept of book reviews and podcasts for the students. Templates are created for various grade levels to help stu-

dents write the book reviews. Video and directions for using Garage Band software are created.

Active participation: Students use the templates to write book reviews and practice reading aloud. Students go to the lab and record their podcasts followed by reviewing their recordings. They add music and sound effects. The podcasts are placed on the school web site (www.runkle.org/Podcasts/index.html).

Source: E. Davis. http://wiki.classroom20.com/Podcasting+ Lesson+Plans Accessed October 6, 2008.

The Wonderful World of Weather (A Real-Time Research Project)

CONTENT AREA/TOPIC: Science, Language Arts, Literacy

GRADE LEVELS: 3–6   **NETS·S:** 4, 5, 6

Description: This project allows students to investigate weather phenomena locally and in places around the world. Because of their ages, they will not be studying complex weather concepts; however, they will develop an understanding of how weather is described in measures such as temperature, wind, and precipitation.

Teacher preparation: Teachers should print out lessons from the web site for: (1) introductory activities, (2) real-time data activities, and (3) language arts activities, as well as other project information. Bookmark the project site at www.ciese.org/realtimeproj .html.

CURRICULUM CONNECTIONS *Continued*

Active participation: Students complete introductory activities, after which they visit provided links to research real-time data regarding weather changes. Students may follow their research period with reports, pictures, or other literacy-related activities. There is a place for student work to be published at the site.

Source: CIESE Real-Time Data Projects. Wonderful world of weather. Retrieved October 10, 2008, from **www.ciese.org/curriculum/weatherproj/html.**

Note: This is one of many projects found at CIESE. Please review other projects at the site.

Virtual Field Trip: The Human Heart: An Online Exploration

CONTENT AREA/TOPIC: Science

GRADE LEVELS: 3–8

NETS·S: 3, 4, 6

Description: Students take a virtual field trip of the Human Heart that is designed by the Franklin Institute. This excellent site provides a wonderful way to virtually visit the human heart and presents information about the development of the heart, the heart structure, vessels, blood, the body systems, monitoring the heart, how to have a healthy heart and the history of heart disease as well as the milestones.

Teacher preparation: Teachers become well acquainted with the site and the materials found there. Decisions are made about the activities (found at the site) for students and how to facilitate their use depending on the grade level of students. The teacher can provide research guide sheets to guide student research. Various topics found at the site can used with various sections of a unit.

Active participation: Students actively participate in this virtual field trip of the human heart. They use the site to complete research on the human heart and possibly use the heart image gallery to complete slideshows with their findings. Enrichment activities are found at the site as well as readings and resources.

Variations: Many topics are well-suited for virtual field trips. Museums often offer activities as well as other places on the Web. Great method to allow students to extend the walls of a classroom.

Source: The Franklin Institute: The Human Heart. Retrieved October 10, 2008. from **www.fi.edu/learn/heart/index.html.**

On the Web

This section includes only a snapshot of web sites that the authors recommend for viewing. To access live links and a larger and continuously updated collection of sites, go to the companion web site at **www.pearsonhighered.com/ obannon2e**.

Evaluation of Web Sites

Kathy Schrock Guide for Educators
http://school.discoveryeducation.com/schrockguide.html
This site developed and maintained by Kathy Schrock, offers a guide for evaluation of web sites for elementary, middle school, and secondary school levels at this page.

Integrating Technology: Games

FunBrain
www.funbrain.com/
Pearson Education sponsors this site that contains Flash Arcades, Web Books, Movies, and the Classic Funbrain collection. There is a new FunBlog for girls and boys in specific age groups. Pearson proves that students can have fun while learning. This site is developed for students in grades K–8.

Online Games
http://arcademicskillbuilders.com/
This site proposes to "engage and educate." Academic Skill Builders present online educational games for learning basic math, language arts, vocabulary, and thinking skills. Increasing fluency impacts three learning outcomes: retention, endurance, and application if while having fun. Try these games with single players or multi-players. Requires a flasher player to access.

Nobelprize
http://nobelprize.org/educational_games/
Play games and simulations based on the achievements of Nobel Prize–awarded achievements at this site. Test and build your knowledge in physics, chemistry, physiology, medicine, literature, peace, and economics. Explore this site and learn while having some fun!

Integrating Technology: Online Projects

The Global Schoolhouse
www.globalschoolnet.org/index.cfm
Global SchoolNet is a network of teachers who practice online project-based learning activities in their K–12 classrooms. Since its beginning, Global SchoolNet has reached more than a million students from 25,000 schools across 100 countries in collaborative learning activities.

CIESE (Center for Improved Engineering and Science Education)
www.k12science.org/currichome.html
Established in 1988 at Stevens Institute of Technology, CIESE helps bring the Institute's technology experience to the K–12 environment through the design of interdisciplinary projects that teachers can use to enhance their curriculum through the use of the Internet. Project opportunities include collaborative projects, projects using primary and archived data, real-time data projects, and partner projects.

WebQuest.Org
http://webquest.org/index.php
This site, recently revised, is "the most complete and current source of information about the WebQuest Model." Visitors may find WebQuests, create WebQuests, link to useful resources, research news, and more. The history of this inquiry-oriented lesson format is shared along with information about the creators, Bernie Dodge, Ph.D. (with Tom March). Contact information for Dr. Dodge is provided along with links to stellar educators in the "Minds We Like" section. This new design offers friendly travel through the information.

Integrating Technology: Virtual Field Trips

Jason Project
www.jason.org/public/home.aspx
The well-known Jason Project is a gateway to adventures in Science. A nonprofit subsidiary of the National Geographic Society, Jason connects students in grades 5–9 with explorers and events to motivate them to learn science. The curriculum is aligned with national standards and can be adapted for lower or higher grade levels. Read more about how to get your students involved in an expedition.

Get Outta Class with Virtual Field Trips
www.educationworld.com/a_tech/tech/tech071.shtml
Great field trips can be taken right in the classroom. Have your students travel to wonderful places that otherwise could not be seen. Education World presents a list of virtual field trips that are already operational to the solar system, other parts of the world, farms, museums and more. Teachers can make their own field trips with some of the templates available. Great strategy for using the huge information sources available on the Web.

Internet Field Trips

http://teacher.scholastic.com/fieldtrp
Sponsored by Scholastic, this site offers field trips for Reading/Language Arts, Science, Social Studies, Math, and K–2. A must-see for every teacher.

Integrating Web 2.0 Tools: Blogs, Wikis, Podcasts, RSS, Social BookMarking

Kathy Schrock's Web 2.0 Tools
http://school.discoveryeducation.com/schrockguide/
edtools.html#Web20_tools
Kathy Schrock shares a list of Web 2.0 tools (free), including aggregators, blogs, database, podcast, and wikis, for teacher evaluation. She cautions that many of the tools are open Internet and because of security issues with open Internet, teachers should use caution when using them with their students.

Blogs in Plain English
www.commoncraft.com/blogs
Commoncraft presents a video introducing the basics of blogs.

Social Bookmarking in Plain English
www.commoncraft.com/bookmarking-plain-english
Commoncraft presents a video introducing the basics of social bookmarking.

Wikis in Plain English
www.commoncraft.com/video-wikis-plain-english
Commoncraft presents a video introducing the basics of wikis.

Key Terms

Internet Service Provider (ISP) (100)
Browser software (101)
DSL (digital subscriber line) (101)
Digital cable (101)
Satellite Internet (101)
Wireless connection (101)
Wireless fidelity (WiFi) (102)
World Wide Web (WWW) (Web) (102)
Uniform Resource Locator (URL) (102)
Web site (102)
Home page (102)
HTML (Hypertext Markup Language) (102)
Hyperlink (102)
Plug-in (102)
Domain name (102)
Cache (103)
Search engine (104)
Subject directory (104)
Meta-search engine (104)

Query (104)
Keyword (104)
Hit (104)
Boolean operator (105)
Wildcard (105)
Modifier (105)
Asynchronous communication (105)
Synchronous communication (105)
Discussion forum (106)
Email program (106)
Listserv (106)
Moderated (106)
Subscribe (106)
Instant messaging (107)
Chat room (107)
Course management systems (CMS) (107)
File transfer protocol (FTP) (107)
Blog (108)
Wiki (108)

Podcast (112)
Social bookmarking (113)
Blocking (115)
Filtering program (116)
Malware (116)
Computer virus (116)
Worm (116)
Trojan horse (116)
Macro-virus (116)
Spyware (116)
Antivirus software (116)
Firewall (117)
Cookies (117)
Phishing (117)
Identity of the author (117)
Publishing body (117)
Objectivity or lack of bias (118)
Accuracy (118)
Currency of the information (118)

Hands-on Activities for Learning

1. Visit the On the Web companion site (**www.pearson highered.com/obannon2e**) and review the sites available.
2. Enter a reflection in your Reflective Technology Blog about ways that you want to integrate the Internet and its services into your classroom.
3. Participate in a WebQuest about WebQuest (**http://webquest.sdsu.edu/webquestwebquest.html**) at the appropriate level with a group of peers within your licensure area and present your findings to your classmates.
4. Using the evaluation tool provided, evaluate a curriculum-based web site that you would like to use with your students to see if the site is a good choice.
5. Conduct research at the WebQuest site (**http://webquest.org/index.php**) and find at least two of the top-rated WebQuests that are aligned with the curriculum for your licensure area. These WebQuests may be used as curriculum resource pages at your classroom web site or added to a collaborative wiki.
6. Create a blog for reflections regarding your growth in technology.
7. Participate in a wiki with your peers to create a collection of curriculum-based sites to place at your web site.
8. Develop an inquiry-based lesson plan using the template provided in student materials of the companion site (or one provided by your instructor) that uses the Web to secure information.

Chapter 6

Word Processing

Teachers:

a. demonstrate fluency in technology systems and the transfer of current knowledge to new technologies and situations.

b. collaborate with students, peers, parents, and community members using digital tools and resources to support student success and innovation.

c. communicate relevant information and ideas effectively to students, parents, and peers using a variety of digital-age media and formats.

d. model and facilitate effective use of current and emerging digital tools to locate, analyze, evaluate, and use information resources to support research and learning.

Frameworks

During the 1980s and early 1990s, a great deal of research on the role of word processing in the learning process was conducted; results suggest that indeed word processing has a positive effect on learning. It appears that students make more revisions (Snyder, 1993), write longer documents (Hawisher, 1989; Snyder, 1993; Bangert-Drowns, 1993), and make fewer simple errors (Snyder, 1993) when using a word processor. The use of word processing has improved students' attitudes toward writing (Hawisher, 1989; Snyder, 1993) and the quality of that writing (Bangert-Drowns, 1993).

A later study examined the use of word processing over longer periods of time with positive results (Owston & Wideman, 1997). Student writing products and processes were studied during a three-year period, beginning in the third grade, at a school where students had routine daily access to word processors and at a nearby school that had only a few infrequently used computers in the classrooms. The study showed that writing quality improved significantly at the school with daily access. Observations support the belief that the use of word processors strongly contributed to the differences. The characteristics of the word processor that seemed to explain the differences were a combination of the ways text was edited, displayed, and manipulated with the computer.

A growing body of evidence points to the word processor as an effective assistive technology (AT) device for students with mild disabilities. Word processors can increase the effectiveness of written work in the areas of organization, structure of writing, and spelling (Day & Edwards, 1996; Lewis, Ashton, Haapa, Kieley, & Fielden, 1999; Hetzroni & Shrieber, 2004). For students with reading and writing deficits, word processors used during the writing process can improve the quality of writing (Raskin & Higgins, 1998; Lewis, 1998). Additionally, word processors can be used as assistive reading devices. Certain word processing features summarize written documents, read text aloud, allow for alteration in the visual display of text, and incorporate rebus or picture symbols to describe a word. These strategies can make reading more accessible for students with cognitive deficits (Edyburn, 2002).

Roblyer (2003) concludes that word processing does improve writing and student attitudes if the student has the time to learn the use of the word processor within the context of writing instruction. This conclusion echoes research findings in the use of technology applications in learning in other areas as well.

Basics

Word processing programs are no longer limited to simple text writing; they have sophisticated features that allow users to create professional-looking documents. Although **word processing** is typically associated with report writing, endless ways of incorporating its power in the classroom exist. Some popular ways that teachers use word processing include the creation of exams and quizzes, lessons plans, and grant proposals. Options for collaboration are available as teachers use the features provided in Google docs and wikis. Further, "classroom" blogs can be created to share information with parents and others. See Figure 6.1 for teacher uses of word processing.

In the Frameworks section, we concluded that research has formed multiple reasons to promote the use of word processing in the classroom. Among these are increased productivity, enhanced appearance, and accuracy. Word processing improves the productivity of students, as all tasks are completed more easily and quickly when these tools are used. The appearance of documents is greatly enhanced, making them easier to read and grade! The use of spell checking, thesaurus, and dictionary features enhance accuracy, and record keeping becomes much easier.

Ways to integrate word processing into student learning include writing assignments such as creative writing, journal writing, outlining, and report writing. In addition, word processing can be used in collaborative writing projects such as the creation of alphabet books and collaborative stories. Web 2.0 tools, including blogs and wikis, offer new ways to collaborate and encourage writing. See Figure 6.2 for student uses of word processing.

Word processing programs may be purchased as **stand-alone programs**; however, it is cheaper for teachers to purchase **integrated software programs** or **software suites**. As mentioned in Chapter 3, integrated software programs contain not only a word processing feature but usually a database, spreadsheet, graphics, and slideshow program in one package. Microsoft Works is an example of an integrated program. The key to the lower pricing is that these programs do not have the advanced features that are found in stand-alone versions or some software suites.

Software suites, such as MS Office, WordPerfect Office, and iWork (for Macs), also have multiple programs, yet they tend to be full-featured programs. Some suites have varying levels of program features; thus, the teacher should research available features and capabilities before purchasing. Open Office is an open source software suite, is free for download, and offers a word processor as well as other programs, as discussed in Chapter 3. Download a free version at the site or

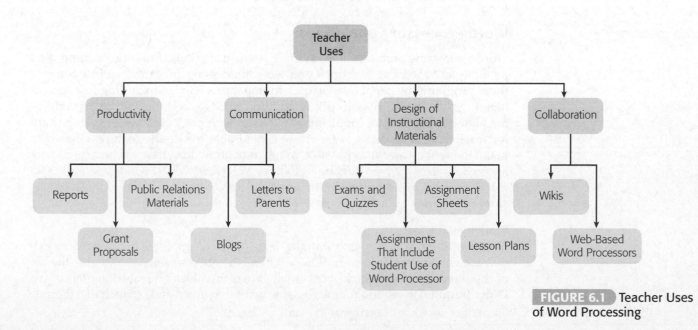

FIGURE 6.1 Teacher Uses of Word Processing

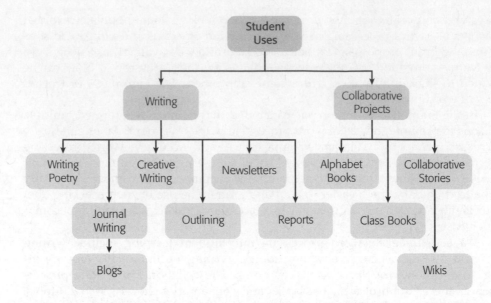

FIGURE 6.2 Student Uses of Word Processing

read about it at **http://why.openoffice.org/why_edu.html**. Google offers Web-based options in Google documents that only require an account to get free access to the tools. Google docs (formerly Writely) is an online space that resembles a word processing document and allows easy collaboration and 24/7 access. Other online word processing tools are Zoho Writer (**http://writer.zoho.com**) and Thinkfree (**www.thinkfree.com**). Adobe Buzzword (**www.adobe.com/acom/buzzword**), a free Web-based word processor, provides improved formatting features, a weakness found in earlier online products. Buzzword, similar to MS Word, has a streamlined interface. A nice feature is Buzzword's ability to import and export documents from a variety of formats as well as produce documents that actually look like what is seen on the screen. This has been coined as WYSIWYP, an acronym for *what you see is what you print*. We expect Web-based versions of software to continue to improve as time moves on, opening many new opportunities for students to create, communicate, and collaborate in friendly online spaces. Obviously, the major focus of our discussion is integrating word processing into learning; however, we would be remiss to omit the capabilities of the tool.

Word Processor Capabilities

Word processing software has multiple useful functions. Entering, editing, and deleting text are basic functions of a word processing program, although today these programs are capable of many additional procedures, including insertion of tables, graphics, and hyperlinks, in addition to advanced formatting procedures for high-quality desktop publishing and even web page creation. It is important for teachers and students to be aware of and able to use the features offered to make the tool as useful as possible. While most functions that are presented here are generic to word processing software, MS Word 2007 (Windows) and 2008 (Mac) form the basis for this discussion. While 2008 is quite similar to the 2004 version, 2007 varies quite a bit from 2003.

Working with Text
Entering, Editing, Saving, and Printing Text   Using Word 2007 involves three primary navigational elements: the Office button, the ribbon, which runs across the top of the screen, and the quick access toolbar, which is located just to the left of the Office button. The ribbon runs across the top of the screen and is much like the side

of a divided notebook in that it has tabs labeled: Home, Insert, Page Layout, References, Mailings, Review, View, and Format. Each of these ribbons has several submenus that are groups of related icons. The groups are labeled across the bottom of each ribbon. Before text can be entered, a document (or file) must be opened. When you open Word, you will see an empty document. To open an additional document, go to the **File** menu in Word 2008 and in Word 2007, go to the Office button; the New and Open options are found under this button. After the document is opened, text is entered using the keyboard and mouse. The mouse is used to place the **I-beam (cursor)** on the paper where the text is to appear. Word processing programs have a feature called **word wrap**, which allows the user to type continually and automatically move to the next line.

The **editing of text** may involve deleting text, or changing it, by cutting, copying, or pasting. In order to make any changes, the text must first be selected. **Deleting text** is completed by selecting it, followed by pressing the delete key on a Mac and the backspace key on a PC. To duplicate or move text, the text must be selected, copied or cut, and "pasted" into an area of choice. These commands are found on the ribbon under the first tab, Home, on the first group called Clipboard in Word 2007. In Word 2008, go to Edit on the Menu. Another very useful feature that most word processors have is the ability to **find and replace**. This feature allows the user to easily alter words or phrases that are used multiple times in a document. To find and replace a word or phrase in Word 2007, go to the Home tab to the Editing group and select Replace. The program will prompt the user to type in the word to find and the word to replace it with. The Find command is located under the **Edit** menu on Word 2008.

Saving text on a regular basis is essential. If a power failure or computer crash occurs, all work that has not been saved is lost forever. There are Save and Save As commands under the File menu (2008) or under the Office button (2007). Use the Save As command to create a backup version of a document or change the name of the document. Use descriptive names for documents so that they can be easily identified, such as midterm.doc. It is essential to have a backup copy of all work, in case there is damage or corruption to a disk. With no backup, all lost work must be completely redone. Needless to say, this is not a desirable option. One good strategy is to occasionally change the name of the document so that new versions will be created each time a sizable amount of work is completed.

After the document is complete, use the **Print** command to send the document to a printer that serves the computer. Preview the document by using the **Print Preview** command. Print Preview allows you to check the final appearance of the document before it is printed. These commands are located under the File menu (2008) or under the Office button (2007).

Formatting

Formatting commands change the look of the document. The entire document or only a paragraph or font may be customized, as discussed in the following sections. The word processor has **default settings**, which are automatically applied unless they are changed. Default settings are, for the most part, useful; however, every user should check the default settings for fonts and other formatting when using any program.

Document Formatting Some formatting procedures dictate the look of the entire document. The orientation of the document and the setting of margins are document formats and are explained in the following paragraphs.

The **orientation** of a document is either *portrait* or *landscape* orientation, which specifies the direction that print is situated on the paper. The default setting is portrait, which indicates that the shorter edge of the paper is the top. With landscape

FIGURE 6.3 Document Formatting: Portrait and Landscape Orientation

orientation, the longer edge of the paper is the top. In Figure 6.3, two options are given for orientation: portrait and landscape. In Word 2008, access to orientation settings is found at File → Page Setup (this means to go to the File menu and select Page Setup). Click the icon that is representative of the desired orientation. Click OK to register the changes. In Word 2007, access to orientation settings is found under the Page Layout tab. In the Page Setup group, click Orientation and then choose the icon that is representative of the desired orientation, as seen in Figure 6.3. **Margins** should be set for each document, unless you want the default margins for the document. Top, bottom, left, and right margins may be set independently for the document. Default margins for a document are 1" for top and bottom margins and 1.25" for left and right margins, and can be changed under Format → Document. Click the appropriate box and make the desired change. Click OK to register the changes. In Word 2007, as shown in Figure 6.4, they can be changed under the Page Layout tab on the Page Setup group.

Paragraph Formatting   The format options found here can be set for the entire document or just a single paragraph. Basic formats in this category are: (1) alignment of the text, (2) paragraph indentions, and (3) line spacing. Each is discussed next, with good design tips for use.

The **alignment of text**, also called **justification**, is the placement of the text horizontally on the page. Text can be placed to the left or right of the page, centered, or justified. Alignments are explained in Table 6.1. An easy way to change the alignment of text is to use the icons on the formatting toolbar (Word 2008). Similar icons are in Word 2007 under the Home tab on the Formatting group as see in Figure 6.5.

Indentations are determined under paragraph formatting (Word 2008). In Word 2007, these are determined in the Home tab on the Paragraph group and on the ruler that is visible across the top of the document. There are three types of indentions: first line, hanging, and block. **First-line indentions** are used to indent the first line of each paragraph in a document and are extremely handy when writing papers with multiple paragraphs. The upper triangle of the left margin marker, located on the ruler, controls the indention position of the first line of text for a paragraph. To set a first-line indention, click and hold this triangle to move the first line to the desired position, as seen in Figure 6.6. Another method of setting indentions is from the menu bar at the Format Paragraph window (2008) or from the Home tab on the Paragraph group (2007).

A **hanging indention** is the indention of all subsequent lines of a paragraph and is extremely handy when developing bibliographies or numbered and bulleted lists. Hanging indentations are seen in the References section of this book. To

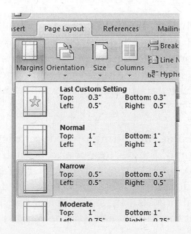

FIGURE 6.4 Document Formatting: Setting

Table 6.1   Text Alignment: Left, Center, Right, Justified

Align left	**Left-justified or left-aligned** is the most common alignment of text and is the easiest to read. In this arrangement, the text aligns on the left of the tab marker and moves to the right with the right margin giving an even or ragged appearance, as seen in this paragraph.
Align center	**Center alignment** of text is commonly used for titles. In center alignment, text is evenly distributed to the left and right of the center. This alignment is a bad choice for text blocks, as it may become difficult to read as demonstrated in this paragraph.
Align right	**Right-justified or right-aligned** text aligns on the right of the tab marker and moves to the left with the left edge giving a ragged appearance, as seen in this paragraph, This is not a good choice for blocks of text.
Justify	**Justified** text is commonly used in books and newsletters. In this arrangement, the text aligns evenly on the left and right margins, as seen in this paragraph. This alignment should be used with caution, as it forces the text to align, which requires uneven spacing between words and can make a document more difficult to read.

set a hanging indent, click and drag the lower triangle of the left margin marker, as shown in Figure 6.7.

Block indentions are indentions on both left and right margins of the paragraph, and are generally used for direct quotes or text that needs to be set apart from the rest of the document text. To set a block indention, left and right margin markers are moved as shown in Figure 6.8. Click and drag each triangle to move the paragraph margins to the desired positions.

Line spacing is the number of lines or the amount of blank space located between rows of text. Common line spacing settings are **single** (no extra space), **double** (an extra line of space), or **1.5** (one and a half line of space). The default setting is single spacing. An easy method for changing the line spacing is to use the icons on the toolbar, as seen in Figure 6.9. For instance, if the document is to be double-spaced, change the line spacing to double before inserting text into the document. If text has already been entered, highlight the text and click on the icon that represents the desired change. Another way to change the line spacing on Word 2008, is to click Format → Paragraph, or on Word 2007, click the small arrow on the bottom right of the Paragraph group. Select the Indents and Spacing tab. Click the Line Spacing menu and select the desired line spacing. Click OK to register the changes.

Font Formatting
Changing the appearance of text is possible by changing fonts. Basic characteristics of **fonts** include (1) typeface, (2) type size, (3) case, and (4) emphasis, as discussed

FIGURE 6.5 Paragraph Formatting: Alignment of Text

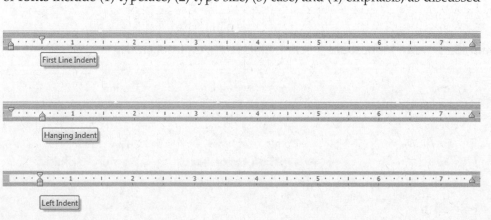

FIGURE 6.6 Margin Markers for a First-Line Indention

FIGURE 6.7 Margin Markers for a Hanging Indention

FIGURE 6.8 Margin Markers for Block Indentions

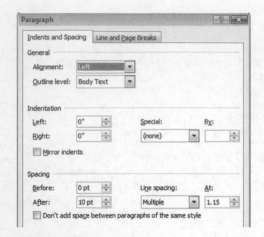

FIGURE 6.9 Setting Indents and Spacing

in the following paragraphs. The most important concern when choosing font formats is legibility.

Typeface There are hundreds of **typefaces** for fonts and all will not be available in word processing programs. Standard fonts are usually found with most computer programs. This is particularly beneficial if you're working on a document that will be printed on a different computer. For example, if you use a really nifty, yet uncommon, font, the computer that is used to print the document may not have the font, thus it will change the font to a default font and change the look of the entire document. If additional typefaces are desired, fonts can easily be made available by purchasing commercial fonts or downloading free ones from the Web and placing them into the appropriate system folder of the computer. Adding fonts to the computer is easy. Go to the Control Panel from the Start menu of Windows, and open the Fonts folder. Drag and drop the new font into this folder. On the Mac, go to the Library within the System folder on the hard drive and open the Fonts folder. Drag and drop to add the new font.

Font Families Fonts are divided into **families** that share common traits. Most fonts are classified as serif, sans serif, monospace, script, Blackletter/Old English, or decorative. Serif or sans serif fonts are the most commonly used in print documents; however, others can be used with caution or to create a particular look. See Table 6.2.

A general rule is to use a maximum of two different fonts in a single document, with variations using effects such as bold, italic, and so on. **Serif fonts** have horizontal "feet" and are the easiest to read in blocks of text. Normally, word processing programs use the Times or Times New Roman font as the default. **Sans serif fonts** do not have the "feet" and are good choices for titles, headings, or for the Web. Sans serif fonts are also good to use when working with young children. Popular sans serif typefaces include Arial, Helvetica, and Geneva. **Monospace fonts** are identified by all characters having the same width. A familiar monospaced font is Courier, which resembles the lettering found on a typewriter. **Script fonts** resemble handwriting, and include typefaces such as Comic Sans and Handwriting. Script fonts should be used sparingly. Some script typefaces are easier to read than others. **Blackletter/Old English fonts** are based on ancient calligraphy. The modern versions within this category still have an old-fashioned look and should also be used sparingly, as they become very difficult to read in narrative. Finally, **decorative fonts** are used to create a feeling or emotion in a particular look. These specialty fonts may be used with holiday documents or lettering for special effects. Examples for all of these fonts are provided at **www.fontmenu .com/site/categories.html**.

Table 6.2 Font Categories: Serif, Sans Serif, Monospaced, Script, Blackletter, and Decorative

Serif	Times	Times New Roman	Caslon
Sans Serif	**Arial**	Helvetica	Geneva
Monospaced	Courier	Courier New	Monaco
Script	*Handwriting*	Comic Sans MS	*Brush Script*
Blackletter/ Old English	Blackletter	**Optima Extra Black**	Century Gothic
Decorative	*Zapf Chancery*	Willow	Birch

Table 6.3 Font Size in Points

Times—18 point	Helvetica—18 point

Fonts can be classified also by their spacing between characters. This spacing is either monospacing or proportionate. **Monospaced** fonts (mentioned earlier), such as Courier, allow the same space for an *i* or an *l* as for an *m*. **Proportionate** fonts are spaced according to the width of the characters, with the *i* and the *m* receiving spacing proportionate to their width.

To change the font (or typeface), use the drop-down menu on the toolbar (2008) or under the Home tab on the Font group (2007). Again, if you click on the small arrow at the lower right of the Font group, the menu that is used on a Mac will open up. If text has already been typed into the document, highlight the text to be changed before selecting the new font. In spite of the fact that gothic, script, or "cute and trendy" typefaces may be acceptable when used sparingly, they are not good choices for blocks of text or most professional documents.

Type Size   **Type size** is measured in points, with approximately 72 points equal to an inch, though all fonts are not measured exactly the same. For instance, Times is a very small font while Helvetica is a larger font; therefore, 18-point Times is not equal to 18-point Helvetica, as illustrated in Table 6.3. Most word processors default to Times or Times New Roman 12. Should a change in size be desired, use the drop-down menus on the toolbar. If text has been added to the document, highlight the text to be changed before selecting the change.

Type Case   Choosing uppercase or lowercase letters (**type case**) has a significant effect on the legibility of text. Setting letters in uppercase should generally be avoided, except in short headings. Downstyle typing, where the only the first word and proper nouns are capitalized, is recommended for headings, subheads, and text.

Emphasis   Fonts may be given **emphasis** by applying bold, italic, and underline as seen in Table 6.4. However, these treatments should be used sparingly. If used too much, nothing will stand out for the reader.

Finally, **special effects** can be applied to fonts, including shadow or embossed effect or superscripts and subscripts. Keep legibility in mind, and never use too many effects. Effects create difficulty in reading if not used with care.

Table 6.4 Applying Emphasis with Italic, Bold, and Underline

Italic is typically used for book or periodical titles or to stress specific words, but is not a good choice for blocks of text because of difficulty in reading.

Boldface attracts attention because it sticks out from the other text in the document, yet becomes difficult to read if used in large blocks of text.

<u>Underlining text is another method of giving emphasis and is often used for headings.</u> This method of emphasis is quite acceptable for print documents, yet unacceptable for Web documents because of confusion distinguishing between emphasis and hyperlinks.

Table 6.5   Numbered or Bulleted Lists

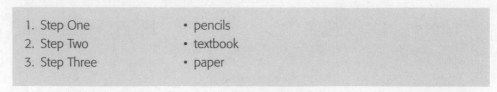

1. Step One   • pencils
2. Step Two   • textbook
3. Step Three   • paper

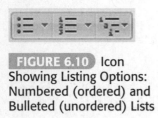

FIGURE 6.10 Icon
Showing Listing Options:
Numbered (ordered) and
Bulleted (unordered) Lists

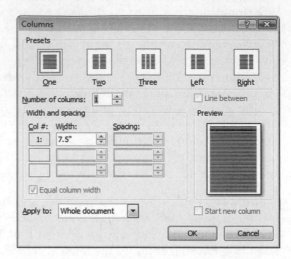

FIGURE 6.11 Document
Window for Formatting of
Columns in Microsoft Word

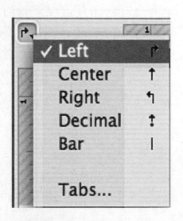

FIGURE 6.12 Tab Icons:
Left, Center, Right, Decimal

More Formatting Options

There are some other formatting options that have not been covered but nevertheless are useful. These include the use of (1) lists, (2) columns, and (3) tabs.

Numbered or Bulleted   Lists can be created by using the numbered or bulleted list icons usually found on the toolbar, as seen in Figure 6.10. These features align the text for easy reading and give the document a professional look. **Numbered lists** should be used when the order of the list is important, such as steps in a sequence. **Bulleted lists** should be used when there is no specific order necessary, such as a list of materials necessary for a writing project. The arrows pictured to the right of these icons move text to the right or left. Examples of bulleted and numbered lists are seen in Table 6.5. The icon to initiate both Numbered and Bulleted lists in Word 2007 are found under the Home tab on the Formatting group.

Columns are typically used in newsletters and newspapers and increase the ease of reading long lines of text. It is easier to read text if it is placed in more narrow columns. The formatting for columns is usually found under the Format → Columns item, which opens a window with column icons, as seen in Figure 6.11. For a PC, under the Page Layout tab, choose Columns on the Page Setup group. Several options of preformatted columnar layouts are there or the user can choose More Columns to format the columns. If the program lacks this feature, columns may be set with tab settings at different points on the ruler.

Tab settings allow the placement of text at specific places on the ruler to align text in columns. Left, center, right, and decimal tabs may be set as explained in Table 6.6. It is important to use tabs rather than using the space bar to align text. Although text may appear aligned on the monitor by inserting extra spaces, it usually is not when the document is printed or viewed on another computer.

Setting tabs is done by selecting one of the icons found on the toolbar, as pictured in Figure 6.12, or in the left corner of the document window followed by

Table 6.6   Setting Tabs: Left, Center, Right, and Decimal

Left tabs	The text aligns on the left of the tab marker.	Mouse Keyboard Monitor
Center tabs	The text is centered on the tab marker and words are distributed across the marker.	Mouse Keyboard Monitor
Right tabs	The text aligns on the right of the tab marker.	Mouse Keyboard Monitor
Decimal tabs	The text aligns on the decimal tab marker; very handy for columns of monetary values.	1.82 .79 10.65

positioning it on the ruler. The icons are slightly different on the Windows and Mac OS X.

An alternative method for setting tabs is clicking Format → Tabs, which opens a window for inserting tab positions and choosing column icons, as seen in Figure 6.13. On Windows, open up the Paragraph group (by clicking on the small arrow) and select Tabs in the lower left-hand corner.

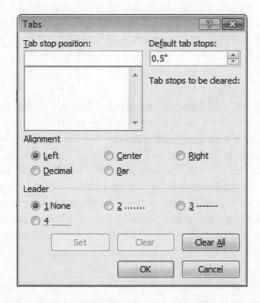

FIGURE 6.13 Window for Setting Tab Positions or Inserting Leaders

Table 6.7   Leaders

Chapter 1	1–10
Chapter 2	11–20
Chapter 3	21–30

Leaders **Leaders** appear as solid, dotted, or dashed lines that fill the space left by tabs; these are commonly used in tables of contents. Setting leaders is done through the tab window located under Format → Tabs, as seen in Figure 6.13. An example of a leader as it might appear in a table of contents is found in Table 6.7. Leaders are found under the Home tab once the Paragraph group is opened up by selecting Tabs from the lower left-hand corner.

Insertions

Many elements can be inserted into a document, especially in the more sophisticated programs. It is our intention to discuss the most basic of these, including page breaks, page numbers, and hyperlinks, and to encourage teachers to review packages to see what is offered in their program.

Page and Section Breaks **Page breaks** are inserted to move to the top of a new page without having to use the return key repeatedly to insert multiple lines. An example might be when you want to move from the title page to page 1 of the document. The option for inserting a page break is usually found beneath the Insert menu, Insert → Break → Page Break in Word 2008 and in Word 2007, go to Insert → Pages group → Page Break. Also, **section breaks** divide a document into different sections, done with Insert → Break → Section Break. Section breaks come in handy when a document needs different formatting in different sections. For instance, if a teacher or student wants to have some of a report in one column and a section in three columns, a good way to avoid problems with formatting is to insert a section break. On your PC, go to the Page Layout tab and in the Page Setup group, click Breaks. Select what style of break you would like to insert.

Page Numbers **Page numbers** are inserted into the document to assist the reader. Page numbers may be inserted in the header (at the top of the page) and aligned to the right or in the footer (at the bottom of the page) and aligned center or right. The option for insertion of page numbers is usually found beneath the Insert menu (Mac) or Insert tab (Windows), along with a setting for the position of the page number.

Headers and/or Footers A **header** or **footer** is located at the top or bottom of the document and is most commonly used for page numbers, a date, a file name, the author's name, or titles of papers. The option for insertion of headers and footers is usually found beneath the View → Header and Footer item. To insert a header, click View → Header and Footer to bring up the header option, as seen in Figure 6.14. In Word 2007, under the Insert tab, in the Header & Footer group, click Header or Footer and choose the design you want. The page number icon has been used to insert a page number in this header. Moving to the footer is easy, using the icons on this toolbar. In the footer in Figure 6.15, the author, page number, and title have been entered.

Hyperlinks Current word processors allow the insertion of **hyperlinks**, a jump to more information. Hyperlinks allow a simple click on text or a graphic to bring you a designated file or a page on the Internet.

The option for insertion of hyperlinks is usually found beneath the Insert menu. The text or picture is first selected followed by going to the Insert → Hyperlink com-

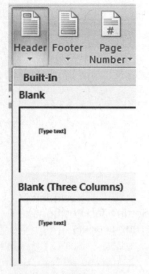

FIGURE 6.14 Header and Footer Window

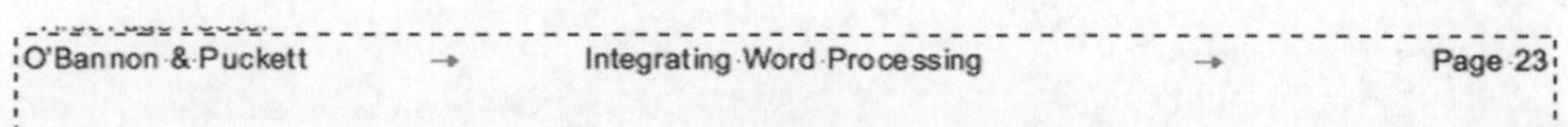

FIGURE 6.15 Footer with Author, Page Number, and Title

O'Bannon & Puckett → Integrating Word Processing → Page 23

mand. The program will then move into a coaching mode and explain what to do in a dialog window where the page location or the URL is linked. PC users will select the Insert tab and then the Hyperlink icon from the Links group.

Tables

Tables are designed with columns and rows and give the document an organized appearance. Usually there is a Table menu on the toolbar. To insert a table in Word, go to Table → Insert Table to bring up a window, similar to the one pictured in Figure 6.16, where the number of columns and rows are entered. In Word 2007, select the Insert tab, in the Tables group, click Table, and then click Insert Table. Then, under Table Size enter the number of columns and rows you wish your table to have.

Tools

A number of commands are found under the **Tools** menu, including the spell-checking feature and access to the thesaurus, dictionary, word count, and mail merge functions. Depending on the version of the word processing program that is being used, the commands will differ; however, the ones mentioned are basic to good productivity.

Spell Checking   The **spell-checking** feature allows the user to check the spelling in the document. The option for spell checking is usually found beneath the Tools or the Edit menu and can be used for checking the entire document, or specific paragraphs or words.

Thesaurus   Many word processors have a **thesaurus** feature that allows the user to find alternative words. The thesaurus is usually found beneath the Tools menu. The word is selected, the thesaurus feature applied, and the program suggests alternatives to the word.

Dictionary   Some word processors have a **dictionary** feature included that allows the user to request a definition for a particular word. The option, if included, is typically found under the Tools menu. The word is selected, the dictionary feature applied, and the program displays definitions for the word.

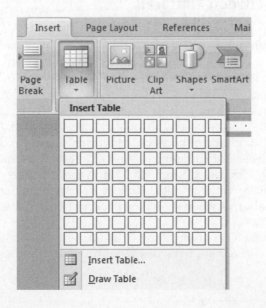

FIGURE 6.16 Insert Table Window

Word Count   Most word processors are equipped with the capability to count the words in a passage. Many times, there is a word limitation or goal for documents. In such cases, the **word count** feature is extremely helpful.

Merge Documents   **Merging** a word-processed document with addresses in a database allows the user to send a letter to multiple people using a simple process. This feature is handy for teachers when sending out letters to all parents throughout the year. A database with names and addresses must be completed for this feature to work. Specifics are found in Chapter 9.

More Formatting Capabilities

Styles   **Styles**, one of the most powerful features in a word processor, facilitate consistency in a document and can save teachers enormous amounts of time as they develop lesson plans, memos, worksheets, and other documents common to their daily routine. Styles, found under the Format menu in Word, instruct the computer to apply a certain format in specific areas of a document, such as the title, the headings, subheadings, body text, captions, and line spacing. A word processor defaults to particular settings in a document that have been set by the manufacturer until changed. Defining styles allows the user to set specific formatting characteristics that will apply to the entire document. Styles, which constitute an advanced technique, are particularly useful when writing long documents, to keep consistency in the various components such as the headings, subheadings, quotes, and captions. Word 2007 has several preformatted styles for your use on the main Home tab under the Styles group. Opening the full styles submenu (by clicking on the arrow in the lower right of the group) brings up each document level for styles allowing you to adjust your styles to suit your individualized needs.

Text Wrap   The **text wrap** feature allows the wrapping of text around a picture. The picture must be selected. The Format menu normally houses the commands for text wrapping. Select the picture or AutoShape option followed by the layout option to see the text wrap options that specify the direction in which the text will be formed around the picture. In Word 2007, when you select the picture, a new menu tab appears called Format. On this new menu tab, the Text Wrapping Icon appears on the Arranging group. Selecting this icon provides all the options needed to format text around an image.

Moving Files between Platforms

Moving files between Mac and Windows platforms is possible; however, it can be frustrating especially when trying to read documents that are created on a later version of software. This is particularly true when new system software is developed such as Windows Vista. Further, cross-platform hiccups occur with some software applications more than others. Current PC models can read a file created on a Mac and sent by email, FTP, or saved to a USB drive. USB drives are not platform-specific and can be used with all platforms. However, those who are new to switching back and forth between platforms should keep in mind that, although it is much easier than in the past, working on the same platform and OS version is probably the safest approach. Otherwise, teachers should note what platform and software version that the initial document is being created in and pay attention to platforms when switching back and forth between older and new versions of software.

In Voices from the Classroom, Amy Graham, a high school teacher, discusses the ways that she and her students use word processing in her foreign language classes.

Voices *from the* Classroom

Working Smarter with Word Processing

Amy Graham

Amy Graham, a French and German teacher for 15 years, serves as Team Leader of Foreign Language Department at Clinton High School in Tennessee. She is active in other roles, having served on the state textbook selection committee and as a state officer in American Association of German Teachers (AATG). She is now serving on her school's leadership team. In addition, she regularly organizes travel to Europe with her language students. This enthusiastic technology-using teacher holds an MA in Instructional Technology and an EdS in Leadership and Supervision. We asked her to share some ways that she integrates word processing in her classroom.

The many changes in the laws that govern education have increased the daily demands on classroom teachers. Does this mean that we have to work harder to be great teachers and to avoid increased legal liability? I don't think so. Rather, we need to work smarter by using technology to meet the multifaceted obligations we are charged with from day to day. I don't mean that we have to master complex programming languages or software packages, but rather use basic tools, like word processors, to their fullest potential and in unique ways. By doing this, we can improve learning and responsibility among our students. We can actually achieve more by doing less.

My many in-class daily operations are always facilitated by word processing. For example, if I wrote everything on the board it would take forever and would barely be legible. Typing the notes prior to class keeps me on track and helps my students know exactly what I have written. I know exactly what I have covered and what I have not. Students who are absent need only ask for the notes and they know what was covered in class and what they need to complete to catch up.

School systems are also requesting more work be done by teachers to equate program content in disciplines in order to implement and succeed at state mandated EOCs (end of course exams) and meet the ever-increasing demands of NCLB. Word processing within wikis facilitates collaboration in a more time-effective and cost-effective manner. Curriculum maps can be simultaneously created, updated, and edited on a class-by-class basis in a secure online environment regardless of schedules and time zones. EOCs can be developed and edited with everyone involved having an equal voice.

But I am not the only one who uses word processing—I require that my students use word processing to type reports, edit information found during research on the Web, type up their notes, and email attachments to themselves and to me. They do other things as well. For example, upon completion of our unit on the *Little Prince,* I divide the students into groups and assign each group specific chapters from the book. Their task is to make a study packet. The study packet includes: (1) a chapter summary, (2) a character list with descriptions, and (3) some activities to complete. These study packets must be typed with headings and page numbers. They use borders and tables, sort columns of information—and turn this in to me in an electronic format (on a disc, CD-ROM, or via email). I review the pages and make copies for the other groups after which each group reviews the material before the final test. Afterward, I have some GREAT activities for next year and since everything is available in electronic format, I can easily make slideshows, worksheets, games, and even the test using their materials. The students have a wonderful study tool, an awesome study session, as well as in-depth knowledge of MS Word.

Yet another way that my students use word processing is during the study of famous French people. The table function is used to create the format of the front page of a newspaper that the students develop into a newspaper concerning aspects of the famous French person they have chosen or been assigned. A timeline descends the left side with several sections including a headline and taglines teasing the reader to "read more on page 3." They modify the table properties and margins, insert images and bulleted lists, and experiment with various font styles and colors. When finished, I take these to a local print shop for printing and hang them in the hallway. Students also use the template to make Information cards, pocket reference cards, and trivia cards on Parisian monuments that can be used to play Trivial Pursuit on a game board which has been produced in MS Word with the graphics functions.

When students are working in groups, wikis are used for collaboration and allow group members to work on the project at home, in the library, or at a friend's house. Most wikis also allow added oversight on the part of the instructor as he or she can monitor all revisions and contributions made by all members ensuring all participate

(Continues)

appropriately. Students working individually on major research papers and projects can profit from periodic review and suggestions from advisors who can monitor progress and ensure more readily that problems are addressed promptly before they become insurmountable.

Word processing plays a big role in the success of students of all ability levels in my class. It aids students with injuries and various issues, which cause them to be absent for several days or to receive instruction from a homebound program for a period of time. It also aids those with more severe learning issues like ADD, dyslexia, and writing and visual barriers. Discussions on the history or the culture of the target language produce lengthy and tedious notes, which I am able to display as we progress through the discussion. But for students with ADD or dyslexia, I print out the notes for them; however, I leave out key terms and dates that they must complete during the discussion. Occasionally for a student with ADD, I simplify the statements so they are easier to study and less distracting, thereby aiding that student's comprehension and ability to study. Also, for students with dyslexia or other reading barriers, I often put individual spaces for the letters of the term or name. They know they are to pay particular attention to filling in each of the blanks and it helps to increase their accuracy. Or, I put a number in parentheses at the end of a blank indicating how many letters are in that particular term. Depending on the severity of the dyslexia, I have even replaced words with images from clip art. I have found that the pictures are easier for some students to study.

Word-processed documents also serve those students with writing barriers—either injuries sustained during the course of the term or an otherwise diagnosed writing disability. It always seems as though the student breaks the hand he/she writes with! Using word-processed notes or allowing students to type them up during class is a great way to keep them engaged and accountable when they could easily fall behind.

We all know there are only so many seats in the front of the class. For the student with visual barriers, the ability to sit anywhere, even in the mid- to rear section of the room with friends is a dream come true if the assignment or notes are reprinted in a larger or bolded font. This is a very simple solution that allows the student access to social partnerships as well as academic information.

Support is essential for all students to succeed. Emailing documents home or to special education coordinators is a simple way to keep all parties involved "in the loop" regarding student progress. All these files are saved on my computer so they are usable from year to year and easily edited to fit the needs of a new student. There is occasionally a learning curve for the students using the software, but most (95%) have used them before or have already completed their keyboarding class before they get to me. I just show them some of the more advanced functions.

I know many great, experienced teachers who feel forced out of education by fears of not being able to comply with IDEA and NCLB. While this might be a little more work in the beginning, in the long term it is a wonderful way to help ALL students and teachers to meet obligations in the classroom and to the school system as well as increase the potential for success for all involved.

Adapting for Special Learners

The word processor is perhaps the most adaptable piece of software for students with special learning needs. Adaptations fall into three categories. First, word processing software can be adapted to improve access to the program itself through the use of a few simple settings. Second, standard word processors can be used to adapt materials to enable student access to general curriculum content. Finally, specialized word processors have assistive features for use with a variety of student needs.

Adaptations That Improve Access to Word Processors

The default settings on word processing software/programs can be changed to accommodate visual and motor needs of many students. Familiarity with the

CURRICULUM CONNECTIONS

There are many ways that word processing tools can assist the teacher and the student in the classroom. Review Figures 6.1 and 6.2 to refresh your knowledge. Here, we share five specific lessons that provide connections to the curriculum using word processing.

A Powerful Web to Weave

CONTENT AREA/TOPIC: Writing Skills
GRADE LEVELS: 1, 2   **NETS·S:** 1, 6

Description: Digital pictures, webbing software, and word processing are used in the five-step process: (1) think, (2) draw, (3) tell, (4) write, (5) share—to assist children to learn to write. Three activities precede the writing activity.

Teacher preparation: At the beginning of school, the teacher takes digital pictures of each student. Because the children are young, the teacher creates a template for them with webbing software such as Inspiration or even a draw tool similar to the one in MS Word.

Active participation:

1. *Preparing to write:* Students are encouraged to think about what they will write about themselves, such as their favorite foods, games, sports, TV programs, or pets.

2. *Planning with webbing:* Students enter information about themselves in the template created by the teacher. Students can put pictures of themselves in the middle of the web.

3. *Writing:* Students use the information from the Web to compose summaries about themselves. The teacher and/or assistants enter the information in a word processor as the students dictate.

Variations: Any program that has text writing capabilities and is grade-level appropriate, such as KidPix Deluxe or HyperStudio 5, can be used.

Source: Etchinson, C. (1995). A powerful web to weave: Developing writing skills for elementary students. *Learning and Leading with Technology, 23*(3), pp. 14–15.

About Me Autobiography

CONTENT AREA/TOPIC: Writing Skills
GRADE LEVELS: 3, 4   **NETS·S:** 1, 6

Description: Digital pictures and word processing are used in this activity and may be used at the beginning of the year to introduce the students to each other.

Teacher preparation: The teacher develops a worksheet with questions that each student is to complete. Questions include such things as: (1) my name is . . . , (2) my family members are . . . , (3) my hobbies are . . . , (4) my favorite foods are . . . , (5) my favorite book is . . . , and so on.

Active participation: Students complete the worksheet with their personal information. They compile the information in rough draft form, which can be reviewed by the teacher before word processing the autobiography. They may add their picture or some graphics to their papers before reading them to the class. The bios could be put into a class book.

Variations: By using other people such as All About Our First President or All About George Washington, the lesson could be varied. A picture could be scanned rather than using the camera. This activity also could be used an as icebreaker for an older audience to present information about themselves to a class or as preparation for creating a web site.

Source: Kamali'i Elementary School. *All About Me.* Accessed October 13, 2008, from **www.kamalii.k12.hi.us/Claris/ke_plan1.htm**.

(Continues)

CURRICULUM CONNECTIONS *Continued*

Rock Star Trading Cards

CONTENT AREA/TOPIC: Science

GRADE LEVEL: 4   **NETS·S:** 3, 6

Description: Students use word processing software and the Web to research an assigned rock or mineral and create a trading card to pass out within the class.

Teacher preparation: The teacher (1) prepares a worksheet with the letters R O C K S written on it and divides the students into small groups; (2) collects, identifies, and labels rocks to use in the lesson.

Active participation:

1. The teacher distributes the worksheet and instructs students to write a sentence that corresponds with each letter and explains what they know about rocks. Then they share their descriptions within their group.
2. Following group sharing, a concept map is constructed with all students supplying ideas from their worksheets.

3. The teacher discusses sedimentary, igneous, and metaphoric rocks.
4. A rock is distributed to each group. Students use the Web to research their rock to determine which category it falls into. They then use the word processor to create a trading card with rock characteristics.
5. Trading cards are shared within the class to reinforce learning. To find out more about this lesson, visit the web site at http://its.guilford.k12.nc.us/act/grade4/act4.asp?ID=529.

Source: Carole Ashby Guilford Middle School. *Rock Star Trading Cards.* Accessed October 13, 2008, from http://its.guilford.k12.nc.us/act/grade4/act4.asp?ID=529.

The Nile

CONTENT AREA/TOPIC: World History

GRADE LEVELS: 6–8   **NETS·S:** 1, 3, 6

Description: Students use word processing software and the Web to research the important part that the Nile River played in ancient Egypt and the way that people lived at that time. They create a newspaper that depicts information from the research.

Teacher preparation: The teacher locates and bookmarks web sites for students to use during the research activity. Students are divided into groups to serve different staffing needs, such as managing editors, and researchers of agriculture, zoology, weather, art, editorial, and advertising.

Active participation:

1. The class works together to produce a newspaper that could have been published in ancient Egypt.

2. The teacher assigns small groups of students to different beats and services, including the ones listed in the preparation.
3. Go over the elements of a news story, including the five Ws (what, why, when, where, and who).
4. Students complete research and write a news story with their findings for the newspaper. To find out more about this lesson, visit the web site at http://school.discoveryeducation.com/lessonplans/programs/nile/.

Source: Wendy Goldfein, upper elementary school teacher, Fairfax County Schools, Virginia, and freelance educational consultant. Accessed October 15, 2008, at http://school.discoveryeducation.com/lessonplans/programs/nile/.

CURRICULUM CONNECTIONS *Continued*

The Digestive System

CONTENT AREA/TOPIC: Health

GRADE LEVELS: 9–12   **NETS·S:** 1, 3, 6

Description: Students use word processing software and the Web to research one common problem of the digestive system and create a brochure that describes the problem, symptoms, and treatment.

Teacher preparation: The teacher locates and bookmarks web sites for students to use during the research activity. Students are divided into groups to complete research on a digestive problem.

Active participation:

1. The teacher reviews the major organs of the digestive system and the function of each, including the esophagus, stomach, small intestine, large intestine, and colon. There is a good overview at **http://school.discoveryeducation. com/lessonplans/programs/digestion/**.
2. The teacher assigns small groups of students to complete research projects on common ailments, such as nausea, diarrhea, constipation, acid indigestion, ulcer, lactose intolerance, or colon cancer.
3. Students determine a title for their brochures and target a specific audience such as children, teens, or adults. They use word processing software to develop the brochure based on their research.
4. Brochures are shared with the class.

To find out more about this lesson, visit the web site at **http://school.discoveryeducation.com/lessonplans/ programs/digestion/**.

Assessment: Rubric.

Source: Joy Brewster, freelance education writer, editor, and consultant. Accessed October 15, 2008, from **http://school .discoveryeducation.com/lessonplans/programs/digestion/**.

following features will enhance the usability of word processing and may reduce the need for more expensive specialized programs.

Zoom Option

The zoom box displays choices to increase the size of the screen display of text without increasing the font size of the printed text. This feature is especially useful for students with limited visual acuity, and for teachers faced with the challenges of age-onset eyestrain. The zoom option is typically located on the Toolbar and/or in the View menu. Although this feature makes reading text on the screen more comfortable, it may not be enough magnification. A separate magnification program may be needed for students with more involved acuity issues (see Chapter 3). Be aware that a larger printed font size and a more easy-to-read font may also be needed for some students. Refer to formatting options listed previously for more information.

Text Color and Background Color

Color of text and the background of the document may be changed from the default setting of black text on a white background. This feature is useful for students who need greater contrast between foreground and background. Some of the more typical high-contrast settings are black text on yellow background, or the inverse. Dark blue and gray are two contrasting colors that are also easier to read. Work with an individual student to determine the most comfortable setting for that student. These settings may be changed in the Format menu; look for these options under Text and under Background.

Speech Recognition

Speech recognition features are included in the newer versions of major word processing programs. This feature is designed to support dictation of words or numbers, thus bypassing keyboard input. In order to use speech recognition, the student must first configure the microphone and train the program to recognize the subtleties of a particular voice by reading prepared text from the setup screen. The program has procedures for distinguishing between text entry and other commands, such as formatting characters, starting a new paragraph, or saving. Speech recognition may serve as a motivator for students with written language difficulties. It can also assist students with labored keyboarding abilities, or people who experience pain while typing. This feature has its limitations, however. Students who must use speech recognition as the only method of input will be better served with more powerful programs, such as Dragon NaturallySpeaking or Via Voice, which work with word processors to input text.

On-screen Keyboards, Writing Pads, and Handwriting Recognition

Newer versions of word processing software have features that support a writing pad for text input. In these formats, the word processor recognizes handwritten text and converts it to a digital format. On-screen keyboards may also be displayed for text correction or for convenience. The use of these devices with students with disabilities has not yet been reviewed in the field's literature, but its potential use for students with written language, motor, or cognitive issues is promising.

Adaptations Using Word Processors That Allow Access to the General Curriculum

Word processing programs also have a number of features that can be adapted for student support. These strategies can be used as a form of assistive technology when teaching basic skills and when accessing general curriculum standards.

Student-Controlled Tools

Spelling and Grammar Checking Spelling and grammar checking features may be turned on (the default) or off in the options section of most word processing programs. When these features are activated (turned on), the student can scan the text for the automatic telltale notices: in MS Word, a red underline for a misspelled word, and a green underline for words, phrases, or punctuation marks that do not conform to standard grammar rules. Right-clicking either notice produces a dialog box suggesting the corrections, and, in the case of grammar notices, explains the rule and suggests options. Students may be encouraged to use these features in several ways, as they type or compose their work, during the editing process, and during a final revision.

When the automatic spelling and grammar checking options are turned off, the teacher may use the word processing program for assessment. Students may then use word processing to take a spelling test, to compose answers to essay questions, or in other forms of writing assessment in which access to spelling, grammar, or thesaurus aids would prevent the measurement of a targeted skill (Council for Exceptional Children, 2000).

Auto Summary Many students with special needs have reading levels far below the level of difficulty of text-based material used by their peers. The text may be too long or too complex. The Auto Summary tool analyzes a document and produces a summary of the main points. For some students, this summary simplifies the reading process and allows choices in the amount of detail presented. This feature gives the user control over the length of the summary in terms of percent of the original. It also gives choices of a format for viewing the summary, such as highlight key points, produce an abstract, create a new document, or hide the original and show only the summary. Auto Summary works best with selection from structured formats, such as textbooks and reports. Results from other forms of literature, such as novels, are less impressive. Auto Summary is activated by customizing the word options feature in the Microsoft Office Button (MS Word 2007). It may also be found in the tools menu in earlier versions (MS Word 1997–2004).

The only drawback to this feature is the difficulty in obtaining a digital version of the text. Much information and many sources of literature are already available in digital format on the Internet (see, for example, Project Gutenberg, **www.gutenberg.net**).

Digital versions of textbooks will become increasingly available for K–12 schools as publishers implement IDEA 2004 requirements for providing accessible text. Until this regulation is fully implemented, scanning into an OCR program or typing the selection into a document are options for print-based sources. Edyburn (2002) proposed the Auto Summary tool as a meta-cognitive strategy that students can be taught to use, evaluating their own need for amount of information within their learning abilities.

Designing Differentiated or UDL Instructional Materials

Readability Statistics   One strategy for selecting reading material that is appropriate for student performance levels is to check the readability level of the text. Readability formulas (Fry, 1977) require the teacher to count the number of sentences and difficult words and apply these values to an equation or points on a chart. Word processors automate this task for the teacher. Obtain a sample of the text in digital format, either by scanning using an OCR program or by typing a sample selection into a document. Activate the word options, proofing tools, select *check grammar with spelling* and *show readability statistics.* Two readability scores are provided. The Flesch Reading Ease test yields a score along a 100-point scale, with higher numbers indicating greater ease of understanding. The Flesch-Kincaid Grade Level rates the text on U.S. school grade level. Both formulas use average sentence length and average number of syllables per word in the calculations. For older versions of Microsoft Word (1997–2004), these features are accessed in the Tools menu.

Document Templates   Students with physical challenges, written language problems, low cognitive skills, or visual impairments may have great difficulty composing written material. Whether the challenge is one of thinking, motor skills, or perception, the challenge for the teacher is to structure a task that will allow the student to express knowledge without hindrance. When the learning task involves communicating summaries or results, consider devising a template to use as a guide. Make generic statements in the document, with spaces or blanks for the student to add specific information; for instance, in a lab report, "When _____ is added, the following reaction occurs." Save the document as a template, with a descriptive name (such as Chemical_reaction_lab_report). When the document is reopened and resaved by a student, the student will be prompted to provide the Save As name (such as Jones_acid_lab_report), leaving the original template document intact. The document template process is used by a number of professionals who must supply specific information within a standard format, such as legal documents, psychological reports, and medical reports. One word of caution when creating templates: MS Word will default to a "templates folder" within the program itself when these documents are saved. Save instead to a documents folder, especially when working on multiple computers.

You or your students can insert comments to define unfamiliar words, perhaps using an online dictionary or thesaurus

FIGURE 6.17 A Comment with a Wave Sound Object Inserted

Literacy Support   Word processing tools can be used to provide a number of literacy supports in documents. Tech Learning (n.d.) has provided an Educators' eZine that reviews the following possibilities.

Comments   Comments are found in the Reviewing tab, Comments group (MS Word 2007), or the Insert menu (MS Word 1997–2004 and 2008). Comments can be used to:

- Define unfamiliar words, perhaps using an online dictionary or thesaurus.
- Provide instructions or other instructional information.
- Provide organizational guidance, by inserting them into an outline to describe what is to be included in each section, with further links to a checklist or rubric.
- Highlight phrases or sections that need changing, providing guidance or comment.
- Provide an organized procedure for peer editing.

A sound recording can be inserted into a comment to provide reading or pronunciation support. Comments may be hidden or shown (Review → Tracking → Show markup) as needed, adding to the UDL features of the text and providing differentiation of instruction. See the example in Figure 6.17 (Lake, 2004).

Forms   The Forms feature can be accessed from the Microsoft Office → Word options → Popular → Show developer tab in the ribbon (MS Word 2007). In earlier versions, this feature is located under View → Toolbars → Forms. Consider using forms for the following:

- Text fields for fill-in-the-blank activities. Set the area to expand to allow as much text as necessary, or control the number of characters that can be typed.
- Check boxes for true/false or yes/no statements.
- Drop-down menu items for choices of answers. (Lake, 2004b)

Highlighting   Accessed from the toolbar or the home tab ribbon (MS Word 2007), the highlight feature can be used to call attention to vocabulary words, headings, and other important features of a document.

Hyperlinks   Consider using hyperlinks to link to definitions or other supporting material. Hyperlinks can be set to link within a document, to another document, or to Internet sources.

Sound   A sound file can be added to the document, accessed from the Insert tab → Text → Object → Wave sound. Teachers may record short sound files to provide reading or pronunciation support; students may use this feature to record answers in the document (Lake, 2004b).

Specialized Word Processors

The specialized word processor features reviewed here are not currently available in typical office suite applications, or are specially designed for use with younger children.

Text-to-Speech Word Processors

Text-to-speech, TTS, or "talking word processor" software offers the choice to read the text displayed within the document. Simple programs merely read the selected text. More sophisticated text-to-speech programs highlight text as it is read by chosen combination: letter-by-letter, or by word, sentence, or selection. Text-to-speech programs support reading, writing, and spelling for emerging struggling readers.

IntelliTalk (IntelliTools, Inc.) is a TTS program with built-in multimedia capabilities. The program includes examples of templates and activities that can be easily modified for any subject area, enabling teachers to develop a variety of instructional supports. Pictures can be attached to specific words, in effect creating a "rebus" system for early writers to express their ideas. IntelliTalk can be used alone or integrated with other multimedia authoring programs in the software package Classroom Suite. These products also integrate easily with switches and other alternate input devices, making them ideal for use with students with physical access barriers. Specific product features include text-to-speech spell-checking capabilities, a large picture library, and a choice of simple word processor picture commands for younger students.

Write:Outloud (Don Johnston, Inc.) is a TTS program that mimics a standard word processor. This product can be used alone or integrated with visual learning, word prediction, and text reading programs in a package called SOLO. Write:Outloud includes the Franklin spell checker and dictionary for grades 3–12, a homonym checker, and a test mode that the teacher can use to restrict access to features that may not be allowed in state assessment situations. It also has a data collection useful for student progress monitoring: word count, average word length, average sentence length, sequential word count, and number of low-frequency words.

Word Prediction

Word prediction, reviewed in Chapter 3, presents the user with possible choices that can be inserted into a word processing document with one keystroke or mouse click. IntelliTalk (IntelliTools, Inc.) is an example of a word processing program with built-in word prediction features. Co:Writer (Don Johnston, Inc.) and Read & Write GOLD (Text Help, Inc.) are programs that work with other word processors to provide word prediction and other text support. Kurzweil 3000 (Kurzweil Educational Systems, Inc.), an electronic reading and study program, also has built-in word processing features with word prediction support.

Rebus-Based Word Processor

A *rebus* is a picture or symbol that is used in place of or to describe a written word. Rebus-enhanced reading programs are sometimes an effective learning strategy for emerging readers or for students with severe reading difficulties. Rebus-based word processors allow the insertion of a picture above an individual word. Most have picture dictionaries of several thousand words and include speech synthesis features. Once a digital version of the text is obtained, it can be copied into this word processor and converted to picture-enhanced text. Rebus-based word processors are recommended as an adaptation to assist struggling readers to independently access classroom-based material (Edyburn, 2002). Two widely used rebus-based word processors are Picture It (Slater Software) and Writing with Symbols (Mayer-Johnson).

Speech Recognition

Speech recognition features and programs were reviewed elsewhere in this text (see the previous section and Chapter 3). The need for a speech recognition program in lieu of the features provided by system and word processing tools may be indicated for students for whom speech is the primary means of input. Dragon NaturallySpeaking, Via Voice, or MacSpeak are available in versions with higher degrees of accuracy, or in versions that accept specialized vocabulary.

Portable Word Processors

Often, the problem experienced by teachers is not how to adapt word processors for student use; instead, it is one of getting enough access to word processors for all students to use effectively. Portable word processors/keyboards can be an effective solution to the lack of adequate computers for word processing instruction and use. Text that is displayed on a small screen can be saved and sent to a printer or transferred to a computer-based word processor for further formatting. Portable word processors/keyboards are low in cost, battery-operated, lightweight, and durable. We have listed some portable word processors in the On the Web section of this chapter and offer quick links at the companion site.

On the Web

This section includes only a snapshot of web sites that the authors recommend for viewing. To access live links and a larger and continuously updated collection of sites, go to the companion web site at **www.pearsonhighered.com/obannon2e.**

Assistive Technology Products

Dragon Naturally Speaking

www.nuance.com/naturallyspeaking/
Nuance, formally ScanSoft, a leading provider of speed and imaging solutions, describes speech recognition software products that work with any open word processor application. Dragon Naturally Speaking now offers recorded speech into text from pocket PCs, Palm Tungsten, and Tablet PC or digital recording devices for PC users while ViaVoice may be used with Mac or Windows.

Intellitalk

www.synapse-ada.com/intellitools/new/IntelliTalk_3.htm
Intellitalk is a word processor with speech synthesis, word prediction, template capabilities, and an extensive picture library suitable for elementary and middle school use. No longer available as a stand-alone product, Intellitalk must be purchased as a part of the Classroom Suite. This site describes Intellitalk and other companion software.

Kurzweil 3000

www.kurzweiledu.com
Developed as a scan and read program to convert printed text to a digitized format, this product also features word processing capabilities with word prediction, dictionary and thesaurus, word translation, speech synthesis, and a sophisticated array of study skills supports to increase learner independence.

Portable Word Processors

Perfect Solutions, Inc.

www.perfectsolutions.com
This vendor offers the Laser PC, a portable word processor with TTS capabilities. Also at this site is a link to the Student Mate, an affordable portable laptop.

Renaissance Learning, Inc.

www.renlearn.com/neo/
Renaissance Learning offers a choice of portable keyboard products. AlphaSmart was purchased by Renaissance in 2005 and these familiar tools for schools are found here. Options include infrared transfer of files, scheduling that is used in schools programs, and wireless Internet access. The Neo and Dana are models that are used extensively in schools.

Software Options—Word Processing

Currently word processing software is offered from commercial sources for a fee, downloaded free from open source groups and as Web-based programs. While we have included a few in each group here, more are found at the companion site at www.pearsonhighered.com/obannon2e.

iWork

www.apple.com/iwork/
Apple offers iWork '09, an exciting software suite that includes a "streamlined" word processor, a slideshow tool and a spreadsheet tool. Pages, the word processing software in this package, is capable of creating many types of documents with ease. Check out iWork '09 for Mac OS X and its ability to give teachers and students options of creating media-rich documents.

Kid Works by Knowledge Adventure

Kid Works Deluxe is designed as a writing tool for PK–4 to build writing, reading and creativity skills. This writing/multimedia tool combines a word processor and paint program to expand student reading and writing skills. Kid Works provides story starters that spark ideas for young students as they create stories, books, and other ideas using the many media elements provided.

Microsoft Office

www.microsoft.com/education/products/overview
.aspx#buildingblocks
Microsoft offers their products for education at this page. There are instructional resources in the form of tutorials, lesson plans and how-to articles. 2007 Office system and 2008 Office for Mac can be accessed from this page.

Open Source Word Processing Programs

OpenOffice.org

www.openoffice.org
OpenOffice.org is a multiplatform and multilingual office suite that offers free downloads from this web site and has a word processing feature. Read about this option and talk with your technology coordinator about the option of using

it with your students. Support is the big drawback to open source. But read about this option for use with your students.

Web-Based Word Processing Programs

Adobe Buzzword

www.adobe.com/acom/buzzword/

Buzzword is a free word processing program offered by Adobe and offers improved formatting. Adobe seems to have overcome some of the issues with earlier programs in getting the screen view to print the way it appears on the screen.

Google Docs

www.google.com

Google offers a word processing program as a part of Google Documents. This program, as with all Web-based options, offers the ability to edit anytime and from anywhere as long as browser software and an Internet connection is provided.

Files can be uploaded, shared, and safely stored on online servers. And best of all, it's free!

Thinkfree

http://member.thinkfree.com/member/goLandingPage
.action

Think Free Office offers a Web-based word processor as well as other programs that are are compatible with MS Office counterparts and are free. Getting an account here allows one gigabyte of free online storage.

Zoho.com

www.zoho.com

Zoho offers a host of programs that are Web-based and free if you have an account. Zoho Writer is an online word processor. This is fully compatible with MS Office counterparts and promote digital literacy and collaboration.

Key Terms

Word processing program (130)
Word processing (131)
Stand-alone program (131)
Integrated software program (131)
Software suites (131)
File (133)
I-beam (cursor) (133)
Word wrap (133)
Editing of text (133)
Deleting text (133)
Find and replace (133)
Edit (133)
Saving text (133)
Print (133)
Print Preview (133)
Formatting (133)
Default settings (133)
Orientation (133)
Margins (134)

Alignment of text/justification of text
  (right, left, centered, or justified)
  (134)
Indentations (first line, hanging,
  block) (134, 135)
Line spacing (single, double, 1.5) (135)
Font (135)
Typeface (136)
Families (serif, sans serif, monospace,
  script, Blackletter/Old English,
  decorative) (136)
Monospaced (137)
Proportionate (137)
Type size (137)
Type case (137)
Emphasis (137)
Special effects (137)
Lists (numbered, bulleted) (138)
Columns (138)

Tab settings (138)
Leaders (139)
Page break (140)
Section break (140)
Page number (140)
Header (140)
Footer (140)
Hyperlink (140)
Table (141)
Tools (141)
Spell checking (141)
Thesaurus (141)
Dictionary (141)
Word count (142)
Merging (142)
Style (142)
Text wrap (142)

Hands-on Activities for Learning

1. Visit the On the Web companion site (**www.pearson highered.com/obannon2e**) and review the sites available.
2. Post a reflection in your technology blog about how you intend to integrate word processing into the grade/subject of your target certification.
3. Re-create one of the lessons listed in the Curriculum Connections section of this chapter in the classroom. During this re-creation, note lessons learned and discuss with classmates.
4. Create a student-centered activity or lesson plan for students in your target certification that uses using word processing as a tool for learning. Align this activity or lesson

with state curriculum standards, NETS·S, and include adaptations for special learners.
5. Insert the activity in your curriculum folder for use at a later time; post at your web site or in your e-portfolio.
6. Use a word processing program that is new to you, preferably a Web-based or open source solution. Discuss, with your peers, the pros and cons of using these software solutions.

Chapter 7 Digital Images

LEARNER OBJECTIVES

At the completion of this chapter, learners will be able to:

- Discuss research related to the effective use of images in teaching and learning.
- Use terminology associated with digital images and their use.
- Acquire digital images using a digital camera, scanner, CD/DVD collection, the Web, and by taking screenshots.
- Examine lesson plans that incorporate digital images into teaching and learning.
- Develop student-centered activities that use digital images in learning.
- Plan and develop lessons that align with state curriculum standards, NETS·S, and require students to use digital images to promote their learning.
- Determine ethical and legal uses of digital images and files in an electronic environment.
- Examine methods for adapting and using digital materials with special learners.

NETS·T ALIGNED WITH DIGITAL IMAGES

1. **Facilitate and Inspire Student Learning and Creativity**

   Teachers use their knowledge of subject matter, teaching and learning, and technology to facilitate experiences that advance student learning, creativity, and innovation in both face-to-face and virtual environments. Teachers:

   a. promote, support, and model creative and innovative thinking and inventiveness.

   b. engage students in exploring real-world issues and solving authentic problems using digital tools and resources.

   c. promote student reflection using collaborative tools to reveal and clarify students' conceptual understanding and thinking, planning, and creative processes.

   d. model collaborative knowledge construction by engaging in learning with students, colleagues, and others in face-to-face and virtual environments.

2. **Design and Develop Digital-Age Learning Experiences and Assessments**

   Teachers design, develop, and evaluate authentic learning experiences and assessments incorporating contemporary tools and resources to maximize content learning in context and to develop the knowledge, skills, and attitudes identified in the NETS·S. Teachers:

   a. design or adapt relevant learning experiences that incorporate digital tools and resources to promote student learning and creativity.

   b. develop technology-enriched learning environments that enable all students to pursue their individual curiosities and become active participants in setting their own educational goals, managing their own learning, and assessing their own progress.

   c. customize and personalize learning activities to address students' diverse learning styles, working strategies, and abilities using digital tools and resources.

   d. provide students with multiple and varied formative and summative assessments aligned with content and technology standards and use resulting data to inform learning and teaching.

3. **Model Digital-Age Work and Learning**

   Teachers exhibit knowledge, skills, and work processes representative of an innovative professional in a global and digital society.

Teachers:

a. demonstrate fluency in technology systems and the transfer of current knowledge to new technologies and situations.

b. collaborate with students, peers, parents, and community members using digital tools and resources to support student success and innovation.

c. communicate relevant information and ideas effectively to students, parents, and peers using a variety of digital-age media and formats.

d. model and facilitate effective use of current and emerging digital tools to locate, analyze, evaluate, and use information resources to support research and learning.

4. **Promote and Model Digital Citizenship and Responsibility**

   Teachers understand local and global societal issues and responsibilities in an evolving digital culture and exhibit legal and ethical behavior in their professional practices. Teachers:

a. advocate, model, and teach safe, legal, and ethical uses of digital information and technology, including respect for copyright, intellectual property, and the appropriate documentation of sources.

b. address the diverse needs of all learners by using learner-centered strategies and providing equitable access to appropriate digital tools and resources.

c. promote and model digital etiquette and responsible social interactions related to the use of technology and information.

d. develop and model cultural understanding and global awareness by engaging with colleagues and students of other cultures using digital-age communication and collaboration tools.

Frameworks

Substantial research is dedicated to the use of pictures (illustrations) and their effect on learning, for both static pictures as well as animated (moving) pictures. This chapter is devoted to static pictures and illustrations. Static pictures are those that show no movement in contrast to animated pictures. Teachers are encouraged to use this information as a framework to guide their design of instructional materials that will be used by their students.

Clearly, the *effectiveness of pictures* used in instructional materials should be a major consideration, as well as the instructional function that they serve. There is general agreement among researchers that pictures or illustrations, if related to the text, can assist learners in understanding text-based instructional materials. In an exhaustive review covering the effects of illustrated text on learning, Levie and Lentz (1982) concluded that learning is enhanced when a picture (illustration) describes the accompanying text information. Peeck (1987) added that this is particularly true when the text is describing spatial relationships. Nonetheless, he stresses that inserting a picture into instructional materials is not always effective, because the reader may fail to see its purpose.

Other researchers (Dean & Kulhavy, 1981; Winn & Holiday, 1982) suggest that photos or illustrations that require learner interaction or further study are the most beneficial in instructional materials. Consequently, teachers should consider using pictures or diagrams that require learner interaction, such as labeling parts or answering questions related to the picture. All of this information concludes that inserting a picture does not necessarily function to assist learning.

Various researchers have offered frameworks identifying the functions that pictures can serve in learning; however, Anglin, Vaez, and Cunningham (2004)

TECH TIP

The effectiveness of a picture depends on its purpose and relation to the text.

TECH TIP

Pictures should always be related to the text.

suggest that the one provided by Levin (1981) has proven useful. In this framework, Levin identifies five primary learning functions that pictures can serve in instructional materials: (1) decoration, (2) representation, (3) organization, (4) interpretation, and (5) transformation. He cautions that the five functions do not each influence learning to the same degree. According to his framework, pictures or illustrations that are used for **decoration** usually have no direct relationship to the text, but serve to break up the text and make it more appealing to the reader. Pictures for **representation** purposes give the reader a more concrete understanding of the text, as they represent objects or activities described in the text. An example might be a picture showing the alignment of stars in different constellations in an explanation of astronomy. Pictures used for **organization** purposes give the text more structure when accompanying a step-by-step or how-to explanation, and are very helpful in providing a framework for a procedure. Pictures used for **interpretation** purposes provide the reader assistance in understanding or interpreting abstract or difficult information. Finally, pictures used for **transformation** purposes aid the reader in transforming or "recoding" the text information by viewing the pictures from the application of mnemonic (devices for memorization) forms.

Including pictures or illustrations in instructional materials greatly enhances learning opportunities for students with special needs. Images are processed by the mind differently than text. Because they present everything at once, rather than in the sequence presented by text, images allow students to examine and learn using their preferred learning style. Using digital pictures provides options for presentation and student expression, which are basic principles for planning universally designed instruction (Rose & Meyer, 2002).

Research offers multiple examples of using digital images to improve the learning outcomes of students with special needs. Short video clips or still images set up authentic problem-based scenarios in a method called **anchored instruction** (Cognition and Technology Group, 1990). These digital anchors have been used effectively in math, literature, vocabulary development, science, and social studies in inclusion-based classrooms (Rieth, Bryant, & Kinzer, 2003; Bottge, Heinrichs, & Chan, 2003). Pictures illustrate social stories for students with autism spectrum disorder or other disabilities for whom explicit teaching in social skills is necessary (Agosta, Graetz, Mastropieri, & Scruggs, 2004). Pictures have also been shown to increase understanding of vocabulary for students with learning disabilities (Slater, 2002).

Three factors should be considered when considering the inclusion of pictures in instructional materials (Morrison, Ross, & Kemp, 2007). The first consideration, **enhancement of learning**, is the most important. Once determination has been made that pictures will indeed enhance learning, their **availability** should be considered. Pictures may be obtained as original art, clip art, and photographs for inclusion in instructional materials. Obtaining digital images, discussed at length in the Basics section of this chapter, should comply with legal and ethical considerations. The third consideration is the **cost of reproduction**. Reproducing instructional materials that contain pictures should be within the available budget. Pictures that are viewed in an electronic format may have little associated cost, yet they depend on the availability of technology resources, such as a computer, software, and a projection system. In contrast, pictures reproduced for print may be quite costly, especially if color is involved.

The following section introduces the basics of obtaining and using digital resources and presents various methods for teachers and students to use these resources for classroom use. In addition, five methods of obtaining digital images are examined, with information that is fundamental to each. Although the majority of the discussion is devoted to digital images, converting materials to digital format is briefly covered. Further suggestions for using digital text are presented in the Adapting for Special Learners section.

Basics

TECH TIP

Pictures in instructional materials enhance learning for students with special needs.

In order to use pictures in computer-based materials, they must be in digital format. There are multiple advantages to digital images, including instantaneous feedback, ease of distribution, ease of editing, and time and money savings—after the initial setup costs of securing the technology resources.

Digital images are quite easy to insert into word-processed documents, slideshows, web sites, email messages, blogs, wikis, and so on. The ease of use and advantages for instruction has made digital imagery a technique popular in classrooms. Some documented ways that teachers incorporate digital images in instructional activities include the design of instructional materials and slideshows, virtual tours and field trips, community mapping projects, sequencing books, email to parents, prompts for writing activities, digital stories, teacher web pages, and teacher *portfolios.* Web 2.0 applications have created more ways to use digital images including inserting in blogs, wikis, and online photo management and sharing applications. Figure 7.1 outlines uses of digital images throughout the teaching–learning process in the areas of productivity, instructional design, communication, and portfolios.

One of the most important ways for teachers to use digital images is to *develop lessons that require their students to take an active role in using digital images to support their learning.* Popular ways for students to incorporate digital images include creating curriculum-related, class, or school newspapers; publicizing a class event or project; writing reports; creating slideshow presentations; creating digital stories, writing letters to ePALS and others; completing scavenger hunts; and developing collaborative books and wikis, web pages, blogs, online photo sharing, and student portfolios (see Figure 7.2). The ways for students to use digital images in learning are limited only by the teacher's imagination. Review additional ideas

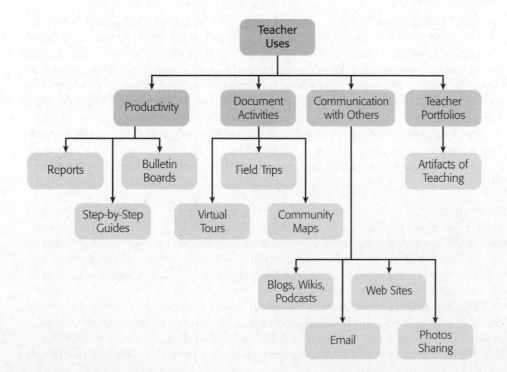

FIGURE 7.1 Teacher Uses of Digital Images

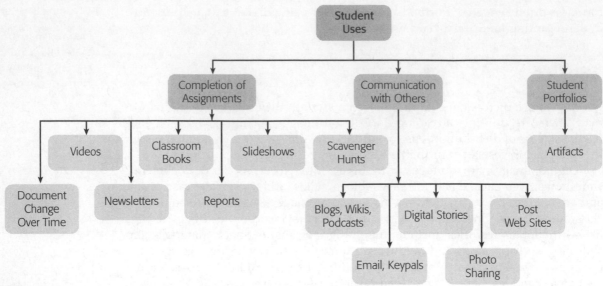

FIGURE 7.2 Student Uses of Digital Images

provided in the On the Web section. Additionally, see the Voices from the Classroom section on page 173 for a teacher's account of how students use digital images to enhance learning.

As teachers incorporate the use of digital images in student learning activities, it becomes necessary for them, as well as for their students, to understand and use basic concepts and terms associated with digital images and their use. We begin as we discuss the structure of a digital image and how resolution plays a part in the digital world, as well as ways to obtain digital images and their legal and ethical uses.

TECH TIP

High resolution images are not needed for electronic output!

Digital Images

A **digital image** is made up of a grid of many tiny squares called **pixels**, short for "picture elements." Each pixel represents a tiny portion of the image as a tonal value (black, white, shades of grey, or color) that defines the image's appearance when viewed with other pixels. An analogy of the structure of a digital image can be made with a tile mosaic, as shown on the left. Each tiny piece of tile in the mosaic, when viewed alone, is quite insignificant; yet, when viewed together, they form a picture. A digital image may consist of thousands or even millions of pixels and is measured by pixel count, the number of pixels that make up the image. The resulting exact physical size is dictated by the monitor or printer resolution, but generally, the more pixels, the larger the image resolution is and the bigger the picture.

Resolution

Understanding **resolution** is fundamental to working with digital images. However, resolution can confuse new learners, because it is measured differently on different output devices such as digital cameras, computer monitors, and printers, which ultimately factor into the way that an image looks electronically on a monitor or in print.

Digital camera resolution is the **pixel count** (maximum number of pixels) that a digital camera can capture in an individual image. This number relies on the potential of the specific camera that is being used and is explained more fully in the digital camera discussion later in this chapter. **Computer monitor resolution**

A digital image is like a tile mosaic, which is made up of many pieces.

is limited to 72 to 96 pixels per linear inch (ppi). High pixel count images are not required for an image to be viewed electronically. In other words, taking a picture at very high resolution is not a good idea if the picture is to be used only for output on computers. A high pixel count image results in a very large image that takes a long time to download and display on a computer monitor.

In contrast, the resolution for images that will ultimately be used in a print environment, such as this book, must be much higher for a quality outcome, and rely on the resolution of the printer that is being used. **Printer resolution** is measured in **dots per inch (dpi)**. The dpi measures the dots of ink per square inch vertically and horizontally. At the printing of this book, printer resolutions range from 300 dpi to 2,400 dpi; however, it is not necessary to use a printer with the highest resolution to get good quality printing. The higher the dpi of the printer, the smaller the dot that is used to make the image. As with digital cameras, the prices of printers are down and the quality is up. A printer that will print at least 300 dpi (300 dots per inch horizontally and vertically) is recommended for general purpose text and graphics; higher quality results with text and graphics require at least 600 dpi, which is considered photo quality. Printers with the highest resolutions are generally designed for professional use. A more detailed explanation is provided online at the Imaging Resource (**www.imaging-resource.com/ARTS/ GSPRINT/GSPRINT.HTM**).

Ways to Obtain Digital Images

Digital images can be obtained by (1) creating original pictures with a digital camera; (2) scanning a photograph, artwork, or text document to create a digital file; (3) copying an image from digital image collections available on CD or DVD; or (4) downloading an image from the Web, and (5) taking a screenshot. The following discussion examines these methods and the pros and cons of each.

The most popular way to create digital images, and avoid issues with copyright, is with a digital camera. Original photos may be taken using digital cameras to provide pictures for specific needs of teachers and students, such as classroom projects, document field trips, or objects of study.

Digital Cameras

Digital cameras are much like traditional film cameras, with essentially the same camera parts and features. The major difference is the way that the camera records and stores images. In a film camera, light passes through the lens and the image is recorded and stored on film. The film, in turn, is processed with little idea of the picture quality until after the film is processed. In a digital camera, light passes through the lens and records the photo on a computer chip called an **image sensor**. The image is stored in **memory** within the camera or on a removable memory device. Unlike with a traditional camera, digital cameras provide the user immediate previews of the image, and allow the user to review, delete, and/or retake the photo.

In a digital camera, resolution refers to the maximum pixel count that the camera can capture and may be expressed in terms of the image dimensions (640 × 480) or as **megapixels (MP)**—1 MP equals one million pixels. In other words, a 2 MP digital camera can capture images up to two million pixels. It is important to consider the MP rating of the camera, as this determines how large a photo can be when printed, as well as the cost of the camera. Most casual users will get a fine result with a 2 MP to 3 MP camera. At the time of the printing of this book, digital cameras range from a resolution of less than 1 MP to 14 MP and higher; however, the higher MP cameras are for professional use and are not needed for the

Table 7.1 **Camera Resolution Translates to Print Size**

Resolution	Size in Print
1 MP	5 × 7 inches
2 MP	8 × 10 inches
4 MP	11 × 14 inches
5–6 MP	16 × 20 inches
8 MP	20 × 30 inches
10 MP	Poster size

classroom. Table 7.1 lists the digital camera resolution needed to print high-quality images at various sizes.

Digital cameras are designed to meet the varying experiences and budget needs of users. Basically, digital cameras are categorized and marketed based on available resolution and features, which are reflected in the price. The following section discusses categories of digital cameras that are available for purchase and explains how each category differs, pointing out good choices for classroom use.

Categories of Digital Cameras

For the purposes of this discussion, digital cameras are divided into three categories: (1) point-and-shoot, (2) semi-professional, and (3) professional. Each category has a range (low end to high end) of sophistication and prices available. Digital cameras have become so popular that features are constantly changing, blurring the lines between categories at times.

Point-and-shoot digital cameras offer the widest selection of models available, and are designed for simplicity of operation for users who want good pictures without having to make a lot of manual settings. Point-and-shoot cameras are a good choice for the K–12 classroom, as they are quite easy to use and can be found under $200. Small in size, they are also the least expensive and easiest to use. These cameras (see Figure 7.3) offer +/− 5 MP as well as an LCD preview screen, removable memory, zoom lens, and built-in flash. Often, basic audio or video recording is available. Video recordings typically range from 30 seconds to several minutes and may also have limited-duration audio capabilities. More sophisticated models of point-and-shoot are available.

For more serious photographers, consideration should be given to moving to a camera in the **semi-professional** or **professional** category, which is not discussed here. Some still-photo cameras can take low-resolution **video** (movies), yet are not adequate for taking more elaborate or professional videos. If more capability is needed, a **digital video camera** or **camcorder** (camera recorder) is capable of shooting video and recording audio as well as taking still photos (see Figure 7.4). As with other digital cameras, digital video cameras come in a range of sophistication and price and are discussed later in this chapter as are **web cams**.

Basic Parts, Features, and Functions of a Digital Camera

Basic parts needed for general operation that are found on most digital cameras are provided here. More information can be found on specific models by going to the manufacturer's web site or reviewing the user guide or manual that illustrates the camera purchased. Additional parts and features may be provided, depending

FIGURE 7.3 Basic Camera Parts (Front and Back of Point-and-Shoot Camera with On/Off, Viewfinder, LCD, Lens, Shutter Button, and Flash) Used by Permission of Sony Electronics Inc.

FIGURE 7.4 Digital Minicam Used by Permission of Sony Electronics Inc.

on the complexity of the digital camera being used. Figure 7.3 shows a typical point-and-shoot camera that might be used in a K–12 setting, with these basic body parts: on/off button, optical viewfinder, LCD screen, camera lens, shutter, and flash.

All digital cameras will have a **power on/off button** or switch that is used to turn the camera on and off, as well as an **optical viewfinder**, the small window that is located on the back of the camera for you to look through and frame the subject of the picture. Optical viewfinders are separate from the camera lens (see next section) and therefore do not give accurate accounts of what the photo will look like, but they do preserve power compared to the LCD screen (explained next), sometimes used as a viewfinder.

To get a more exact preview of what the photo will look like, viewing through the **LCD screen** is recommended. This small screen, found at the back of the camera, is built into most digital cameras, and allows better framing of a picture before taking it, and previewing after taking it—useful, for instance, to determine whether to keep it. The use of an LCD screen, though very handy, drains battery power quickly. Even though the screen provides a more accurate image of the capture, using the LCD screen as a viewfinder is not recommended if the camera is needed for longer periods of time.

Camera Lenses

The **camera lens** serves as the eye of the camera and allows light to enter so that a picture can be taken. Camera lenses differ in quality and the ability to capture images at varying distances. Digital cameras have a fixed focus or a zoom lens. **Fixed-focus lenses** have a fixed focal length that has been calculated and cannot be changed regardless of the distance involved in the picture. Fixed focal length is customary on very inexpensive point-and-shoot digital cameras.

Zoom lenses, more preferable by far, are becoming quite common on entry-level cameras, and allow you to vary the focal length, or view the subject closer or farther away without physically changing locations. In other words, the user can zoom in to view the subject at close range without moving too close. A zoom lens is either optical or digital—optical is a far better choice. **Optical zoom** is an actual zoom that uses the lens of the camera to bring the subject closer. Optical zoom is expressed in terms of a number followed by an X such as 3X, or 6X, 8X, etc., which indicates the number of times the focal length is doubled. In other words, a camera that has 3X optical zoom would be capable of zooming triple the focal length. The casual user's needs are probably met at 3X to 6X. In contrast, **digital zoom** manipulates a portion of the image. The camera crops the center portion of the picture and enlarges it to give the illusion of optical zoom, resulting in a loss of image quality. Avoid cameras that offer only digital zoom. Camera lenses are made of plastic or glass; glass lenses are better than plastic ones. The camera lens, like a human eye, is delicate and can easily be damaged or scratched. Protection for a camera lens can be provided by a lens cap that fits over the lens when it is not in use.

Shutter

The camera **shutter** controls light and motion and lets light enter through the lens when the shutter button is pressed to take the photo. A simple explanation of this process is that as the shutter button is pressed to allow light to enter the lens, the image is recorded on the image sensor and becomes a digital file. In more expensive cameras, this process is facilitated by what is known as the **adjusting aperture**, which controls the amount of light entering the camera in various lighting situations. When using cameras with an **autofocus feature**, pressing the shutter

TECH TIP
Using the LCD drains battery power quickly!

TECH TIP
Optical zoom provides a more accurate zoom and is expressed in a number followed by an X.

TECH TIP
Glass lenses are far better than plastic.

TECH TIP

Shutter lag can result in blurring of the picture.

button will center the subject, and automatically focus and take the picture. The time that elapses between pressing the shutter button and actually taking the picture is called **shutter lag**. Lag time may result in the object movement and blurring of the photo. Avoid this by pressing the button halfway down to start the process. Keep the button pressed halfway until you are satisfied that the best moment has arrived and then press it fully; this technique should help eliminate blur. As a general rule, more expensive cameras have less shutter lag.

Flash

At times, there will not be enough light to get a good picture. The **flash** is a control on the light that is shown on a picture. The flash on a digital camera is not very high powered, but works well for casual use. Some camera models provide an automatic setting that allows the camera to determine whether there is enough light for the shot and activate the flash if more light is needed.

TECH TIP

"Red-eye" results from taking pictures in low-light situations.

A common problem experienced by many is known as **red-eye** (eyes of people or animals appear red) and is a result of shooting photos of people or animals in low-light conditions. A simple explanation is that eyes are dilated in low-light conditions, with the pupils becoming quite large. The flash reflects off the red retina and gives the eyes a red glow in the photo. Some camera models have settings that reduce red-eye effect. Because red-eye does not occur in bright light, other ways to decrease red eye is to avoid taking photos outside after dark or in darker rooms. Keep in mind that if editing is needed, image editors have features to get rid of red-eye effects.

Memory Sources

Digital cameras need a **memory source** to store images. Memory is offered as **fixed memory** or **removable memory** (see Figure 7.5). Older or very inexpensive models of cameras offer fixed memory, meaning that a limited amount of memory is offered within the camera for storage. This limits the number of photos that can be taken at a given time. Newer or more advanced models offer some type of removable storage, such as a memory card, that can be inserted and removed from a slot in the camera and allows the storage of many more photos. Removable memory is far superior to fixed memory, because (1) it offers more space, (2) it is erasable and reusable, and (3) the transfer of images to the computer is easier.

The model of digital camera will determine the type of removable memory that it uses. The most popular types of removable memory include different types of flash memory cards including CompactFlash, Secure Digital, and Memory Sticks. These cards come in various storage capacities and are physically different and therefore not interchangeable. **Compact flash (CF)**, once considered the ultimate in flash memory, has lost ground to **SecureDigital (SD)** for point-and-shoot cameras although they are common to many high-end digital camera models. SD cards are available in standard and high capacity and can be used in a variety of cameras. SD is the most common type of flash memory and has higher transfer rates than CF. **Memory Sticks (MS)**, developed by Sony, are limited in compatibility to Sony cameras and camcorders with the exception of Samsung, which uses MS in their media. Generally speaking, the cards provided with cameras at purchase (for all formats) usually offer little storage space. However, memory in each format can be purchased in sizes up to 16 GB. If the camera has removable memory capabilities, there will be a slot or slots, typically located on the side of the camera, for the insertion and ejection of the memory source.

Memory is an important consideration when buying a digital camera. The number of images that can be stored in a camera depends on (1) the capacity of storage available, (2) the resolution at which the photos are taken, and (3) amount of compression used. It is wise to have extra memory on hand.

FIGURE 7.5 Removable Memory

Power Sources

Digital cameras are dependent on either batteries or an AC adaptor as a source of power. The camera's manual will specify the type of battery that can be used. If the camera uses AA batteries, it is quite important to get NiMH (nickel-metal hydride) rechargeable batteries, which are somewhat inexpensive versus other types. Many newer models use LiIon (lithium ion) batteries. Although these batteries are more expensive, they last much longer than NiMH batteries, are rechargeable, and thus are preferable. There will be a battery compartment, typically located on the bottom of the camera, with a cover for the insertion and ejection of the batteries.

An AC power adaptor, pictured in Figure 7.6, gets its power from an electrical outlet, thus eliminating the concern of dying batteries. Even so, adaptors are rarely included with the purchase of a digital camera. If an adaptor is not included, it is a wise purchase. Keep in mind that the use of the LCD preview screen and the flash quickly drains batteries, so it is quite important to conserve battery power in order to use the camera for longer periods.

Connectivity

After capturing the images, they must be transferred to a computer and edited, printed, or archived for later use. Connectivity or transferring images from the camera to the computer has become quite an easy process, but it is very important to make sure that the camera can communicate with the computer being used. Different camera models typically transfer images to a computer in one of four ways: (1) connecting the camera directly to the computer by a USB or FireWire cable, (2) connecting a card reader to the computer and inserting the removable memory card, (3) connecting a dock to the computer and placing the camera in the dock for the transfer, or (4) using wireless connectivity. Wireless connectivity is offered on the newest generation of cameras. After the transfer has been completed, the photos can be edited with photo software.

Camera Software

Software is needed for the camera to communicate with or "talk" to the computer. This special software, called **driver software**, translates between the computer operating system and the specific camera. Newer computer operating systems (Windows XP, Vista, and Mac OS X) are designed for use with digital cameras and have the driver software already installed for many camera models.

Software is also required to edit images, and a program is usually included on a CD that comes with the camera; the user manual will describe the installation process. Typically, the software for entry-level camera models has limited features; nevertheless, it may be adequate for use by teachers and students. Adobe Photoshop Elements, a simplified version of Photoshop, offers nice editing options, is quite affordable for the classroom, and is far easier to use than its complex cousin. Trial Windows and Mac versions of Adobe Photoshop Elements can be downloaded from **www.adobe.com/digitalimag/main.html**. Photo Express by Ulead offers similar features; trial versions can be found at **www.ulead.com/pe/runme.htm**. Corel's Paint Shop Pro trial versions and educational pricing information are available at **www.corel.com**. As mentioned earlier, GIMP is an open source image manipulation program and may be downloaded at no charge from **www.gimp.org**.

Camera Accessories

A few camera accessories should be considered when purchasing digital cameras, including carrying cases, removable storage sources, power sources and chargers, tripods, and cleaning supplies. Carrying cases protect the delicate camera parts

FIGURE 7.6 Power Sources for Digital Cameras
Used by Permission of Eastman Kodak Company

from bumps and bad weather. Some models come with a case, but purchasing one is essential if yours does not. Carrying cases can also provide extra space for additional accessories such as cables, extra batteries, and storage. Extra removable memory such as memory cards are needed to avoid running out of memory when you fill up a card. The same is true for batteries discussed earlier in this chapter in the Power Sources section. It is always a good idea to have at least two batteries to make certain that you always have a charge. Battery chargers allow batteries to be recharged after each use, which is critical if the camera is needed for long periods. Tripods, commonly used by professionals, are attached to the camera to prevent any movement. Many cameras are equipped with a tripod mount, a screw to attach the tripod to the camera. Finally, cleaning supplies, such as cloths to clean the lenses, prolong the life of the camera.

Key Purchasing Considerations

When buying a digital camera, five considerations are essential to keep in mind: (1) available budget, (2) image quality, (3) image storage, (4) connectivity, and (5) battery life of the camera model. A summation of each is provided here.

Determining an available **budget** and sticking to it are vital when being introduced to new and dazzling features and well-trained sales personnel. The purpose of the camera should be considered, which includes determining how it will be used and who will use it. As discussed earlier, there are several major categories of cameras, each with many models of varying features and prices. It is easy to get excited and buy more camera than is needed for most classroom use.

Image quality is related to the resolution range of the camera (see the previous discussion). The resolution that is needed depends on how the pictures will ultimately be used or output. As mentioned previously, images that are displayed in an electronic format do not require a resolution as high as those that will be printed. Although image quality is typically associated with resolution, other criteria should be considered, such as the quality of the camera lens, the image sensor, and compression capacities.

Image storage, or how the camera stores images, is very important when considering a purchase for classroom use (see earlier discussion of memory sources). Removable memory is far superior to fixed memory.

Connectivity (transferring the images to the computer) provides easy options for teachers; this method of transfer should be taken into consideration during the purchase considerations. A camera that transfers through a USB connection requires a computer with a USB port.

Finally, the **battery life** required for the camera being considered is quite important (see power sources). Having a camera that offers rechargeable batteries such as the ones described earlier is by far the most cost-effective alternative.

We have established the many good uses for photos in learning environments and you are ready to move forward to taking some pictures. As with learning to use most tools, practice using the camera parts will help greatly. Grab a camera and take some photos following these simple steps. Keep in mind that teachers should be very comfortable with the technology before teaching students to use a tool. Because readers will have various models for practice, the steps are designed to guide basic picture taking and are not specific for all camera settings.

Using a Digital Camera to Take a Still Photo

1. *Get ready.* If the camera is a new tool, take the time to get acquainted with available features of the model being used. If the camera uses a battery for power or if the images will be saved to a removable storage such as a memory card, make sure that these are inserted into the camera.

2. *Power on the camera and adjust settings.*   Power on the camera, remove the lens cover, and make adjustments to settings (such as camera mode, or automatic mode to set focus, exposure, flash, and white balance).

3. *Take the photo(s).*   Using the viewfinder, frame the target. Adjust the zoom accordingly and press the shutter button to store the photo.

4. *Preview the photos and delete unwanted images.*   Using the LCD screen, preview the photos. Delete unwanted photos or retake photos if needed. Keep in mind the capability of the storage that the camera affords.

5. *Transfer the images to the computer.*   After the photo(s) to keep have been selected, transfer them to the computer for storage or editing.

6. *Edit the photo(s).*   Modifications can be completed after the photo is transferred. The amount of editing that can take place will vary with the software being used; however, even the most basic should allow the photo to be lightened, darkened, cropped (cut away a portion of the picture), or resized. Keep in mind how the photo is going to be used (electronic or print) and save the photo at the resolution needed.

7. *Save the file.*   Archive the edited photo for later use. The camera automatically names each photo with numbers. Each photo that is to be saved should be renamed with a descriptive name and the proper image extension. Keep in mind that a camera typically saves photos as jpeg files. Saving your work to a public computer is not a good idea as it can easily disappear! To be certain that your pictures will be available to you when needed, save the photos to a personal storage device such as a USB, CD, or personal Web space.

> **TECH TIP**
> Never save files to a public or lab computer if you want to be sure your work is safe.

> **TECH TIP**
> Always back up your work.

Graphic File Formats

Images should be saved in or converted to a specific format; which one depends on how the picture will be ultimately used. We will discuss the differences in bitmapped (raster) and object-based (vector) files and the basics of working with them. In addition, we will look closer at six common graphic formats that teachers and students will use. Each has its own characteristics, uses, disadvantages, and advantages. Image files, like other files, should be saved with a descriptive name, followed by a period (dot), followed by a three-letter extension that identifies the image format. See Table 7.2.

Raster vs. Vector

There are many graphic file formats and more are appearing and disappearing frequently as we move forward with technology. So many in fact, it is quite easy to get confused, nevertheless quite necessary to have a general understanding of what it's all about if you are going to experience more success and less frustration. The types that we provide are not all-inclusive but are the most common.

Graphic files are divided into two categories: **object-based** (also called **vector graphics**) and **bitmapped** (also called **raster graphics**). It is important for teachers and students to understand that all graphics are not created equal and when resizing needs to occur, this basic understanding will make the process a less frustrating one. Object-based or vector graphics are created and stored in the computer as a set of mathematical instructions that identify shapes, curves, and lines, and because of that can be resized, rotated, and/or stretched without distortion. Object-based graphics are developed in drawing programs or with drawing tools and include arrows, circles, shapes, and so forth and take much less space than bitmapped graphics.

In contrast, bitmapped graphics are composed of many tiny squares (pixels or dots) that make up a grid. A digital image is represented as a grid of pixels. All

Table 7.2   Image Formats Are Defined by End Use of Image

File Name	File Extension	Major Uses	Characteristics	Raster/Vector
Windows Bitmap	.bmp/BMP	Used with Windows OS and Windows programs	Usually uncompressed	Raster
Graphics Interchange Format	.gif/GIF	Best the for Web, use with flat, solid colors. Supports animated images.	Lossless but only supports 8 bit color (256 colors)	Raster
Joint Photographic Experts Group	.jpg, jpeg/JPEG	Best for the Web, camera storage use for photos	Lossy compression, supports full color	Raster
Portable Network Graphics	.png	Best for the Web; not supported by older browsers.	Lossless compression, full color	Raster
Tagged Image File Format	.tif/TIFF	Used for print-based documents; huge files.	Lossy (using .jpeg compression and lossless using LSW compression)	Raster
Portable Document Format	.pdf/PDF	Used to "freeze" the format of documents and hold the links intact.	Supported by Adobe Acrobat Reader	Raster/Vector
Photoshop	.psd	Identifies a file created in Photoshop.	Supported by a few other programs. Can be converted to .tiff or .gif depending on end use.	Raster
Flash	.swf	Identifies a file created in Flash animation application	Player needed to play these files on the Web.	Vector
Adobe Illustrator	.ai	Identifies a file from Adobe Illustrator		Vector
Adobe Freehand	.fh	Identifies a file from Freehand		Vector

images obtained with digital cameras, scanners, camcorders or screen captures are bitmapped images as well as those created with paint programs. Bitmapped graphics (raster) are affected by resolution. Thus, when a bitmapped image is changed, the image will distort or get fuzzy if not changed correctly. The category for all graphics with this composition includes familiar formats as .gif, .jpg, .png, and .tiff.

Images should be saved in or converted to a specific format depending on how the picture will ultimately be used. Image file formats that are widely accepted for Web publication are .gif and .jpeg. Another format, .png, was originally developed several years ago to replace .gif format but has not been widely accepted by browsers. The latest browsers do recognize .png. Image files accepted for printed documents may vary by the program being used; however, .tiff format will give high quality for most print jobs. To determine which formats are friendly with the program being used; search the Help section of the program for graphic file types that you can use in documents. In addition, there should be a troubleshooting area of the Help section to assist in determining why files may not work well. Teachers, as well as older students, should understand basic information regarding file types that are best suited for Web documents as well as documents that will be printed. Review the files types that follow as well as their major characteristics.

BMP   Bitmap (BMP) files are somewhat confusing as many refer to these files as simply those that are composed of many tiny squares, pixels, or dots that make up a square or grid, which are indeed referred to as bitmapped files. Yet, a true bitmap file is native to Windows-based computers and should be used there. These files are not supported by the Web and should not be used in high-end print applications.

GIF   Graphic Interchange Format (.gif/GIF, pronounced as *gift* without the t) file format was developed by CompuServe in the late 1980s to transmit images over the Internet. It remains one of the two primary formats for image files that are used on the Web. GIF files use a compression scheme that keeps files to a minimum; yet, GIF images are limited to 256 colors. If the image has limited colors and has large areas of a color, use GIF.

JPEG   The **Joint Photographic Experts Group** (.jpg, .jpeg/JPEG, pronounced *jay peg*) is one of the primary formats accepted by the Web, and supports full color. This format is a good choice for photographs, but is not a good choice for print documents. Most digital cameras will automatically save pictures to a .jpeg format.

PNG   A **Portable Network Graphic** (.png/PNG, pronounced as *ping*) is a format that is pixel-based and was developed for the Web to replace GIF files, support full color, and maintain a lossless compression. PNG is a great improvement over the capabilities offered by GIF but is not accepted by older browsers. The new browser versions are supporting this format more fully. PNG is not a good choice for print.

TIFF   Tagged Image File (.tif or Tiff/TIFF) format is commonly used in desktop publishing and is the best choice when quality is required in print documents. Do not consider Tiff files for the Web!

PDF   Portable Document Format (.pdf/PDF) documents are Adobe's attempt at a universal file format that protects the formatting of a document when it crosses platforms and computers. Detailed graphics can be created, saved in PDF, and look exactly like they were created, even when opened on a computer without the specialized software or fonts. The Adobe Acrobat Reader is used to read these documents if the original program that created them is not available, and is a free download from the Adobe site (**www.adobe.com**).

Compression

As discussed earlier, high-resolution digital images result in very large file sizes, causing difficulty in storing, transferring, and/or viewing on the Web. Images must be "compressed" or reduced in file size to store or transfer or use on the Web. Image compression allows the reduction of the file size; however, if overdone, compression can also affect the image quality. Lossless and lossy compression approaches are characteristic to various file types.

Lossless and Lossy Compression

Lossless compression means that there is no data loss during the compression process. GIF uses a lossless method of compression. In other words, when the image is created, the original image is reduced to make it as small as possible. Obviously, GIFs are limited to 256 colors meaning that it is quite good for images with few colors but not for photographs.

TECH TIP

There is no recovery of the quality after an image has been overcompressed using the lossy approach.

During a **lossy compression** approach, each time compression takes place some of the data is lost. Compressing multiple times will result in a noticeable loss of quality of the image. JPEG uses a lossy compression approach meaning that during the compression process, some of the pixels are thrown away to make the image smaller. Each time the image is compressed, more of the pixels are thrown away reducing the color quality of the image.

Scanners

A scanner converts analog data into digital data by analyzing an image or text, and makes a copy of it in digital format that can be saved to a computer. The file can then be edited as needed and added to a digital environment such as a web page, email message, or multimedia presentation. The computer that will communicate with the scanner during the scanning process must be connected to it and have specialized software loaded, most of which will be packaged with the scanner at purchase.

As with digital cameras, there are various types of scanners. The following section presents categories of scanners that are available to consumers for purchase and explains how each category differs, as well as good choices for classroom use.

Categories of Scanners

For the purposes of this discussion, the authors have divided scanners into three major categories: (1) flatbed, (2) film, and (3) sheet-fed. Although there are additional types of scanners, such as bar code scanners, the primary focus here is on the type most common to the PK–12 setting: the flatbed scanner.

A **flatbed scanner**, the most commonly used and versatile type of scanner, works much like a traditional copy machine. The item to be scanned is placed face-down on a glass bed, the lid is closed, directions are given to the scanner, and the scan takes place. Flatbed scanners allow easy scanning of photographs, documents, pages from books or magazines, maps, and less traditional items such as coins, leaves, or fabric. These scanners are useful in the classroom and have become quite affordable.

A **sheet-fed scanner** resembles a portable printer and is much more limiting than a flatbed scanner. The subject to be scanned must be fed into the scanner and moved through the scanner during the scanning process—this obviously limits the types of items that can be scanned. Many will scan single sheets of paper while some models have document feeders. Nevertheless, the resulting scan tends to be less exact than a flatbed scanner.

A **film scanner** is used to scan 35 mm film or 35 mm slides. Often called slide scanners, the best outcomes will come from scanning the original film or negatives. Scanners that produce good results are expensive and difficult to use. Fulton (2005) warns that 35 mm adaptors are being packaged with some flatbed scanners, yet do not yield a great quality result.

Basic Flatbed Scanner Components, Features, and Functions

Basic parts needed for general operation and found on most flatbed scanners are provided here. More information can be found on specific models by going to the manufacturer's web site or reviewing the user's guide provided with the scanner at purchase. Additional parts and features may be provided, depending on the complexity of the scanner being used. Figure 7.7 displays a typical flatbed scanner that might be used in a PK–12 setting, the scanner bed, and lid.

The **scanner bed** is the glass surface on which the item to be scanned is positioned. The bed is located under the **scanner lid**. The scanner lid covers the scanner bed during the scanning process and when the scanner is not being used.

Scanner software is needed for the scanner to communicate with or talk to the computer. This software, called a *scanner driver,* is required to allow the scan to take place. This software should be provided on CD/DVD with the scanner at purchase; the user's manual describes the install process.

The types of scans that will be completed influence the software needed. The software is very important—everything is done with the software. Most scanners will have very basic software bundled, which is sufficient for novice users. However, it may be necessary to upgrade the software to get more features. The two major types of software that are used with scanners are image editing and OCR. **Image editing software** is needed when scanning graphics. The image editing software packaged with the scanner will allow basic adjustments such as brightness, contrast, color balance, cropping, resizing, and rotating. The quality of this software and thus the features are typically limited. If more advanced features are desired, full-featured programs are discussed earlier in this chapter under camera software.

Scanning a page of text results in a graphic of the text that is not editable. In order to decode the graphic to real text that can be edited, **optical character recognition (OCR)** software must be used. Usually an entry-level OCR program will be bundled with the scanner. Entry-level OCR produces scan results that require further editing for the characters that were not accurately converted to text. Although functional for occasional use or demonstration, if the scanner will be used extensively for digitizing text, more sophisticated or advanced OCR software such as Kurzweil 3000 or Read & Write (TextHelp) is easier to use and more accurate. Further discussion on the use of OCR software can be found in the Adapting for Special Learners section later in this chapter.

Connectivity and Compatibility   Transferring images from the scanner to the computer is an easy process. The scanner is directly connected to the computer by a cable. The most common connections are parallel (the slowest transfer), SCSI (pronounced *scuzzy*), USB, or Firewire. The latest models offer USB connection, and will provide more speed for the transfer. High-end scanners offer FireWire connections and very fast transfer of large amounts of data. If a scanner is being shared at a station, students can save the scans to a USB or other storage device.

System Requirements   The scanner must be compatible with the computer that it will be connected to. For example, if the computer is using Windows XP, Vista, or Mac OS X, the scanner must provide software drivers for those systems. In addition, the connection ports that are needed for transfer must be available on the computer.

The flatbed scanner must be connected to the computer that will receive the digital files before it is functional. In addition, the scanner software must be loaded on the computer. It is always a good idea to read the manual that comes with the particular model that is being used. Many times, such manuals are provided on disks instead of as printed copies.

Using a Flatbed Scanner

1. *Get ready.*   If the scanner is a new tool, take some time for orientation to learn available features of the model being used. This software, usually provided with the scanner, must be installed on the computer that will receive the scanned file. Follow the directions for installation or check with the tech coordinator/support at your school.

2. *Open the scanner software.*

3. *Place the subject.*   Lift the lid of the scanner and place the subject (photo, document, map) to be scanned face-down on the scanner bed. Align the subject with marking cue located in one of the corners. Close the lid. Note:

FIGURE 7.7 Flatbed Scanner

TECH TIP

A scan is only as good as the original that is being used. In other words, if the original has problems, these problems will be apparent in the scan as well.

TECH TIP

Any marks or lint that appear on the scanner bed will become part of the scan as well. If these are noticeable on the scanned file and are not a part of the original document, clean the scanner bed with a mild detergent or glass cleaner.

TECH TIP

Refer to info on graphic file types on best use.

Most flatbed scanners will allow the lid to expand or be removed for thicker documents such as books.

4. *Scan the subject.* The software will usually have a File menu with a Scan or Acquire or Import command to begin the scan. Choose this command. The resolution can be changed at this time if the image will be used in electronic format.

5. *Preview the scan.* The software should allow you to preview the scan before the actual scan takes place to determine whether adjustments need to be made. If the preview is acceptable, continue with scan process. If not, make adjustments and preview again.

6. *Edit the scan in the software.* Modifications can be completed after the scan is complete. The amount of editing that can take place will vary with the software being used; however, even the most basic software should allow the scan to be lightened, darkened, cropped, or resized.

7. *Save the file.* Archive the edited scan for later use. Always save images on a removable storage drive over which you have full control, such as a USB.

CD-ROM Collections

Commercial CD-ROM collections of clip art and photos typically consist of multiple CDs/DVDs digital images. These collections are quite easy to use in electronic documents. The quality is very good, but the size of an image may vary, which should be considered if it is to be used online. An index in print format is often provided that identifies the CD that holds the picture with a small graphic image and corresponding number. An example of a CD collection is the *Big Box of Art* by Hemera, which can be purchased at Amazon.com and is quite reasonably priced for the classroom.

Using a CD Collection to Gather Digital Images

1. *Orientation with the user guide.* Read the instructions for installation of the CD software and use of the collection. Knowing how to find a particular photo in a large collection of multiple CDs is necessary to avoid wasting hours searching. In addition, access to possible technical support must be determined.

2. *Install the master disk.* Using the identification steps identified in the instructions, locate the picture or clip art desired.

3. *Search for images.* Collections offer a variety of ways to search for images. During the time that you're becoming familiar to the user's guide, you should learn the method that is used with the particular collection. Some will allow searches by keyword, such as *dog* or *flower.*

4. *Save the image.* to an application or storage device. Typically the image can be dragged and dropped to an application, such as the word processor, or to a storage device. The directions may be a bit different for Windows and Macintosh platforms, but each should be described in the user's guide. Clicking on the image and using File/Save As will allow saving to a specific destination folder.

5. *Edit the images.* Modifications can be completed after the transfer is complete. The amount of editing that can take place is limited with packaged software; however, resizing and cropping are standard options.

Web Collections

Collections of digital images available from the Web offer clip art, photographs, fonts, icons, animations, and sound. Access to these collections may be free for use, require a yearly or monthly subscription, or have a fee for each picture used. The sites that require a subscription usually provide many good-quality images. Search engines can locate such sites, and you will find some listed in the On the Web: Digital Images section of the companion web site. Although "free" immediately gets a teacher's attention, many free sites have a large number of pop-up screens and distracting advertising.

Google (http://images.google.com) offers a comprehensive image search tool, Google Images, that works with keyword searches for images. The tool brings forth a selection of images matching the keyword, with the size of the image as well as the site that it originally comes from. It is important to note that many schools block Google images, thus making it useless during school hours. In addition, teachers should be aware of copyright considerations and caution students about using such photos in web sites. Downloading images from the Web is very easy and can be completed using the following steps.

Using the Web to Download Images

1. *Open the browser software and locate the image resource.* It is imperative to establish ownership of the images and determine whether they can be used. Some images may be used in the classroom under fair use doctrine, but there are still restrictions on Web publishing. Sites that allow downloads should provide information about the restrictions on their use as well as the citations that must remain on the document or in the credits.

2. *Download and save an image.* Once an image has been located and ownership has been established, the image should be selected and downloaded from the Web to your computer. The process is similar on Mac or Windows machines. On a Mac computer, click and hold the image, select Save As from the pop-up dialog box, and specify where the image should be saved (such as a storage drive). On a Windows computer, right-click the image, select Save As from the pop-up dialog box, and specify where the image should be saved (such as a storage drive). On both Mac and Windows platforms, an image can be saved to the desktop by simply clicking on the image and dragging it to the desktop.

Legal and Ethical Use of Digital Images

Copyright law addresses the legal and ethical use of works created by others. **Fair Use law** places a limit on the use of copyrighted works so that these works can be used without getting permission. It is very important for teachers and students to understand and comply with such laws when working with digital files.

The medium that a teacher or student is working within makes a difference as there is variation in what can be done in the classroom for educational purposes. These copyright or fair use laws are at times misunderstood. In this section, we look closely at the use of photographs, illustrations, and sound and video files that can be accessed, scanned, or downloaded from the Web, videotapes, or DVDs and used in multimedia projects by teachers and students.

Illustrations and Photographs

Teachers and students may use a complete photo by a photographer, but may use no more than five from a particular photographer. If there is a collection of photos involved, only fifteen photos or 10 percent of the collection (whichever is less) can be used without permission. For instance, photographs from a school yearbook would fall into the collection category and, thus, could not be scanned and put into an electronic slideshow if more than 15 were going to be used, without getting permission from the photographer. Taking original photographs alleviates some responsibility; even so, it is important to check school and district policy regarding

> **TECH TIP**
>
> Fifteen photos or 10 percent (whichever is less) of a photo collection can be used without permission.

TECH TIP

To use photos of students, always get parents' permission.

the photographing of students. Preservice teachers should be aware that there are strict school policies regarding photographing students without parent permission. If permission is granted, it is important to clarify how the picture will be used and what medium will be used. This information should be addressed with the technology coordinator or administration of the school.

Resources from the Web

One major consideration to keep in mind is where and how the Web resource is going to be used as mentioned previously. Images, sound files, and video can be downloaded from the Web for use in student projects and teacher-developed lesson activities; nonetheless, they may not be reposted to the Web without advance permission.

TECH TIP

Do not post students' names with photos.

This requirement, often misunderstood by teachers, is passed to students. Using the resource in face-to-face learning situations is fine. However, reposting to the Web, perhaps in a "student spotlight" project, is illegal without proper permission. In addition, make sure that the resource has been legally acquired by the particular web site. If student pictures are posted on the Internet, signed parent permission must be given and the names of students must never be posted.

Music, Lyrics, or Music Video

A portion may be used not to exceed 10% or 3 minutes of the work. Further, the melody or character of the work may not be changed.

TECH TIP

Ten percent or 3 minutes (whichever is less) can be used.

Video for Viewing

Teachers may use legitimately acquired videotapes (purchased or rented) and DVDs in the classroom for instructional purposes in a face-to-face learning environment. Copies may be made for archival purposes or for loss due to damage or theft if replacements are not offered at a reasonable price.

Video for Integration in Projects

Students may use legitimately acquired (legal copy, not home recorded) videotapes, DVDs, multimedia encyclopedias, QuickTime movies, and video clips from the Web in the classroom for instructional purposes in a face-to-face learning environment.

TECH TIP

Consider using videos found on TeacherTube or YouTube.

Digital images are used across the curriculum at different grade levels in various ways. In her Voices from the Classroom section, Vicki Wells shares how she integrates digital images into the learning experiences of young students.

Basic Parts, Features, and Functions of a Camcorder (Video Camera-Recorder)

While video cameras, commonly called *camcorders*, are different from point-and-shoot cameras, they are still digital cameras and have similar parts that have been discussed. New models are small enough to fit in your pocket and can be found for under $300. Basic parts needed for general operation that are found on most digital video cameras are provided here. More information can be found on specific models by going to the manufacturer's web site or reviewing the user's guide or manual illustrations with the video camera at purchase. Additional parts and features may be provided, depending on the complexity of the digital video camera being used. Figure 7.4 (p. 160) shows a typical video camera that might be used in a K–12 setting, with these basic body parts: on/off button, eyepiece (viewfinder), grip, record button, built-in microphone, LCD screen, lens, shutter, and flash.

Video File Formats

Video converts to a video file type. See Table 7.3 on page 174 for the most common video file types.

Voices *from the* Classroom

Using Digital Images in Early Learning
Vicki Wells

Vicki Wells has over 25 years of teaching experience. She is the curriculum and instructional facilitator at an inner city school. In this new position, she is part of a team that has developed a plan for acquiring projectors, document cameras, and new computers for classroom teachers. She provides support for these teachers as they develop lessons to integrate this technology into their teaching. Prior to this, Vicki served eight years as a first-grade teacher in another inner city school. Her first-grade classroom had seven computers of varying ages and models and a SMARTBoard. In addition, she had a laptop and digital camera that she used to integrate technology into learning activities for her young students. She extended her ability to integrate technology into classroom instruction through her participation in a PT3 (Preparing Tomorrow's Teachers to Use Technology) grant with the University of Tennessee. We asked Vicki to share her experiences with integrating digital images into classroom instruction.

In first grade, there are many opportunities to use digital images in classroom instruction. First graders love to make books. Using a digital camera personalizes the books we make. Not only do the books have pictures of the students, but also of their environments. I use digital images to record classroom activities such as field trips and special units of study. From these collections of pictures, we make books for the classroom library. I also have used digital images in Microsoft PowerPoint slideshows for open house nights and classroom instruction.

One of the ways that I have used digital images in classroom instruction is in a math unit on shapes. One of the objectives of the unit is for students to make the connection between their environment and plane and solid shapes. First, I made a PowerPoint slideshow that was a

Shape Hunt. I found examples of the plane and solid shapes on our school campus. I made a close-up picture for the students to (1) identify the shape and (2) identify where that shape could be found at our school. The students were eager to participate in the guessing game. In the next step of the lesson, the students went on shape hunts on our school campus to find more examples of the shapes that we had studied. They used the digital camera to take pictures of the examples they found. My teacher intern used their pictures to create a class book that has become a class favorite of all the students.

In social studies, one unit of study is identifying the helpers in our school, such as the principal, the school nurse, the secretary, and other important people on the school staff. The students developed questions for interviewing the staff members. With my teacher intern's support, the students made appointments and interviewed people on the school staff. During the interview, they took their pictures using the digital camera for another class book. This activity developed interviewing skills and helped the students build relationships with staff members.

There are many benefits to using technology in classroom instruction. Technology can meet the different learning styles of students. It also adds another dimension to the strategies that a classroom teacher has for meeting the goals for student achievement. Children are always excited to use computers and digital cameras. This excitement creates a positive environment for learning. One of the challenges to using technology with young children is the need for the classroom teacher to have some extra support from a teacher intern, parent, or assistant. Technology with young children works best when the teacher is able to have the students work in small groups and there is adult support for those students.

Web cams are digital cameras that send images over the Internet (see Figure 7.8). Popular uses include sending video clips through email, videoconferencing, chatting in real time and sending video over the Internet. To do this, a digital camera is attached to the computer through a USB port. The camera can take video or still shots. There are ways to successfully use these tiny cameras in the classroom. Teachers might want to search EarthCam (**www.earthcam.com/**), the largest Web cam Directory that lists Web cams all over the world. Education World (**www.education-world.com/a_tech/sites/sites081.shtml**) provides a number of ways to incorporate Web cams into the classroom.

FIGURE 7.8 **Web Cam**
©2008 Logitech. All rights reserved. Image used with permission from Logitech.

Table 7.3 Video File Formats

File Name	Description
MPEG (Moving Picture Experts Group)	A common audio/video file format that is often used with digital cameras or camcorders to capture small video clips.
MPEG-4 (.MP4)	Used for streaming and downloadable Web content and is the current format used in cameras and camcorders.
Quicktime (.QT)	Used for storing and playing movies with sound. Developed by Apple, but not limited to Apple operating systems. Quicktime files typically appear with .MOV file extensions when used in Windows.
Windows Media	Microsoft's video format for Windows only (.WMV for video and .WMA for audio). This is the default format for Windows Media Player.
Real media (.RM)	A media file format used by RealPlayer for audio/video and can be downloaded or streamed. It works with a Web browser and the Real Player plug-in.

Adapting for Special Learners

The techniques for obtaining digital images that are introduced in this chapter are essential tools that make it possible and practical for teachers to differentiate instruction for learners who experience physical, visual, and cognitive barriers to learning. Digital images can be incorporated into software products used by learners with special needs, such as text-to-speech (TTS) word processors (IntelliTalk in Classroom Suite), presentation and multimedia composition tools (Microsoft PowerPoint, HyperStudio, IntelliPics Studio in Classroom Suite, or KidPix Deluxe), and visual learning tools (Inspiration, Kidspiration). Once developed, these materials can then be used in a variety of formats: computer-based, overhead slides, or print. When images are digitized, the same or similar materials can be used by a variety of learners, thereby increasing access to the general curriculum.

Digital Text

The skills learned in this chapter for obtaining digital images also have applications for digital text materials. When text is offered in digital formats, learners who are blind, who are English language learners, or who have certain learning disabilities can access it through conversion to Braille, by having a computer "read" the material using TTS software, or by translating certain words. The accessibility of digitized formats produced prior to 2005 varied considerably among the publishers, however. Some were easily accessed in alternate formats; others are not. IDEA 2004 now requires publishers to provide textbooks in an accessible format using National Instructional Materials Accessibility Standards (NIMAS, 2005). NIMAS files are sent to a national repository, the National Instructional Materials Access Centers (NIMAC).

Bookshare is an organization that maintains a digital library of books from a variety of sources, including U.S. K–12 textbooks from the NIMAC repository. Recent funding from the U.S. Department of Education has made access to *Bookshare's* extensive library of textbooks and other instructional literature free to all K–12, postsecondary, and graduate students in the United States who receive special education services and qualify under the 1996 Chafee Amendment. In order to obtain these services, proof of a print disability must be submitted to *Bookshare,* either through an individual subscription or through an institutional

CURRICULUM CONNECTIONS

The following lesson summaries integrate digital images with curriculum topics. Each summary presents a content area, grade level(s), NETS·S alignment, brief description of the lesson, teacher preparation needed for the lesson, active participation of the students, and suggested variations. If the lesson was adapted, the original source is provided.

Life Cycle Sequencing

CONTENT AREA/TOPIC: Language Arts, Reading
GRADE LEVELS: 1, 2   **NETS·S:** 2, 6

Description: Activities that involve sequencing allow students to distinguish the order of events in stories or historical events and aid reading comprehension. Sequencing provides a foundation for breaking large tasks into controllable pieces that must go together in the proper order. This lesson allows students to practice sequencing events by using pictures from a story that they must place into the order that they occurred.

Teacher preparation: Teachers should scan the pictures from the site "From Caterpillar to Butterfly" or download the pictures from the Web at **www.dcboces. org/sufsd/nassau/vitek/butterfly/**.

Active participation: Students read and discuss the book in the classroom. The pictures may be kept in digital format and students may insert them into a word processing program or a slideshow in the proper sequence. They could also be printed for students to sequence when not using the computer. Students place the pictures of the life cycle of a butterfly in the proper order.

Variations: This activity could be completed with any story that students are reading or any historical event.

Source: Lesson plans page, butterfly unit: life cycle sequence. Accessed October 15, 2008, from **www.lessonplanspage.com/ more/ScienceLAArtMathMDButterflyUnit2-CaterToBFly12.htm**.

Counting Big Book

CONTENT AREA/TOPIC: Language Arts, Reading
GRADE LEVELS: K–2   **NETS·S:** 2, 6

Description: This lesson uses the digital camera to capture photos of sets of numbers.

Teacher preparation: Teachers choose a theme such as blocks, balls, dolls, or similar ideas to represent their sets of numbers.

Active participation: The teacher, teacher's assistant, or a parent helper takes pictures of the number sets after the students arrange the pieces. Pictures are printed and used by the students to practice the number sets. They can make a booklet or a poster to compare their work with those from other groups.

Welcome to Our Class

CONTENT AREA/TOPIC: Language Arts, Social Studies, Art
GRADE LEVELS: K–6   **NETS·S:** 2, 3, 4

Description: In this lesson, which is designed to enhance reading and writing skills, a class uses digital cameras to create a resource book that identifies important people (class members, teachers, adminis-tration, nurse, custodian, and so on) and areas (media center, cafeteria, and so on) in the school. The book can be used by incoming students and parents to make them feel more comfortable in a new class.

(Continues)

CURRICULUM CONNECTIONS *Continued*

Teacher preparation: The teacher develops a data sheet for students to complete with special information about themselves. The teacher plans the content for the book. Helpful content might include daily schedules, class policies (such as quietly walking to lunch), or anything that the teacher decides is important. Each page has pictures and titles to help new students more easily fit into their new surroundings. Ideas to consider are: pictures and names of individual students (or small groups), teachers and aides they will work with, office staff and administration they may encounter, and the school nurse. Be sure to include special areas in the classroom and in the school, with descriptions of what happens there. Include photos of your class rules being demonstrated by students.

Active participation: The book topics are demonstrated by students and pictures are collected. The book can be put into print or digital format or both. It also makes a nice looping slideshow for the parent's conference night.

Know Your Community

CONTENT AREA/TOPIC: Language Arts, Social Studies
GRADE LEVELS: 3–5   **NETS·S:** 2, 3, 6

Description: Students pick an area of interest about their city to research, photograph, and describe. Areas of interest might include medical facilities, schools, or parks, or the teacher might decide to have an assortment of areas represented.

Teacher preparation: Teachers determine the areas of interest. Depending on the age of the students, teachers provide appropriate structure for the activity.

Active participation: Photos are collected and students write descriptions of the pictures. Books in print or electronic format can be made with these pictures and descriptions.

Variations: This activity could be varied using other topics that teachers choose. It also could be printed and posted on a bulletin board.

Focus on Safety

CONTENT AREA/TOPIC: Language Arts
GRADE LEVELS: 4, 5   **NETS·S:** 2, 6

Description: Digital pictures and slideshows are used in this project, which provides safety rules for students to follow as they travel to and from school.

Teacher preparation: The teacher discusses the need for safety rules and asks the students to discuss such rules with their parents and develop individual lists of rules.

Active participation: Students finalize a list of safety rules to be researched, schedule interviews with selected experts (PE teacher, sheriff, custodian) at the school or in the community for research, stage demonstrations of rules being violated or followed, and take pictures to include in a slideshow. They write and narrate an audio track to accompany the slideshow.

Variations: This activity could be varied using many other topics, such as playground behavior/rules, lunchroom behavior/rules, behavior for collaborative projects, and so on. It also could be printed and posted on a bulletin board.

Source: Juanita Edge, Joan Kirby, East Dale Elementary School: Focus on Safety.

CURRICULUM CONNECTIONS *Continued*

Focus on Life

CONTENT AREA/TOPIC: Science

GRADE LEVEL: 7

NETS·S: 2, 3, 6

Description: Digital pictures and word processing are used in this inquiry-based project, which provides a basis for yearlong inquiry to allow students to photograph various stages of authentic processes.

Teacher preparation: Students are given the option of working by themselves or with partners and may deal with simple observations or experiment with simple or complex topics as they participate in a "photo-tivity."

Active participation: Students choose the specimen for their photo activity. Some examples include the growth cycle of a tadpole or a sugar maple. The photos are taken throughout the change process and are accompanied with a paper that explains the scientific reasoning involved in the changes noted.

Variations: This project could be adapted in other content areas by photographing various phases of construction or design for industrial arts or showing how to measure time according to shadow lengths in math. If cost is a big factor, an entire class could work together to produce a joint photo activity.

Source: Eugene Schmidt, Alan B. Shephard Jr. High School.

membership maintained by the school or district. Once verified, with agreements to abide by copyright restrictions in place, students and their teachers may download these electronic materials. *Bookshare* maintains a web site (**www.bookshare.org**) where teachers may learn about their services and registration procedures.

Although NIMAS books are digitized using a standard accessible format, the files must still be opened by a text reader program. Two complimentary ebook readers are available for text obtained through *Bookshare*. The *Read:OutLoud Bookshare Edition ebook reader* (Don Johnston, Inc.) is designed specifically for individuals with learning disabilities. It offers TTS and other literacy supports, such as electronic highlighting, note-taking options, and embedded reading comprehension strategies that align with state educational standards. *The Victor Reader Soft Bookshare Edition* ebook reader (HumanWare) is intended for people who are blind or who have low vision.

As stated earlier, *Bookshare* files are restricted to students with disabilities who qualify under the Chaffee Amendment. This refers the 1996 amendments to the Copyright Act, Section 121, which allows "a nonprofit organization or governmental agency that has a primary mission to provide specialized services relating to training, education, or adaptive reading or information access needs of blind or other persons with disabilities," to create alternate formats of printed work without seeking permission from the copyright holder (NLS, 1996). *Bookshare* and other NIMAS files are available for students with print-based disabilities, and that verification must be made by qualified medical personnel. As with most legislation, implementation issues have raised certain ambiguities. Students with certain disabilities may not qualify as medically based (some forms of ADHD or emotional disorders). Further, IDEA regulations still require that accessible text be available for any student with disabilities who would benefit. And individual determinations of student eligibility for accessible text are time consuming for teachers and for districts. To address these issues, disability, technology, and publishing groups are working together to develop approaches—which would make text available in multiple formats accessible to all. Until these approaches are widely available, however, teachers may still be faced with the problem of obtaining text in a digital format for some students. One way of converting print material into digital text is to use a scanner and OCR software.

As currently interpreted (Stragman, Hall, & Meyer, 2004; Stahl, 2004), the Chafee Amendment permits teachers who work with students with disabilities to digitize printed text materials in order to provide a version that is accessible. Teachers and schools are in compliance with this amendment if the material is used on an individual basis with students who have disabilities that affect their ability to read printed materials. The amendment restricts further reproduction or distribution of these materials. In other words, it may be acceptable to convert portions of a science text from print to audio file for a student with a learning disability, but it is not acceptable to make copies of that file for everyone in the class.

Although most technology experts agree that converting print-based text to a digital format through scanning is a time-consuming process, for some individuals it is the only available alternative to print. For students who must use digitized text frequently, dedicated software programs such as Kurzweil 3000 or Read & Write Gold have the most accurate and efficient OCR capabilities and an array of definitional and syntactic reading supports. Other affordable methods for these adaptations include copying the OCR-converted text file into a text-to-speech program, such as IntelliTalk, Write:OutLoud, or the speech tool in Microsoft Office. Internet searching will produce a number of other low-cost or free-ware screen reader options. These lower-cost methods are effective for showing teachers the processes for converting text, and for occasional student use or evaluation, to determine whether the conversion to such a format would assist the learning outcome. While low cost and free downloads are always popular among teachers in resource-challenged schools, a caution is in order. Many school districts restrict the download of free screen-reader programs, and many of their features have the potential for conflict with other software. Be sure to check with the school or district technology coordinator regarding procedures for obtaining these programs.

Scanning large amounts of text using a flatbed scanner is time consuming. Sheet-fed scanners, explained earlier, are faster, but they require the book or document to be taken apart or copied initially onto flat sheets of paper. Many of the newer photocopy machines have options that allow a scan to be saved in PDF format, which can then be opened in many text-to-speech software programs. This option may save time when converting some types of printed material.

Some students don't require extensive text-to-speech support, but do need occasional help with reading or note taking. For these students, scanning smaller amounts of text is more useful. The Reading Pen (WizCom Technologies) is a handheld scanner with built-in OCR software. This pen scans words, directly from the printed page, which can then be read, translated, and defined. Larger selections, such as phrases or sentences, can be stored for later transfer to word processing programs or a handheld device such as a PDA.

Obtaining text in a digital format, when and where needed, can still be problematic for some students. With the continued development of digital materials in accessible formats, teachers may need to take the lead in informing school district personnel about the possibilities of digital images and text in supporting the achievement of students with special needs. The Center for Applied Special Technology and LD OnLine (2007) as well as NCTI and CITEd (2007) offer further information on sources and tools for accessing digital text.

On the Web

This section includes only a snapshot of web sites that the authors recommend for viewing. To access live links and a larger and continuously updated collection of sites, go to the companion web site at **www.pearsonhighered.com/ obannon2e**.

Copyright and Fair Use for Educators and Students

Copyright and Fair Use
www.pbs.org/teachers/copyright/
PBS Teachers presents explanations about Copyright Law and Fair Use, Guidelines for Off-Air Recording, and recent Fair Use guidelines for educational multimedia. You will also find FAQs about these issues.

Copyright and Fair Use in the Classroom, on the Internet, and the World Wide Web
www.umuc.edu/llbrary/copy.shtml
The University of Maryland presents excellent information at this site that is from their library. Many of your questions will be answered here in a user-friendly environment.

Digital Collections: Free or Subscription-based

Clipart.com
www.clipart.com/en/index
This site offers a subscription-based collection of clipart, photos, web graphics, illustrations, fonts, and sounds. Compatible art for Web- and print-based documents. There are special school rates available.

CoolCLIPS
www.coolclips.com/index.htm
This site, offered by New Vision Technologies in Canada, offers royalty-free access to many clips that can be used by teachers and students for projects. There is an image license agreement that appears at the site that should be reviewed and adhered to when the clips are downloaded and that advise that all clips are screen resolution and cannot be redistributed without written permission.

Discovery School Clip Art Gallery
http://school.discoveryeducation.com/clipart/
The free clip art gallery, provided by Discovery School, has many categories of images available for student and teacher use if accompanied by a credit. Please read the copyright information at this site and document as requested for permission for use.

Free Photography
www.freestockphotos.com
This site serves as a portal for free photo web sites. There are some restrictions that can be easily identified.

Pics for Learning
http://pics.tech4learning.com
This is an image library for students and teachers and is copyright friendly. The images have been donated by teachers, students, and others who give permission for the images to be used.

Digital Cameras, Scanners, and Reviews

Digicamhelp
www.digicamhelp.com
This guide for digital camera beginners and beyond, originally started by an educator to help her less technical friends, has since transformed into pages that present information on digital cameras and photography. This information-rich site connects the reader to a buying guide, features, accessories, taking pictures, working with images, and more.

How a Digital Camera Works
http://electronics.howstuffworks.com/digital-camera.htm
This site details the inner workings of a digital camera, detailing the process from capture to output.

How Scanners Work
www.howstuffworks.com/scanner.htm
This section of howstuffworks.com presents both basic and in-depth information about flatbed, sheet-fed, handheld, and drum scanners. A drop-down menu makes the information quite convenient to the reader.

Integrating Digital Images in Learning

Educational Uses of Digital Storytelling
http://digitalstorytelling.coe.uh.edu/
Published at the University of Houston and written by Dr. Bernard Robin, this page explains the steps to creating a digital story. Storytelling is a vital skill with many applications. An overview of digital storytelling, examples of digital stories, software applications to use, how to evaluate as well as many resources are shared.

Quick! Get the (Digital) Camera!
www.educationworld.com/a_tech/tech/tech148.shtml
This article, published by Education World, is shared by a tech coordinator in South Dakota and presents ways that students use digital cameras in learning in grades K–12. Share the neat ideas from Craig Nansen.

Using Technology in the Classroom
http://schristensen.basd.k12.wi.us/lessonideas/primary/
Find lesson ideas that include using digital cameras with elementary, middle school, and high school curricula at this site. Activities for the older students include the use of slideshows and other multimedia software.

Key Terms

Decoration (156)
Representation (156)
Organization (156)
Interpretation (156)
Transformation (156)
Anchored instruction (156)
Enhancement of learning (156)
Availability (156)
Cost of reproduction (156)
Digital image (158)
Pixel (158)
Resolution (158)
Digital camera resolution (158)
Pixel count (158)
Computer monitor resolution (158)
Printer resolution (159)
Dots per inch (dpi) (159)
Digital camera (159)
Image sensor (159)
Memory (159)
Megapixels (MP) (159)
Point-and-shoot digital camera (160)
Semi-professional digital camera (160)
Professional camera (160)
Video (160)
Digital video camera (160)
Camcorder (160)

Web cam (160)
Power on/off button (161)
Optical viewfinder (161)
LCD screen (161)
Camera lens (161)
Fixed-focus lens (161)
Zoom lens (161)
Optical zoom (161)
Digital zoom (161)
Shutter (161)
Adjusting aperture (161)
Autofocus feature (161)
Shutter lag (162)
Flash (162)
Red-eye (162)
Memory source (162)
Fixed memory (162)
Removable memory (162)
Compact flash (CF) (162)
SecureDigital (SD) (162)
Memory Sticks (MS) (162)
Driver software (163)
Budget (164)
Image quality (164)
Image storage (164)
Connectivity (164)
Battery life (164)

Object-based file (165)
Vector graphics (165)
Raster graphics (165)
Bitmap (BMP) files (167)
Graphic Interchange Format (GIF) (167)
Joint Photographic Experts Group (JPEG) (167)
Portable Network Graphic (PNG) (167)
Tagged Image File (TIFF) (167)
Portable Document Format (PDF) (167)
Lossless compression (167)
Lossy compression (168)
Flatbed scanner (168)
Sheet-fed scanner (168)
Film scanner (168)
Scanner bed (168)
Scanner lid (168)
Scanner software (169)
Image editing software (169)
Optical character recognition (OCR) software (169)
Copyright law (171)
Fair Use law (171)

Hands-on Activities for Learning

1. Visit the On the Web companion site (**www.pearsonhighered.com/obannon2e**) and review the sites available.
2. Write a reflection in your Reflective Technology Blog about ways to integrate digital images into learning activities with the target population that you will be teaching.
3. Use the digital camera to complete a scavenger hunt appropriate for your students.
4. Use Photo Sharing software such as Flickr or Picasa to create an album and share photos on the Web.

5. Use iMovie or Windows Movie Maker to create a movie from still shots. Insert titles, transitions, effects, and audio to enhance the topic.
6. Develop a lesson that is aligned with state curriculum standards and requires that K–12 students use digital images to promote their learning. List ways that would be appropriate to adapt the lesson for special learners.
7. Develop a scenario or quiz of situations for students that would allow them to determine whether you have legal rights to use digital files.

Diagrams, Maps, and Webs

LEARNER OBJECTIVES

At the completion of this chapter, learners will be able to:

- Discuss research related to the effective use of visual learning tools, specifically diagrams, maps, and webs, in teaching and learning.

- Use terminology associated with diagrams, maps, and webs and their use.

- Examine learning activities that include diagrams, maps, and/or webs.

- Create a concept map, story map, or web that depicts an appropriate curriculum topic using mapping software.

- Plan and develop a learning activity that aligns with state curriculum and NETS·S and requires PK–12 students to actively use mapping software to promote their learning through analysis of a story map, a character map, a vocabulary word, a curriculum concept, or a comparison/contrast of a curriculum topic.

- Discuss methods for using visual learning tools, specifically diagrams, maps, and webs with special learners.

NETS·T ALIGNED WITH DIAGRAMS, MAPS, AND WEBS

2. **Design and Develop Digital-Age Learning Experiences and Assessments**

   Teachers design, develop, and evaluate authentic learning experiences and assessments incorporating contemporary tools and resources to maximize content learning in context and to develop the knowledge, skills, and attitudes identified in the NETS·S. Teachers:

   a. design or adapt relevant learning experiences that incorporate digital tools and resources to promote student learning and creativity.

   b. develop technology-enriched learning environments that enable all students to pursue their individual curiosities and become active participants in setting their own educational goals, managing their own learning, and assessing their own progress.

   c. customize and personalize learning activities to address students' diverse learning styles, working strategies, and abilities using digital tools and resources

   d. provide students with multiple and varied formative and summative assessments aligned with content and technology standards and use resulting data to inform learning and teaching.

Frameworks

Visual learning is identified as a graphical means of working with ideas and presenting information (Inspiration, 2006). Visual learning is commonly associated with graphic organizers. Graphic organizers, described by Dye (2000) as visual displays that make information easier to learn and understand, include concept maps, story maps, advance organizers, semantic maps, and webs. Visual learning approaches include the use of illustrations, photographs, diagrams, and graphs to facilitate the learner's ability to understand complex information.

Learning visually is based on the work of David Ausubel in the early 1960s. Ausubel believed that graphic illustrations organized information to help students learn. Ausubel proposed that visuals such as maps facilitated learning, especially when the learning included unfamiliar or abstract ideas. The construction of a visual map directs learner attention and reinforces concepts. This tool also serves the organizational purpose of helping students remember material by increasing the depth at which content is processed.

Ausubel also believed that new knowledge is reliant on previous knowledge. In other words, students learn by constructing a network of ideas and adding to these ideas. Construction of knowledge begins with learner observation and recognition of things around them based on concepts they already possess. Concept maps are useful in clarifying links between old and new knowledge.

Several cognitive learning theories support the use of visual learning tools and provide the foundation for explaining why graphic organizers support the learning process. These theories include dual coding theory, schema theory, and cognitive load theory. **Dual coding theory** suggests that learners code information in both verbal and nonverbal formats. Both can be addressed with visual learning tools and thus make retention of information easier. **Schema theory** proposes that schemas (networks of information) exist in a learner's memory. These schemas make up prior knowledge. Visual learning tools assist learners in linking the existing schemas to new knowledge. Finally, **cognitive load theory** explains that there is a limit to the information that can be processed at one time. If that limit is exceeded, no learning will take place. Visual learning tools can reduce the load and make learning possible.

The Institute for the Advancement of Research in Education (IARE) conducted a study of existing education research on the benefit of graphic organizers. This study used the definition set by Section 9101 of No Child Left Behind (NCLB) Act when identifying 29 scientifically based research studies that concluded that visual learning improves student performance in the areas of literacy development (vocabulary skills, writing skills, and reading comprehension), critical thinking and higher-order thinking skills, retention and recall of information, problem solving, and organization (IARE, 2003).

Basics

Although there are other software options, the most popular diagramming software is Inspiration (http://inspiration.com/Inspiration). This software tool, designed by Inspiration Software, Inc. and typically used with students in grades 6–12, allows them to create an illustration of their ideas in diagram or outline format. The software is used across the curriculum for brainstorming, webbing, diagramming, planning, concept mapping, organizing, and outlining.

A simplified version, Kidspiration (http://inspiration.com/Kidspiration), created for grades K–5, helps young students develop thinking, literacy, and numeracy skills using visual learning techniques. This program strengthens word recognition, vocabulary, comprehension, and written expression. New to Kidspiration are visual math tools to help students build reasoning and problem-solving skills. There are Web-based versions that provide immediate access if you have a computer with an Internet connection and a browser. In 2009, Inspiration created Webspiration, which is currently in beta. Lerman (2006) reports that one of the best versions is Gliffy (**www.gliffy.com**). Because it is Web-based, students can collaboratively work on projects as they create, edit, and share information. The basic version is free while the premium version is $5 per month. Be sure to review the examples provided at the top of the site.

Teachers can integrate visual learning tools to support a variety of subjects in a variety of different ways, as seen in Figure 8.1. The strategy allows teachers to clearly identify student misunderstandings revealed by incorrect or misdirected labels or links. The process encourages students to see contradictions or gaps in information and provides a basis for questioning, creativity, and discussion. The process also supports organizational skills and nonsequential thinking.

Uses of Diagrams

There are various types of **diagrams** that assist learning; each has its place in various curriculum activities. Concept maps, idea maps, storyboards, and webs are popular ways to integrate the use of diagrams in the K–12 classroom.

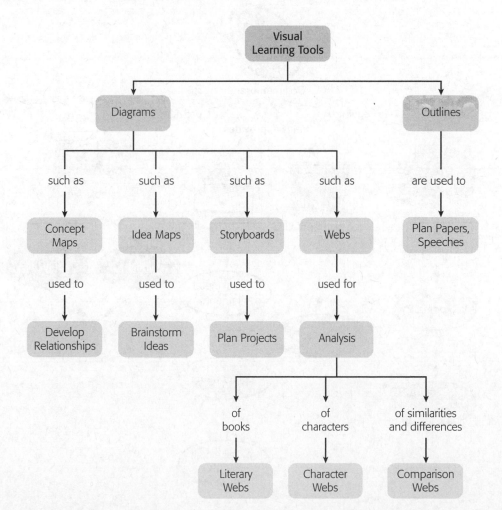

FIGURE 8.1 Uses of Visual Learning Tools

Concept Maps

Joseph Novack at Cornell University developed concept mapping in the early 1980s. A **concept map** is a hierarchical diagram showing the relationships between concepts. It begins with the most general and progresses to the specific. Often used to represent scientific or historical concepts, the map contains propositions and two or more concept labels (or items, questions, and so on) linked by words that describe their relationship. The map shows relationships between concepts through these linking words and arrows that indicate the direction of the relationship. An example of a concept map appears in Figure 8.2.

Idea Map (Brainstorming)

Idea maps are created during brainstorming sessions. **Brainstorming** is an approach used to facilitate spontaneous thinking and generate ideas. Judgment is suspended during the process. This approach allows students to view a concept from other perspectives and to develop critical-thinking skills. Long used in classrooms, brainstorming is greatly enhanced by using diagramming software such as Inspiration. (See Figure 8.3.)

The basic process is simple, yet in order to make the session productive, the teacher should incorporate some structure. First, a focus statement of what to accomplish should be written and displayed where students can see it. If the statement is too general, students will not know where to start.

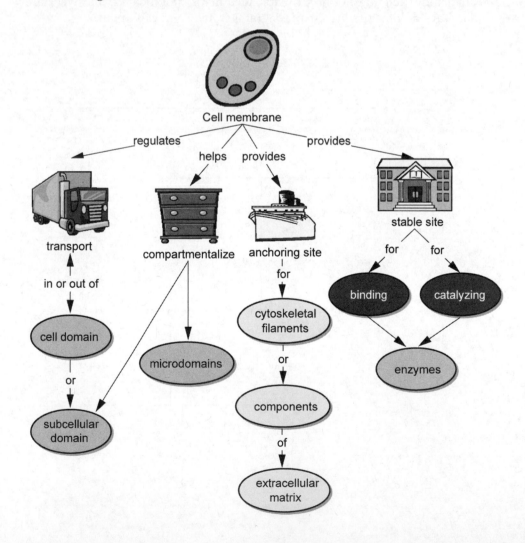

FIGURE 8.2 Concept Map: Cell Membrane
Source: © 2008 Inspiration Software®, Inc. Diagram created by Jessica Schwind in Inspiration® by Inspiration Software®, Inc. Used with permission.

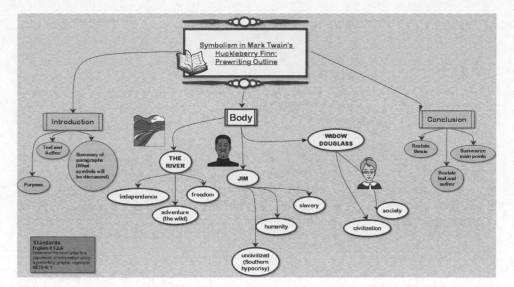

Next, the teacher should determine whether to serve as the scribe (recorder) who enters the ideas into the program or to appoint a student to this role. This decision depends on the developmental levels of the students and their familiarity with the program. Next, the students should be allowed to freely generate ideas, while the scribe enters these ideas into Inspiration. After the ideas are entered, students cluster related ideas and eliminate redundancies or ideas that do not fit. Students then determine directional links between information with appropriate labels. Finally, students can analyze and refine the map.

Web

A **web** (in this context) is a visual map that illustrates how different pieces of information relate to each other. A web has a main idea in the center, with different kinds of information connected to it. There are a variety of webs, including literary webs, character webs, comparison webs, and prewriting webs.

A *literary web* facilitates understanding, as students analyze stories to determine specific information about the plot, characters, or theme. A *character web* allows the student to identify various traits of the characters in the story, which is particularly useful for complex stories. Figure 8.4 provides an example of a character web. A comparison web allows students to compare and contrast information to determine the connections (see Figure 8.5). Many topics lend themselves to this use of visual learning and include people, places, or events. Venn diagrams, often used in teaching and learning, fit into this category of diagrams. *Prewriting webs* are used during the writing process. Students enter the main idea in the center and brainstorm ideas about their paper. After the brainstorming session, the student organizes and transfers the information to an outline that can serve as a guide for writing.

Storyboard

A **storyboard** is a visual means of planning for a project such as a multimedia presentation or web site. Each symbol can represent each card or a page. Figure 8.6 is an example of a storyboard showing the navigation of a nonlinear slideshow that could be used as a tutorial or study guide on a topic.

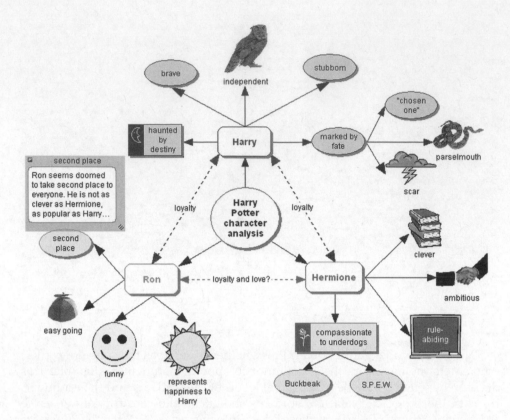

FIGURE 8.4 Character
Web: *Harry Potter*
Source: © 2008 Inspiration
Software®, Inc. Diagram
created in Inspiration® by
Inspiration Software®, Inc.
Used with permission.

Uses of Outlines

Outlines

Use **outlines** to create a hierarchical structure for ideas for a paper, speech, or project.

Visual Learning Capabilities (Inspiration)

Visual learning tools—the most popular of which is Inspiration—have multiple useful features.

Working with Inspiration

Working with Inspiration is quite easy even for those new to the program. Free downloads are now available for the major platforms, at **www.inspiration.com**. The program should be installed on the hard drive. In this section, a step-by-step guide will guide you through the steps. If Webspiration becomes a reality, this can be done through a Web browser with an account.

Opening the Program   Before work can be completed, a new document (or file) must be opened. Double-click the icon to open the program. Inspiration opens in diagram view, which is where information is constructed (see Figure 8.7).

Saving a File in Inspiration   It is a good idea to save your document file regularly, and it should always be saved to a place that is easy to locate. The first time that a file is saved, the Save command is used, and the file is given a descriptive name so that it is easy to find later. Inspiration files add an .isf extension.

Transferring a File in Inspiration   Inspiration files can be transferred to a word processing program of your choice (Microsoft Word, Apple Pages, or OpenOffice) by

Life Becomes Fiction
Charlotte Brontë and Jane Eyre

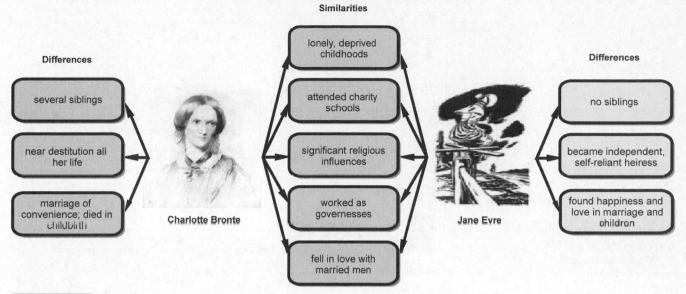

FIGURE 8.5 Comparison Web, Life Becomes Fiction: Charlotte Brontë and Jane Eyre

Source: © 2008 Inspiration Software®, Inc. Diagram created in Inspiration® by Inspiration Software®, Inc. Used with permission.

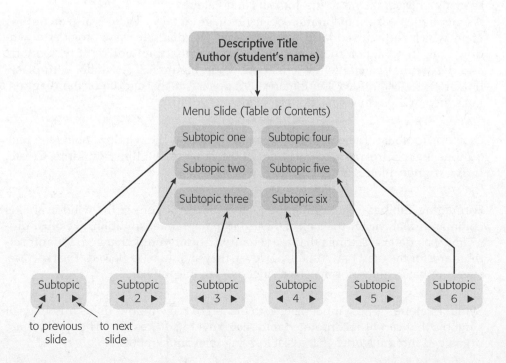

FIGURE 8.6 Storyboard Example

Toolbar

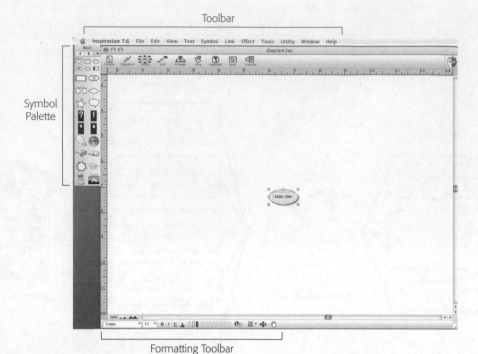

Symbol
Palette

Formatting Toolbar

FIGURE 8.7 Diagram
View in Inspiration
Source: © 2008 Inspiration
Software®, Inc. Diagram
created in Inspiration® by
Inspiration Software®, Inc.
Used with permission.

selecting the Transfer button on the toolbar. The word processor is opened, and the
file can be viewed in outline or diagram modes.

Exporting a Diagram
Diagrams and outlines can be exported to HTML files for the
Web by going to the File menu and choosing Export.

Working in Diagram View: The Toolbars and Palette
As mentioned earlier, Inspiration opens in diagram view. There is also an outline
view, which is discussed later in this chapter. The diagram view provides a window with the **diagram toolbar** at the top, the **formatting toolbar** at the bottom,
and the **symbol palette** to the left, as shown in Figure 8.7. A symbol with placeholder text ("Main Idea") automatically appears in the middle of the diagram.
Let's look at these toolbars and the palette a little closer.

Diagram Toolbar
The diagram toolbar, at the top of the window, holds the nine
buttons that control particular features of the program: Outline, Rapidfire, Create,
Link, Arrange, Note, Hyperlink, Spell, and Transfer.

Formatting Toolbar
The formatting toolbar, at the bottom of the window, holds
commands that change the look of the text in a diagram. Inspiration, like other programs, has default settings that are set automatically until changed. Default settings are, for the most part, useful; however, they should be reviewed. The typeface,
size, emphasis, and color may be changed using this toolbar.

Symbol Palette
The symbol palette, to the left of the window, holds hundreds of
symbols that can be incorporated into diagrams to add realism. The symbols are
organized into categories that assist locating relevant symbols.

Working in Diagram View: Creating a Diagram

Entering a Main Idea   The placeholder text should be changed to the main idea topic of the diagram. Information radiates from the main idea. Symbols may be added as linked symbols or unconnected symbols that will be linked at a later time.

Adding Linked Symbols   Adding linked symbols is completed by using the Create or Rapidfire tool. Linked symbols can be added with the Create tool by clicking on the main idea symbol and clicking on the point on the Create button that signifies the location for the next symbol. This may be continued until all linked symbols are entered.

Linked symbols can also be added with the Rapidfire tool quickly in an open form structure by: (1) clicking the Rapidfire button located on the diagram toolbar; (2) clicking on the starting point symbol; and (3) clicking on additional symbols. Rapidfire places attention on getting the information onto the paper quickly, with organization and placement of the ideas to be completed later. When this tool is active, the Rapidfire icon appears inside the symbol.

Adding Unconnected Symbols   Inspiration will automatically create a symbol that is not linked by pointing and typing in the diagram window. This feature is useful in cases when you are not yet sure where to position the text.

Linking Symbols   Linking the symbols in a diagram is used to indicate the relationship between ideas. Linking symbols can be completed by: (1) selecting the starting point symbol for the link (perhaps the main idea); (2) selecting the Link button on the diagram toolbar; and (3) selecting the symbol where the link is to end. The process continues until all links are complete. At this time, the Link tool is turned off.

Adding Text on a Link   A text box appears on a link when the link is selected. Inserting text into the text box defines the relationship between the symbols.

Adding a Note to a Symbol   Notes provide a method to expand ideas, as the symbols provide little writing space. A note is available for each symbol in a diagram, though they may not be used. A note is added by: (1) selecting the symbol; (2) selecting the Note button on the diagram toolbar; and (3) entering the desired text.

Arranging the Diagram   When the diagram is completed, the Arrange tool organizes the diagram into a readable format. To arrange the diagram: (1) select the Arrange button on the diagram toolbar; (2) select a pattern in the Links menu; (3) select a pattern in the diagram type list; and (4) select OK to close the tool.

Adding a Hyperlink   Hyperlinks can be easily inserted into the diagram for Web access. To insert a hyperlink: (1) select the text in a symbol; (2) select the Hyperlink button on the diagram toolbar; (3) type the Web address in the Link To box; and (4) deselect the Hyperlink button to deactivate it. Hyperlinks provide a way to take the reader to a web site for more information or to a video.

Working in Outline View

As mentioned earlier, Inspiration offers an outline view, in which work can be entered or edited. (See Figure 8.8 for a sample of different views.) While working in the diagram view, Inspiration is creating an outline of your work in the background. To see the outline, click the Outline button on the diagram toolbar. The diagram switches to an outline, showing the symbols as topics and subtopics and the text on the notes is visible.

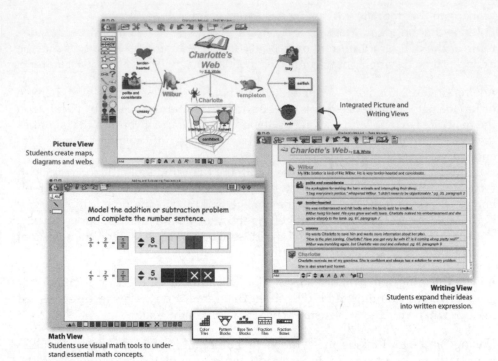

FIGURE 8.8 Young Learners Use Picture View, Integrated Writing View, and Math View in Kidspiration
Source: © 2008 Inspiration Software®, Inc. Diagram created in Kidspiration® by Inspiration Software®, Inc. Used with permission.

Adapting for Special Learners

Many students with disabilities and/or language differences have problems with comprehension, vocabulary development, and abstract reasoning when information is presented in text. Students exhibiting these types of learning difficulties typically have not learned to use strategies for learning new material efficiently. They often confuse the probability of success with the effort it takes to learn. For example, they might spend hours rereading an assignment when studying for a test, or reading a passage straight through, skipping over unknown terms and not stopping to question whether they understand what they are reading. When their efforts do not bring the result or grade they expect, they blame the task (the test was stupid) or the teacher (she never liked me anyway), or themselves (I am just plain dumb). Successful students are more strategic. They might spend the same amount of time reviewing vocabulary terms, finding key ideas from text and notes, and developing diagrams of major concepts.

Visual learning strategies are among the evidence-based practices used to assist struggling learners (Bulgren, Schumaker, & Deschler, 1988; Gardill & Jitendra, 1999). These strategies are reported in the literature under a variety of names: concept maps, story maps, advanced organizers, story webs, or semantic maps. They are used to help students understand the structure and content of text and to organize ideas for writing, note taking and vocabulary development. Training students to use visual learning strategies is essential to their effective use.

The advantage of using a diagramming software program such as Inspiration is that it gives both teachers and students flexibility. Working in a digital environment enables one to quickly adapt the display of information or to add additional supports. The content may be transformed in appearance or in format (for example, increasing the size of the screen, or having the text read aloud). The student

CURRICULUM CONNECTIONS

A Powerful Web to Weave

CONTENT AREA/TOPIC: Language Arts
GRADE LEVELS: 1, 2   **NETS·S:** 1, 6

Description: Digital pictures, webbing software, and word processing is used in the five-step process—Think, Draw, Tell, Write, Share—to assist children to learn to write. Three activities precede the writing activity.

Teacher preparation:

1. *Preparing to write.* At the beginning of school, the teacher takes digital pictures of the students to use in the project. Students are encouraged to think about what they would write about themselves, such as their favorite foods, games, sports, TV programs, pets, and such.

2. *Planning with webbing.* Use a webbing program such as Inspiration or a drawing tool in a word processing program and create a template for students to enter information about themselves. Students can put the picture of themselves in the middle of the web.

3. *Writing.* Students use the information from the web to compose a summary about themselves. Teachers or assistants enter the information in a word processor as the students dictate it.

Variations: Any program that has text writing capabilities can be used, such as KidPix Deluxe or HyperStudio5.

Source: Etchinson, C. (1995). A powerful web to weave: Developing writing skills for elementary students. *Learning and Leading with Technology,* 23(3), pp. 14–15.

Amazing Words

CONTENT AREA/TOPIC: Language Arts
GRADE LEVELS: 1–8   **NETS·S:** 1, 3, 6

Description: In this lesson, students complete a template that the teacher has developed to broaden their understanding of vocabulary words. Students are actively involved with technology and complete the template with antonyms, and synonyms, as well as creating sentences with the word.

Preparation: The teacher develops a vocabulary list. It could be composed of unusual words or simply words that are connected to learning. Explain the definitions of the words and their derivations. Using a Language Arts Vocabulary template that has been developed, the teacher enters the word and the definition in the open note. The template could be provided in Inspiration as well. Note: Dictionaries, thesauruses, and other language references should be made available to students.

Active participation: Students fill in the remainder of the template, which includes antonyms, synonyms, and sentences using the words.

Variations: Other categories for additional information about the word may be added, such as singular or plural versions of a noun, or tenses of a verb.

Source: Inspiration (2002). Amazing words. Achieving Standards with Inspiration 7, pp. 2–3.

(Continues)

CURRICULUM CONNECTIONS *Continued*

Timelines

CONTENT AREA/TOPIC: Research, Writing
GRADE LEVELS: 1–8   **NETS·S:** 1, 6

Description: In this lesson, students are actively involved on the computer creating timelines using curriculum connections determined by the teacher.

Teacher preparation: Teachers determine topics that would be appropriately represented in a timeline. The options are endless; ideas can be found in the On the Web section of this chapter. The beginning of school is a great time to introduce the concept of timelines by creating one in which holidays, school events, and vacations can be posted. Photographs can be added to tell the story of the event as it happens, as well as newspaper clippings of current events as they happen. This activity will get students ready and eager to use concept maps in learning information.

Active participation: Students use Inspiration software to construct a timeline of events. Timelines could be developed for story events from a book the students are reading, things students did on a class field trip, or personal journal entries. Other ideas include timelines that serve as records of important events in the past, such as the Civil War, the development of the Internet, or the life of a famous scientist.

Source: Education World Timelines: Timeless Teaching Tool. Retrieved October 13, 2008, from **www.educationworld.com/ a_lesson/lesson044.shtml**.

Brainstorming Maps

CONTENT AREA/TOPIC: Prewriting Strategies
GRADE LEVELS: 3–12   **NETS·S:** 4, 6

Description: Students actively participate in a brainstorming session preceding a writing lesson and see mapping software modeled by the teacher or fellow students. Students may participate as scribes as determined by the teacher. This lesson can be repeated with various topics throughout the year.

Teacher preparation: Teachers can use brainstorming as a group technique for generating new, useful ideas; promoting creative thinking; and creating a map of ideas. Teachers choose a topic for brainstorming and designate a time limit for brainstorming activities. Teachers act as facilitator of the process and may or may not act as the scribe on the concept mapping tool. Teachers should explain the ground rules of brainstorming to the students to get the most out of the activity. Such rules include: (1) all answers are welcome and there are no wrong answers; (2) be creative with answers; (3) attempt to give high-quality ideas; and (4) "hook on" to the ideas previously generated.

Active participation: Students join in the session, making suggestions that are appropriate for the topic. They may receive the visual of the map after the session to assist a writing assignment on the topic.

may link to explanatory files or web sites for additional information. As stated repeatedly throughout this text, visual learning software is another example of using a tool to build in options that support learning differences from the beginning, reducing the need to modify or create alternate assignments or adapt for special learners after the fact (Rose & Meyer, 2002). The following supports can be used with visual learning software.

Voices *from the* Classroom

Visual Learning Software in the Curriculum
Kevin Thomas

Kevin Thomas was a high school language arts teacher for 15 years. For the last seven years of his tenure in secondary education, Kevin taught at an inner city high school. We interviewed him concerning the insights he was able to garner from his attempts to integrate visual learning software into the curriculum.

My freshman English class had just completed a unit on Shakespeare's *Romeo and Juliet.* I was quite disappointed with the scores on the unit test. At the time, I was just learning about the potential benefits related to the use of technology in the classroom. One of the software applications I had recently learned about was a visual learning program called Inspiration. I decided to use Inspiration for the next unit on Homer's *Odyssey* to see if there were improvements.

The lesson that I designed using Inspiration was twofold. The first part of the lesson required the students to create a character map of all the characters in the story. I created a rubric that graded the students based on the inclusion of basic design features such as a heading, categories, subcategories, linking words, spelling/grammar, and notes. Students were also graded on the depth of their inclusion of various characters, as well as the notes that they included to describe the characters. Other categories that the rubric included related to the use of appropriate icons and the logical arrangement and originality of the design. The second part of the lesson allowed the students to make a choice. They could create a concept map that outlined the various conflicts in the story or they could create a plot line. A rubric was also designed to guide these activities.

This weeklong lesson began in the computer lab, with a half hour spent on learning the basics of Inspiration and then letting them work in pairs while I moved around to assist. Let me say that at no other time in the semester did the students work as well as they did during this lesson. They were all completely engaged in the use of this technology.

Of course, I was thrilled by the way that the students responded to the software, but I was interested in whether it would affect their retention of information. The timing of the lesson was the week before the unit test and was designed as a review. By engaging the students in reflecting on the story, would they improve their comprehension and ultimately demonstrate this on their unit test? That was the million-dollar question, and the resulting answer was "yes." Granted, this was not a scientific test, but the class average for the unit test on the *Odyssey* was higher than that for *Romeo and Juliet.* I do not know what part the concept map lesson played in this improvement, but I do know that the students were actively (excitedly) engaged in using the software while they were being forced to go back through the entire *Odyssey* looking for specifics related to characters, conflicts, and plot details.

Yet, there were challenges. As is the case with all aspects of education, planning is essential. The mobile computer lab had to be reserved in advance. Further, because our school did not have the software, it was necessary for me to download 20 trial copies onto the laptops, which was an extremely time-consuming process.

In my current job, in the School of Education at Bellamine University, I help students understand not only the benefits of the integration of technology into their curricula, but also the challenges they will often encounter while trying to utilize technology in their classrooms. Hopefully, as was my experience, I help them realize that the benefits garnered from such use by their students outweigh any cost they may incur.

Visual Supports

A printed version provides all students with a study copy or an outline from which to begin developing responses to an assignment. The display, as viewed on the screen, may be changed to accommodate student preferences—the diagram and text size may be enlarged, high-contrast color combinations could be added. Students needing magnification can be accommodated with the magnifier program (see Chapter 3), a larger monitor, a projected image, or a large "smart board" for the display. Students who are blind may use screen reading software in the outline view of the visual learning program.

Auditory Supports

The visual display may be read aloud using the text reading and voice note options to accommodate students with either visual or reading limitations.

Motivational, Interest, and Cognitive Supports

Digital formats are not one-dimensional; they can easily link the learner to other places. Teachers may take advantage of this transportability by planning for features that hold student interest, accommodate a shorter attention span, or provide cognitive support. For example, hyperlinks can be added to most visual learning software programs. This capacity may be used to connect to a definitions page in a word processing program, or to an Internet site that illustrates the concept with a video clip. The teacher may add these links to aid in the presentation of the material. Similarly, the student, depending on technology skills and abilities, may add hyperlinks to demonstrate what has been learned.

Some students with disabilities have difficulty with the complexity of a program such as Inspiration. Consider using Kidspiration software as an alternative to simplify the cognitive demands of the display and the learning task at hand. While Kidspiration is intended for students in grades K–4, the simplified commands may be easier to use for older students who need the support.

Learning Strategy Support

Visual learning software, when paired with other evidence-based learning strategies, is effective with diverse learners in general education settings. Anderson-Inman and colleagues (1996) reported using Inspiration to teach students with learning disabilities how to study a textbook. Using the structure of a concept map, students were shown a three-step process. The students first created a skeleton of the chapter by typing in the headings and subheadings. They then read each paragraph and recorded key phrases or ideas in new symbols linked to each heading or subheading. The third step was to self-test their knowledge by hiding or showing (using expand or contract functions) material under each heading (Anderson-Inman, Knox-Quinn, & Horney, 1996). Other studies pair the use of visual learning software with content-area literacy strategies (Puckett & Brozo, 2004; Brozo & Puckett, 2009).

Some students with disabilities may need help with the writing process, and features of visual learning software can be used to provide these supports. Templates provided in the programs can provide ideas for how to develop a visual map of the concept being studied. Once a diagram is completed, the outline view may be exported to a word processor so that other cognitive supports, such as a dictionary, thesaurus, word prediction, or text-to-speech, may be accessed to aid in the writing process.

Draft:Builder (Don Johnston, Inc.) is a visual learning program specially designed to support the writing process. Draft:Builder is a part of a suite of products called *Solo,* and contains many features that are similar to Inspiration, with a slightly different user interface. Students enter items into an outline, from which they gather information and form ideas. Both the outline and the visual map are displayed in a split-screen format. Notes may be added to the outline using "drag and drop" features. The program interfaces with the other programs in *Solo:* word prediction (Co:Writer) and text-to-speech (Write:Outloud). Outline templates for different writing purposes that are patterned on evidence-based strategy research are included in the program. These include outlines for essay, compare and contrast, interview, grouping, and expository reports. Documentation also includes research references for each strategy.

On the Web

This section includes only a snapshot of web sites that the authors recommend for viewing. To access live links and a larger and continuously updated collection of sites, go to the companion web site at **www.pearsonhighered.com/obannon2e.**

Integration of Diagrams, Maps, Webs, and More

The following web sites include many ideas for including visual learning in the curriculum:

Curriculum Integration from Inspiration Software
www.inspiration.com/Examples/Search
Inspiration software offers a section specifically for curriculum integration. Drop-down menus offer access to curriculum ideas for language arts, reading, math, science, and social studies plus cross curriculum, meeting standards, and test prep for grades K–12.

Education World: Timelines: Timeless Teaching Tool
www.educationworld.com/a_lesson/lesson/lesson044.shtml
Education World shares great examples of how to use timelines to document changing times and putting these changes into perspective in the elementary and above curriculum. Find lesson ideas for all grade levels.

Fifty Uses of Inspiration and Kidspiration
www.uwstout.edu/soe/profdev/conceptmap/50uses.html
This site at the University of Wisconsin, Stout, presents 50 ideas for the integration of visual learning tools in the curriculum.

Graphic Organizers by Scholastic
www2.scholastic.com/browse/article.jsp?id=2983
Scholastic provides information about graphic organizer patterns, reading comprehension organizers, story elements (character, plot, setting, sequence), organizers, and assessment at this site.

S.C.O.R.E: Graphic Organizers
www.sdcoe.k12.ca.us/score/actbank/torganiz.htm
Schools of California Online Resources for Education (SCORE) provides many resources for teachers. At this site, explanations of various graphic organizer configurations are presented as well as their usefulness in the classroom.

The Graphic Organizer
www.graphic.org
This site is maintained by Greg Freeman and eVisions.net and provides materials that can be duplicated for educational purposes. The site suggests that graphic organizers (mind maps or concept maps) are powerful tools that can be used to enhance learning.

Software Options

Draft:Builder by Don Johnston, Inc.
www.donjohnston.com
This site provides information on products, research, and services for Draft:Builder software and *Solo*, its suite of integrated literacy supports.

Kidspiration
www.inspiration.com/Kidspiration
Kidspiration is a version created for learners in grades K–5 so they can learn to categorize and group ideas, organize thoughts, and communicate. Trial software can be downloaded for 30 days.

Inspiration
www.inspiration.com
Inspiration software provides this site to inform interested readers about this visual learning tool. Found here is information about Inspiration, Kidspiration, visual learning, curriculum integration, No Child Left Behind, Inspiration for Palm, and much more. Trial software can be downloaded for 30 days.

Gliffy
www.gliffy.com
Gliffy is a Web-based diagramming software that allows you to create and share flow charts, diagrams, and more. Students can build their 21st century skills as they create, share, and collaborate. This sight provides examples and a blog for comments. There is a basic version and a premium version. Gliffy Basic is free and the premium is $5 per month for individuals.

Key Terms

Visual learning (182)	Concept map (184)	Outline (186)
Dual coding theory (182)	Idea map (184)	Diagram toolbar (188)
Schema theory (182)	Brainstorming (184)	Formatting toolbar (188)
Cognitive load theory (182)	Web (185)	Symbol palette (188)
Diagram (183)	Storyboard (185)	

Hands-on Activities for Learning

1. Visit the On the Web companion site (**www.pearsonhighered.com/obannon2e**) and review the sites available.

2. Write a reflection in your blog about ways to use diagrams, maps, and webs in the classroom.

3. Use diagramming software to have a brainstorming session in the classroom.

4. Re-create one of the lessons listed in the Curriculum Connections section of this chapter to simulate the activity in the classroom. During this re-creation, jot down lessons learned and discuss with classmates.

5. Develop a student-centered activity that requires K–12 students to use diagramming software to create a concept map from a topic in the curriculum that is aligned with state curriculum standards.

6. Develop a student-centered lesson that requires K–12 students to create a storyboard for a multimedia project that is aligned with state curriculum standards.

7. Insert the activities or lessons into the curriculum file of a teacher portfolio.

LEARNER OBJECTIVES

At the completion of this chapter, learners will be able to:

- Discuss research that supports the use of databases in K–12 instruction.
- Use terminology and capabilities associated with databases.
- Examine lessons that incorporate use of databases into teaching and learning.
- Develop student-centered activities that use databases as a tool for learning.
- Plan and develop a lesson that aligns with state curriculum and NETS·S standards and requires students to use a database to promote their learning.
- Determine appropriate methods of adapting databases for special learners.

NETS·T ALIGNED WITH DATABASES

2. **Design and Develop Digital-Age Learning Experiences and Assessments**

   Teachers design, develop, and evaluate authentic learning experiences and assessments incorporating contemporary tools and resources to maximize content learning in context and to develop the knowledge, skills, and attitudes identified in the NETS·S. Teachers:

   a. design or adapt relevant learning experiences that incorporate digital tools and resources to promote student learning and creativity.

   b. develop technology-enriched learning environments that enable all students to pursue their individual curiosities and become active participants in setting their own educational goals, managing their own learning, and assessing their own progress.

   c. customize and personalize learning activities to address students' diverse learning styles, working strategies, and abilities using digital tools and resources.

   d. provide students with multiple and varied formative and summative assessments aligned with content and technology standards and use resulting data to inform learning and teaching.

Frameworks

Databases are used so often and in so many ways that it is difficult to imagine what our world was like before their common use. From directory assistance to medical records and airline reservations, businesses and individuals use a variety of databases to quickly and efficiently store, retrieve, and modify records. Databases also have their place in teaching and learning.

Databases can be thought of as an electronic version of a card file or a filing cabinet. Records, analogous to index cards or file folders, contain defined pieces of information, or fields, such as last name, Social Security number, or zip code. Just as in a filing cabinet or card box, these records can be sorted or filed in any order, by any one of the fields (such as by last name). But unlike a card file or filing cabinet, electronic databases provide users the option of quickly changing the sorting order in numerous ways. Additionally, the information within each record, because it is digitized, can be transported to other files or applications, such as word-processed reports, letters, or labels, without moving or corrupting the original file.

In the classroom, teachers and students can create databases to help keep track of information from data collection and to sort through disconnected facts to find relationships. Using databases in research projects makes the process of analysis and presentation of results easier and more efficient.

Research studies cite the ability of databases to facilitate the use of higher-order thinking skills, an essential element of the newer, constructivist teaching strategies. Databases are useful for teaching young students such higher-order skills as classifying and keyword searching (Hollis, 1990; Jankowski, 1994). Jonassen (2000) supports the belief that databases can help teachers accomplish constructivist principles and help students analyze relationships, look for trends, test and refine hypotheses, discover likenesses and differences, and arrange information in more useful ways.

Nonetheless, Roblyer (2003) reminds us that simply having students use databases does not ensure that these skills will be mastered. Teachers play a critical role in developing curricular uses of databases. In addition to teaching students how to use a database, teachers must guide the questions that the data is meant to answer and continue to ask questions during data analysis. The role of mentor during the process is evident here; teachers must guide the inquiry and facilitate discussion of results in order for students to develop the desired research and problem-solving skills. Further, Roblyer (2003) suggests that, if left alone, students may regard simple lists of results as a measure of success.

These cautions are supported by data from studies of classroom use of databases. Collis (1990), after reviewing six studies looking at instructional use of databases, concluded that students need guidance when using databases in developing and using the information. A need to consider completeness, accuracy, and relevance was evident. Students had difficulty designing questions from which to develop queries, and thought that the task was complete when any kind of data resulted.

Ehman, Glenn, Johnson, and White (1992) found similar results when using databases in social studies. Their study examined the use of databases to teach problem-solving skills in eight social studies classrooms (grades 5–12) where the teachers and students had a fairly strong knowledge base of computers and database software. The pivotal role of the teacher in the inquiry process was again evident. Teachers who were successful had clear plans from the beginning and offered feedback and reinforcement during the process. Their lessons were highly structured, initially identifying the problem to be solved and offering clear expectations to students. In order for problem solving to occur, the students had to be comfortable with the software tool that was being used. Large databases were overwhelming, overloading the students with information. When database fields were carefully defined, the students understood the concepts but tended to use their time poorly when they had inadequate plans for data collection and analysis. This sometimes resulted in critical information that was missing in the database. Further, these findings revealed that teaching with databases required more time than other instructional strategies and were best taught in small groups.

Databases should be used repeatedly throughout the curriculum if teachers want to achieve the maximum effect. Rawitsch (1988) proposed this notion after he studied the use of computer databases to aid the development of higher-order thinking skills with 339 eighth graders. Using databases to solve problems cannot be a one-time activity, but rather must be taught repeatedly. His comparison of work styles using computer and paper databases revealed that students liked working with computers better and solved more problems than with paper databases, but also that the tasks initially took longer.

In conclusion, databases are powerful tools for teaching **higher-order thinking skills**, **problem solving**, and **research strategies.** The open structure of databases makes them ideal for implementing constructivist strategies and practices. However, despite the power of databases, reliance on the software alone will not ensure that students will build the research skills necessary. The teacher must remain an integral part of the learning process, designing well-structured projects and posing well-articulated questions in order for the students to be successful with problem-solving strategies.

Basics

Databases offer a variety of uses for teachers and students. For instance, teachers can use databases to organize student information that can later be merged into word processing documents to serve as personalized letters to parents, compile bibliographies of relevant books and articles, record equipment and materials available, and keep examples of lesson plans. Databases can be developed for use with elementary, secondary, or postsecondary students. Important skills that teachers can teach when involving databases in teaching and learning include research and study skills, organization skills, and problem-solving skills. Students may be introduced to existing databases and given research questions to locate, or they can design and develop databases related to areas of study. The extent of the development will, of course, depend on the developmental stage of the student. See Figure 9.1 for teacher and student uses of databases. Although databases are most commonly used in social studies, they are also useful in other content areas, such as science and language arts.

Choosing a Database Tool

As mentioned in Chapter 3, database programs may be purchased as stand-alone programs, integrated software packages, or software suites. A well-known stand-alone database program is FileMaker Pro (**www.filemaker.com**). Integrated programs provide access to a database feature as well as a word processor, spreadsheet, graphics, and slideshow program. Microsoft Works (**www.microsoft.com/products/works/default.mspx**) is an example of an integrated software program.

Software suites, as you remember, tend to provide full-featured programs. Software suites include MS Office (**www.microsoft.com/en/us/default.aspx**), WordPerfect Office (**http://apps.corel.com/lp/wpo/**), as well as the open source solution OpenOffice.org (**www.openoffice.org**). Both MS Office and WordPerfect

FIGURE 9.1 Teacher and Student Uses for Databases

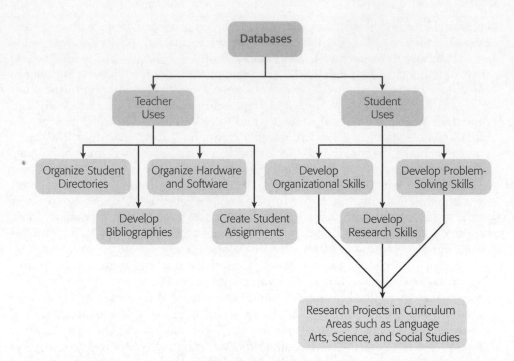

Office have versions that they term "Standard" versions and "Professional" versions. Neither has a database in the Standard version, yet the Professional versions have full-featured database tools. OpenOffice provides a database tool that, if used, brings database software to your classroom at no cost. Zoho Creator (http://zoho.com) is a Web-based database application that is free and offers 24/7 accessibility, making it worth a try.

New to the Inspiration family is Inspire Data, a product created by TERC through a grant from NSF and marketed by Inspiration. This program contains many curriculum-based databases that students can use as the basis to formulate questions and interact with the data. Graphs may be plotted, such as the one shown in Figure 9.2. Further, new databases can be created using the tool, and manipulation of the resulting data can be completed. A neat feature of this product is its template for an online survey that students can run to collect data. This tool definitely merits a look from teachers.

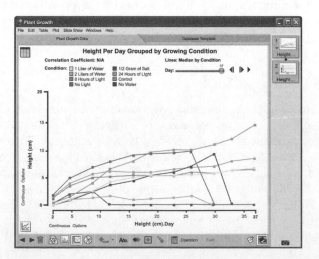

FIGURE 9.2 Plant Data Graph
Source: © 2008 Inspiration Software®, Inc. Graph created in Inspire Data® by Inspiration Software®, Inc. Used with permission.

Database Organization and Capabilities

Databases are tools that can organize, store, and search for information. Even though there is a variety of such software titles with varying levels of sophistication and capability, all are organized into fields, records, and files. It is important for teachers and students to understand database organization and capabilities and to be able to use each to make the tool as useful as possible.

Fields, Records, and Files

A database is organized into fields. A **field** is the smallest category of information in the database. For instance, information found in a database about the U.S. presidents might include the following fields: Last Name, First Name, Spouse's Name, Dates of Presidency, Birthplace, Died in Office, and so on. The field indicates the type of information that will be located in that section of the database, hence the field Dates of Presidency would contain the years involved in the term of office.

A group of fields related to a collection of information constitutes a **record**. For instance, in the database about presidents, all the fields of information for George Washington would be part of the same record. The fields in a record can be displayed in a logical order by manipulating the design of the layout in a record. Similarly, all of the records in the database make up a **file**. For instance, the records for all of the presidents would constitute the database file.

Database Capabilities

After information is entered into the database, the records can be manipulated in various ways to provide easier access to information through sorting techniques, answers to questions through the use of queries, or printing a report. Database records can also be merged with word processing documents resulting in personalized letters. After input of data is complete, the data can be sorted according to criteria such as alphabetical or chronological order. In a database about U.S. presidents, the information can be randomly entered and then sorted into chronological order of dates of presidency.

One of the most significant features provided by a database is retrieving information quickly through the use of **queries**. Running a query permits the user to select certain criteria and find any and all records that match the criteria. In other words, data can be narrowed to certain information in a query (such as all presidents whose birthplace was Virginia from a database on U.S. presidents).

A **report** can be developed in the program; this will summarize the information in a database in an easily read format. Reports can be printed containing information from the entire database or from a query only.

Finally, the **mail merge** feature allows the customization of letters by merging information from a database (such as title, name, address) with a word processing document (such as a letter). This capability is quite a useful, time-saving tool for teachers needing to correspond with large numbers of parents, students, or others.

Constructing the Database

Constructing and using a database is a simple procedure when following a sequence of steps, regardless of the software used as a tool. Planning is fundamental to developing a database that has power in the classroom. The designer must carefully think about the purpose of the database, who will use it, and the questions that the database is to reveal. Teachers—or students, under direction of the teacher—should progress through the following five steps to create effective databases:

1. *Plan the database.*   Planning the database is a crucial step for the resulting product to effectively function in the classroom and reveal the information that

the teacher wants highlighted. The purpose of the database and the information needed determine the fields to include.

2. *Construct the fields.*   Recall that fields are the smallest categories of information in the database. Fields are combined to create records. Constructing the fields is a simple sequence of steps that the teacher or student follows to create the fields in the database structure. For instance, in a database about U.S. presidents, fields might include last name, first name, political party, term started, termed ended, years in office, and order of service, as well as any others that the teacher might wish to have.

3. *Student research to find the data.*   In this step, the teacher can design the database shell (fields and layout) and students can get involved, or older students can develop the shell themselves. Using Web resources (**www.whitehouse.gov/history/presidents/**) selected by the teacher or books, students investigate answers to insert into the designated fields. A research guide sheet can be developed by the teacher to guide the research process.

4. *Enter the data.*   After locating the information required for the database, the students log (insert) the information into the field categories.

5. *Develop queries.*   Queries are questions that can be answered by the information within the database. To answer queries, the database is sorted or filtered to locate specific information. For instance, consider the database that holds information about the U.S. presidents. Perhaps the teacher wants the students to find out how many presidents died while in office. The student would develop a filter that would sort the data to reveal that information. *Important!* Keep in mind that in order to query information, the field *must be* in the database plan.

Creating a Database with Microsoft Excel

As mentioned earlier, several database programs exist, yet some of the commercial programs are either part of a professional package that schools may not have access to, or have a steep learning curve making them difficult for young students. MS Excel, normally considered a spreadsheet program, can be used as a database tool. Any school that has the MS Office Suite has access to Excel; it is developed for both Windows and Apple platforms and it can be used with Web-based tools in Zoho Sheet (**www.zoho.com**) and Thinkfree (**www.thinkfree.com**). Thus, the authors determined Excel to be a good tool to use in the following steps. The screenshots follow the five-step process discussed in the previous section to create a database on U.S. presidents. Most of the tasks needed for databases are available in Excel with the exception of a field for pictures, and single records cannot be printed.

1. *Open Excel.*   Open a new worksheet as pictured in Figure 9.3. Save the file as presidents. The program will add the .xls extension to identify that the file is an Excel file. The data will be inserted into the worksheet in the **columns** and

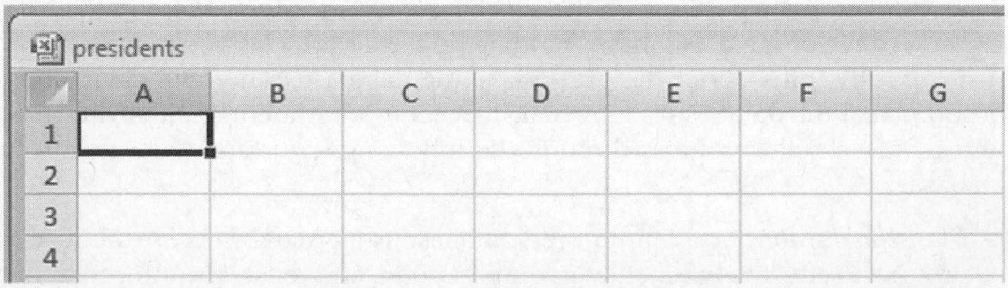

FIGURE 9.3 Excel Worksheet with Columns and Rows

	A	B	C	D	E	F	G
1	Last Name	First Name	Political Party	Term Started	Term Ended	Years in Office	Order of Service
2							
3							
4							
5							

FIGURE 9.4 The Fields

rows. The columns will serve as fields of information. Each row of information will create a record for each president.

2. *Construct the fields.* Enter the **field names** in the top row cells of each column, as pictured in Figure 9.4. The field names for this database are Last Name, First Name, Political Party, Term Started, Term Ended, Years in Office, and Order of Service. Teachers must plan the fields carefully to yield the information that the students can find. Save the database again after entering the fields. It is always important to save work often!

Excel does not have the option for pop-up menus, radio buttons, and check boxes—all handy options in database records. **Radio buttons** are used when a list of two or more options are needed but restrict the selection to only one option. **Pop-up menus** are used when many options are needed but limit the selection to one. **Check boxes** are useful when multiple options as well as selections are needed. A single check box allows the option to turn on or off, such as daily medication needed. These options will have to be completed with other measures.

3. *Enter the data.* After entering the field names, the data can be entered in each row, as seen in Figure 9.5. It is important to carefully enter the data. Errors will result in students not being able to find the correct information when sorting the data.

4. *Sort the data.* The data can be entered in any order (see Order of Service in Figure 9.6). For instance, as data is entered into a database, the records are not necessarily arranged in any certain order. Sorting the data arranges the records by the selected field in ascending (A–Z) or descending (Z–A) order. Or in this case, the data can be sorted by the order of service. To sort the data in Excel, go to a Sort records window that will display the fields in the database, as pictured in Figure 9.6. The field names are listed in the **field list**. The order for the sort must be specified. In this sort, the teacher would like the records arranged in the order that the president served. Thus the Order of Service field is selected and moved to the Sort order box. Ascending order is chosen, followed by OK to alert the computer that all commands are entered. The result of this sort is seen in Figure 9.7.

It is possible to sort information using more than one field. In other words, you could sort the data by order of service and then by political party, so the result would be the order of the service that the presidents served in

	A	B	C	D	E	F	G
1	First Name	Last Name	Political Party	Term Started	Term Ended	Years in Office	Order of Service
2	George	Washington	Federalist	1789	1797	8	1
3	John	Adams	Federalist	1797	1801	4	2
4	Thomas	Jefferson	Democratic-Republican	1801	1809	8	3
5	James	Madison	Democratic-Republican	1809	1817	8	4
6	James	Monroe	Democratic-Republican	1817	1825	8	5

FIGURE 9.5 Entering Data

	A	B	C	D	E	F	G
1	First Name	Last Name	Political Party	Term Started	Term Ended	Years in Office	Order of Service
2	Andrew	Jackson	Democratic	1829	1837	8	7
3	George	Washington	Federalist	1789	1797	8	1
4	James	Madison	Democratic-Republican	1809	1817	8	4
5	James	Monroe	Democratic-Republican	1817	1825	8	5
6	John	Adams	Federalist	1797	1801	4	2
7	John	Tyler	Whig	1841	1845	4	10
8	John Quincy	Adams	Democratic-Republican	1825	1829	4	6
9	Martin	Van Buren	Democratic	1837	1841	4	8
10	Thomas	Jefferson	Democratic-Republican	1801	1809	8	3
11	William Henry	Harrison	Whig	1841	1841	1 month	9

FIGURE 9.6 Sort Data to Show the Order of Service for the Presidents

	A	B	C	D	E	F	G
1	First Name	Last Name	Political Party	Term Started	Term Ended	Years in Office	Order of Service
2	George	Washington	Federalist	1789	1797	8	1
3	John	Adams	Federalist	1797	1801	4	2
4	Thomas	Jefferson	Democratic-Republican	1801	1809	8	3
5	James	Madison	Democratic-Republican	1809	1817	8	4
6	James	Monroe	Democratic-Republican	1817	1825	8	5
7	John Quincy	Adams	Democratic-Republican	1825	1829	4	6
8	Andrew	Jackson	Democratic	1829	1837	8	7
9	Martin	Van Buren	Democratic	1837	1841	4	8
10	William Henry	Harrison	Whig	1841	1841	1 month	9
11	John	Tyler	Whig	1841	1845	4	10

FIGURE 9.7 Results of Sort to Show Order of Service

each of the political parties. There are some databases where more than one sort is an advantage.

5. *Query the data.* Data may be manipulated to provide information by performing a query. Queries are searches for information and provide one of the most significant features of the database. When querying a database in Excel, the student instructs the program to **filter** the database to locate specific data. For instance, the teacher may want the students to know which presidents were Whigs. This would be done by using the **AutoFilter**. Select the appropriate field where the information is recorded (in this case, Political Party, see Figure 9.8) then go to Data/Auto, as seen in Figure 9.7. *Whig* is selected from the political parties, and presidents who were Whigs are filtered and shown, as in Figure 9.9. When a more complex search is needed, the Match records operation should be used. Go to List or Browse mode. Select Organize/Show all records. Go to Organize/Match records.

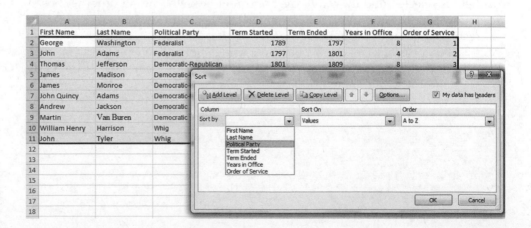

FIGURE 9.8 AutoFilter Tool to Show Presidents by Political Party

	A	B	C	
1	First Name	Last Name	Political Party	▾
2	George	Washington	Federalist	
3	John	Adams	Federalist	
4	Thomas	Jefferson	Democratic-Republican	
5	James	Madison	Democratic-Republican	
6	James	Monroe	Democratic-Republican	
7	John Quincy	Adams	Democratic-Republican	
8	Andrew	Jackson	Democratic	
9	Martin	Van Buren	Democratic	
10	William Henry	Harrison	Whig	
11	John	Tyler	Whig	

FIGURE 9.9 Results of AutoFilter Tool to Show Presidents Who Were Whigs

The AutoFilter can also be used in various other ways. The teacher might want the students to know the presidents who served less than four years. Eight of the presidents died in office; four were assassinated; and four died of various diseases. Roosevelt died in office but was in his fourth term, so we should find that seven presidents served less than four years. Let's see if we do.

To complete a filter to discover which presidents did not serve at least four years, go to Data/Filter as you see in Figure 9.10. Drop-down arrows appear on each field column. Click the drop down for Years in Office and you will see the options listed in the database. The options in this one are 0 years to 8 years. Since we are trying to solve for the presidents that served less than four, we deselect four and eight. When we do this, the filter is completed and the results are pulled up as seen in Figure 9.11.

Mail Merge

One of the most valuable features of a database is the ability to create a **mail merge**. The mail merge operation allows the customization of letters. This feature is quite useful for teachers when corresponding with large numbers of parents. A customized letter can go home with every child that is addressed to the parent in a formalized way. To create a mail merge, a word processing document (a letter) is merged with the information (contact information) from the database. While the process is explained here, Excel is not capable of merging records. Database software must be used for merging letters.

FIGURE 9.10 Applying a Filter to the Presidents Database to Solve Which Presidents Served Less Than Four Years

	A	B	C	D	E	F	G	H
1	Last Name ▾	First Name ▾	Term Began ▾	Term Ended ▾	Years in Offic ▾	Political Part ▾	Order of Servic ▾	Died in Office ▾
10	Harrison	William Henry	1841	1841	0	Whig	9	Died of pneumonia
13	Taylor	Zachary	1849	1850	1	Whig	12	Died of gastroenteritis
14	Fillmore	Millard	1850	1853	3	Whig	13	
21	Garfield	James	1881	1881	0	Republican	20	Assassinated
22	Harding	Warren	1921	1923	2	Republican	29	Heart Attack
23	Kennedy	John	1961	1963	2	Democrat	35	Assassinated
24	Ford	Gerald	1974	1977	3	Republican	38	

FIGURE 9.11 Results of the Filter Showing That Seven Presidents Have Served Less Than Four Years

Creating a Merged Document

1. *Open the database and a blank word-processing document.*   In order to merge the contents of a database with a word processed document, the database and the word-processed document must both be open. The open database and the word-processed document are seen during the merging process. As the letter is being written, the appropriate fields (such as first name) are automatically inserted into the letter from the database in the form of a **placeholder**.

2. *Merge field information.*   The development of the letter is continued and placeholders for the fields are inserted in the places where you want to merge information from the database. Placeholders are field names that have double parentheses around them, showing that field information will automatically be inserted when the document is printed. Keep in mind that you *must* insert all punctuation such as commas and periods, as the software does not do this for you.

3. *Print the letters.*   After the completion of the letter, the Mail Merge dialog box will be open. Click Merge. A Mail Merge destination dialog box will open, which will give the option of sending the documents to the printer. The print command will send all of the letters to the printer and the resulting letters will be personalized.

Adapting for Special Learners

Students with special needs who are included in general education classrooms should not be excluded from participation in database projects. As stated earlier, database software is a powerful tool for teaching problem solving and higher-order thinking—skills needed by students with special learning needs as well. Anticipating the needs of diverse learners during lesson planning can assure all students' successful participation in most database projects. The following are some considerations that may assist in a positive learning outcome.

Lessons that are designed with cooperative learning components lend themselves to a natural inclusion of diverse academic needs and learning styles. Learners with challenges can participate quite successfully within small cooperative groups that are responsible for assigned segments of the project. Students who need additional support for academic tasks may get help either from their peers or through specific AT strategies. For example, finding adequate information from web sites may present reading challenges for some students. A number of technology solutions can provide scaffolding for this task. If slow and laborious reading is the problem, screen-reading programs, such as Read & Write GOLD (TextHelp, Inc.) or Kurzweil 3000 (Kurzweil Educational Systems), can provide text-to-speech reading, definition, and translation capabilities for material from the Internet. Look for multilevel, translatable Web-based sources that differentiate among reading and language abilities—for example, the education web sites provided by NASA (http://starchild.gsfc.nasa.gov/docs/StarChild/StarChild.html).

Teachers may vary the length and complexity of text by pasting it into Auto Summary (in MS Word) to reduce the selection to a specified percent of the original. Edyburn (2002) refers to this strategy as *cognitive rescaling* and has reported its successful use with adolescents. Word predication programs, such as Co:Writer (Don Johnston, Inc.) or Read & Write GOLD (TextHelp, Inc.), can ease input difficulties caused by either poor motor coordination or difficulties with word retrieval.

CURRICULUM CONNECTIONS

The Horror of War

CONTENT AREA/TOPIC: Social Studies
GRADE LEVELS: 3–8   **NETS·S:** 3, 4, 6

Description: Students complete research using the Web to determine facts regarding the wars of the teacher's choice.

Teacher preparation: Teachers locate sites for safe student research. Teachers create a research guide sheet to assist the student research. Questions are limited only by the teacher's goals for the lesson. Some questions would include the name of the war, the location, the date the war began, the date the war ended, and the number of casualties. Keep in mind that the database will provide answers for students if the fields with the information are included.

Active participation: Students actively participate in this research of wars. They use the sites to complete research of the facts about each war. The data is entered in the database and queries are performed to bring forth answers.

Variations: Many topics are well suited for research using the Web and other media. This lesson could be redesigned with many different topics in social studies.

All About Mammals

CONTENT AREA/TOPIC: Science
GRADE LEVELS: 3–5   **NETS·S:** 3, 4, 6

Description: During their study of mammals, students complete research using the Web to determine facts about mammals.

Teacher preparation: Teachers locate sites for safe student research. Teachers create a research guide sheet to assist the student research. Questions are limited only by the teacher's goals for the lesson. Some questions could include name, type (monotremes, marsupials, placental), diet, habitat, life span, behavior, and communication.

Active participation: Students actively participate in this research of mammals. They use the sites or other media to complete research about the different mammals. The data is entered in the database and queries are performed to bring forth answers.

Variations: Many topics in science are well suited for research using the Web and other media. This lesson could be redesigned with many different topics in science.

Students with more severe physical or visual disabilities may have access to further specialized equipment that can be used to participate in a database research project. Students who are blind or visually limited may use more highly specialized and dedicated screen readers (JAWS, for example) or magnifiers. Students with physical limitations may input with single-switch applications instead of mouse and keyboard. Any of these applications work well with standard products such as databases. An assistive technology specialist can assist the teacher in adjusting any of these more specialized technology applications.

On the Web

This section includes only a snapshot of web sites that the authors recommend for viewing. To access live links and a larger and continuously updated collection of sites, go to the companion web site at **www.pearsonhighered.com/obannon2e.**

Integration Ideas with Databases

Discovery School
http://school.discoveryeducation.com/
Lessons that use databases in research activities are found at Discovery School, a searchable site. The lessons that are presented here are only a sample.

Earth and Beyond
http://school.discoveryeducation.com/lessonplans/activities/earthandbeyond/
In this one-week lesson, students in grades 6–8 or 9–12 investigate global warming, lunar exploration, space travel, Mars exploration, or terraforming, and develop a plan for the future.

Health Database
www.eduref.org/cgibin/printlessons.cgi/Virtual/Lessons/Health/Nutrition/NUT0003.html
This lesson is designed for grades 2–5 and places students in inquiry learning as they log the information about their lunch menus to determine if they're getting a balanced diet.

Lesson Plane
www.lessonplanet.com
This site sponsored by Educational Planet offers Web-based resources, tools, and services. In 2002, the company launched Lesson Planet, which provides many lesson plans; however, to have complete access, there is a fee. There are three membership options that can be researched at the web site. Lessons that include the construction of databases can be found at this site.

Mathematicians Are People Too
http://manassas.k12.va.us/round/ClassWeb/Volz/database_lesson.htm
This database lesson designed for students in grades 5–8 allows students to learn about the lives and contributions of mathematicians as they complete Internet research and compare and contrast these findings.

Science Hits
http://school.discoveryeducation.com/lessonplans/activities/sciencehits/
Students in grades 6–8 or 9–12 listen to a recording of "The Elements" by Tom Lehrer (1960) and write their own song for recalling scientific information. Research is completed with online databases.

Wartime Posters
http://school.discoveryeducation.com/lessonplans/activities/wartimeposters/
In this U.S. history lesson, students conduct research about the political, economic, sociological, and historical factors in the United States prior to World War II and take a position based on their research. Research is completed with students using online databases.

We the People
http://school.discoveryeducation.com/lessonplans/activities/wethepeople/
In this U. S. history lesson, students research to gather images from newspapers, magazines, television, and/or the Internet and show how the meaning of the Preamble is reflected in current American culture. Research is completed with students using online databases.

Software Options: Databases

Proprietary Database Solutions

FileMaker Pro
www.filemaker.com/solutions/k12/index.html
Travel to the Filemaker site to find special offers for K–12 educators with award-winning database software. Download a thirty-day trial of the latest version to see if it's a match for you and/or your students.

Inspire Data
www.inspiration.com/InspireData
Inspiration has recently published Inspire Data, a program that holds many databases that can be used for problem solving and graphing. This nifty tool provides database software so new databases can be created when students gather data. Try out a trial! Great for the types of inquiry and problem solving that 21st century learners need.

Microsoft Access

http://office.microsoft.com/en-us/access/FX100487571033
.aspx

Microsoft Corporation offers Microsoft Access, a powerful database program, with Office Professional but not the standard MS Office. While powerful, this software requires a high learning curve.

Open Source Database Solutions

Base

www.openoffice.org/product/base.html

OpenOffice, an open source suite, offers a database option, Base, a free download. Take a look and see if this is a good choice for your classroom.

NeoOffice

www.neooffice.org/neojava/en/index.php

NeoOffice is a full-featured set of office applications for Mac OSX, based on OpenOffice. Take a look and see if this is a good choice for your classroom. Free downloads are available.

Web-Based Databases

Zoho.com

http://creator.zoho.com/

Zoho offers a host of programs that are Web-based and free if you have an account. Zoho Creator is an online database application. It is fully compatible with MS Office counterparts and promotes digital literacy and collaboration.

Key Terms

Higher-order thinking skills (199)	Queries (201)	Pop-up menu (203)
Problem solving (199)	Report (201)	Check boxes (203)
Research strategies (199)	Mail merge (201)	Field list (203)
Database (201)	Column (202)	Filter (204)
Field (201)	Row (203)	AutoFilter (204)
Record (201)	Field name (203)	Mail merge (205)
File (201)	Radio button (203)	Placeholder (206)

Hands-on Activities for Learning

1. Link to other On the Web resources found on the companion web site (**www.pearsonhighered.com/obannon2e**).
2. Examine the ways that databases are appropriate for teacher use and for student use.
3. Examine some lessons that have been implemented by teachers.
4. Explore the features of a database in MS Access, Filemaker Pro, or other database software.
5. Re-create one of the lessons listed in the Curriculum Connections section of this chapter to simulate the activity in the classroom.
6. Using a database program, create a collection of information about U.S. presidents. Create fields for name, age when elected, date of birth, date of death, cause of death, party, name of wife, number of children, number of terms served, vice president, and place of burial. Research the information for these fields for all of the U.S. presidents. Use the database to answer the following questions: (1) Which presidents were under 50 when elected? (2) How many presidents were members of the Whig Party? Who were they? (3) Which U.S. presidents were assassinated? Decide on other questions that would be appropriate for students to query.
7. After this project, note lessons learned and discuss them with classmates.
8. Locate databases on the Web, such as the one that you queried to discover information about the American presidents, that would be appropriate for helping your students to develop inquiry skills.
9. Develop a lesson that uses databases in learning and is appropriate with grade levels within your licensure area. Align the lesson with state curriculum standards and NETS•S standards. The lesson should involve K–12 students in research, study, and problem solving skills and may use a database on the Internet or a student-—constructed database. Save the lesson into the curriculum file for your teaching portfolio.

10 Spreadsheets

LEARNER OBJECTIVES

At the completion of this chapter, learners will be able to:

- Discuss research related to the use of spreadsheets in teaching and learning.
- Use terminology associated with spreadsheet tools.
- Explain the organization and capabilities of spreadsheet software.
- Identify ways to incorporate spreadsheets into teaching and learning.
- Use spreadsheet software to create an interactive spreadsheet to serve as a tool for assessment or practice.
- Examine methods of adapting and using spreadsheets with special learners.

NETS·T ALIGNED WITH SPREADSHEETS

2. **Design and Develop Digital-Age Learning Experiences and Assessments**

   Teachers design, develop, and evaluate authentic learning experiences and assessments incorporating contemporary tools and resources to maximize content learning in context and to develop the knowledge, skills, and attitudes identified in the NETS·S. Teachers:

   a. design or adapt relevant learning experiences that incorporate digital tools and resources to promote student learning and creativity.

   b. develop technology-enriched learning environments that enable all students to pursue their individual curiosities and become active participants in setting their own educational goals, managing their own learning, and assessing their own progress.

   c. customize and personalize learning activities to address students' diverse learning styles, working strategies, and abilities using digital tools and resources.

   d. provide students with multiple and varied formative and summative assessments aligned with content and technology standards and use resulting data to inform learning and teaching.

Frameworks

A spreadsheet is a computerized record-keeping system initially designed to replace print-based accounting systems. This application software program was originally developed and is most commonly used for business accounting. Yet the spreadsheet is a powerful tool for the K–12 classroom to increase cognitive skills, such as problem solving. They are very useful in answering "what if" questions. For example, changes made to the data result in new calculations, such as "What if John's grade on the last test was increased by 20 points?" A change in one cell automatically recalculates all affected cells, as well as recalculating John's final grade.

Jonassen (1996) reports that spreadsheets are cognitive tools for strengthening mental functioning. Further, they are rule-based tools that require users to write rules and identify relationships and patterns in the data, requiring abstract reasoning by the user (Vockell & van Deusen, 1989).

Numerous authors have explored the use of a spreadsheet as a cognitive tool. Although most spreadsheets use math to some extent, that does not limit the use of this software to math teachers and math classes. Nevertheless, studies reveal that spreadsheets have been used in math classes to replace the calculator since the late 1980s. Such studies include using spreadsheets to demonstrate multiplicative relationships in elementary math (Edwards & Bitter, 1989), answering mathematical story problems (Verderber, 1990), finding roots in precalculus (Pinter-Lucke, 1992), assisting children in understanding large numbers (Parker & Widmer, 1991), and implementing problem plans with arithmetic problems (Sgroi, 1992). Lewis (2001, 2002) promotes the use of spreadsheets to support the math curriculum at all grade levels. Her examples are aligned with national technology and NCTM standards.

Spreadsheets have been used to calculate quantitative relationships in chemistry and physics classrooms (Jonassen, 1996). Such studies include calculating the size of a model of the Milky Way (Whitmer, 1990), solving complex problems in chemistry (Misovich & Biasca, 1990), and solving rate equation problems (Blickensderfer, 1990). Albrecht and Davis (2000) used spreadsheets in elementary science classrooms as students completed research and created a spreadsheet with elements, symbols, and the percentages of each that are found in the human body. In addition, spreadsheets were used to compare the atmosphere of Earth and Mars.

Jonassen (2000) suggests a six-stage approach to using spreadsheets to develop higher-order thinking. The first stage involves having students work with existing spreadsheets, both manipulating the data in the spreadsheet and entering new data into an existing template. In the second stage, the teacher guides the students in planning a spreadsheet. In the third stage, students adapt existing spreadsheets or create new ones that others will complete. In the fourth stage, the complexity of the content increases. In the fifth stage, existing spreadsheets are extended by adding new variables. The sixth and final stage is a reflective period for students.

Basics

Spreadsheets can be used for a variety of classroom activities, but their major function is to generate numeric information and graphical representations of that information. As mentioned in Chapter 9, databases were found to be a good way to support constructivist teaching practices. Spreadsheets support constructivist teaching practices as well. According to Jonassen (2000), spreadsheets can be used to *organize information, describe relationships, generate new rules, promote abstract reasoning,* and *support problem-solving activities.*

Spreadsheets facilitate storage, calculation, and presentation of information. The process involved in defining values, formulas, and functions involves analytical skills and encourages deeper processing of information. Students must use abstract reasoning as they create and interpret spreadsheets. These software tools enable learners to consider options and implications of conditions and hypothesize about outcomes.

The flexibility of chart and graph options provided in spreadsheet packages encourages this type of analysis and facilitates active learning. Graphs represent abstract numerical data in a concrete, interesting, and clear way. Graphs frequently make it easier to understand the data and further encourage the development of analysis and interpretation skills.

It is important that students be able to accurately construct and interpret graphs as the use of visual representations grows. Visual literacy is an important skill because so much information is presented graphically. Students should be able to name, describe, and correctly interpret the information conveyed in charts and graphs.

Spreadsheets can also assist teachers with tracking and calculating grades, lesson plans, rubrics, classroom inventory, club budget, or charting students' growth and development. In addition, interactive worksheets can be constructed by using spreadsheet software. More explanation about how to use spreadsheet software to create interactive worksheets is presented later in this chapter and the directions are provided at the companion web site for this chapter. See Figure 10.1 for teacher and student uses of spreadsheets.

There are a number of sites provided in the On the Web section and on the companion web site that provide spreadsheet activities, graphing, and more. After learning how to use the tool, go to the site and see what is there to help you integrate spreadsheets into your curriculum.

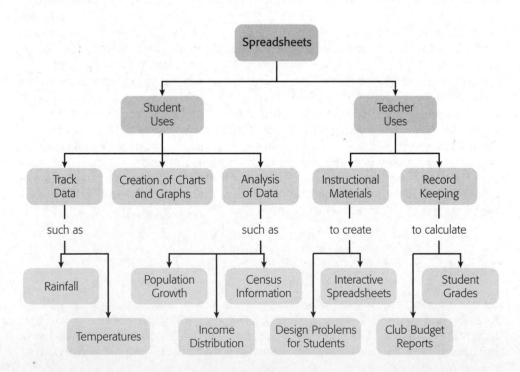

FIGURE 10.1 Student and Teacher Uses of Spreadsheets

Choosing a Spreadsheet Tool

As mentioned in Chapter 3, spreadsheet programs may be purchased as stand-alone programs, integrated software packages, or software suites. In addition, there are Web-based and free spreadsheet programs that can be used and are discussed in the last paragraph of this section. Integrated programs provide access to a spreadsheet feature as well as word processor, database, graphics, and slideshow programs. As you will recall, Microsoft Works (**www.microsoft.com/products/works/default.mspx**) is an example of an integrated software package.

Software suites, as you remember, tend to provide full-featured programs. Software suites include MS Office (**www.microsoft.com/en/us/default.aspx**), WordPerfect Office (**http://apps.corel.com/lp/wpo/**), and Apple iWork (**www.apple.com/iwork**), as well as the open source solution OpenOffice.org (**www.openoffice.org/**). Excel is the spreadsheet program in MS Office and Quattro Pro is the spreadsheet solution in WordPerfect Office. Apple offers a relatively new spreadsheet application in iWork named Numbers (**www.apple.com/iwork/**). OpenOffice, an open source software suite, offers a spreadsheet tool named Calc, which if used brings spreadsheet software to your classroom at no cost.

Web-based, free spreadsheet tools are now available and offer access from any computer with an Internet connection and browser software. One such tool is provided by Google, as part of the Google documents, called Google spreadsheet. To use this tool, sign up for a Google account if you do not have one, and go to Google docs. In the drop-down menu, as seen in Figure 10.2, click on Spreadsheet and a worksheet will open for you. There are also spreadsheet solutions in Zoho (**http://zoho.com/**) and Thinkfree (**www.thinkfree.com**).

> ### TECH TIP
> Web-based spreadsheet programs provide 24/7 access to students with Internet access and a browser, require no purchase or space on the hard drive, and are cross-platform.

Spreadsheet Organization and Capabilities

Spreadsheets were the earliest of the application software programs developed for computers. These programs process calculations more rapidly and accurately than other tools used for the same purpose, such as calculators. It is important for teachers and students to understand spreadsheet organization and capabilities to make the tool as useful as possible.

Spreadsheet Organization

A spreadsheet document, sometimes referred to as a **worksheet**, consists of a grid of columns and rows that intersect to form cells. Cells hold the data (numbers or text) that the user inputs into the spreadsheet. Figure 10.3 displays a worksheet grid with columns, rows, and cells.

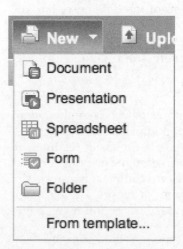

FIGURE 10.2 Drop-down Menu and Worksheet from Google Spreadsheet

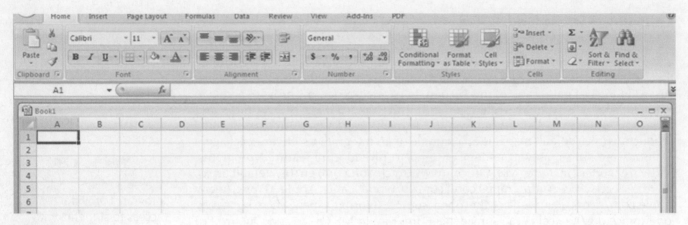

FIGURE 10.3 Worksheet Grid with Columns, Rows, Cells, Cell Address Box, Quick Access Buttons, and Formula Bar

Columns, Rows, and Cells   The **columns** are the vertical divisions of the spreadsheet and are labeled across the top of the worksheet. Each column is represented by a letter, starting with A. The **rows** are the horizontal divisions of the spreadsheet and are numbered down the side of the worksheet. Each row is represented by a number, starting with 1. More powerful programs allow many rows. The intersection of a row and a column is called a **cell**. Each cell has a unique address, consisting of the column letter and row number. For example, the first cell in the spreadsheet is A1. Spreadsheets store the data in these cell addresses making the information quite easy to scan and read. To insert data in a cell, the cursor is placed in the cell and the data is typed into the entry bar. The cell that is actively being used is called the **active cell**.

After the spreadsheet document is opened, it should be saved with a descriptive name to remind the user what information is found there.

Formula Bar and Address Box

Other elements of a spreadsheet include the data entry bar, sometimes called a formula bar, the cell address box, and several buttons that provide shortcuts to various actions, all of which are seen in Figure 10.3. Keep in mind that all of these elements will be provided in a spreadsheet program, even though they may not look exactly like the examples provided here. The **data entry bar** (formula bar) is located under the menu bar of the document. This is the area where the data is entered into the spreadsheet; however, the cell destination for the data must first be selected to specify where the data will go.

The **cell address box**, generally located at the left of the data entry bar, displays the active cell or the cell that is currently selected. This box allows the user to know where the data will go in the spreadsheet. For obvious reasons, knowing this becomes very important to ensure that the numeric information is inserted into the correct cell.

Spreadsheet Capabilities

After the data (**labels** or **values**) is entered into the spreadsheet, it can be manipulated in various ways to provide easier access to the information through performing calculations to reach answers, formatting the data for easier reading, creating a graphical (graph or chart) display of the information, or printing a report. Additionally, well-designed spreadsheets can be inserted into word processing documents to enhance a professional-looking document or report. These capabilities are explained next, with directions for each provided in the following pages.

Entering Data into the Spreadsheet   Only two types of data, **numeric** and **alphabetic**, are entered into spreadsheets. Numeric data consists of numbers (val-

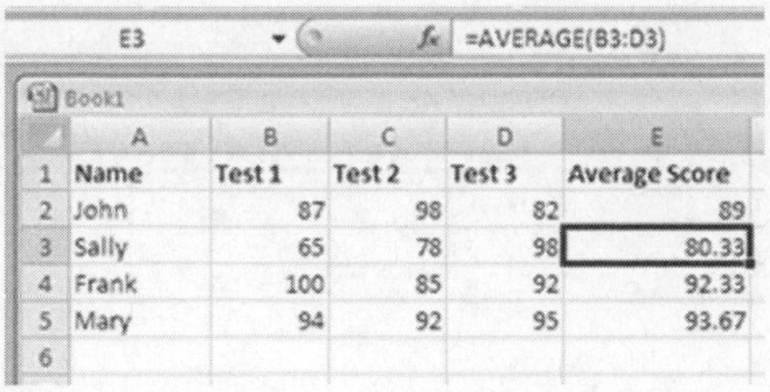

	E3		f_x	=AVERAGE(B3:D3)

Book1

	A	B	C	D	E
1	Name	Test 1	Test 2	Test 3	Average Score
2	John	87	98	82	89
3	Sally	65	78	98	80.33
4	Frank	100	85	92	92.33
5	Mary	94	92	95	93.67
6					

FIGURE 10.4
Spreadsheet with Cell Range

ues). Alphabetic data, or labels, provides descriptors for the columns and assist them in reading the spreadsheet. Labels cannot be manipulated mathematically. Data is entered into the spreadsheet by placing the cursor in the cell and typing the data on the keyboard.

Performing Calculations in the Spreadsheet   There are a number of spreadsheet elements, including a range of cells, formulas, and functions, which are used in performing calculations. In addition, the **fill down** and **fill across** features provide a shortcut for making a calculation copy to additional cells.

A **range of cells** is a grouping of cells for mathematical calculation. Ranges of cells are expressed by specifying the first and last cells in the range separated by a colon (B2:D2). To select a range of cells, click and hold in the first cell, drag the mouse to the last cell in the selection, and release the mouse. The address of the selected range will appear in the entry bar. In Figure 10.4, a range of cells (B3, C3, D3) is selected to calculate an average of student grades.

Spreadsheets perform calculations through the use of formulas. A formula is a set of instructions that the software follows to produce a value for a cell. To manipulate the data using formulas, the user places the cursor in the cell where the resulting data should appear and enters the formula in the entry bar; the result appears in the designated spreadsheet cell. A formula must start with the equal (=) sign for the spreadsheet to recognize it as a formula. Figure 10.4 presents a formula (in this case, for averaging) in the data entry bar.

Functions are formulas that are the most commonly used in spreadsheets; examples include sum and average. Sum adds the numbers in a specified group of cells and average calculates the average of a set of numbers. Functions are built into the features of the spreadsheet. To manipulate data using functions, the user places the cursor in the cell where the resulting data is to appear, selects the function, and presses the return key to see the calculation. Figure 10.4 uses the average function.

When a formula has been entered into a spreadsheet, it can be copied to more cells by using the fill down or fill across commands. This feature is a huge time saver. To use this feature in MS Excel, select the cell that will display the calculation. Enter the formula in the formula bar and press the return key to display the answer. Click to select that cell and drag across the cells to copy the formula. Press the return key to see the results in all selected cells.

Formatting the Data   Using formatting procedures in spreadsheets increases the ease of reading. Formatting includes the alignment of data, the font used, format of numbers (such as currency), and insertion of borders and patterns. In addition, the cell width and height can be adjusted so that a larger amount of text is visible.

The **alignment of data** in spreadsheet cells is similar to text alignment used in word processing. The cell data can be aligned to the left, right, or center of the cell. It is important that all categorical data (labels or numbers) have the same alignment for ease of reading. Numeric data defaults to the right and alphabetic data

TECH TIP

A range of cells is separated by a colon. "B3:B10" means all cells between B3 and B10.

TECH TIP

Always use = to start a formula.

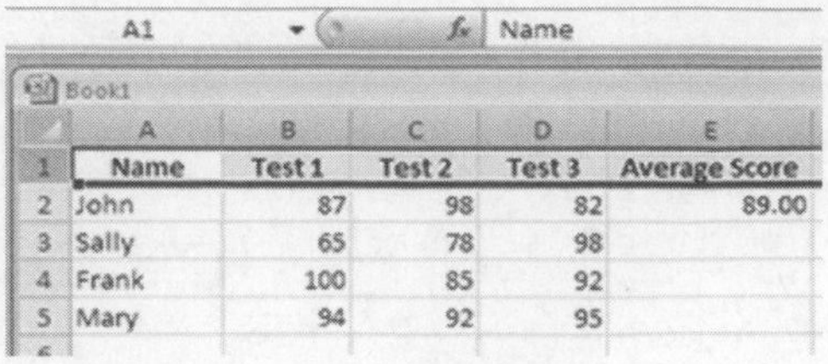

FIGURE 10.5 Center Alignment of Alphabetic Data (Labels)

to the left. If there is a sizable amount of text for the cell, **cell wrap** can be turned on, which allows the text in the cell to wrap to the next line. Figure 10.5 displays data after center-aligning the labels.

As with word processing, the font (typeface) may be changed in the spreadsheet worksheet. It is important that all categorical data (labels or numbers) in the spreadsheet use the same font. The font normally defaults to Geneva 9. Figure 10.5 displays changes in the font formatting in the labels from normal text to bold text.

Numbers may be formatted in a variety of ways, such as for currency, percentages, or fixed numbers (using place value). Dates and times can also be formatted for the spreadsheet.

Sorting the data in a spreadsheet can help organize, analyze, and interpret the data. To sort data in a spreadsheet:

1. Select the cell that you want to sort.
2. Choose Sort from the Calculate menu.
3. Specify which row or column determines the order of the sort.
4. Specify the sort order as either ascending (A–Z or 1–100) or descending (Z–A or 100–1).
5. Select a direction for sorting (vertical for rows and horizontal for columns).

Figure 10.6 displays the result of a sort on names in ascending order.

Creating Graphical Representations (Charts and Graphs) from Spreadsheet Data Spreadsheet data can be transferred to a **chart** or **graph** for ease of reading. Charts provide a visual description of data in the spreadsheet and graphically reveal relationships that might otherwise be overlooked. Since the chart relates the data in a spreadsheet, any changes to that data updates the graph. There are a number of chart formats available in spreadsheet programs. Some of the most commonly used are bar charts, line charts and graphs, pie charts, and pictograms. Each chart is best suited for particular data. **Bar charts** are typically used for comparing data or rankings. **Line graphs** are great to show change over time. **Pie charts** are best for showing percents of the whole, and **pictograms** use pictures rather than bars. Pictograms are often used with young children.

Printing a Report An entire spreadsheet can be printed or simply a portion of it. Each software program will handle this task a bit differently but will provide direc-

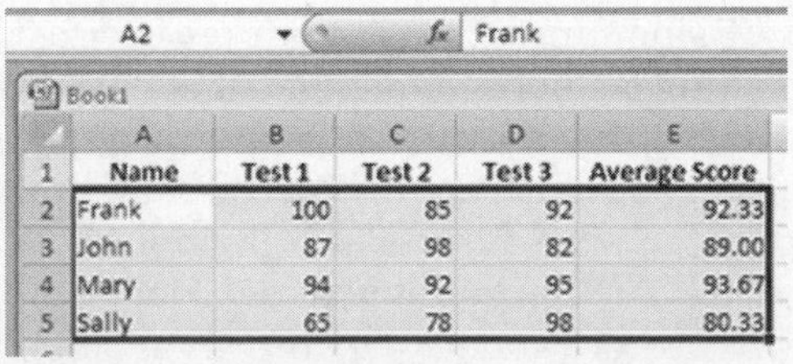

FIGURE 10.6 Sort on Names in Ascending (A–Z) Order

tions in the Help section of the program. Review the options available in a spreadsheet program for print details. Keep in mind that some software titles have limited features compared to more sophisticated programs, which is the reason that they can be used with young learners. Work within a program's capabilities; if more is needed, move to a more powerful program.

Constructing the Spreadsheet

Constructing and using a spreadsheet is a simple procedure:

1. *Open the spreadsheet program that is available.* Save the file with a descriptive name depending on the data in the file. The program will add an extension that identifies the document as a spreadsheet file.
2. *Enter the title.* The title of the spreadsheet should identify the contents when printed in report form. If the spreadsheet calculates student grades for a given semester, an appropriate title might be Ms. Smith's Fall Math Grades. If the spreadsheet calculates the budget for the school band, an appropriate title might be Anywhere Middle School Band Budget 2010–2011. If the spreadsheet calculates rainfall during the month, an appropriate title might be Rainfall September, 2010.
3. *Enter column and row labels.* The column labels identify the contents in the columns, just as the row labels identify the row contents. In the spreadsheet of student grades, the columns might be labeled for weekly tests as Wk. 1, Wk. 2, and so on (or identifiers for assignments), and the rows would be identified by the student names. In the spreadsheet activity for the M&Ms activity shown later in this chapter, the columns are named by student groups and the rows identify the possible colors of the candy.
4. *Enter the data.* The data to be entered into the cells is dependent on the contents of the spreadsheet. Grades obviously would be added over the course of the grading period, whereas for the M&Ms activity (shown later in this chapter), the data is entered as the groups report.
5. *Enter formulas and functions as appropriate.* Formulas calculate the data. The formula that is entered is dependent on what calculation is needed. If the sum of numbers is needed, use a formula or function that sums the appropriate cells.
6. *Check the calculations and adjust formulas as needed.* If the calculation does not reveal a logical answer, the formulas should be checked immediately to see whether the formula was entered correctly.
7. *Format the data to increase ease of reading.* Formatting the contents of a spreadsheet makes the spreadsheet easier to read. As mentioned earlier, format the data by changing the alignment, the font, the values, the insert border, or patterns as desired.
8. *Set print options.* Print options include the orientation of the spreadsheet, the number of copies, and whether the information is printed with or without the gridlines. At times, the grids make the document easier to read. Set the options and use print preview to see whether you are actually increasing the readability when you take away the gridlines. When you're satisfied, print the document.

Janet Smith designed the interactive spreadsheet shown in Figure 10.7 to use with high school English students. The content is taken from "Jabberwocky," a poem of nonsense verse by Lewis Carroll, and is part of the novel, *Through the Looking Glass* (1872). Although the poem contains many nonsense words, it follows poetry form and structure perfectly. Because of this perfect form and conventional structure of grammar, it is often used for study in middle and high schools to teach the semantics of the parts of speech.

Name: Jan Smith
Date: November, 2008

Directions: Using the poem "Jabberwocky" by Lewis Carroll, identify the parts of speech of the following nonsense words by how they are used in the context of the poem.

Nonsense Words	Parts of Speech	Correct?	Points
1. Jabberwock	noun	Correct!	10
2. slithy	adjective	Correct!	10
3. toves	noun	Correct!	10
4. gyre	verb	Correct!	10
5. gimble	verb	Correct!	10
6. frumious	adjective	Correct!	10
7. vorpal	adjective	Correct!	10
8. galumphing	verb	Correct!	10
9. frabjous	adjective	Correct!	10
10. wabe	noun	Correct!	10
		Your Score --->	100

FIGURE 10.7 Interactive Spreadsheet Created in ThinkFree

Voices *from the* Classroom

Going below the Surface: Tapping into the Interactive Capabilities of Spreadsheets

Allison Watkinson

Allison Watkinson has taught in urban schools for 15 years. Her teaching experience ranges from early grades to high school mathematics, including Advanced Placement Calculus. She has authored and been awarded several grants to facilitate the integration of technology. The largest, a federal grant for $200,000, funded an iBook for each certified teacher in her school and allowed her to serve as the technology coach to train and support these teachers as they integrated technology into the curriculum to improve students' academic achievement. Allison introduced, with great success, interactive spreadsheets as a component of this training. We asked her to explain why she believes this strategy is effective in the classroom in various content areas and grade levels.

Spreadsheets are a great way to collect data and visually display that data. Graphs and charts provide us with a far better picture of what the data is doing than the tabular record of that data. However, if that is as far as you go with using spreadsheets, you are not taking full advantage of the power of spreadsheet software.

Through the use of simple logic statements, a teacher can create an interactive spreadsheet that matches what is being taught in the classroom and state/district curriculum standards. The interactive spreadsheets allow students additional practice or a quick assessment of skills learned. The interactive spreadsheets are self-grading and, when used as drill and practice, provide students with immediate feedback about the correctness of their answers. Interac-

tive spreadsheets can be printed and completed by pencil if the technology has broken down; of course, in this case the teacher would grade the activity by hand.

When working with a spreadsheet at the computer, the student enters the answer to a question in a response cell. The computer then compares the student's answers to the teacher's expected answer. If the answers are the same, the student is given positive feedback, and if a numerical grade is desired, points are awarded for the correct response. If the answers are not the same, the student is given negative or corrective feedback and no points. Students want to do well, so if they answered incorrectly, they will keep trying until they get the right answer. In drill and practice spreadsheets, students generally work hard to earn a score of 100. In quizzing or testing conditions, students do not receive feedback for each response and do not see their score until all questions have been answered.

When I first began creating interactive spreadsheets, I designed spreadsheets for use in the math curriculum. However, as I became more proficient in writing logic statements and spreadsheet formatting, I created spreadsheets for all content areas in kindergarten through 12th grades. Most students love working on the computer and interactive spreadsheets provide numerous opportunities for additional practice without the groans of doing another paper worksheet!

When examining the results of our standardized test data, we discovered an area of deficiency for multimeaning words. This deficiency was occurring across grade lev-

Voices *from the* Classroom *Continued*

els, throughout the school. Our teachers knew they taught multimeaning words and concluded that a major problem was that students were taught and assessed in the classroom in a manner different from the way they were tested on the state tests. Several teachers worked with me in developing interactive spreadsheets for students to practice the formats they would see on the standardized tests for multimeaning words. Allowing children to practice what they had learned in the format in which they would be tested allowed them to be more successful on the standardized test. The third grade teacher who used the interactive spreadsheet in her classroom had a 3.5 NCE point gain from the previous year on the vocabulary subtest. The only other teacher in third grade who had a positive gain had a one-point gain. A gain of zero points indicates that the students have gained one full year; a negative gain indicates that students lost ground; and a positive gain indicates that students gained more than one year's academic achievement during the year. With No Child Left Behind (NCLB) legislation it has become increasingly important to expose students throughout the year to the standardized test format they will see during their high-stakes test. Interactive spreadsheets are the perfect way to experience this format.

Interactive spreadsheets are also a wonderful way to differentiate and individualize instruction for the different instructional and interest levels in the classroom. Students can even be brought into the process by writing review questions and answer choices for a quiz or test. These questions and answer choices can then be used in an interactive spreadsheet.

Students always need more practice in using homonyms such as *their, there, they're* and *to, too, two.*

My fifth-grade students liked using interactive spreadsheets to practice choosing the correct homonym for the sentence. They were then inspired to create their own sentences using these homonyms and requested that I create more spreadsheets using their sentences for additional practice.

Science and social studies are also perfect for creating interactive spreadsheets. In science, writing questions about water and life cycles, parts of plant or animal cells, and the solar system are some examples of topics for which interactive spreadsheets can easily be written for either drill and practice or assessment. In social studies, providing descriptions of Civil War battles or important people and then asking students to give the name of the battle or the person is so much more fun than filling out a paper worksheet and waiting for a teacher to grade it. Students can be provided with a word bank from which to choose the answers if total recall of the answer is not important to you.

Spreadsheets are extremely powerful, especially when you learn how to use formulas and logic statements. Gathering data and creating graphs or charts from that data touches only the visible part of the iceberg! Going below the surface and tapping into the interactive capabilities of the spreadsheet will help ensure your students are more engaged in the learning process and also enable you to create worksheets that match what you are teaching and your state and district curriculum standards.

Please visit my web site to access more about interactive spreadsheets at **www.allisonwatkinson.com/interactive/index.html**.

Adapting for Special Learners

Most teachers can employ practices that include all students in the excitement of spreadsheet learning. Students with hearing barriers should have little difficulty accessing spreadsheet software. For gifted students, spreadsheets can free them from laborious manipulation of numbers and allow them to see the progression of calculations on the screen as they are generated. For students with vision, cognitive, and physical barriers, teachers may wish to consider the following solutions.

Vision Barriers

For students with low vision, the text may be too small, the contrast between the page and the type may be indiscernible, or the page may not be viewable at all. A simple solution is to adjust the actual worksheet display for personal preferences.

CURRICULUM CONNECTIONS

Beginning Letters Bingo

CONTENT AREA/TOPIC: Language Arts
GRADE LEVELS: K, 1   **NETS·S:** 4, 6

Description: Students use the computer to create personal Bingo boards, which will be used to review the letters in the alphabet in an instructional game format. Each student creates their board by moving a picture from the picture bank and the beginning letter for that picture in a spreadsheet cell. Each bingo board is printed for the student and used for a bingo board during the instructional game.

Teacher preparation: The teacher uses spreadsheet software to create a template using rows and columns like a regular Bingo board. The columns are labeled *B, I, N, G, O* and the rows *1, 2, 3, 4, 5* so that the cell addresses would be B1, B2, and so on. Having a "free" center spot is optional. After the template is created, it can be reused for different lessons. The teacher creates a picture bank at the bottom of the page that corresponds to the beginning sounds of the chosen letters. The teacher may want to review the pictures at the bottom of the screen and review beginning letters.

Active participation: Students create a board by dragging a picture from the picture bank into individual cells on the spreadsheet. They then enter the beginning letter of each picture in its cell by typing the letter. After the computer work is complete and the extra pictures are deleted from the page, the students (with help) save and print their pages and play Bingo; as the teacher calls out letters, the students place an X on the picture that begins with the letter in the cell.

Variation: This creative instructional game can be modified for older students by using vocabulary words from a chapter of study in science, social studies, or a foreign language.

Source: Lewis, P. (2001). *Beginning letters Bingo, Spreadsheet Magic* (pp. 14–16). Eugene, OR: ISTE Publications.

List 2

CONTENT AREA/TOPIC: Language Arts (spelling and vocabulary)
GRADE LEVEL: 4   **NETS·S:** 4, 6

Description: This lesson allows students to practice spelling words, alphabetize, and find synonyms using a spreadsheet and spell checking features. Students can be provided with a word bank from which to choose the answers if total recall of the answer is not important to the teacher.

Teacher preparation: The teacher creates a template with a spreadsheet program providing one column for entering the spelling list and one column for writing a synonym for each word. The teacher creates step-by-step directions at the top that explain exactly what the student needs to do.

Student participation: Students follow the directions to enter their spelling words, check spelling, sort alphabetically, and find and enter synonyms.

Variations: This lesson may be adapted for vocabulary for any content area, or rather than synonyms, the student can find homonyms.

Source: Lewis, P. (2001). *Spelling list 2, Spreadsheet Magic* (pp. 82–83). Eugene, OR: ISTE Publications.

CURRICULUM CONNECTIONS *Continued*

Word Search

CONTENT AREA/TOPIC: Language Arts

GRADE LEVELS: 4, 5   **NETS·S:** 4, 6

Description: This lesson allows students to practice recognizing and spelling vocabulary words.

Teacher preparation: The teacher provides instructions and a spreadsheet template to create a word search grid along with vocabulary or spelling words.

Student participation: Students enter vocabulary into a grid in any direction and fill in the remaining boxes with random letters creating a word puzzle. By sav-

ing one version with the words in red font, they also create an answer sheet for their puzzles.

Variations: This may be adapted for synonyms, antonyms, foreign languages, or vocabulary for science or social studies.

Source: Lewis, P. (2001). *Word search, Spreadsheet Magic* (pp. 84–85). Eugene, OR: ISTE Publications.

M&Ms

CONTENT AREA/TOPIC: Mathematics

GRADE LEVEL: 4   **NETS·S:** 4, 6

Description: This lesson allows students to estimate, record, and analyze data using a spreadsheet. Students use a spreadsheet program to enter data to be analyzed.

Teacher preparation: The teacher asks students what they think is in a typical bag of plain M&Ms. How many colors are represented? What are the colors? Are there the same number of colors in each bag? If not, what color is represented the most? How many total M&Ms are in a bag? The teacher should record all of the responses. The teacher breaks the class into small groups of two or more and gives each group a bag of M&Ms.

Student participation: Student groups open their bags of M&Ms and record the number of each color on an index card. Each group enters their findings in a blackboard spreadsheet where the column labels are

Red, Yellow, Green, Orange, Blue, and Brown. Each group enters their results into the cells. A spreadsheet program is used to enter the data from the class. Formulas are entered to calculate averages of each color. A pie graph of the averages is created.

Variations: This activity can be varied depending on the developmental levels of the students and the preference of the teacher. Students problem-solve to find such things as: (1) which color appears least? most? (2) the ratios of colors; (3) if a bag of M&Ms contains 100 M&Ms, how many reds are expected? yellows? greens? oranges? blues? browns? This activity could also be completed using other candy that comes in a variety of colors, such as Skittles.

Source: Niess, M. (1992). Mathematics and M&Ms. *The Computing Teacher,* 21(1), pp. 29–31.

(Continues)

CURRICULUM CONNECTIONS *Continued*

One Out of Two Homes in America

CONTENT AREA/TOPIC: Mathematics/Statistics and Probability
GRADE LEVELS: 6–8   **NETS·S:** 2, 4, 6

Description: Students become scientists as they participate in an online project to test a hypothesis, collect and analyze data, and make decisions based on the gathered data. One out of Two Homes in America is online at http://allisonwatkinson.com/appliances/index.html/.

Teacher preparation: The teacher registers the class for participation in the online project. The teacher then introduces the class to the web site and prints the survey for student data collection.

Active participation: Students survey two households and enter data online. Students return to the site on Monday or Wednesday to use spreadsheet software to start analyzing data.

Variations: Students design their own survey, collect data, and enter results into a spreadsheet for analysis. Students write their own questions to be answered from data.

Source: Watkinson, A. (2003, 2008). *One out of two homes in America.* Accessed October 15, 2008, from http://allisonwatkinson.com/appliances/index.html.

Area and Perimeter of Rectangles

CONTENT AREA/TOPIC: Mathematics/Measurement
GRADE LEVELS: 6–8   **NETS·S:** 4, 6

Description: Students use a teacher-created interactive spreadsheet to practice calculating area and perimeter of rectangles. Students receive immediate feedback. The template can be found at: http://allisonwatkinson.com/interactive/area.html.

Teacher preparation: The teacher downloads the interactive spreadsheet for students to practice using formulas to solve area and perimeter problems. Formula information and instructions for creating original interactive spreadsheets are also available on the web site.

Active participation: Students use the interactive spreadsheet to practice solving area and perimeter problems.

Variations: Students and teachers create their own interactive spreadsheets to practice solving area and perimeter problems for other quadrilaterals.

Source: Watkinson, A. (2003, 2008). *Area and perimeter of a rectangle.* Accessed October 15, 2008, from http://allisonwatkinson.com/interactive/area.html.

Zoomed-in views can provide some magnification of the worksheet, and cells can be viewed in a variety of font sizes, styles, and colors. The background color can be changed to provide higher contrast between the page and cell contents. Some spreadsheets (including MS Excel 2003 and later versions) also offer text-to-speech capabilities, speaking the contents of each cell when the Enter key is pressed. For students who require further adjustments, computer control panel settings adjust the display contrast (accessibility options). Beyond what is available in basic computer settings, magnification and screen reading software can be used with most spreadsheet programs. See Chapter 3 for further discussion.

Cognitive Barriers

The advantages that spreadsheets give most students in developing higher-order thinking skills apply to students with cognitive barriers as well. In the past, students with learning problems were not provided the opportunity to develop higher-order thinking skills until basic skills in reading and computation were mastered. Current emphasis on standards-based learning for all students is changing this emphasis from merely obtaining correct answers to explaining how the process of obtaining answers works (Anderson & Anderson, 2001). Because spreadsheets are among the technology options used to teach this process, these students should not be excluded from this valuable tool. Teachers should be encouraged to move student awareness toward planning, creating, and extending spreadsheet use as a tool for problem solving.

Beyond making sure that these students are included in learning the many uses of spreadsheets, other adaptations include using the charting and graphing features to serve as memory aids, or providing further explanations of concepts that are not understandable in print. When reading the text in cells presents a barrier to understanding the information, a screen or text reader—such as those recommended for students with visual barriers—may be useful (see the section on screen readers in Chapter 3).

Physical Barriers

Students with physical barriers can still access spreadsheets, as adaptations are available for any form of computer input. Keyboard adjustments include filter keys to adjust the rate of key stroke acceptance, sticky keys to allow typing with one hand, or on-screen keyboards (see software chapter, Chapter 3). Basic hardware adaptations, such as mouse and keyboard alternatives, are discussed in Hardware, Chapter 2. Voice recognition options, which allow cell input using the voice, are available in system tools in newer versions of Microsoft products or as separately purchased programs.

On the Web

This section includes only a snapshot of web sites that the authors recommend for viewing. To access live links and a larger and continuously updated collection of sites, go to the companion web site at **www.pearsonhighered.com/obannon2e.**

Integration Ideas with Spreadsheets

Center for Engineering and Science Education
www.k12science.org/collabprojs.html
Multiple collaborative projects, in which students can participate and calculate different types of data, are provided here. Teachers can allow class participation or simulate the activity in the classroom using spreadsheet software. Find unique projects for your classroom at this site.

Franklin Online Institute
www2.fi.edu/
Ideas and resources for real-world data to be analyzed and/or graphed. Multiple spreadsheet lessons can be found after doing a search.

What percentage of your class is right- or left-handed?
http://math.rice.edu/~lanius/Algebra/rightleft.html
This activity, hosted by Rice University and developed by Cynthia Lanius with Math Forum, allows student participation in a data collection and analysis experiment that allows students to use spreadsheets to record and graph real data. Try it!

Web-Based Spreadsheet Options

Google Spreadsheets
http://docs.google.com/
Google spreadsheets is a part of the Google Documents collection. Try this Web-based solution to spreadsheet software and have access 24/7 as long as you have a computer with an Internet connection and a browser.

Zoho.com
www.zoho.com
Zoho offers a host of programs that are Web-based and free if you have an account. Zoho Writer is an online word

processor. Zoho Creator is an online database application. Zoho Sheet is an online spreadsheet. These are fully compatible with MS Office counterparts and promote digital literacy and collaboration. There is a presentation tool as well as a wiki and more.

ThinkFree

www.thinkfree.com

ThinkFree Office offers Web-based word processor, spreadsheets, and presentation programs that are compatible with MS Office counterparts and are free. Getting an account here allows 1 gigabyte of free online storage.

Spreadsheet Tutorials

Interactive Spreadsheets

http://allisonwatkinson.com/interactive/index.html

This site is developed by Allison Watkinson, a former math and technology teacher. This talented teacher shares information about interactive spreadsheets including the directions for making these electronic sheets as well as sharing a number of spreadsheets created by teachers.

Jan's Illustrated Computer Basics: Working with Numbers

www.jegsworks.com/Lessons/numbers/index.html

Jan Smith, a mathematician and teacher, designed this site that holds basic information about computer literacy. The site is rich with pictures and includes information on computer types, software applications, hardware devices, and much more. This section of her site is Working with Numbers: Spreadsheets and discusses not only the interface and navigation in MS Excel, but also formatting issues, formulas, and analysis with "what if" explanations. This is available in English or Spanish.

School Spreadsheet Safari

http://library.thinkquest.org/J0110054/

This site is presented by ThinkQuest as a finalist in 2001and presents a nice overview of spreadsheets with a definition, spreadsheet vocabulary, the basics, the history through 2001, classroom activities, a scavenger hunt, puzzle, quiz, and references. A site map assists navigation. The only drawback is the distraction of the animated gifs but it is well worth the visit.

Key Terms

Worksheet (213)	Numeric data (214)	Chart (216)
Column (214)	Alphabetic data (214)	Graph (216)
Row (214)	Fill down (215)	Bar chart (216)
Cell (214)	Fill across (215)	Line graph (216)
Active cell (214)	Range of cells (215)	Pie chart (216)
Data entry bar (214)	Functions (215)	Pictogram (216)
Cell address box (214)	Alignment of data (215)	
Label (214)	Cell wrap (216)	
Value (214)	Sorting the data (216)	

Hands-on Activities for Learning

1. Visit the On the Web companion site (**www.pearsonhighered.com/obannon2e**) and review the sites available.
2. Write a reflection in your reflective technology blog about ways to integrate spreadsheets into learning situations with the target population that you will be teaching.
3. Re-create one of the lessons listed in the Curriculum Connections section of this chapter to simulate the activity in the classroom. During this creation, note lessons learned and discuss these with classmates.
4. Create an interactive spreadsheet to serve as a practice/review for your students. The content should be aligned with curriculum standards and NETS·S.
5. Insert the spreadsheet into the curriculum file for your portfolio.

11 Multimedia Tools

At the completion of this chapter, learners will be able to:

- Discuss research related to the effective use of multimedia in teaching and learning.
- Use terminology associated with multimedia tools and their use.
- Examine ways to incorporate multimedia tools into learning activities to promote student learning and creativity.
- Create a multimedia slideshow using presentation software.
- Examine digital stories and describe their purpose and use in learning.
- Create a digital story following the guidelines set forth in the text.
- Apply safe, legal, and ethical use of digital files (images, video, and music) included in multimedia development and correctly document resources.
- Discuss methods for adapting multimedia tools with special learners.

NETS·T ALIGNED WITH MULTIMEDIA TOOLS

1. Facilitate and Inspire Student Learning and Creativity

Teachers use their knowledge of subject matter, teaching and learning, and technology to facilitate experiences that advance student learning, creativity, and innovation in both face-to-face and virtual environments. Teachers:

a. promote, support, and model creative and innovative thinking and inventiveness.

b. engage students in exploring real-world issues and solving authentic problems using digital tools and resources.

2. Design and Develop Digital-Age Learning Experiences and Assessments

Teachers design, develop, and evaluate authentic learning experiences and assessments incorporating contemporary tools and resources to maximize content learning in context and to develop the knowledge, skills, and attitudes identified in the NETS·S. Teachers:

a. design or adapt relevant learning experiences that incorporate digital tools and resources to promote student learning and creativity.

b. customize and personalize learning activities to address students' diverse learning styles, working strategies, and abilities using digital tools and resources.

c. provide students with multiple and varied formative and summative assessments aligned with content and technology standards and use resulting data to inform learning and teaching.

3. Model Digital-Age Work and Learning

Teachers exhibit knowledge, skills, and work processes representative of an innovative professional in a global and digital society. Teachers:

a. demonstrate fluency in technology systems and the transfer of current knowledge to new technologies and situations.

b. communicate relevant information and ideas effectively to students, parents, and peers using a variety of digital-age media and formats.

4. Promote and Model Digital Citizenship and Responsibility

Teachers understand local and global societal issues and responsibilities in an evolving digital culture and exhibit legal and ethical behavior in their professional practices.

Teachers:

a. advocate, model, and teach safe, legal, and ethical use of digital information and technology, including respect for copyright, intellectual property, and the appropriate documentation of sources.

b. address the diverse needs of all learners by using learner-centered strategies and providing equitable access to appropriate digital tools and resources.

Frameworks

Multimedia is a combination of more than one type of media and media functions—text, graphics, audio, animation, and/or video—to communicate a message. In the past, multimedia had been identified, rather broadly, as the simultaneous use of multiple types of media devices to deliver a message. But as technology has advanced, emphasis has moved from multiple devices to multiple media delivered through one device—the computer (Moore, Burton, & Myers, 2004). This combination of multiple media using one device is referred to in research as **multiple-channel communications**.

In the early days of the Internet, scientists were excited when they were able to transfer information and data using only text. Today, using text as a single mode of communication seems quite bland. Research suggests that adding additional types of media can assist understanding of the text by the reader, especially when that text is complex. As you will recall from Chapter 7, substantial research supports the addition of pictures to text if the picture is related to the text and serves a function in the instructional materials. This claim is further supported by dual coding theory, which suggests that two types of information, pictorial and verbal, function to support learning in different ways and are thus better than only one type. Adding additional media, such as audio or video, can support communication and learning by creating interest.

Research has generally agreed upon the merits of multimedia. Rieber (1990) looked at 13 research studies in which animation was used in computer-based learning to determine its significance on learning. Of the 13 studies, he found that five revealed significant effects. He concluded that (1) animation should be used only when it matches the learning task, (2) the greatest contribution of animation is with interactivity, and (3) when learners are new to the curriculum, they can miss important cues delivered by the animation. Reiber further reported that the functions of animation in learning have been to (1) gain attention, (2) for presentation, and (3) for practice. The combination of text, graphics, and full-motion video; the ability to navigate within a hypertext space; and being in a context-rich environment can increase the learning and motivation of learners (Moore, Burton, & Myers, 2004). Jonassen (2000) suggests that **multimedia presentations** get and hold students' attention due to the multimodal nature of the software; the different media appeal to the different senses. He suggests that this is necessary to capture the attention of students who are living in today's technology-rich, video-conscious information age. But researchers also suggest that caution is warranted. When using multichannel communication, learning will increase when the channels complement each other. When the information is redundant, there is no improvement in learning, and when the information is inconsistent, is on different channels, or is distracting, learning actually decreases (Jonassen, 2000).

Consequently, with all the excitement generated by this appealing technology, it is the design of the product—regardless of whether the product is a slideshow, a podcast, a digital story, or a web site—that determines how well it provides the merits identified as advantages. Adding multiple media channels without thinking about purpose or using care in selection can destroy the message by creating distraction for the learner. In other words, the learners get so intrigued with the bells and whistles that the message is lost in the technology.

How important should using multiple channels of media be to student success in today's classrooms? Multimedia enhances communication, encourages interaction, provokes thought, and (it is hoped) causes the retention of knowledge. The emphasis should not be on the technology, but rather on the delivery of the message. Sophisticated multimedia slideshows can make weak content appear stronger. Teachers still need to keep the focus on the curriculum, on the learning objective, and on the learning outcome. Multimedia software tools offer an excellent way to engage students in learning while allowing them to be creative and to construct their learning.

There are several ways to communicate in worlds of multimedia depending on what you are working with: CDs/DVDs, the Web, and through iPods. Previous chapters and discussions have built your knowledge appropriately with many of the same digital tools used in multimedia, thus giving you the skills to build a multimedia presentation. We begin with a multimedia environment applicable to CD/DVD and move to the Web environment in the next chapter. Because our society is quickly moving toward a digital communication system, it is necessary for all teachers as well as students to be able to work comfortably in the digital and multimedia environments. Although designing for each type of media is not without added preparation time, the results merit the extra work.

The following section presents terms basic to multimedia tools, techniques, and software common to the K–12 classroom. Many types of inquiry-based lessons and ideas are examined, as well as various methods for teachers and students to use these resources in teaching and learning. A relatively new strategy, digital storytelling and its uses in education, is examined. Further suggestions for using multimedia can be found in the Adapting for Special Learners section.

Basics

There are many ways that teachers find multimedia software helpful with the design of instruction, including the use of multimedia presentations to accompany demonstrations or discussions in class, creation of virtual tours to art galleries and faraway lands, documentation of field trips, community mapping projects, the creation of tutorials, or documenting change over time. Digital stories have become a favorite strategy in learning environments as students use digital tools to tell stories. Digital storytelling is discussed later in this chapter and associated web sites are provided at On the Web: Multimedia located at the companion web site. Podcasts, briefly discussed in Chapter 5 as part of Web 2.0 applications, are another use of multimedia and one that is clearly aligned with 21st century skill sets. We'll discuss podcasting a bit more and point to ways to use this technology in learning.

Teachers should get students actively involved as quickly as the students are developmentally capable of using technology. Typical ways that students may use multimedia tools to construct their learning is to develop multimedia slideshows to accompany reports or inquiry-based projects. Such reports can vary according to grade levels and are limited only by the teacher's imagination and eagerness to use active methods of learning. Figure 11.1 presents typical ways that teachers and students integrate multimedia throughout the teaching-learning process in the areas of design, documentation, and student reports. Slideshows can assist the delivery of instruction (it is delivered to the whole group), small group collaborative

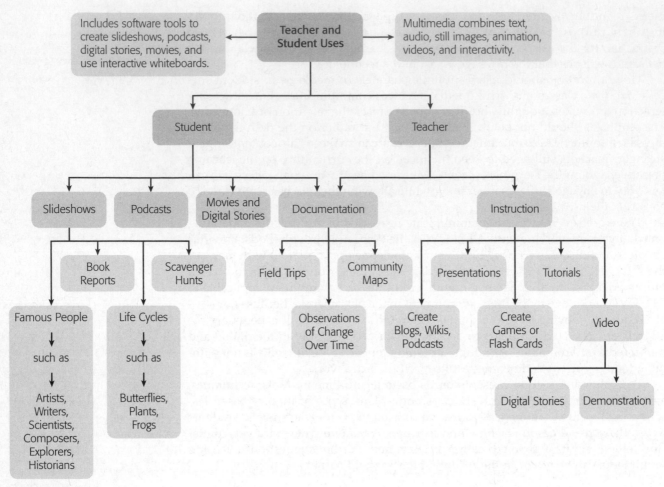

FIGURE 11.1 Teacher and Student Uses of Multimedia/Presentation Tools

work, and team-building types of skills. An increasingly popular way to use multimedia is for students as well as their teachers to create digital stories, podcasts, and e-portfolios.

Student projects can become elements of a student showcase published at the class web site or put on a rolling display during parent-teacher conferences. Review additional ideas at the sites provided at the On the Web section of this chapter, which provide more vision with regard to integrating multimedia tools in instructional activities in various curriculum areas. Additionally, the Curriculum Connections section provides lesson plans that teachers have implemented and the Voices from the Classroom section includes an account of how students and teachers are using digital images and multimedia slideshows in both high school and early elementary art classes.

As teachers incorporate the use of multimedia tools into student learning activities, it is necessary for them and their students to feel comfortable and confident with the hardware and software being used. Everyone should be familiar with the terms associated with these tools and their use, the ways to obtain the media (pictures, audio, video), and the safe, legal, and ethical uses of such media as well as knowing how to document resources used. We begin by defining multimedia components and move to the multimedia software packages that are commonly used in K–12 schools.

Multimedia, Hypermedia, and Its Capabilities

A multimedia presentation consists of a combination of more than one type of media and the media functions to translate the message through text, graphics (clip art, drawings, photos), audio, animation, and/or video. In this discussion, we look at each of these elements and identify information that is important about each as it applies to multimedia presentation (slideshow) tools.

The **text** is the wording; the printed information for the slideshow that is entered using the keyboard. The text format differs in slideshows from that used in other printed documents. The text in a slideshow is typically written in bulleted statements that highlight the main ideas and act as a guide for an oral presentation. Long sentences are not recommended. Be mindful that this tool is primarily developed to use when a person is speaking, making a report, presentation, or demonstration. The language that is used in the slideshow should be spell-checked to protect the credibility of the speaker. In addition, technical jargon should not be used without explanation unless the audience understands such language. Readability is greatly affected by the selection of the typeface, and its size and style.

Sans serif fonts such as Arial or Verdana are much easier to read than others in headlines, electronic format, or on the Web. It is important to use platform-safe fonts: fonts that are common on both Mac and Windows platforms. The font must be on the computer from which the slideshow is ultimately displayed, or must be added to the presentation machine's system folder for access. If the font is not on the computer that displays the show, the default font will appear, which can change the entire look for the slideshow. Bullets (•) can be traditional or novelty (☞) and are generally a character variation of the font being used. If the font is not on the computer that displays the show, the bullets will appear as strange symbols or seemingly random letters of the alphabet. The font size used is larger on slideshows such as Microsoft PowerPoint, because it is primarily used to project onto a screen. The typical font size for titles defaults to Arial 44, the first level header to Arial 32, the second level of headings to Arial 28, the third level to Arial 24, and the fourth level to Arial 20. These sizes will vary depending on the typeface that is used or the amount of text that is placed on a slide.

Care should be taken in choosing a display template that provides contrast in the text and background so that the audience can easily read the message. The number of different font types should be limited to two or three in one slideshow—and the third one should be used only when a different title font is needed for effect. Be consistent throughout the show with the type, sizes, styles, and colors of fonts that are used. It is important to refrain from using underlining in electronic documents as it signals a hyperlink. If you want to use emphasis, use bold or italic text and leave underlines for hyperlinks to web site or other documents.

The second type of media is **graphics**, and includes an assortment of both still and moving pictorial items. The most commonly used are "static" or still graphics, which includes photos, clip art, icons, drawings, tables, graphs, and maps. There are also dynamic or "moving" graphics, which include animations and video. The instructions or help section of the software that is being used for developing slideshows (such as MS PowerPoint, Apple's Keynote, OpenOffice Impress or the slideshow applications in Web-based tools such as Google Docs, Zoho.com, or Thinkfree.com) should be examined to determine which graphic file formats work best with the software. Teachers should apply best practices to working with images in a multimedia slideshow. As you may recall from Chapter 7, digital images can be saved or converted to one of several formats, depending on how the picture will be used. Each format has its own characteristics, uses, advantages, and disadvantages. File formats for static graphics that work best with slideshow

TECH TIP

Use platform-safe fonts.

TECH TIP

Consistency in type sizes, styles, and colors in a slideshow is a must!

TECH TIP

- GIF files are limited to 256 colors
- JPEG files support full color: best for photos

TECH TIP

A slideshow with too many graphics will become bloated and may crash.

software are **raster graphics**. Recall that raster graphics are those that are created using pixels and include bitmapped files, gif files, and jpeg files. **Bitmapped files** include many of the types of images used in slideshows. Bitmapped graphics include images such as photos from digital cameras, scans, or photo collections; screenshots; and images from paint programs. Bitmapped graphics are made up of pixels or dots, and as you will remember, the more pixels, the higher the quality of the photo—and—the larger the file. Therefore, you will want to reduce the resolution of the graphic to the resolution of the computer screen that you'll be working on. You'll have good quality photos as well as a smaller slideshow file. Bitmapped graphics are very fast to load in slideshow software. The **Graphics Interchange Format (.gif/GIF)** file format, one of the two primary formats used on the Web, also does fine in most slideshow tools. Consider that while the GIF files use a compression scheme that keeps file size to a minimum, the images are limited to 256 colors. GIF files are small and thus do not bloat the size of the slideshow file, and load quickly. The **Joint Photographic Experts Group (.jpg or .jpeg/JPEG)** file format is one of the primary formats accepted by the Web, and supports full color. JPEGs are acceptable for most slideshow software, yet lose information (pixels) each time they are compressed. Refer to Chapter 7 for a review of compression.

Although graphics add interest and meaning to text, a slideshow can become quite bloated in size as images, video, and audio are added. The graphics used should be limited and chosen to enhance the message. Thus, if you're taking photos with a digital camera, remember that high-resolution pictures are not required for electronic documents and should be adjusted for the computer. Although many multimedia slideshows contain only text and graphics, the use of audio can add another dimension to communication.

Audio files may serve as background music to enhance a story, sound effects to set the mood or create an emotion, or voice files for narration. Working with audio can be very simplistic; very young students are able to record and embed their voices, or it can be extremely difficult, needing the direction of audio professionals. It is the intent of this discussion to leave teachers with basic understanding about how to use audio files, as well as to discuss the advantages and disadvantages of their use.

To use audio, a teacher or student must first locate and acquire it. Acquiring audio is done by creating the audio file or obtaining it from a secondary source. The specific method depends on the project goals, the available budget, and time. If you or a friend is musically inclined or have a good voice for narration, audio can be recorded easily enough using a microphone and recording device. Similar to digital images, the Web abounds with audio files that are free or nearly free for download. The downside is the time involved in searching for what is needed. Another idea is to visit a computer or music store and ask for suggestions, or go to the public domain where music that is no longer protected by copyright can be found free of charge. Finally, another alternative, and perhaps the best one for busy teachers, is to buy a CD with an assortment of sound effects or use one of the free programs like Garage Band to grab audio. After locating and acquiring the audio files to be used, the audio is "captured," or recorded, and saved to the computer.

The process is similar, though not always the same, across platforms and software. Generally, open the software that you are using to edit the audio file and go to File → Capture. This makes a recording of the audio file. The audio, if something other than voice narration, may need some editing. However, inserting sound effects files should not require this step. Save the file in the authoring tool that you're working with. This depends if you're working with slideshow software, creating a digital story, or a podcast. The steps to record a sound are found later in this chapter. Remember: When using audio, "less is more." Although audio can enhance the message considerably, audio used poorly or overused becomes very annoying quickly. Another best practice is to equip the classroom with quality headphones and speakers. The audio output should be tested on various computers, as the quality of output is dependent on the speakers available.

The fourth media that may be used is **video**. Video files may serve as documentaries of field trips, demonstrations of procedures or behaviors, reports by student groups or special speakers, scenarios for students to watch and then find answers to questions, or even digital yearbooks. Video files are acquired by creating original video using a video camera or obtaining video from a secondary source, including the Web or prerecorded video clips on CD-ROM or DVD. Video can be shot at various times and put together with transitions and music to create a nice yearlong history. The intention of this discussion is only to acquaint teachers with basic video and the advantages and disadvantages of using it. One major challenge when working with even basic video or trying to watch video on your own computer is the huge size of video files. Storage room for video clips should be carefully planned.

Choosing a Multimedia Presentation Tool

A number of software titles can be used to create multimedia slideshows including Microsoft PowerPoint, Apple's Keynote, and OpenOffice Impress. In addition, there are Web-based choices such as the presentation application in Google Documents, Zoho.com, and Thinkfree.com. All are capable of constructing linear presentations of information, and most can easily construct nonlinear presentations for the creation of tutorials if needed (see Figure 11.2). The more flexible PowerPoint and Keynote are capable of importing graphics, sound, and movies in a rather sophisticated (though friendly) interface. In addition, an old favorite—HyperStudio 5 (**www.mackiev.com/hyperstudio**)—has been redesigned and has many new features including supporting the ability to export to a podcast or video. Go to the On the Web: Multimedia on the companion web site to travel to these web sites, read more about these programs, and download free trial versions.

Because this is a book to assist teachers with integrating digital tools into the curriculum, we have provided tutorials at the companion site that will guide learning specifics about software tools. Here we have provided steps to creating a slideshow in Microsoft PowerPoint 2007 that can be used in most multimedia slideshow tools.

Steps to Creating a Multimedia Slideshow

1. *Get ready.* This step includes planning the slideshow. It is a mistake not to think about the content and its position in the slideshow. Outline the slides to make sure that no important points are left out.
2. *Launch the software.* If the software is a new tool, take some time for orientation to learn the available features. Even if the software is somewhat familiar, each new version includes new features.
3. *Open a new presentation.* Go to File → New Presentation. In PowerPoint (PPT) 2007, a presentation is automatically opened for you. If you would like to open an additional new presentation, click on the Office button and select New. In PPT 2008, a presentation is automatically opened for you. To open an additional new presentation, go to File → New Presentation.
4. *Save the presentation.* Save the presentation to the hard drive or a removable storage drive by using the File → Save As command. In PPT 2007, click the Office button and select Save or Save As command. Give the file a descriptive name. Most programs automatically insert an extension at the end of the file, identifying the file as a PowerPoint file, a Keynote file, OpenOffice Impress, and so on. For example, if the slideshow is a presentation on the United States,

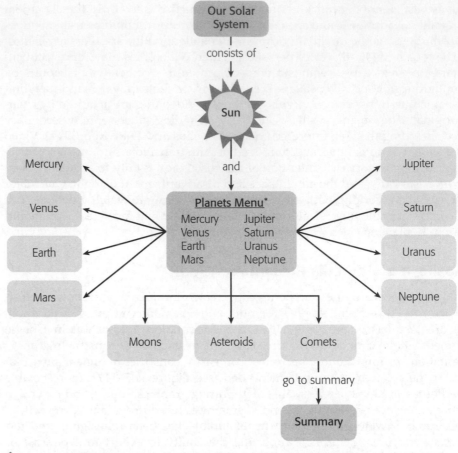

FIGURE 11.2 Nonlinear
Presentation Using a Menu

* At the time of printing, Pluto was ruled not a planet but some astronomers are trying to overrule that decision.

the name might be *us_states.ppt* for a slideshow created in PowerPoint. In PPT 2008, go to File → Save As and give the file a descriptive name.

A recommended practice is to save the development in versions so that you can go back to an older version if necessary. An essential practice is to keep a backup of each change. In other words, the first version would be *us_states.ppt*. The next time the show is changed, it should be saved as *us_states2.ppt*. When the show is complete, the final version can be named *us_states_final.ppt*.

5. *Format the master slide.* Formatting the master slide dictates the "rules" for the entire show. Setting the formatting here can be a time-saver; however, if you want flexibility to change slide layouts for your information, formatting the master slide is not a good idea. Be sure to follow the tutorial to change fonts, sizes, and colors, accordingly. In PPT 2007, you must switch to the View tab and select Slide Master on the Presentation Views palette. Each descending level of slide organization can be formatted here in terms of font, background layout, etc. to maximize and facilitate consistency throughout the slideshow. In PPT 2008, go to View → Master → Slide Master and you will be able to change text styles.

6. *Enter the slide content.* The slide content should be entered in the Outline view in PowerPoint for fastest entry. If this is an option in the software that you are using, it is a time-saver. Once the text is entered in the slides, the other components can be added.

7. *Spell check the content.* All slideshow software should have a spell check feature. Misspelled words cause authors to lose credibility quickly. This should be done each time a sizeable amount of content is entered, and always again before the presentation.

8. *Select a design template.* The design template that you choose should enhance the content of the topic and should not interfere with the lettering on each slide. There are limited design templates within a program and there are many that are found on the Web if you want to take the time to look.

9. *Select the slide layout that is appropriate for each slide.* You may want to use a slide layout template as a placeholder for a photo or object by choosing one that leaves some space and come back later and insert the photos. Once you have formatted your master slide layout in PPT 2007, when you select New Slide from the Slides palette on the Home tab, each new slide you insert will carry the formatting with it from the Master Slide setup completed previously. The same holds true for PPT 2008. If you wish to use various layouts for your information, it may not be wise to format the Master Slide.

10. *Insert the graphics that you have collected for the slideshow.* Make sure that all of your digital image files are at the resolution of the computer (72–96).

11. *Add slide transitions to move from slide to the slideshow.* Transitions provide a method of moving from one slide to the next smoothly. However, some of the transitions will distract from the content. Choose the transition wisely. PPT 2007 offers many new options for transitions. Once the slides are completed, switch to the Animations tab. Hover your cursor over each option for transitions to watch the transition and how it affects the slide. In the slide sorter view, select all the slides (CTRL + A) and select one of the transitions to apply it to all the slides in the presentation. In PPT 2008, go to the slide sorter view and select all the slides in the slideshow. This version of PPT also offers many new options for transitions. Test a few until you find one that pleases you. Choose a transition for the entire show.

12. *Test your show in slideshow view.* It is imperative that all navigation works. Once you are satisfied, save your slideshow as a PowerPoint Show (.pps). This allows the show to present at full screen upon clicking, which is very convenient.

Digital Stories

Storytelling has been going on for centuries. We continue storytelling as we provide a modern use with as digital stories. **Digital stories** are narratives, told from a point of view, that have been turned into multimedia productions. Digital stories combine a mix of still images or video, music and audio narration (author's voice), or text that tells the story and can vary in length and present powerful messages. The Educational Uses of Digital Storytelling (**http://digitalstorytelling.coe .uh.edu**), created at the University of Houston, reports that digital stories can recount historical events, explore life in a community or share personal tales. Chris King (**www.creativekeys.net/StorytellingPower/article1004.html**) explains that a good story is one that touches people in some way, has substance, needs conflict and resolutions, and creates vivid images in the mind of the listener. A good story is sincere and one that you would love to tell. There are seven elements of storytelling according to the Center for Digital Storytelling (CS) in Berkeley, California (**www.storycenter.org/index1.html**). These seven elements are: (1) point of view (what is the main point of the story?), (2) a dramatic question (what is the key question that keeps the attention of the audience and is answered by the end of the story?); (3) emotional content (serious issues that come alive in the story and relate to the audience); (4) the gift of your voice (a way to personalize the story and assist the audience's understanding); (5) the power of the soundtrack (music that supports or exaggerates the story); (6) economy (use enough content to tell the story without "overloading" the audience); and (7) pacing (the rhythm of the story; how quickly or slowly it moves forward). Bernajean Porter, author of Digitales, stresses that authors must "live in their stories" to develop creative tension for their audiences. There are a number of digital stories that may be viewed at the University of Houston site as well as many other sources found at the

TECH TIP

Creating a slideshow in a Web-based program allows the options of displaying from the Web account or downloading as a .ppt document.

companion site. Digital stories provide an avenue for students to use digital tools to push the limits of their creativity and construct products using 21st century skills.

Choosing Software for Digital Stories

There are a number of proprietary software titles that can be used to create digital stories and a huge collection of tools that have been created with storytelling in mind. Table 11.1 presents some of the well-known software used in the development of digital stories. It does not matter which ones you use as long as you come out with a story that you can put in a form that others can use such as on the Web so that others can download and share the message. Since digital stories have pictures, it is reasonable to think that you would need access to **edit images**. There

TABLE 11.1 Software Used for Digital Storytelling

Software for Video Creation			
Title	**Platform**	**Cost**	**Features**
Apple iMovie www.apple.com/ilife/imovie	Mac only	Included free with new computer models	Easy to use; supports full motion video clips, generally supports only .mov format
Adobe Premiere Elements www.adobe.com/products/premiereel	Mac OS X or Windows XP or Vista	Priced for educators	Greater learning curve than others; scaled-down version of the more expensive professional version; full featured
Microsoft Photo Story 3 www.microsoft.com/windowsxp/using/ digitalphotography/photostory/default .mspx	Windows XP or Vista only	Free	Easy to use; supports still images only; played back with Windows Media Player on PCs running Windows
Windows Movie Maker www.microsoft.com/windows/windows media/player/default.aspx	Mac OS X or Windows XP or Vista	Included with the operating system since 2000	Easy to use; new version bundled with Vista. Only outputs files in AVI and WMV formats.
Software for Image Editing			
Adobe Photoshop Elements www.adobe.com/products/ photoshopelwin/ www.adobe.com/products/ photoshopelmac/	Mac OS X or Windows XP or Vista	Priced for educators	Easy to use; scaled down version of the more expensive professional version; full featured
The Gimp www.gimp.org	Linux, Unix, Windows: XP and Vista, Mac OS X	Free, Open source	Easy to use; support of .jpeg, .gif, .png, .psd, and .tiff formats
Software Players Needed for Playing Audio/Video Files			
Windows Media Player www.microsoft.com/windows/windows media/player/default.aspx	Windows only	Free	Audio and video player
iTunes www.apple.com/itunes/download	Mac OS X and Windows	Free	Easy to use, allows purchase of music, movies, TV shows, applications, podcasts, and audiobooks to play computer or iPod
QuickTime Player www.apple.com/quicktime/download	Mac OS X and Windows XP and Vista	Basic is free; Pro version may be purchased	Audio and video player with tight compression and small files; full screen playback

are several titles that you may choose from including Adobe Photoshop Elements for Windows or Macs, Paint Shop Pro for Windows only, or a favorite open source selection is the GIMP. Video creation is easy with MS Photo Story 3 or Windows Movie Maker if you're a Windows user, and iMovie if you're a Mac user. These can be used to "drop-in" still images or video clips, add transitions and sound, and make great stories.

Apple iMovie is video editing software that is designed for Mac computers. iMovie not only can be used to import video but also works well with digital still photos. Various themes, effects, transitions, and audio clips are included with the software and are quite easy to insert into a project for a more professional and interesting show. Even the most novice user can create professional looking results with this easy-to-use software. iMovie can be used for video slideshows, movies, or a combination and is a good tool for creating digital stories. Movie Maker for Windows in similar in operation to iMovie.

A large window shows the "viewer" where "effects" and the movie can be viewed. The images seen at the upper right are "thumbnails" (small images that represent the larger image) of the images that are stored on the hard drive of the computer or on an external storage device and may be used in the movie. The rows, seen at the bottom, show the photos that have been inserted into the project and are organized like a storyboard. The images can easily be selected and moved around if desired.

Audio can be in the form of background music and/or voice narration. While there are more expensive selections, audio editing can be completed with Audacity, a free and fully functional audio editor for Windows, Mac, and Linux users. You can find active links to all software at the companion site at On the Web: Multimedia. Garage Band, a part of iLife, allows you to record your own music. It may be necessary to have the players or download the latest versions of these. iTunes is a player for Mac and PC and is boasted by Apple to be your iPod's best friend, which has a lot of merit. iTunes gives lots of perks such as the ability to download music, movies, podcasts, audiobooks, and more. Go to the companion site and read all about it. QuickTime player is available for Macs or PCs with XP or Vista operating systems. It is free download. Windows Media Player is for XP and Vista is built into the system software. Table 11.2 presents information about common audio/video files, the players needed to open the files, and the characteristics of each.

BubbleShare (**www.bubbleshare.com**) is a Web-based digital story application. Using this software, the images are uploaded and the narration is recorded on the computer microphone for each image. Comic bubbles are overlayed with text. BubbleShare is reported to be simple enough for nonreaders to create a story. There are many other tools that come and go but Alan Levine offers *The Fifty Tools for Telling Stories* at **http://cogdogroo.wikispaces.com/StoryTools**.

Steps to Creating a Digital Story

1. *Get ready.*   If the software tools are new tools, take some time for orientation to learn the available features of the tool being used. Even if the software is somewhat familiar, each new version includes new features. It is a mistake not to take ample time to plan the story as well as gather the resources. The success of the story will depend on this. There are several steps that should be completed. You will need to select a topic for your story. After deciding on a topic, you will have to locate the media, including images, audio, and the content for the story. Each of these steps is discussed in step 2.
2. *Locate the media.*   You will need to select a topic and locate the resources for the project. Folder organization is the best way to stay organized. Create a folder on your hard drive or external storage drive such as a USB and file as

Table 11.2 Common Audio and Video File Formats

File Type	File Extension	Player Programs Needed to Open Files	Characteristics
Audio Video Interleave File	.avi	Apple QuickTime Player www.apple.com/quicktime/	Video file created by Microsoft. Typically uses less compression that .mpeg and .mov.
Apple QuickTime Movie	.mov	Apple QuickTime Player www.apple.com/quicktime/	Multimedia format for saving movies and other video files. Compatible with Mac or Windows.
Apple QuickTime	.qt	Apple QuickTime Player www.apple.com/quicktime/	Video file that was initially developed by Apple. Compatible with Mac or Windows.
Flash Movie	.swf	• Adobe Flash Player or Web browser with Flash plug-in installed www.adobe.com/products/flashplayer/ • Adobe Media Player http://get.adobe.com/amp/	Files that are created on Flash. Compatible with Mac or Windows. Can be played through the Web with the proper plug-ins.
MPEG (Moving Picture Experts Group) Video File	.mpg	• Apple QuickTime Player www.apple.com/quicktime/Microsoft Windows • Media Player www.microsoft.com/windows/	Common video format that was standardized by MPEG. Incorporates MPEG 1 or MPEG 2.
MP3 (Moving Picture Experts Group) Audio file	.mp3	• Apple iTunes www.apple.com/itunes • Windows Media Player www.microsoft.com/windows/	Audio files used for music or audio books. Much smaller file than .wav or .aif files. Supported by iPods and MS Zune and mobile phones that can play MP3 files.
MPEG-4 (Moving Picture Experts Group) Video File	.mp4	Apple QuickTime Player www.apple.com/quicktime/	Video format that was standardized by MPEG that uses MPEG-4 compression, a standard used for sharing video files on the Web.
Real Media File	.rm	RealNetworks RealPlayer or Web browser with the RealPlayer plug-in installed www.realplayer.com/	Media file format used by RealPlayer. Compatible with Mac or Windows. May contain audio, video or both. Can be downloaded or streamed (played as it downloads).
Windows Media Video File	.wmv	Microsoft Windows Media Player or Web browser with the Windows Media Player plug-in installed.	Video or audio file that is compressed with Windows Media compression.
Windows Media Audio File	.wma	Microsoft Windows Media Player or web browser with the Windows Media Player plug-in installed	Audio file that is compressed with Windows Media compression. Used for playing music on the Web.
WAVE Audio File	.wav	• Apple iTunes http://www.apple.com/itunes/ • Windows Media Player	Similar to an .aif file but uses a complex format. Generally more common on Windows systems and gives CD quality.
Audio Interchange File format	.aif or .aiff	• Apple QuickTime Player www.apple.com/quicktime/ • Apple iTunes www.apple.com/itunes/ • Windows Media Player www.microsoft.com/windows/	Audio files. Developed by Apple. CD quality.

Table 11.2 Common Audio and Video File Formats *Continued*

File Type	File Extension	Player Programs Needed to Open Files	Characteristics
MIDI (Musical Instrument Digital Interface) File	.mid or .midi	• Apple QuickTime www.apple.com/quicktime • Windows Media Player www.microsoft.com/windows/	Audio file for musical instruments.
Real Audio File	.ra	Real Player or Web browser with the RealPlayer plug-in installed www.realplayer.com/	Audio file developed by RealPlayer. Common format used for playing audio through a Web browser.
Real Audio Media	.ram	Real Player or Web browser with the RealPlayer plug-in installed www.realplayer.com/	Audio file developed by RealPlayer. Proprietary for delivering and playing streaming audio on the Web.

Source: www..filcinfo.com on May 13, 2009.

you find. You will need to collect images, audio, and content information that will tell of the story. Search for the images that you will use for your story: photos, illustrations, maps, charts, and so on. After you find what is needed, continue your search for the audio that will assist the storyline. The kind of story you decide to tell will dictate the audio needed. The music that you will need to set the mood, along with speeches (think of a story about Martin Luther King and a story about him without part of his famous speech wouldn't be a story), interviews or sound effects should be located. The information that will be the main content should be located. The information might come from web sites, newspapers, or other types of documentation.

3. *Select the media.* Make your selection of images, audio, and content and ready them for the creation of the story. You might edit images or select the sequence that the images will be presented.
4. *Write the script.* The content should guide the narration. You will have to determine the point of view that you will take before beginning your writing. After your script is complete, you are ready to record it.
5. *Record the script.* Record the script using a microphone directly into your computer.
6. *Import the media.* Using the software—iMovie, Photo Story, or Windows Movie maker—import the images into the software, followed by the music and finally by the narration. You will save your movie file as directed.
7. *Preview your movie and upload to the Web.*

Podcasts

As mentioned in Chapter 5, **podcasts** allow individuals (called *podcasters*) to create and distribute multimedia to an audience who can access and listen to audio (voice and music) files through an Internet connection or mobile device. Podcasts, named by combining *iPod* and *broadcast,* provide an abundance of opportunities for teachers and students as they create digital audio on various topics. Podcasts can be strictly audio files or can contain video as well. Podcasts can be downloaded and listened to or watched at the user's convenience. You can listen to it on your computer or your iPod when it's convenient. There are podcasts on every topic that you can think of and provide a great way to "be there at a distance." Typically, podcasts are MP3 audio files so these can be played on any MP3 player or your computer.

Creating a podcast is a simple procedure once you get the hang of it. Equipment is minimal. You will need a computer with a high-speed connection (DSL or cable), a microphone, and software that will allow you to record sound to your computer. New computer models have built-in microphones, which could provide one option for a microphone; however, it might be wise to invest in a headset with microphone if you wish to make podcasting a habit. Software options are shared in step 2. After you have the equipment and software, you're ready to plan and script the podcast.

Steps to Creating a Podcast

1. *Plan the podcast.*   Like so many projects in technology, the planning part of the podcast is the most tedious. The podcaster must determine the purpose of the podcast, the format of the podcast (audio or video), and the equipment/software to use.
2. *Record and edit: Audio.*   Should you choose to create a podcast in audio format, you will have to record and edit the audio. As mentioned earlier, Audacity is a free recording and editing program that works well with Windows and Mac platforms. Garage Band, a favorite of Mac users, comes bundled with new Macs as a part of iLife. After editing the audio to your liking, the file must be saved as an MP3 file.
3. *Create an MP3 File.*   The Web standard file format for podcasts is MP3. Neither Audacity or Garage Band record the audio in MP3 format so the audio file must be "exported" or "converted" to an MP3 file. In Audacity, go to File and select Export as MP3. Save the file as a descriptive name that will identify the podcast in an iPod or on the Web. In Garage Band, export to iTunes and then convert to an MP3 file.
4. *Upload to the Web.*   These files are very large so do not be tempted to email them to your friends or students. If you have a web site that resides on a server, you simply upload the audio file to the server and insert a hyperlink to the file. Remember to move the file to the server as well so that others may access the file to download it and listen to it.

Safe, Legal, and Ethical Use of Digital Information

Copyright and **fair use laws** address the legal and ethical use of multimedia content. Such laws are very important for teachers and students to understand and comply with when working with digital files. The medium that a teacher or student is working within matters, as there is a difference in what can be done with copyrighted materials, what is covered by fair use laws, and how these laws are at times misunderstood, resulting in unintentional misuse. If multimedia files such as slideshows are going to be used within the classroom environment, in projects or for instruction, teachers and students are covered by fair use policies. When publishing these projects on the Web, the teacher and students are far more likely to be in copyright violation and thus need to make sure that the images, audio, or video contained within the project are not protected by copyright. Many teachers believe that if documentation is given for the source, then it is OK to use. That is wrong. If the ultimate destination for a multimedia project is the Web, the images, audio, and video files used must follow copyright policy. Copyright and Fair Use for Educators presents an updated list of information for educators at **www.ipsd.org/Uploads/NVHS_CopyrightAndFairUseForEducators2008.pdf**. This was developed some time ago and has been updated in 2008. You can download a handy chart from this site. An excellent web site, designed by Baruch College of the City University of New York, is found at **www.baruch.cuny.edu/tutorials/copyright** and allows visitors to interactively find facts regarding using multimedia in teaching. Intended for the faculty at this university, the site is open to all readers. Lerman (2006) reports that the site provides a quick and easy-to-follow explanation for using media in teaching. While this is designed for university classrooms, it answers basic questions to using copyrighted materials.

Text   Teachers and students may use a selection of text that is 10 percent or 1,000 words (whichever is less).

Illustrations and Photographs   Teachers and students may use single works by a photographer, but not more than five works of a particular photographer. If there is a collection of photos involved, only 15 images or 10 percent (whichever is less) can be used without permission. An example is that pictures cannot be scanned from a school annual and used in a multimedia document without getting permission from the photographer. Taking original photographs alleviates some responsibility. However, it is important to follow school and district policy regarding the photographing of students. Normally, there will be a strict school policy on photographing students without parents' permission. If permission is granted, it is important to clarify how the picture will be used and what medium will be used.

Music   Up to 10 percent but not more than 30 seconds of a copyrighted work (CD, audio clips from the Web) may be used by teachers and students.

Video   Students may use legitimately acquired (legal copy, not home-recorded) videotapes, DVDs, multimedia encyclopedias, QuickTime movies, and video clips from the Web in the classroom for instructional purposes in a face-to-face learning environment. Students may also use portions of copyrighted works legally. The limit is 10 percent or 3 minutes (whichever is less) of motion media.

Resources from the Web   One major consideration to keep in mind is where and how a Web resource is going to be used. Images, sound files, and video can be downloaded from the Web for use in student projects and teacher-developed lesson activities, yet, they may not be reposted to the Web without permission. This is often misunderstood by teachers and therefore by their students. Using the resource in face-to-face learning situations is fine. However, reposting to the Web, perhaps in a student spotlight page, is illegal without proper permission. In addition, make sure that the resource was legally acquired by the particular web site. There are many sites that offer free files, thus there is really no reason to steal ones that are under copyright. There are also items that are in **Creative Commons** (http://creativecommons.org), a nonprofit group that is dedicated to helping people share their creative work. There is a creative commons search tool (http://search.creativecommons.org) to assist media that can be shared. A short video explaining CC can be accessed from On the Web: Multimedia at the companion site.

Adapting for Special Learners

Using multimedia software and presentation programs gives teachers advantages and flexibility in adapting the curriculum. Multimedia software can engage all four learning modalities: visual, auditory, tactile, and kinesthetic. Using multimedia is an effective way to design lessons considering universal design for learning (UDL), a concept first presented in Chapter 1. Recall that the first element of UDL concerns how information is presented. Using multimedia software supports recognition learning when it is used to present a concept in multiple ways. Using these authoring tools, a concept can be presented or reinforced using images, music, voice, video, or text. Additional support can be offered through links to definitions, translations, models of possible solutions, or web sites with background information. The second element of UDL gives students options for how they will show what they have learned. Students who have difficulty with written expression benefit from being able to talk about what they know and to illustrate their learning through either drawings or graphics. Multimedia programs have the capacity to offer these supports electronically, giving students the choice of using drawings, diagrams, pictures, text, sounds, and audio (voice recordings) to express their learning. The third element of UDL looks at student interest and motivation. Multimedia software can encourage interactivity, collaboration, and exploration of

(*text continues on page 244*)

Voices *from the* Classroom

Integrating Technology into My Art Classroom
Melanie Hammond

Melanie Hammond is beginning her sixth year as an art teacher in grades K–12. During that time, she has worked with high school, middle school, and elementary students, and is currently assigned to a primary school, teaching grades 1–2. She has a BA in Studio Art and has an MA in Teacher Education. We asked her to share her views of how technology enhances teaching and learning in the art classroom and how she uses multimedia slideshows during her instruction.

I have often found integrating technology into the art classroom to be very helpful. It has helped me work more efficiently as a teacher and has enabled me to better communicate my lessons to the students. My students have found it to be a helpful tool for generating new ideas and more creative subject matter from which to work. Art teachers can be a rather mixed lot when it comes to technology: they tend to love it or hate it. I personally think it is very beneficial, so long as it's used when practical and does not completely replace the notion of a handmade object. Students are often very interested in working in digital media to create art. The study of digital photography, film, and other images are an important part of an art curriculum, especially at the middle and secondary grade levels.

As a teacher intern, I was fortunate enough to have a mentoring teacher who was rather enthusiastic about technology. Through some hard work, begging, and grant writing, he had acquired quite a bit of technology for his classroom: big-screen TVs, a dozen computers, digital cameras, color printers, Photoshop software, and so on. During that year I had fun exploring the potentials for technology integration in an art curriculum. Many of the students who were resistant to pencil, paint, and paper projects were often happy to work away on a digital image. As a teacher, I enjoyed their enthusiasm, but wanted to get them excited about more traditional media as well.

One of the primary struggles my students often faced was coming up with original and creative source material. The use of technology seemed to be a natural fit for this problem. One day we took the digital cameras and set up photo shoots around the classroom. The students took pictures of themselves in front of backgrounds that had a lot of pattern and contrast. The photos were then placed in Photoshop and students altered them by making them high-contrast images. The students cropped the images on the computer, printed copies, and traced the outlines onto linoleum blocks. The students then employed traditional printmaking techniques to carve and print the images. The results were both strikingly modern and undeniably traditional, and the students loved the entire process. In later years I've had students use the same techniques to do paintings as well.

When I began teaching at the elementary level, I inherited a classroom with very limited technology. Having been fortunate enough to have a lot technology access in my previous classrooms, I was shocked to find only a chalkboard and several boxes of art posters waiting for me. I thought to myself; "What am I going to do without my PowerPoint presentations?" and "I have 1,400 grades to give every six weeks and I am supposed to do it on paper?" It all seemed extremely difficult if not impossible to manage. As the year passed by I did procure a computer to keep grades with, but it had been passed along from at least five previous owners and was perpetually crashing. I pulled out my posters and used them for examples instead of PowerPoint presentations. I found the posters to be really limiting. I could only teach about artists that were in my poster collection and the collection never seemed to have the images I really wanted. Another drawback was that the images in the collection frequently contained only one image by a particular artist, and it was hard to help students really identify an artist's style with only one image to show them. I thought about ordering more poster sets, but decided against it when I saw how steep the prices were. I managed to get by that year with what I had and I still had a great year. A good teacher usually finds ways to make whatever is available work.

Over the next few years I talked a lot to my principal and school technology team about how I use technology in the classroom, and through their wonderful support and assistance, I now have all the equipment I need. I have a reliable laptop and an Activboard. I use the Activboard in my classroom to do drawing demonstrations, have interactive flipcharts, play art review games, and watch video clips about artists. I am able to introduce each lesson with a slideshow and use the Internet to take my students to the Louvre, the National Gallery of Art in Washington, D.C., or any other kid-friendly art web sites. I can now share the artwork that I want the students to see and multiple works by the same artist. The students really enjoy using the Activboard and it has really helped me increase the overall level of interactive learning in my classroom. In just a few years time I have learned that while technology is not essential to good teaching, it can make teaching a lot easier and learning more exciting and interactive for my students.

CURRICULUM CONNECTIONS

The following Curriculum Connections are summaries of lessons that integrate multimedia slideshows with curriculum topics. Each summary presents a content area, grade level(s), NETS·S alignment, brief description of the lesson, teacher preparation needed for the lesson, active participation steps of the students, and suggested variations. If the lesson was adapted, the original source is provided.

Picture-Perfect PowerPoint

CONTENT AREA/TOPIC: Language Arts

GRADE LEVEL: K   **NETS·S:** 1, 6

Description: Students, after learning to take photos with a digital camera, take pictures throughout the school, and draw pictures to represent items that start with the letter "P" to use in a slideshow, recognize and use inventive spelling to attempt to spell words that begin with P. The collection builds until the each child has at least one item in the show. Some scanned pictures may also be used if needed.

Teacher preparation: The teacher, with the help of parent-assistants, aides, or preservice teachers, teach the children the basic ways to use a basic digital camera. The basic parts of the camera are taught to the children, as is the care of the camera and how the digital pictures are moved from the camera to the computer.

Active participation: The teacher discusses the letter P and words that begin with P. Photos can be taken in the schoolyard (such as a pole) or at the farm (a pig) or in the classroom (a paper) and/or children can draw and color items to go into the collection. Electronic books are made with the pictures and each child records the name of the item on their slide. This presentation can be shared at the parent conferences or with the school as an enriched curriculum with technology.

Variations: This lesson could be done featuring other letters in the alphabet. See the outcome of one implementation at the On the Web section of this chapter.

Source: Picture Perfect PowerPoint, lesson from Lesson Library, a PT3 funded project: 2001–2004.

The Four Seasons

CONTENT AREA/TOPIC: Science

GRADE LEVELS: 1–2   **NETS·S:** 1, 6

Description: Students, after learning to take photos with a digital camera, take pictures throughout the year to use in a slideshow to distinguish between the typical landscape, stages of the trees, flowers, and clothes that are characteristic of the different seasons. The collection builds until the four seasons are represented. Some scanned pictures may be used to represent the summer months if school is not in session.

Teacher preparation: The teacher, with the help of parent-assistants, aides, or preservice teachers, teach the children the basic ways to use a basic digital camera. The basic parts of the camera are taught to the children, as is the care of the camera and how the dig-

ital pictures are moved from the camera to the computer. The teacher discusses what to look for that is descriptive of each season. Photos can be taken in the schoolyard, on a field trip, scanned from drawings, and scanned from traditional photos.

Active participation: The photos are collected and students write descriptions of the pictures. Electronic books are made and shared with the class each season, at the parent conferences, or with the whole school.

Variations: This activity could be varied using other topics that teachers choose. It also could be printed and posted on a bulletin board.

(Continues)

CURRICULUM CONNECTIONS *Continued*

Greek Gods and Goddesses

CONTENT AREA/TOPIC: Language Arts, Social Studies

GRADE LEVELS: 6–8   **NETS·S:** 1, 3, 6

Description: This lesson is designed to have students actively engaged in inquiry-based learning about a Greek god or goddess and to share their findings in a multimedia slideshow at the conclusion of the research.

Teacher preparation: The teacher locates helpful web sites such as **www.mythweb.com**, **www.loggia.com/myth**, **www.crystalinks.com/greekgods.html**, or others that will provide information needed for student research. To save time, sites chosen should be bookmarked on computers or presented at a web page that students can access. The teacher should also create a research data sheet to accompany the research project that outlines the information that is needed. The requirements for the slideshow are defined and a rubric is developed.

Active participation: Students may be paired or otherwise grouped for the active participation segment of the lesson and are assigned a Greek god or goddess to research. Using the web resources provided or other types of resources, the students research to find information regarding their assignment and complete the data sheet before moving on to the slideshow software to create their presentation.

Assessment: Monitor students. Check answers for accuracy. Depending on developmental ability of students, assistance will be given with technology. The presentations are given to the whole class and the teacher evaluates according to the criteria set forth for the assignment.

Variations: The topic can be changed using Roman gods or other content appropriate for the curriculum.

Source: Adapted from a lesson from Beth Dudney, a participant in Project ImPACT 2002–04, a PT3 funded project.

Learning about Crawfish

CONTENT AREA/TOPIC: Science

GRADE LEVEL: 6   **NETS·S:** 1, 3, 6

Description: This unique long-term lesson gives students an opportunity to collect crawfish and document their life cycles. After the collection period, students watch specimens in a tank in the classroom to determine their gender, watch the molting process, regeneration of lost claws, and hatching of baby crawfish from eggs. The processes are documented with digital photos and placed in a collection. Finally the photos for use are chosen, captions are written, and the slideshow album is developed.

Teacher preparation: The teacher carefully plans the crawfish collection period and secures parent volunteers to go on expeditions. The materials necessary for the lesson, including aquariums, digital cameras, and microscopes, are secured in anticipation of the first arrivals.

Active participation: Students search their neighborhoods for crawfish habitats and record their activities to share with the class. Specimens are brought to class and placed in one of several aquariums (obviously this lesson occurs in an area where the specimens are plentiful). During the collection process, students are studying and writing research papers on crawfish to provide foundation knowledge. In addition, they watch movies and read books, and talk with experts. During the weeks that follow, they watch and document the various processes that occur during the life cycle of these creatures. The slideshow acts as a teaching tool for future students and sets the stage for another inquiry-based project with a different specimen.

CURRICULUM CONNECTIONS *Continued*

Assessment: The teacher monitors the process of the inquiry into real-world learning. Reports are graded as well as digital collections and finally the collection in the slideshow.

Variations: Other animals to be considered could be earthworms, fish, insects, or specimens determined by the teacher.

Source: William Fuchs, Teacher. Nimitz Middle School, San Antonio, TX. www.kodak.com/global/en/consumer/education/lesson-Plans/lessonPlan093.shtml.

Planning a Trip of a Lifetime

CONTENT AREA/TOPIC: Social Studies/Mathematics

GRADE LEVELS: 6–8   **NETS·S:** 1, 3, 6

Description: The goal of this unit is to promote awareness of money management, as well as encourage the understanding of the culture, history, attractions, and expenses associated with different locations. In this lesson, students plan a "trip of a lifetime" to a specified location (i.e., New York City) for five days and four nights but must remain within an allocated budget as they plan lodging, food, transportation, and entertainment. Their plans and success in managing their money is presented to class members in a slideshow presentation.

Teacher preparation: The teacher develops a guide sheet to facilitate inquiry with specific information that must be researched for the project. The research would include the location of the city, the distance from their location, the special attractions in that city, and the transportation options, culture, and history. The class is divided into student teams of four for research. The teacher chooses locations within the United States (by region, population, or other criteria) for students to target their research. Selections might include New York City (**www.nycvp.com**), Chicago (**www.choosechicago.com**), San Francisco (**www.onlyinsanfrancisco.com**), Memphis (**www.memphistravel.com/**), Atlanta, Boston, Phoenix, Orlando, Detroit, Cleveland, Seattle, and so on. Web sites such as the chamber of commerce in each location (see above) could be bookmarked or placed at a research web site to start research.

Active participation: Each student team plans for a trip for four (yourself and three friends) to travel to an assigned or chosen destination for 5 days and 4 nights.

The cost of a plane ticket (or other means of travel), the hotel room, food, attractions and recreation, souvenirs, and other miscellaneous expenses must be considered. While the hotel that you choose is a decision of your group, consideration should be taken about the distance of the lodging from the attractions. Documentation must be provided with digital pictures of the choices in the final slideshow presentation: a picture and name of the hotel/motel used by the group, at least three pictures of different restaurants that you plan to eat at (restaurants cannot be generic fast-food places, such as McDonald's; restaurants must be exclusive to the city you are visiting), at least four pictures and names of attractions or recreation of which your group plans on taking advantage, and at least two pictures and names of free events or activities that your groups will visit.

Assessment: Based on the amount of points that will be available through this assignment, create a rubric for each required item. For example, within the rubric, accuracy and completion of the research could be considered as well as the design and number of slides, hotel information, mode of transportation, and so forth. *Optional:* Create a student assessment sheet so students can assess peer contributions to the overall project.

Variations: The lesson could be varied with travel out of the United States and could be utilized to teach money conversions.

Source: E. Peters Rowe, Teacher, grade 3. Norwood Elementary, Knoxville, TN.

(Continues)

CURRICULUM CONNECTIONS *Continued*

Digital Reenactments

CONTENT AREA/TOPIC: Foreign Language, History, Literature

GRADE LEVEL: Any   **NETS·S:** 1, 6

Description: Students use digital pictures and slideshow software to create a comic-strip style synthesis of a piece of literature or time period in history.

Teacher preparation: The teacher collects digital cameras and blank disks for the groups. A box of miscellaneous items that can be used for costumes, props, and the like is useful. Halloween masks are also useful items to keep on hand. The teacher divides the class into collaborative groups.

Active participation: This lesson requires two or three days, depending on the length of class periods. Days 1–2: After the text is completed in class, it is divided into sections, each of which is assigned to a student group. The groups assign roles and create a storyboard for their section of the text. They use blank note slides printed from MS PowerPoint. The dialogue and narration for each slide is written on the lines and the positioning of each person in the picture is drawn/sketched—stick figures are fine. Any backdrops should also be noted. The instructor reviews the material for accuracy and/or omissions. Students prepare lists of items that they will bring the next day for completing the project. Days 2–3: The teacher returns the pages to the student groups and allows time for review of comments and suggestions. Then the students begin taking the digital pictures needed to complete the project. They should note the file number of each photo on their papers. After all the pictures are taken, the groups go to the lab and begin the compilation process.

They bring the images into MS PowerPoint, where they edit them as needed. They then apply dialogue and narration to each of the slides. They can also apply fancy transitions and sound effects that enhance the story. The final products are then shown (in order) to the class as a whole.

Variations: This activity could be varied to present a student's life, or to re-create a time period or sequence of events in history. In mathematics, it could re-create the steps in solving a proof or equation or the various stages in completing a project in any class. In science, you could use the stages of a life cycle.

Source: A. Kelly Graham, Clinton High School, Clinton, TN.

---

interests far beyond the confines of the printed page. The use of multimedia shows great promise for improving student learning and motivation to learn.

Examples of multimedia programs that incorporate principles of UDL include two products designed in collaboration with researchers at the Center for Applied Special Technology (CAST). Wiggle Works is a beginning literacy series that provides a blend of reading, writing, listening, and speaking in a flexible and customizable environment. It is available in English and Spanish versions and is produced and distributed by Scholastic, Inc. Thinking Reader uses unabridged core literature titles to provide students in grades 5–8 with instruction and practice in key reading strategies. The program embeds choices of prompts, hints, model answers, and corrective feedback into the text. It includes human voice narration with synchronized highlighting to build fluency, and a contextual glossary with Spanish translations for students who are English language learners. Accessibility features include adjustable font size and options for keyboard navigation for blind users or switch access, text captioning, and screen reader compatibility. It is produced and distributed by Tom Snyder Productions, a division of Scholastic.

Balanced Literacy (IntelliTools, Inc.) is another example of a multimedia reading program that incorporates universal design principles. Designed for struggling readers and students with special needs, the interactive format provides instruction in five components of effective K–2 reading instruction: phonemic awareness, phonics, fluency, vocabulary, and comprehension. The program has a series of overlays that can be used with IntelliKeys, an alternate keyboard, and with switch access. Lessons correlate to NETS·S standards, and the English language learning and early literacy standards of most states.

These commercial products provide highly developed examples of UDL strategies as applied to reading programs. But most of these strategies are quite simple and actually are easily applied within most multimedia authoring programs. Students who experience cognitive, hearing, vision, and physical barriers may find additional support using the adaptations listed in this section.

Cognitive Barriers

Many of the multimedia software and presentation programs reviewed in this chapter can be successfully used with students with cognitive barriers. Many younger students enjoy using drawing programs, such as KidPix Deluxe. Other programs, such as PowerPoint, can be used as launch pages, hyperlinking a screen to specific web sites or other files for assigned activities. For students who are confused by the standard keyboard, programmable keyboards may be used with multimedia programs. IntelliKeys (by IntelliTools, Inc.) can be programmed to accept keyboard navigation commands and shortcuts. A customized printed-paper overlay, developed using a companion program (Overlay Maker), is placed on the IntelliKeys keyboard. Printed areas indicate where the student is to press in order to interact with the screen. IntelliKeys may also be used with switches and onscreen scanning programs. Although multimedia programs can support almost any learning activity, teachers often feel hindered by the time it takes to create such examples for the classroom. Classroom Suite (IntelliTools, Inc.) is an integrated software package with a multimedia program (IntelliPics Studio), text-to-speech word processor (IntelliTalk III), and electronic math manipulatives (IntelliMathics). This software package has numerous templates for developing multimedia activities for book reports, writing prompts, adaptive books, quizzes, math activities, spelling practice, and basic phonics activities. Teachers add their own content to the template examples. The screen interface is simple and intuitive for students with cognitive disabilities as well as for general classroom use. Universal access features, such as onscreen scanning for switch users and an interface with the programmable keyboard (IntelliKeys), are built-in software options. This vendor also supports an online community of teachers who share activities authored using the software program.

Hearing Barriers

Adaptations that increase accessibility for students with hearing barriers offered in previous chapters apply to multimedia as well. These include providing captioned or text-based descriptions for all pictures, animations, and clips with sound. If using a commercially produced multimedia program that incorporates sound without captions, be sure that the student has an interpreter or other form of interpretive assistance (such as a note taker) to ensure that the information is communicated. An emerging multimedia technology for the deaf and hearing impaired is the Sign Smith Studio, developed by Vcom3D, Inc. These are animated American Sign Language files that translate English text into American Sign Language or Signed English. The files can be captured to a variety of formats that can be incorporated into many different multimedia programs. Further information can be obtained from the company at **www.vcom3d.com**.

Vision Barriers

Multimedia programs can present access barriers for people who do not use sight for obtaining information. These barriers are similar to those discussed in previous chapters. Authoring solutions may include providing a narrative description of all animations, text descriptions of all pictures, large fonts, and pages that have a logical, consistent layout. For students who are color blind, adjust the images accordingly. Screen adjustments include magnification and/or screen reading software. Consult the options listed in Chapter 3 for specific programs and vendors.

Students with vision barriers are not the only individuals who can feel frustrated when viewing multimedia presentations. Who among us has not suffered through a lecture or presentation in which a well-intentioned teacher presented visuals with full screens of words written in 12-point type? When projecting a multimedia program, preview the presentation as if you were the audience, checking for any slides that might cause potential eyestrain.

Physical and Language Barriers

Students with physical barriers can still access multimedia programs, as adaptations are available for any form of computer input. Keyboard adjustments include filter keys to adjust the rate of keystroke acceptance, sticky keys to allow typing with one hand, or onscreen keyboards (see Chapter 3). Basic hardware adaptations, such as switches and other mouse and keyboard alternatives, are discussed in Chapter 2. The IntelliKeys keyboard works well with most multimedia products, as well as with the Classroom Suite developed by IntelliTools. For students with language barriers, certain augmentative communication devices (such as those offered by Pretke-Romich) can be programmed to navigate the multimedia program, thus eliminating a second layer of input.

On the Web

This section includes only a snapshot of web sites that the authors recommend for viewing. To access live links and a larger and continuously updated collection of sites, go to the companion web site at **www.pearsonhighered.com/obannon2e.**

Assistive Technology

Sign Smith Studio
www.vcom3d.com/signsmith.php
Sign Smith Studio has been purchased by Vcom3D, which is where you can now find information about this product. This software translates English text into American Sign Language or Signed English files that can be incorporated into many different multimedia programs. Sign Smith Studio has been recently upgraded to 3.0. Read about the new features that have been added at the company blog.

Thinking Reader
www.tomsnyder.com/Products/product.asp?sku=THITHI
Thinking Reader is a multimedia program that includes a series of core literature titles used in grades 5–8. It is designed in conjunction with reading experts using principles of universal design for learning. Titles may be purchased separately or as part of a set.

Wiggle Works
http://teacher.scholastic.com/products/wiggleworks/index.htm
Read about Wiggle Works, a beginning literacy multimedia program developed using principles of universal design for learning.

Digital Stories

Teach Digital: Curriculum by Wes Fryer: Digital Storytelling
http://teachdigital.pbwiki.com/digitalstorytelling
Information presented in a PB wiki presents information about digital stories, music, copyright, podcasting, Voice Thread, and sources for free images.

The Educational Uses of Digital Storytelling
http://digitalstorytelling.coe.uh.edu/
The University of Houston presents this informative site that discusses the educational uses of digital storytelling. You will find examples, software, the seven elements for storytelling, directions for how to design and develop your story, and more. This is a great help to the new storyteller!

Interactive Learning Sites

Biology in Motion
http://biologyinmotion.com/
This interactive site has animations and simulations for students in the sciences.

Interactive Curriculum Resources
www.globalclassroom.org/ecell00/javamath.html
This site provides many interactive math, language arts, science, social studies, and other sites that the teacher can browse and select for their study pages for their students. The Global Classroom provides this page. Flash Player is needed to see the animation and they will provide the link to download if you do not have access to it.

Powers of Ten: Molecular Expressions: Science Optics and You

http://micro.magnet.fsu.edu/primer/java/scienceopticsu/powersof10/

This site allows you to move through space toward Earth in successive powers of ten. Developed by Florida State University, this offers a photo gallery and a movie gallery with tutorials and other teacher resources as well as student activities.

Integration Ideas

Creating Multimedia Projects

www.adobe.com/education/instruction/adsc/

Adobe has created a list of ways to use multimedia projects in the classroom that includes many content areas. You will need Adobe Acrobat Player to read this document.

20 Ways to Use Multimedia in Your Classroom

www.sonycreativesoftware.com/education/sellsheets/academic_20ways.pdf.

Sony provides this document that presents 20 ways to use multimedia in your classroom. This list, in PDF format, suggests team video reports, slideshow presentations, multimedia portfolios, and podcasting, among other great suggestions.

Multimedia in the Classroom

http://fcit.usf.edu/multimedia/overview/overviewb.html

This site, presented by Florida Center for Educational Technology at the University of South Florida in partnership with Pinellas County School District, explains that multimedia activities allow students to build 21st century skills: to work in teams, express their knowledge in numerous ways, solve problems, revise their work, and construct knowledge. Such activities build collaboration, and allow students to work with real-world skills and communicate with different audiences. Go to the web site to review the DDD-E or Decide, Design, Develop and Evaluate model.

Web-Based Multimedia Slideshow Tools

Google Documents

http://docs.google.com

Google Documents offers a presentation tool. As with all Web-based software, users have 24/7 access to presentations on the Web as long as they access to the Internet and a browser. Try it out for a free solution for your classroom. Keep in mind that you must sign up for a Google account.

Zoho.com

www.zoho.com

Zoho offers a host of programs that are Web-based and free if you have an account. Zoho Show is a presentation tool. These are fully compatible with MS Office counterparts and promote digital literacy and collaboration.

ThinkFree

www.thinkfree.com

ThinkFree Office offers Web-based word processor, spreadsheets, and presentation programs that are compatible with MS Office counterparts. Trial versions can be downloaded for thirty days. The office suite can then be purchased for approximately $50. Getting an account allows 1 gigabyte of free online storage for the trial period.

Key Terms

Multimedia (226)
Multiple-channel communication (226)
Multimedia presentation (226)
Text (229)
Graphics (229)
Raster graphic (230)

Bitmapped file (230)
Graphics Interchange Format (.gif/GIF) (230)
Joint Photographic Experts Group (.jpg/JPEG) (230)
Audio (230)
Video (231)

Digital story (233)
Edit images (234)
Podcast (237)
Copyright (238)
Fair use laws (238)
Creative Commons (239)

Hands-on Activities for Learning

1. Visit the On the Web companion site (**www.pearsonhighered.com/obannon2e**) and review the sites available.
2. Write a reflection in your reflective technology blog about ways to integrate multimedia projects into learning situations with the target population that you will be teaching.
3. Use a presentation tool to construct a slideshow that will serve as an example for a report that you wish students to complete. For instance, if you will be having students give book reports, create one to serve as an example for your students.
4. Using the information provided and the software of your choice, create a digital story.
5. Using the information provided and the software of your choice, create a podcast that is appropriate for the learners in the target population that you will be teaching.
6. Develop a scenario or quiz of situations for students that would allow them to determine whether they would be within the legal rights to use the images, sound, and audio for multimedia slideshows, digital stories, or podcasts.

LEARNER OBJECTIVES

At the completion of this chapter, learners will be able to:

- Discuss research that supports the development of usable, accessible Web design.
- Use terminology associated with basic Web design.
- Describe various methods used to create web pages and the pros and cons of each.
- Establish a web site account and create a homepage (index.html).
- Create a folder structure for the organization of Web files, transfer files between local and remote computers, and work with graphics for the Web environment.
- Discuss the safe, ethical, and legal use of images, audio, and video in a Web environment.
- Distinguish between information suitable for school versus classroom web sites.
- Examine classroom web sites that serve as communication, showcase, and instructional tools for students and parents.
- Identify elements that facilitate accessibility in web pages for all learners.
- Plan, design, and publish an accessible classroom web site to serve as a communication and resource tool for students and their parents for curricular purposes.

NETS-T ALIGNED WITH WEB AUTHORING

1. **Facilitate and Inspire Student Learning and Creativity**

   Teachers use their knowledge of subject matter, teaching and learning, and technology to facilitate experiences that advance student learning, creativity, and innovation in both face-to-face and virtual environments. *Teachers:*

   a. promote, support, and model creative and innovative thinking and inventiveness.

   b. engage students in exploring real-world issues and solving authentic problems using digital tools and resources.

   c. model collaborative knowledge construction by engaging in learning with students, colleagues, and others in face-to-face and virtual environments.

3. **Model Digital-Age Work and Learning**

   Teachers exhibit knowledge, skills, and work processes representative of an innovative professional in a global and digital society. *Teachers:*

   a. demonstrate fluency in technology systems and the transfer of current knowledge to new technologies and situations.

   b. collaborate with students, peers, parents, and community members using digital tools and resources to support student success and innovation.

   c. communicate relevant information and ideas effectively to students, parents, and peers using a variety of digital-age media and formats.

   d. model and facilitate effective use of current and emerging digital tools to locate, analyze, evaluate, and use information resources to support research and learning.

4. **Promote and Model Digital Citizenship and Responsibility**

    Teachers understand local and global societal issues and responsibilities in an evolving digital culture and exhibit legal and ethical behavior in their professional practices. *Teachers:*

    a. advocate, model, and teach safe, legal, and ethical use of digital information and technology, including respect for copyright, intellectual property, and the appropriate documentation of sources.

    b. address the diverse needs of all learners by using learner-centered strategies and providing equitable access to appropriate digital tools and resources.

Frameworks

Although the Web is still considered young, many changes have taken place since scientists first developed interest in using a computer network to exchange documents in the early 1980s. At that time, standard HyperText Markup Language (HTML) was developed, as well as a browser program, to allow these scientists to exchange their research. The emphasis then was the exchange of text-based information rather than graphical presentation. Because of the ease and lack of expense, the Web rapidly grew into a popular means of publishing. Because standard HTML was not designed for visual appeal, it greatly limited effective communication. Graphic designers realized its lack of appeal for publication purposes and adapted it for graphic page design. Since that time, the Web has grown into a massive information resource, giving teachers and students access to huge amounts of information. With this growth has come more demand for ways to make this environment easier to use. Today, there is a building collection of research devoted to design issues that potential Web authors should consider when designing even the most simplistic web site. The purpose of this chapter is to review what is known about designing web sites that are easy to use and accessible to all, especially those in the targeted viewing audience. The target population, for a teacher/designer, is primarily the students, their parents or guardians, and other teachers and administrators. Because of the importance of these issues, the U.S. Department of Health and Human Services provides a web site, **www .usability.gov**, that features research-based usability guidelines. Usability.gov provides guidelines for "designing usable, useful, and accessible Web sites and user interfaces." They report that the usability of a site is the measurement of four factors: (1) ease of the reader to move about the site, (2) the efficiency of the design, (3) how easy it is to learn and recall how to use the site, and (4) the satisfaction experienced by the site visitor. Web designers agree that usability is crucial to designing pages that are useful to readers.

Research-based Web design and usability guidelines (**www.usability.gov/ pdfs/guidelines.html**), sponsored by the federal government's Department of Health and Human Services (revised in 2008), are available for purchase from the web site. Although we realize that teachers and/or students are not professional Web designers, creating web sites that are useful to the readers is a consideration for anyone who publishes in this environment. **Usability** can be greatly enhanced by following these basic guidelines. Designing usable and accessible web sites is very important as teachers move into the role of author/designer for classroom sites. In addition, this information should be modeled and passed along for student designers.

Lynch and Horton (2009) emphasize that Web design includes two processes; the **planning process** followed by the **development process**. The time devoted to planning, as with all project-based development, is time well spent and ultimately results in time saved; nevertheless, it is the part of the process that is most often avoided by those new to design. These authors suggest systematic planning focusing on several specific elements that they identify as the "process, interface design, site design, page design, typography, editorial (writing) style, graphics, and multimedia." Each element is detailed in the online version of the *Web Style Guide*, Third Edition (**www.webstyleguide.com/index.html**), or in the print version listed in the References section at the end of the book. Although this well-respected resource is not necessarily aimed at a new designer or teacher, these authors do an excellent job of discussing basic design fundamentals for those who want to design and develop a web site that can be of use and accessible to all. Similar information is supported by other authors (Williams & Tollett, 2006; Horton, 2006), though each presents the fundamentals somewhat differently. It is important that teachers realize that it doesn't take a professional designer to create a well-designed page(s) that students and their families will be anxious to use as a resource guide. It is with that premise that this information is presented. We begin our discussion by introducing basic terms and reviewing the many benefits of publishing on the Web for schools and teachers. This discussion is followed by options for creating web sites and designing a classroom site with the tool of your choice.

Basics

A **web page** is a document created using **HTML (HyperText Markup Language)** code and uploaded (transferred) to a **server** to become accessible on the Web. Each web page typically contains text, graphics, and hyperlinks and has a unique address called a **URL (Uniform Resource Locator)**. Often, web pages contain audio and video clips and since the new Web 2.0 tools have surfaced, many web sites contain blogs for communicating with readers. Depending on the site and its purpose, podcasts may be available for download to access speeches and such. A collection of related and hyperlinked web pages together make up a **web site**. A web site always has a **homepage** that serves as the entry point to the site, and should contain an index and an introduction to the site to tell the reader what the site provides. Many new tools have made the design of web pages the old-fashioned way—requiring a lot of technical expertise—unnecessary. We discuss the benefits of publishing a web site as well as methods to use in the next paragraphs.

Benefits of Web Publishing

There are multiple reasons for schools and individual teachers to publish web sites. The cost of publishing on the Web is much less than the cost of print-based publishing. The use of color is basically free and the ability to make instant revisions and updates as well as to archive information is possible without stacks and stacks of paper. Distribution is basically free with exception of the designer's time and the Web space, and the visitors can "tune in" over and over. Other advantages include the ability to request a quick reply on a form, including some video or audio, and linking learners to a huge amount of information. Further, teacher sites can have a classroom blog, which can be used to communicate with students and parents on weekly happenings. Podcasts can also be downloaded from teacher sites that share all kinds of information in audio and video format.

If the design of school web sites and classroom web sites are well thought out, visitors will know when to go to the school site versus when to link into their child's classroom. The information found on school sites is somewhat different

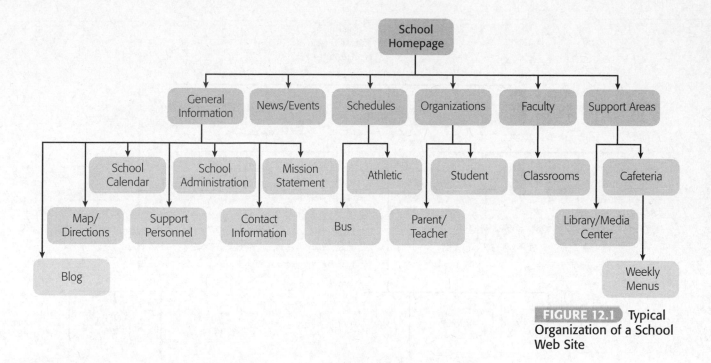

FIGURE 12.1 Typical Organization of a School Web Site

than what is found on classroom sites, although both provide valuable information. Typically, the school web site will link to a faculty section that will list individual teachers. The classroom site should provide a link back to the school homepage to assist navigation for the readers.

Organizing Appropriate Information

The information found on a school web site should be somewhat general in nature and apply to the entire population at that school rather than a specific grade level or teacher. *A Teacher's Guide to School Web Sites* (**http://fcit.usf.edu/websites**), developed by the Florida Center for Instructional Technology at South Florida University (2004), presents an excellent outline of information that a school should consider when designing or revising the web site that will represent the school. Keep in mind that the site was developed in 2004 and therefore it does not include references to the inclusion of the Web 2.0 tools.

Useful categories for school sites are presented in Figure 12.1 and include general school information (such as the address, contact information, and map), school administration, school policies (such as policies for snow days, dress code, attendance, and behavior), calendar of events, extracurricular activities, school newsletters (with monthly editions), parent involvement such as the parent/teacher organization (PTO), volunteers, or fundraising and important links of interest to the audience who will visit. Within each of these and other categories, more specific information is provided. A good way to decide what may be important to a specific school would be to brainstorm with teachers and parents to see what additional information they would like to access.

Teachers can develop classroom web pages that serve as a communication tool to share information with students, parents/guardians, and other teachers. Typically, members of a school faculty are listed on a faculty page with links to the teacher's classroom site, if available. If the politics are such that teacher web sites are difficult to update, it may be a good idea for teachers to consider having their classroom site housed at Google or other Web servers that provided easier access

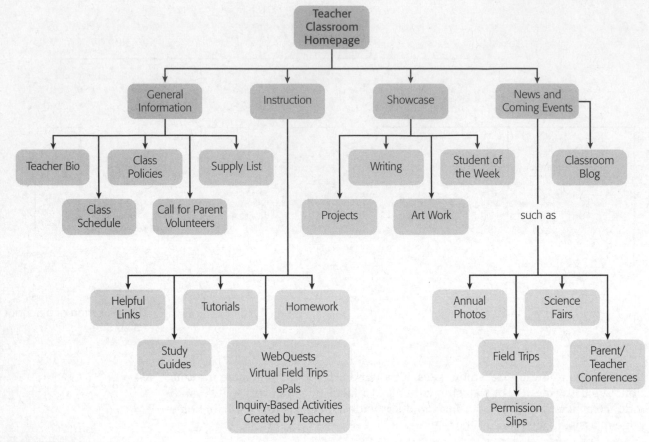

FIGURE 12.2 Typical Organization of a Teacher/Classroom Web Site

for revisions. This advice is not meant to get teachers to move outside of school policy; however, many times, teachers are policed to the point that it interferes with their ability to keep their sites current.

Information found on individual teacher/classroom pages may vary depending on grade levels and school policy; typical items include general information such as a class schedule, class supply list, class policies, and requests for parent volunteers. A classroom blog could reside in this section to let parents know what is happening in the classroom. A biography page could be included that provides information about the teacher's formal training, certifications, awards, and other personal information, if desired. Instructional information might include a homework page, study guides, problem-based learning activities such as WebQuests, or project sites, and curriculum links. Showcase sections are popular to display student work. A section might be included to announce upcoming events. A blog might be housed in this section or simply serve the entire site. New teachers should be aware that school/district policies govern the publication of student pictures and information published on the Web. It is important to research these policies and to abide by them. It is also important for teachers to provide easy navigation back to the school homepage for topics that are related to the entire school population. Planning the information that resides on school and classroom sites will result in useful sites. Figure 12.2 presents the organization of a typical teacher/classroom site, showing the homepage that links to the major sections and some example secondary pages within each section. Organizing in sections simplifies the navigation scheme and makes it easier for the reader to learn.

Methods for Creating Web Pages

Methods for creating web pages have changed for individuals who don't have the time to learn HTML code or other more complex editing programs. The Web-based tools that characterize the Web 2.0 world are free and friendly and do not require technical skills. Teachers and students are able to work in Web-based friendly spaces that react similarly to a word processor. However, we would be remiss if we did not mention all methods of Web design. There are three ways to create pages that we will discuss. Each method has pros and cons and varies in complexity, learning curve, and features offered. The methods include: (1) writing HTML code, (2) using a WYSIWYG editor, and (3) using a Web-based content managed tool.

Initially, all web pages were created by "hand-coding," or writing HTML (HyperText Markup Language) code directly. Although writing the code is very time consuming and is no longer mandatory, now that newer and easier options are available, it is helpful to have a basic understanding of HTML to read and troubleshoot problems if you're working in a WYSIWYG editor.

WYSIWYG (pronounced *wizzy-wig*) is an acronym for "what you see is what you get," and describes a group of editors that allow the designer to work in a document area similar to that of a word processing document. Text, graphics, and tables can be inserted and look very similar to how they will appear through browser software. Knowledge of HTML coding when using these editor programs is not mandatory, because the software program writes the HTML code in the background while the page is being created. Although WYSIWYG programs are typically easy to use, are focused on design rather than code, and provide quick options for inserting page elements such as tables, at times the HTML written in the background can be atypical, causing problems later. It is helpful, of course, to know basic HTML to make changes in the code if needed. WYSIWYG programs in the recent past were bountiful; however, it appears that Web-based tools have taken their share of the market. The well-known programs include Adobe Dreamweaver (Mac or Windows; **www.adobe.com/products/dreamweaver**), Microsoft Expression Web (Windows only; **www.microsoft.com/expression**), and KompoZer (Mac, Windows, or Linux; **http://kompozer.net**), a very easy editor that requires no technical knowledge.

Web-based programs, such as Google Sites (**www.google.com**) and Weebly (**www.weebly.com**) and/or a Weebly account, are free and offer a space to create and revise pages as needed. All that is required is a computer that is connected to the Internet, a browser, and a Google and/or a Weebly account. WordPress (**http://wordpress.org**) is a blog tool that provides more features than basic blog tools and can be used for building a web site. A site that is developed in WordPress by Tim Stahmer, an IT Specialist for the Fairfax Public Schools is *The Top 101 Web Sites for Teachers* resides at **www.assortedstuff.com/top101**. As you examine this useful site, you will notice that the fact that it is Web-based does not limit the clean design that is possible. ClassnotesOnline.com (**www.classnotesonline.com**) allows teachers to create a full-featured class web page at no charge. This site is template driven so creating a page is quite easy. The information may be public or private and provides fill-in-the-blank answers to questions. There are a variety of items that teacher may include on their page including class supplies, class calendar, class links, class news, and more. It is important to keep in mind that as time passes, one can expect more Web-based and content-managed solutions to appear. Designing web sites that require serious technical skills are becoming a thing of the past.

Regardless of the method used for designing web pages, space on a server or Web host must be obtained unless you are using a Web-based tool that provides the space for you. By now, you may have chosen a software tool (or had one chosen for you). Before you start thinking about what will be at the site, if you are not using a Web-based tool, you must obtain space on a server at your school or elsewhere to place the final site so that someone can see and use it.

Obtaining Server Space

For preservice teachers, a limited amount of server space should be provided free, as long student status is retained at the university. Many universities provide undergraduate and graduate students a certain amount of space on the university server that may be used once the account has been established. Even if a preservice teacher decides to use a Web-based program for designing a classroom page, having space on a server allows the storage of documents.

For practicing teachers, space may be provided by the school or district; the amount in both instances will vary by institution, as will the policies for storing information. If neither situation is applicable, server space may be purchased or Web-based tools may be used as previously discussed. The university, school district, or commercial host will have a specific process for securing the space on their server. Check with the support staff to see what has to be done. After the space has been obtained, a folder structure for the organization of files should be completed (see next section). If the teacher has decided to use a Web-based tool, like one of the ones that we have mentioned, the space is provided when an account is secured. If students are using a Web-based tool, the information is entered directly on the page and there is no need for storing the pages on your computer or external storage device. However, if students are using Web editors, building a folder structure to hold web pages is essential.

Building a Folder Structure for Organization

There are several things that need to be done after the planning process and before the development process begins. Building a **folder structure** to organize the Web files and naming those files that will become part of your site are important tasks, as these files lay the foundation for what comes later.

Carefully organizing the Web files in folders results in files that are easier to locate, revise, and delete as updates occur. Storage space is typically limited for university students or teachers at school sites. Consequently, if files are not maintained or become inactive or outdated, open space can be assigned quickly. Many new Web authors will fail to foresee that there may be multiple Web projects in their future. Reorganization is a huge undertaking that requires extensive time, which teachers don't have. Consequently, starting the organization process early and passing organizational habits along to students is good design strategy.

A folder structure is used for organization, similar to folders in a file cabinet or on a computer. This type of organization will result in HTML documents, graphics, and other associated files that are easy to locate because they are filed away in folders, also referred to as **directories**. The process starts with the creation of a base folder called the **root folder** to serve as a container for all Web files. There is a **universal homepage** that serves as an entry point to the Web files. The homepage is named index.html or index.htm or occasionally default.html. The name to use will be specified by the systems administrator of the server that hosts the site.

In addition to the universal homepage, the root folder holds project folders for each major project. Each **project folder** holds all of the files that are associated with a particular site, including a homepage that serves as the entryway for that particular project as well as any associated files. Like the homepage, all of the document files will include the .html (or .html) extension, identifying the document as a Web document. In addition to the homepage, and associated document files,

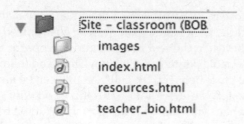

FIGURE 12.3 Folder Structure/Organization for a Typical Teacher/Classroom Web Site

there should be a folder to hold all images for the project named Images. All graphics that go with the project should be stored in the images folder. Figure 12.3 displays a typical folder structure for a classroom site that a teacher might initially create when designing the site on a Web editor and uploading to a server. Obviously as more pages are created, more files would be seen.

After the folder structure has been created, files that are contained there should follow certain common practices to allow them to work correctly and be easy to locate. One such practice is **naming the files**. All files are given an identity and an extension that identifies the type of file that it is. File names should be descriptive and short! The longer the filename, the more difficult it becomes to type correctly. Yet the filename should be descriptive enough to jog the memory of the designer. Use only lowercase letters for naming files. This is not mandatory, but it is easier to keep the naming scheme organized. There can be no spaces used, so to separate letters insert an underscore (_), hyphen (–), or tilde (~). The underscore is difficult to read in a URL. The authors suggest choosing one way to separate words and use it each time to lessen confusion.

All web pages must have a **file extension**, which identifies the type of file. All Web documents have the .htm or .html extension added to identify the document as an HTML file. Typically the .htm extension is used on the Windows platform and the .html on Macs. Other files for the Web have extensions that identify them as well. When these files are created, the program typically puts the correct extension on the document. For instance, you have learned that converting a word-processed document to PDF will preserve the formatting. MS Word documents have the .doc extension. Documents converted to PDF have a .pdf extension. The same is true for graphics. A graphic that is saved as a GIF file should end in the .gif extension. A graphic that is saved as a JPEG file should end in the .jpg or .jpeg extension.

Basic Web Page Components

Basic components are used in even the simplest of web pages, including text, tables, images, hyperlinks, and a navigation scheme. In this section, we review each of these components and explain how they fit into a Web environment.

Text　Similar to inserting text into a word processing document, before **text** can be entered in a Web editor, a document (or file) must be opened. This option is typically under the File menu. After the document is opened, text can be entered, edited, and saved via procedures similar to those used in a word processor. The writing can be created in a word processor and copied and pasted into the Web editor page. If you work this way, it is very important to complete all formatting in the editor program. Time is wasted by inserting formatting procedures earlier, as it will not be recognized or copied over. The editor is writing the code in the background so any formatting done previously is ignored.

Tables　Tables offer a way to control the layout of web pages so that they appear well organized when viewed through different browsers. **Tables** contain rows and columns similar to those in word-processed documents. Text and hyperlinks can be inserted in tables, and the background color can be customized. **Cell padding** is the (adjustable) margin between the text in a cell and the border of the cell. More cell padding (up to a reasonable degree) will improve the readability of the information. **Cell spacing** is the distance between the cells. A table can be inserted within a table, and this is called a **nested table**. Although this is a good way to control the layout, care must be taken when working with nested tables; some browsers do not handle them well. Nested tables should be used minimally to avoid downloading problems as well as accessibility issues. Tables can also be problematic for screen readers, as the cells interrupt the ability of the reader to scan the text.

TECH TIP

Hyperlinks used for navigation can be relative, absolute, or anchor links.

Hyperlinks   **Hyperlinks** are used in web pages to move to different pages or sites. There are four categories of links that can be created, each having a different purpose: internal links, external links, anchor links, and email links. **Internal (relative) links** are those that jump to pages within the same site. In contrast, **external (absolute) links** jump to pages on another site. **Anchor links** are a type of internal link used to jump to information on the same page and are used to avoid the need to scroll through long pages of information. Anchor links are usually used in conjunction with the "back to top" links providing the reader with easy ways to navigate up and down a long page. If the entire page is viewable on the screen at one time, there is no need to insert anchor links. Finally, **email links** take the reader to an email message window that is preaddressed to the author of the web page, giving the reader a way to contact the author by email. Methods are somewhat different for each of these links and may be handled a bit differently in different editors.

TECH TIP

Email links are inserted by using mailto: email address.

To create an *internal link*, select the text that your readers will click on in order to link to another page and move through the steps to link the new location. *External links* are completed by linking to a page that is not within the site but are external to your site. After selecting the text for the link, type in the URL of the external location in the link box. The easiest and safest way to enter a URL is to copy and paste from the actual site so that no typing errors will be created. *Anchor links* are often found in a navigation bar at the top of a page to allow the reader easy travel within the long page. To insert anchor links, scroll down the document to the location (heading). Insert a named anchor icon. You will have to assign a name to the anchor. Travel back up to the navigation bar and select the corresponding text. Insert the name of the anchor in the link box. *Email links* are entered using the following steps in either an editor or with the HTML. Type a descriptive phrase that will signal the reader that they may contact the author by clicking the link. An example might be "contact me" or "contact the teacher" or something similar. Select the text. In the link box or HTML code, enter the following: mailto: your email address. By pressing the return key, the email address should be activated.

Images   Inserting an **image** into a web page is similar to inserting one in other types of documents, with a couple of important differences: a graphic inserted into a page on the Web must be included in the project folder and uploaded to the remote server along with the page in order to be seen on the Web. (This is not true with Web-based software as the image is embedded.) Also, there are two primary formats to which digital images can be saved or converted for use on the Web. Each format has its own characteristics, uses, disadvantages, and advantages. Image files are saved with a descriptive name, followed by a period (dot), followed by a three-letter extension that identifies the file format. File formats that are most commonly used for Web publication at the current time are .gif and .jpeg. However, new browsers now recognize .png files.

As you will remember from previous discussions, the Graphic Interchange Format (.gif) was developed to transmit images over the Internet. It remains one of the two primary formats used on the Web. GIF files use a compression scheme that keeps files to a minimum, yet they are limited to 256 colors. The Joint Photographic Experts Group (.jpg or .jpeg [pronounced jay-peg]) format is one of the primary formats accepted by the Web. This format supports full color and is a good choice for photographs.

Planning the Process

The Web design process begins as the teacher determines the purpose of the site, establishes the goals of the site, identifies the target audience for the site, and outlines the content for the site. For example, a teacher's purpose for a classroom site might be as a communication tool for students, their parents or guardians, and other teachers. Therefore, the purpose and the target audience are established. The goals of the site might be to provide information for new students and homebound students, to provide assistance to students with their homework, to showcase outstanding student work, or to document activities for parents. Classroom web sites can be useful for communication, as well as a good area for students to access instructional resources, and for spotlighting student work, along with other things. The site could even have different sections for the expected visitors, such as an area for parents or guardians or other teachers. You may decide to have a way that parents can communicate with you through a blog. If so, the purpose of the blog will have to be planned. After the *general purpose*, the *target audience*, and the *major goals* are clearly defined, you can write the content to meet those goals.

Teachers designing sites should take into account technology considerations such as which browsers the site will support and the bandwidth required, so as not to overwhelm the connection speed of the average visitor. In other words, the teacher must determine what information the target audience of the site wants and needs and what technology resources they must have to easily access it. After all, if the readers cannot easily get to the information at the site, it is a sure bet that they will never return. For example, if a teacher wants to provide video clips of activities at school, the reader will need certain browser plug-ins to play the videos, and will have to wait a very long time for videos to download on a slow connection.

Planning the Design of the Interface

Planning continues with the design of the **site interface**, which involves creating pages that are independent and easy to navigate. Web pages are very different from pages in print; a design that works in print does not necessarily work on the Web. Specifically, each web page needs to be designed to stand on its own, independent of the remainder of the site. For example, when a reader visits one page within the site, all information should be available for that reader to easily find it again. This independence is achieved by providing certain information to the reader on each page. An easy way to recall the information that should be on each page is the who/what/when/where refrain familiar to authors. This information is generally placed in navigation bars at the top or bottom of each page and consists of who designed the page (author's identity and the ability to contact the author), what the page is about (descriptive title that appears when the page is saved as a bookmark/favorite), when the page was created and/or last revised, and where the page originates on the Web (the URL of the homepage). Figure 12.4 displays a typical navigation bar/footer with links provided to the homepage and each of the major section pages, as well as the author's identity, revision date, and the URL of the place that the page resides on the Web. Using as Web-based application, much of this is determined for you, which eliminates some of the structure so that you can concentrate on the information that you put there.

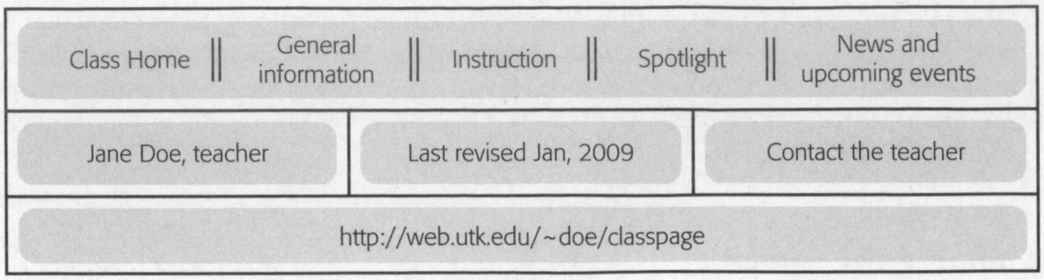

Class Home ‖	General information ‖	Instruction ‖	Spotlight ‖	News and upcoming events
Jane Doe, teacher		Last revised Jan, 2009		Contact the teacher
http://web.utk.edu/~doe/classpage				

FIGURE 12.4 Navigation Bar and Essential Information in a Web Page Footer

Designing the site interface also includes planning the **navigation system** for the site, which will prevent readers from getting lost or arriving at a **dead-end** or **orphaned page** (page that has no navigation except to use the Back button). Readers need easy access to the starting point (homepage) of the site and each major section from every page in the site. Although classroom sites may be quite small at first, it is best to assume future growth, consider major sections wisely, and add pages within these sections or add new sections as the site grows.

Planning the Design of the Site

The **site design** includes the organization of the information in the site. This is simply planning what sections/pages will be in the site and what information will be found on each. Web sites vary tremendously, although all are designed as information resources and should contain certain common elements, including a homepage that provides an index and a site summary and navigation bars. The homepage serves as the entry to the site and is the most visited page. The importance of this page cannot be understated. The homepage should contain an **index (table of contents)** for easy navigation to each major section, as well as a summary, which tells the reader what is contained at the site. Navigation bars can also be located at the bottom or top of the page (see Figure 12.5) to provide easy movement to the major sections in the site. Creating a **paper prototype** or **storyboard** for the site that shows the homepage and other main section pages allows the teacher/designer to get a clearer picture of what the site will ultimately become. All storyboards should include the navigation plan that will be used. Figure 12.5 displays a typical storyboard presenting the pages and navigation among them.

Planning the Design of the Page

Planning the design of the pages within the site includes choosing the colors for the page background and text, typefaces, page elements, and page length, and considering accessibility issues.

Web pages must be designed with contrasting backgrounds and text to increase readability, and each page within a site should use consistent colors throughout. Although it seems fun to have lots of interesting colors used in a single web site, it is quite confusing to the reader. There are many web pages that are difficult to read because the colors of the background and text have little contrast or the background color or image makes reading very difficult. It doesn't matter how "cute" the background is or how brilliant the message is if it cannot be read. The most legible color combination consists of a white background with black text. If white is not appealing to you, use another neutral background. Dark pages with white or light text are easy to read because of the contrast but reading many pages in that combination begins to be difficult after a time. Also, using bright colors such as bright yellow or neon quickly becomes very hard on the eyes. Some nice examples are shared at **www.edtech.vt.edu/edtech/id/interface/text.html**.

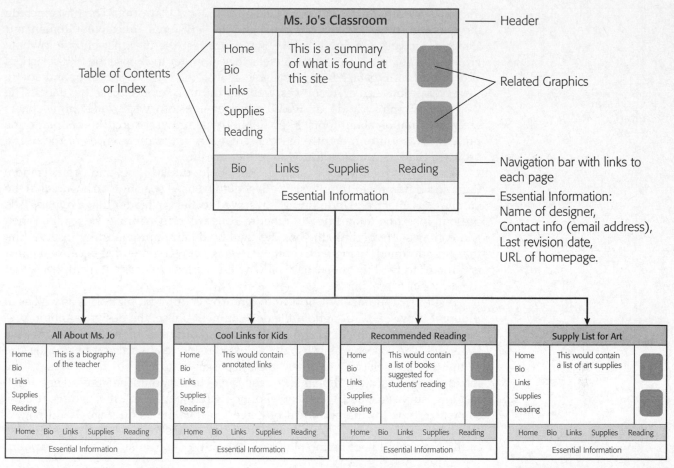

FIGURE 12.5 Storyboard for a Typical Classroom Web Site

A **hierarchy** or level of importance should be established for the content of each page. In other words, the most important content should appear at the top of the page so that the reader can easily locate it.

The length of the page should be considered. Single pages are quicker to download than multiple ones, although readers do not like to scroll through long Web documents that seemingly continue forever and cause disorientation quickly. If you need a longer page, be quite sure that you have provided easy navigation through anchor links so that your reader will not have to scroll excessively.

A major barrier for learners who rely on assistive tools, such as speech synthesizers, is the difficulty experienced when the page is designed in tables that include many cells. These tools read the information in a linear fashion, cell by cell. This method becomes very difficult with nested tables.

Planning the Typography

The typography that should be used in web pages is different from that used in print. The teacher/designer must choose the typeface, typestyle, type size, line spacing, and word spacing to make a web page visually appealing and easy to read. These elements are explained in this section.

The **typeface(s)** chosen for web pages affect the reader's ability to read the onscreen information. Although serif typefaces are easier to read in print, sans serif typefaces are easier to read on a computer screen. Sans serif typefaces are recommended in both environments for headers and subheads. Another potential problem results from using a typeface that is not on the reader's computer, thus changing the entire look of the page. Recommended are cross-platform typefaces that are typically found on both Mac and Windows platforms. The fonts include the sans serif fonts Arial and Verdana and the serif fonts Times New Roman and Georgia, as well as a few others. Some editors let the designer choose a whole group or list of fonts. This selection tells the computer to choose the first selection, and if the first typeface is not available choose the second selection, and so on. Visit **www.motive.co.nz/resources/webfonts.html** to review these typefaces. The Web Typography Guide at **www.webstyleguide.com/wsg3/index.html** shares great information about fonts. Keep in mind that browsers on different platforms present fonts a bit differently in size. However, in the preferences of the user's browser, the size can be adjusted for easier reading.

Typestyles refer to styles such as italic, bold, underlining, and capitalization. Italic and bold provide emphasis; both should be used sparingly to ensure that the emphasis is effective. Underlining is reserved to cue the reader that a hyperlink is present. Inserting underlines for other reasons will only confuse the reader. When text contains a hyperlink, the browser will by default automatically insert a link that is underlined. Using ALL capital letters is not recommended because the text is difficult to read for more than a few words. It fails to create the emphasis that the designer is seeking.

A specific **type size** will appear differently on different platforms as well as in different browsers. Throughout the development phase, the designer should preview the page on both Mac and Windows platforms, as well as in multiple browsers. The size of type is usually adjusted using relative sizing in that the size of the type is "relative" to other sizes. If possible, do not use these tags, as the resulting type is often too small or too big. There should be consistency in all headers, subheads, body text, and captions across pages. In other words, use the same size type for the body text on page 1 of the site as on page 3 and page 9 (when you get there). The easiest way to control text is to use style sheets. The size of the type should not be too big (over 14 point) or too small (less than 10 point) for body copy on the Web.

Line spacing is also called **leading** (pronounced *ledding*), a term from former times when printers would place pieces of lead between the lines of text. Keep in mind that if the spacing between your lines is too close, it makes the text harder to read. If there is too much white space between the lines of text, the text is hard to read.

If you are using a **Web-based application**, you may be limited on some of these choices such as line spacing. However, it is important to follow good design principals with color and type no matter what tool you are using. Get acquainted with the features and use the program to the fullest. You, of course, will have to make the decision whether 24/7 access for your students and easy editing is worth what you give up in design features in some of the more advanced editors such as Dreamweaver.

Writing for the Web

Writing content for publication on the Web is different than writing content for publication in print, because of the differences in the media. Many new designers fail to take these differences into consideration when designing web pages.

One of the differences is readability (how easy it is to read long pages of text). Reading long blocks of text in a Web environment is much more tedious than in a printed page or book. The typical reader on the Web does not like to read large amounts of text online, preferring to quickly scan the information. Consequently, the writing should be very concise and presented in short blocks of text or bulleted (unordered) or numbered (ordered) lists. Numbered lists should be used when the sequence of events or items is important. In addition, the writing must take into consideration the targeted audience. If that audience is primarily elementary students, the writing must be in language that they can read and understand. Obviously, it would be quite different for an older group of students. If the page is aimed at children and their parents, the page must be written for the students' reading level and perhaps have a special section for parents. The line length for text can hamper reading if it is long and spread across the browser page.

Using Graphics and Multimedia on the Web

As with graphics that are inserted into print documents, the graphics that are inserted into web pages must meet certain specifications. The graphics inserted into a web page should be used wisely and should be limited to images that enhance the content, are meaningful, and add value to the text. Having unrelated graphics is a waste of time and contributes nothing to the page. It is essential for the teacher/designer to consider the download time (time it takes to get the information to the user's desktop) for graphics for the audience. Graphics that are used for web sites must be saved in an appropriate format for the Web, meaning GIF, JPEG, or PNG files. While PNG files are acceptable by the Web, older browsers do not recognize them so be sure to test pages with PNG files on various browsers. Use alternative text (alt.tags) for each graphic that is placed in the site. **Alternative text** presents a text version of each graphic and can be used by screen readers for learners with visual limitations (see Adapting for Special Learners).

The way the image will ultimately be used should be considered when taking a photo with a digital camera or scanning. Photos captured at high resolution for print documents, such as brochures, provide the most distinct results, and also result in very large files. A computer monitor, in contrast, can display an image only at 72–96 ppi (pixels per inch). Thus, if an image is captured at high resolution, the result will be a large image when displayed through the browser. If photographs are being considered for the web site, make sure to take that into consideration.

Most importantly, copyright laws are in full force when a teacher is publishing on the Web. Much of the fair use guidelines that teachers often rely on do not protect the teacher as designer, because web sites become public upon upload. Also, photographs of students should be published according to the policies of the school; if allowed at all, these usually require parents' permission. Students should not be photographed alone and names are not typically published with the photo for Web publication. Refer to Chapter 11 to review the copyright policies for digital media.

Other multimedia elements used in classroom web sites includes audio, video, slideshows, and animation. Key to the use of multimedia are three concerns: (1) accessibility, (2) download time, and (3) copyright and school policies regarding the contents of video of students. These areas of concern are echoed by additional research studies such as those found in the research-based Web design and usability guidelines mentioned earlier. Animation should be used cautiously, because the movement quickly becomes a distraction. The constant blinking of any element becomes quite distracting and annoying quickly. Commonly used examples of bad design choices include animations that continue forever, animated pictures that are commonly seen in email (such as the opening and closing of a mailbox . . . over and over and over). Although "under construction" signs are a bad design choice, animated ones are even worse. It is probably a better idea to just not have the page available at all than to create one and have it say only "under construction." Animation is a wonderful tool, if used creatively and to make an abstract concept easier to understand, yet beware of the pesky distractions that are so often seen.

A poor choice of colors, the use of graphics with no alternative text (alt tags), and the use of complex tables all hinder accessibility issues. There is additional information in the discussion found in the Adapting for Special Learners section of this chapter as well as resources found in the On the Web: Web Authoring virtual site.

Prior to Developing Your Site

TECH TIP

If you are using Web-based software, such as Google Sites or Weebly, applying for an account gives you space on the server hosted by the company.

1. *Apply for Web space.*   If you are using a Web editor and uploading your pages to a server at your school, you will have to obtain space. In order to apply for space, you will need to obtain a Web account. If you are a university student and your university offers web space, apply for this space. Seek advice if this information is not readily available. Each student is assigned a username (user id) and initial password that are used to access and transfer Web files. Typically, a temporary password is issued that you should change to secrure your account. If you are a teacher, seek support from your technology coordinator. If you are using a Web-based site such as Google sites or Weebly, apply for an account at the site. Once the account is approved, you are automatically allocated the amount of space that the site provides to account holders.

2. *Create a universal homepage.*   This step is only necessary if you are using an editor and uploading to a server. Move to the bottom of the paragraph for directions for Web-based tools. In all public_html folders, there should be a universal homepage that serves as the entry page for all of your projects. A generic page is typically generated when the account is assigned, and will require personalization. The homepage is typically named index.html, or default.html, or main.html; however, only the Web server administrator can tell you specifically how to name your homepage. This homepage should be linked to the project that you will be creating. Each time that you create a future project, a folder for that a project should be created to hold its files. Remember, organization is the key to sanity for the busy teacher. If you are using a Web-based tool, such as **Google Sites**, the first page that you create will serve as your homepage and you do not have to worry about specific naming schemes because this is done for you by the site.

You may be thinking that Web-based development eliminates much of the technical expertise for the teacher and you're right. Yet, you need to be aware that with that ease, you give up some of the cool features that can be created with advanced editors like Dreamweaver. Most of the Web-based tools have some really cool templates and as long as you concentrate on creating clean and easy-to-read pages, these tools offer teachers many perks.

Steps for Development

1. *Plan the site that will be created.*   Following the steps provided earlier in the chapter, determine the purpose of the site, the target audience, and the goals of the site to be designed. Determine the technology that is required to access the site. Next, plan the interface design that will be used to create a site that is usable and is easy to navigate. Then, plan the site design. How many major sections will be in the site? How many pages in each section? What colors will be used throughout the

project? What typeface will be used for headings, for text? Storyboard out the initial plan drawing in the navigation scheme. After the planning of the site, begin development.

2. ***Create a folder structure to organize your project files.***   Create a folder to hold the files for the Web project. Name the folder to reflect the project. Remember that folders should be named with brief, yet descriptive names using no more than eight characters in the name: all lowercase characters with no spaces. For instance, if your project will be the creation of a site for your classroom, a proper name for the folder would be "classroom." Within the project folder, create a folder named "images" to hold all of the graphics used in the site.

3. ***Create a homepage for the project site.***   Create a page to serve as the homepage for the project site and save it as index.html in the project folder. The homepage for the project should present a hyperlinked index (table of contents) for the project as well as a summary of what will be found within the project pages. For instance, if you are creating a classroom site, review the diagram in Figure 12.2 and determine the sections (or pages) that will be featured in your site. These sections (or pages) will appear in the index on the homepage along with a summary of what is found at the site.

4. ***Create additional pages for this site.***   Other pages for the site should be developed and saved in the project folder. Each page should be named using the same naming scheme as outlined in step 2. For instance, if you are creating a classroom site, review the diagram at the beginning of the chapter and determine what pages you will develop. If you want a section for general information at your site, typical pages might be classroom policies, classroom schedule, teacher bio, and so forth. In that case, these pages might be named policies.html, schedule.html, teacher-bio.html and would be saved in the project folder.

These steps change somewhat for teachers who are using a Web-based tool. Yet, I emphasize the importance of completing a plan. Step 1 should be carefully completed. It is a mistake to move directly to the tool and begin development without a plan. Planning, while tedious, will facilitate the development of a well-designed site that is pleasant to look at, easy to read, user friendly, and provide the information the user needs.

Transferring the Files to the Remote Server

After the project files are complete, they must be uploaded (transferred) to the Web server for viewing. There are various ways for the transfer to take place depending on the software or technique used for Web design. If a Web editor is used, the program may have a built-in FTP (file transfer protocol) application. FTP is used to transfer files over the Internet. Each time you're downloading something from the Internet, you're using a form of FTP in your browser software. To upload files, you want a secure way to transfer them, so you would use a special software called an FTP client or a Web editor that has the feature. Dreamweaver has a built-in FTP feature making the transfer of files easy using the drag-and-drop method. If working in a program without this feature, an FTP client may be used such as WS-FTP or Fetch. This process is explained below.

1. ***Launch the FTP software.***   There are many FTP programs that are reviewed at tucows.com for Windows and Apple OS computers and are available for download, some of which are free. We provide generic information and links to Web tutorials for two quite familiar FTP clients: Fetch (fetchworks.com) for Apple

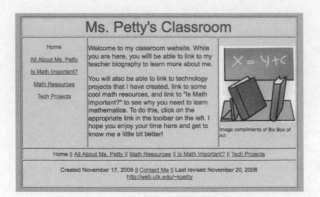

FIGURE 12.6 Classroom
Web Site Created in
Dreamweaver by Kelly Petty
(Reprinted with permission)

Computers and WS_FTP at (**www.ipswitch.com/Products/WS_FTP/**) for Windows users. These sites offer tutorials for the latest versions and also free thirty-day trials.

2. *Connect to the remote server site.* Select File → New Connection and complete the dialog box. The information requested will typically be the same in any connection: Host computer, your username, and your password for your Web account. The Hostname field asks for the name of computer (server name) that provides space for your account; the username is your Web username, and the password is given to you for your Web account. Connect by clicking Connect and the remote window appears.

3. *Transfer files to the remote server.* When the remote window appears, you will see the files that are on the remote site. You should be able to see your universal homepage. The universal homepage (that provides entry to your Web space) should be uploaded each time a change is made. The project folder should be uploaded. The PUT command allows the user to PUT files on the remote server. The GET command allows the user to download files that are on the remote site to your local computer. You may also drop and drag the files to the server. Make sure that the files go where you want them to go in order to keep your organization. After the selection is transferred, check your pages.

4. *View your pages on the Web.* After the files are transferred, check the transfer by using your browser to see if the new pages or updates can be seen. If you are

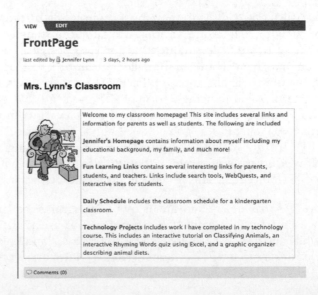

FIGURE 12.7 Classroom
Web Site Created in PB
Works by Jennifer Lynn
(Reprinted with permission)

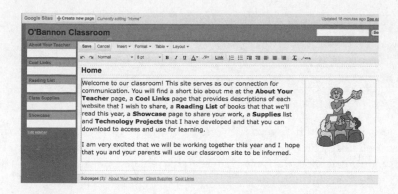

FIGURE 12.8 Classroom Web Site Developed in Google Sites by the Author

working with updating files, if the changes are not seen, make sure that you refresh your browser and try again.

If you are using a Web-based editor, you simply have to design, edit, revise, and save the page. When you choose the Save button, the page is immediately available. Take some time to view some of the teacher web sites at On the Web: Web Authoring at the companion site.

As described in this chapter, teachers may use various tools to develop classroom web sites. Figures 12.6, 12.7, and 12.8 show web sites developed by preservice teachers using different tools and slightly different formats.

Adapting for Special Learners

When authoring a web site, attention to accessibility helps to make the site usable by the widest range of individuals. An accessible web site is designed in a consistent and logical manner that makes possible the use of physical supports, such as screen readers, alternatives to mouse control, or different browsers. Students with physical, cognitive, perceptual, hearing, or low-vision barriers are more able to navigate an accessible site without assistance. Although designing a fully accessible site can be technically demanding, there are a few simple guidelines that teachers and students can follow to make the site available to the widest possible audience. The Web Accessibility Initiative (WAI) of the World Wide Web Consortium (W3C) developed guidelines for accessible Web design. Key concepts from Web Content Accessibility Guidelines are summarized in the following discussion. Further information can be found on the WAI web site (**www.w3.org/wai**). The WAI site also provides a number of free or open source web accessibility evaluation tools that authors may use to test the accessibility of their pages.

For classroom use, teachers and students may wish to use a simple method to test for screen reader accessibility. The free browser Opera (**www.opera.com**) has features that allow one to view the page in an accessibility layout and to test for any images that may have missing or invalid ALT attributes, which would render information unusable by screen readers. Although other browsers also have this feature, it is easily accessed under the view menu, styles option in Opera.

Page Design

Following a few suggestions for consistent page organization structure makes it easier for individuals using magnification, screen readers, or handheld computers to find their place on the page, and is the best practice in web site design. Creating or using a template structure for each page helps to ensure this consistency. When designing each page, keep the screen uncluttered, and leave considerable space

(*text continues on page 269*)

CURRICULUM CONNECTIONS

African Safari

CONTENT AREA/TOPIC: Technology, Science
GRADE LEVELS: K–2, 3–5   **NETS·S:** 1, 3, 6

Description: Students become familiar with words that are common to Africa as well as research some of the wildlife that live there. Students can choose an animal of their own or research one from the list that is provided including a lion, tiger, cheetah, elephant, zebra, giraffe, or an alligator.

Teacher preparation: Teachers should divide the students into groups and download the page with questions that the students should discover during their research.

Active participation: Students research their animal to find answers to the questions provided by the quest. They are to find pictures of the animal too. They use the pictures and information from their research to create a poster. They, then, write a one-day journal as if they were the animal. The journal would tell the daily routines, activities, and adventures. Finally, the student writes a reflection about the activity. The posters are shared with the class.

Assessment: A downloadable rubric is included for grading.

Source: Celzo, C. (2007). Accessed May 8, 2009, from http://questgarden.com/47/75/0/070310184951/.

Folklore Creatures: Myth or Reality?

CONTENT AREA/TOPIC: English, Language Arts, Social Studies
GRADE LEVELS: 6–8   **NETS·S:** 3, 4, 6

Description: Students explore various folklore creatures and form opinions based on their research as to whether the creature exists. The creatures include the New Jersey Devil, Big Foot, Loch Ness monster, and the Abominable Snowman.

Teacher preparation: Teachers should review this entire project in order to be clear about the activity. Teachers should decide whether this project is best completed by placing the students in pairs, groups of three, or individually.

Active participation: Students take on the role of international researcher from a famous university. They select one of the creatures and complete research to form an opinion about its existence. Students use search engines to find sites and evidence to support their claim. They create a slideshow with at least five slides and make a three- to five-minute presentation.

Assessment: A rubric is provided for grading.

Source: Press, M. (2007). Accessed May 6, 2009, from http://questgarden.com/06/13/4/070302111225/.

History of Geometry

CONTENT AREA/TOPIC: Technology, Mathematics, Science, Social Studies, Language Arts, Visual Arts
GRADE LEVELS: 9–12   **NETS·S:** 3, 4, 6

Description: Students create a timeline outlining the evolution of geometry. The project is intended to show how geometry has helped the world throughout history.

Teacher preparation: The teacher divides the class into teams of four. The computer lab is scheduled for student research. The rubric is printed out for the students.

Active participation: The students research the history of geometry using links that the WebQuest provides to find information on how Ancient Egypt, Babylon, China and India, Greek (Classical and Hellenistic), Middle Ages, Islamic, 17th, 18th, and 19th centuries, and modern day–20th century to the present contributed to geometry.

Assessment: A rubric is provided for grading.

Source: Webster, D. (2007). Accessed May 6, 2009, from http://questgarden.com/43/63/4/070108070106/.

Voices *in the* Classroom

A Virtual Classroom That Is Smarter Than SMART Board

Paul Gigliotti

For the past 10 years, Paul Gigliotti has been igniting a passion for Social Studies and learning within his students through the use of educational technology. Paul Gigliotti retains a BS in history from Baldwin Wallace College, Berea, Ohio, as well as an MA in educational technology from Cleveland State University, Cleveland, Ohio. During his distinguished career he has been awarded the "Parent Teacher Association's Lifetime Achievement Award" in 2007 as well as the prestigious "Ohio Middle School Teacher of the Year Award" in 2008. Paul has been a featured speaker at the "National Council for the Social Studies" and at the "Ohio Middle School Association." As an Adjunct Professor, he has developed and taught a series of graduate courses in educational technology for Ashland University, Ashland, Ohio. Paul explains how his use of an extensive course web site, as well as a mimio interactive whiteboard, has greatly enhanced student performance within his classroom.

One of the greatest challenges today in education is how best to teach the 21st century student. Today's young people are uniquely "wired" having been reared in a world that has seen the blossoming of the Technology Revolution. Over the past several years, technology has transformed the world in a way that has not been experienced since the Industrial Revolution. While computers, cell phones, and the Internet might be new to some, 21st century students have known nothing else. Adolescent learners have grown up in a world full of technology that provides them with instant access to information, entertainment, and communication. Just like the advent of the factory changed manufacturing years ago, today's Technology Revolution must also change the way we look at effective teaching. In order to encourage 21st century student success, educators must do their best to adapt traditional teaching strategies to a new digital world.

It was based on this premise that I began to work on my course web site (**www.mrgigliotti.com**) nearly a decade ago. Since that time, mrgigliotti.com has evolved into a virtualized extension of my daily classroom. My class web site is designed to engage students in active learning by taking the traditional history being taught in the classroom out into the digital world to which my students are more accustom. The web site is a medium by which my students can master content knowledge within a multi-media digital framework rather than a dusty old book. It also permits the use of digital differentiation for students at various ability levels. When students log on to the web site, they have 24-hour-a-day access to a multitude of valuable classroom resources such as: class notes, review questions, grades, podcasts, interactive Internet-based assignments, mimio interactive whiteboard files, document and presentation downloads, wiki work spaces to collaborate on projects, a virtual agenda, contests, surveys, and even daily video of each class session. Most of all, my web site serves as an effective means by which to get students interested in course content and to become motivated learners. Today my web site receives thousands of hits from not only current students, but also past students, and even teachers and students from other schools across the country and around the world.

Over the years, many of my colleagues have approached me with a desire to create a web site for their classes and looking for advice. However, in those discussions my fellow teachers almost always identify two main reasons why they do not feel that they could create a similar class web site. Many teachers have told me that they lack the time and technical ability to digitize their courses. What many teachers do not realize, however, is that a web page does not have to be elaborate to be effective. There are always options for teachers to overcome those obstacles and to put content online for their students.

It is usually at this point in our conversation that I explain to them the very humble beginnings of my own web page and its decade-long evolution. When I started my site, I was a first-year teacher with little time and even less knowledge of Web design. My web site began as an awkward two-column, one-picture site with ads for all sorts of interesting products gleaming down the right-hand side of the screen. I had found a server willing to host educational web sites for free who provided a long and difficult-to-remember URL address as well as a basic text-only template where I would post daily assignments and class notes.

After a year or so, my desire to improve my web site and to make it a more valuable resource for students drove me to learn more and more about Web design, Web applications, and programming code

At the start of my third year of teaching I had learned enough to leave the confines of my text-only template.

(Continues)

Voices *in the* **Classroom** *Continued*

That summer, I purchased space on a server for $9.99 per month and registered my very own and easy-to-remember URL (**www.mrgigliotti.com**). I went to the college bookstore and with my graduate student discount I purchased a copy of Microsoft FrontPage. FrontPage was one of many Web design applications at the time that worked much like a word processor and that allowed you to build and publish a web page without knowing much about programming code. That summer, after extensive paper and pencil planning, I built and published my new and improved virtual History course.

Each year since that time, my web site has continued to see major changes and upgrades. I have continued to learn more about programming and applications so that I can keep up with the rapid changes occurring online. My web site has had to become more dynamic each year as the technology on the Internet becomes more interactive. In order to make my virtual content connect with students, I have had to add some of the latest Internet trends to my site. For example, a few years ago downloading music to MP3 players and iPods was all the rage within the schools. I knew that I could capitalize on that popularity, so I began to record my own podcasts that went over course material. Students began downloading my files before tests and studying using their trendy iPods instead of a notebook. That audio revolution only lasted a few years as new video sites such as YouTube began to capture the students' attention. The logical extension of my site, therefore, was to add my own Internet videos. Today there are three cameras within my classroom that record class content. Video of class each day is posted to my web site much like the video sites the students use at home. I have even recorded video at the Grand Canyon and the Alamo for my students.

Another major addition to my classroom and my web site has been my mimio interactive whiteboard. For years I had tried to use a SMART Board in my classroom with only minimal success. Then, at a conference I was introduced to a new Newell Rubbermaid product called "mimio," which turns any hard flat surface into an interactive surface. I took a mimio back to my classroom and began to use it with my students. It was not long before I was hooked. My mimio became the cornerstone of my class-wide instruction. My mimio functioned much like the SMART Board, only it is wireless, ultra portable, more reliable, and only cost about a third of the price. Now each day in class my mimio turns an old-fashioned dry erase board into an interactive surface that motivates and engages my students. My classroom instruction is now powered by my mimio Studio software that allows me use materials that I already had to create dynamic and engaging lessons. Those lessons are then saved and posted on my web site as just one more engaging strategy for connecting with high-tech students. It is clear that this interactive technology encourages learning and mimio's low price tag makes it a much smarter option for schools than other boards. Undoubtedly, as technology continues to advance, my web site will also continue to evolve. At the printing of this "Voice," the ability to hold live virtual courses that could be used as review sessions or for distance learning is currently on the drawing board.

My experience over the years has taught me that every teacher can and should establish a web site as a means by which to connect with their 21st century students. Teachers who are interested in virtualizing their courses can always find a way to get their materials online regardless of their technical skills. The first piece of advice that I give to teachers excited about starting their own web page is to plan, plan, and when they are done go plan some more. In our conversations, I always ask them to start off by envisioning what a class web site would include and what it would look like if they had no technical obstacles to overcome. I ask them to sketch out the type of design they would use and to include a list of desired content. Teachers can use this as a goal for where they would like to take their site. In the meantime, I ask them to assess their own technical abilities and other obstacles that might stand in their way in order to find a path to a virtual course that might work best for them. Unlike years ago, today there are numerous web page options available to teachers of all ability levels. The Technological Revolution that has changed our world must find its way into education in order to connect with 21st century learners, and a course web site is the best place to start.

around each item. When using color, avoid dark or brightly colored backgrounds and provide a high contrast in color between text and background (black text on a cream or yellow background is desirable; a bright red background with purple text is particularly unreadable and offensive to most). Avoid tile backgrounds; these can obscure the text. Beyond aesthetics, be considerate of people with color deficiencies. Color may be used for interest and attention, but should not be the only method of conveying information. The WAI website offers a number of online tools that simulate color combinations that are hard to discern. Vischeck (**www.vischeck.com**) offers a test for color blindness compatibility.

Images and Animations

To accommodate students with visual barriers, provide text descriptions of all images and animations. Most web site developers accomplish this by providing alternative (alt) text, which is read by screen reading software for each image. A second useful feature is to place the letter "d" next to each image. Hyperlink this letter to a text file that provides a description. This alternative approach is also useful for individuals who are working on older computers or slower Internet connections; they may set the browser's settings so that pictures do not automatically load, thereby increasing speed of access to the information.

Images are a powerful way to convey the meaning of the information, but they must be used wisely. Images that are clarifying for some individuals may be a nuisance for others. Accessibility guidelines use the term *eye candy* to describe images that are appealing but do not directly relate to the content. Pages with an excess of eye candy are confusing to those with cognitive impairments. They are also annoying to those using screen readers, who must wait for the description to be read and discern how or if it relates to the information presented. If using eye candy, recognize its purpose and do not provide a text description. To accommodate people who use screen readers exclusively, provide the option to link to the same page of text provided without images or animation.

Audio and Video

To accommodate individuals who are deaf, who are hearing impaired, or who have older computer equipment, find alternative methods for accessing the information conveyed by audio and video clips. Provide transcripts of audio and captioned descriptions of all video.

Although beyond the scope of this text, the National Center for Accessible Media (NCAM; part of the Corporation for Public Broadcasting and WGBH) has developed a program called the Media Access Generator (MAGpie) to assist developers in creating captions and audio descriptions for digital media. More information can be found at their web site, **http://ncam.wgbh.org/webaccess/ magpie/**.

Hyperlinks

Hyperlinks (hypertext links) should convey meaning when read out of context (not just "click here"). This convention makes the site more understandable for everyone, especially people using screen readers or students with cognitive barriers. Avoid placing more than one hyperlink on any one line.

Plug-in Features

If using plug-in features, such as a Flash program, provide alternative content for the information. Users then have a choice of access to the information. Some accessibility adaptations, such as screen readers, do not respond well to plug-ins, and their use on older machines can be problematic.

Charts and Graphs

Provide summaries of all charts and graphs. The summaries are useful if the information cannot be obtained otherwise. Some charts and graphs are hard to read or understand when using magnification, screen reading, or other personal access features.

Tables

Because most screen reading programs read horizontally across the page, tables need to read sensibly line by line. Provide a description of the table and summarize the information it contains. (For example, "This table charts the number of ice cream treats purchased by each grade at Miracle Elementary School and the type of ice cream (vanilla, chocolate, or other)." WAI guidelines recommend the use of tables only if the data needs to be presented in tabular form. Otherwise, use style sheets for controlling the layout and positioning of text and images on a page.

Titles

Write meaningful titles. This simple procedure makes navigation more convenient, accessible, and understandable for everyone.

Language Use

The wording of web sites should be very clear, without slang or jargon, to accommodate people whose first language is not English. Also, consider how someone from another region of the United States or other English-speaking countries might interpret the words. Write out all acronyms (such as Parent Teacher Student Organization for PTSO).

On the Web

This section includes only a snapshot of web sites that the authors recommend for viewing. To access live links and a larger and continuously updated collection of sites, go to the companion web site at **www.pearsonhighered.com/obannon2e**.

Assistive Technology

Color Blindness
http://vischeck.com
Vischeck offers links to a simulation of color combinations that are hard to discern by people with color blindness. This web site also provides a check for web site compatibility.

Media Access Generator (MAGpie)
http://ncam.wgbh.org
The Corporation for Public Broadcasting and WGBH National Center for Accessible Media (NCAM) has developed a program, called the Media Access Generator (MAGpie), to assist developers create captions and audio descriptions for digital media.

Sign Smith Studio
www.vcom3d.com/signsmith.php
Sign Smith Studio has been purchased by Vcom3D where you can find information about this product. This software translates English text into American Sign Language or Signed English files that can be incorporated into many different multimedia programs. Sign Smith Studio has been recently upgraded to 3.0. Read about the new features that have been added at the company blog.

World Wide Web Consortium (W3C)
www.w3.org
This International World Wide Web Consortium develops Web standards, and guidelines to promote long-term growth of the Web. Read about the activities of W3C at this page.

Free Software for Creating Websites

There are a number of free options for the creation of web pages. These Web-based tools no longer require technical skills as in the past. Such tools allow users to work in an environment similar to a word processor. Free options are great for the budget but are currently limited on features.

Google Sites
www.google.com/sites/help/intl/en/overview.html
Offered by Google, this free tool allows making and sharing a web site easy. There is no HTML necessary to create the page. Custom look. Try this new tool out. Examples are provided.

Moodle
http://moodle.org
Moodle is a Course Management System (CMS) that is similar to Blackboard with the exception that it is free. Web sites may be created in Moodle for use with students. Moodle contains a wiki.

Weebly
www.weebly.com
Weebly provides free domain hosting for building web sites with space limited to 5 MB. Space for 100 MG can be purchased at the rate of $2.99/month with a two-year subscription. This Web-based tool has a drag-and-drop interface and requires no technical skills. Many professional designs assist the creation of professional-looking web sites. A blog feature allows teachers to communicate with parents and students.

Cool Classroom Sites

Classroom Site: Molecules in Motion
www.jsriley.com/ASFS_RM_149/ASFS_index.php
Travel to Molecules in Motion, hosted by kindergarten teacher Jeffery Riley at Arlington Science Focus School, to see ways that teachers can use the Web to communicate what's happening in their classes. A link to a student section is offered as well. At this site, a classroom blog offers insight into what is happening in this classroom with young learners.

Mr. Leahy's Class
www.beavton.k12.or.us/jacob_wismer/leahy/leahy.htm
This exemplary, award-winning classroom site, developed and maintained by fourth-grade teacher and technology facilitator Dave Leahy, spotlights student projects, featured pages, as well as suggested curriculum links.

Mrs. Nelson's Class
www.mrsnelsonsclass.com/home.aspx
This kindergarten teacher's site is full of great information for her students, parents, teachers, and other visitors. There are curriculum units, an ongoing section for teacher resources, classroom news and page that bios this outstanding teacher. The resource categories include Literacy Centers, Play Centers, Class Management, Themes and Units and teaching resources. It's not wonder that this teacher's site has captured numerous awards.

Mr. Smith's 5th Grade
http://mclean.usd259.org/smith/links.htm
Visit this unique classroom site developed at a Science Technology Magnet Elementary School in Kansas. The classroom site has been featured at Eduhound and is truly a wonderful example of teachers and students in action. There are archives at this site as well as features that include four major sections for news, pictures, students, and links.

Web Design and Usability

Jacob Nielsen's Top Ten Mistakes in Web Design
www.useit.com/alertbox/9605.html
This well-known expert on usability shares design mistakes that are common, yet disasterous, for the user.

Usability.gov
http://usability.gov
This web site, sponsored by the U.S. Department of Health and Human Services, offers links to information on Web accessibility and resources for Web authoring.

Key Terms

Usability (249)
Planning process (249)
Development process (249)
Web page (250)
HTML (HyperText Markup
   Language) (250)
Server (250)
URL (Uniform Resource Locator) (250)
Web site (250)
Homepage (250)
WYSIWYG (253)
Folder structure (254)
Directories (254)
Root folder (254)
Universal homepage (254)

Project folder (254)
Naming the files (255)
File extension (255)
Text (255)
Tables (255)
Cell padding (256)
Cell spacing (256)
Nested table (256)
Hyperlink (256)
Internal (relative) links (256)
External (absolute) links (256)
Anchor links (256)
Email links (256)
Image (256)
Site interface (257)

Navigation system (258)
Dead-end or orphaned page (258)
Site design (258)
Index (table of contents) (258)
Paper prototype or storyboard (258)
Hierarchy (259)
Typeface (259)
Typestyles (260)
Type size (260)
Line spacing (leading) (260)
Web-based applications (260)
Alternative text (261)
Google Sites (262)

Hands-on Activities for Learning

1. Visit the companion web site (**www.pearsonhighered.com/ obannon2e**) and review the sites available.

2. Write a reflection in your reflective technology blog about how you plan to use a classroom site with the target population that you will be teaching.

3. Move through each of the steps described in the chapter to plan the classroom web site for your classroom. What is the purpose of your web site? Who is the target audience? What are your major goals?

4. Create a storyboard for a classroom site that you will develop as part of your study. The storyboard should show a homepage, major section pages, and subsection pages. The navigation for the site should be indicated by arrows.

5. Using the storyboard, create a web site for your classroom using the suggestions from this chapter. If you are a teacher in preparation, your site can be modified during your student teaching experience or your internship year. During this creation, jot down lessons learned and discuss these with classmates and your instructor or mentor teachers.

6. In your classroom site, create a homepage that will serve as the entry point. Be sure that your homepage contains an index that provides easy navigation to the major sections of the site as well as a summary of the site that identifies the information that is found there. The summary should welcome visitors to the page and tell them what they are going to find there.

7. In your classroom site, create a "teacher bio" page that presents professional information about you. This might be information such as your educational institutions, special skills that might be of interest such as "highly motivated to use technology to enhance learning," professional organizations, as well as a personal snapshot of hobbies, pets, family, etc. Look at some examples that other teachers have written. Since this will be on the Web, carefully consider information that you want to share. The information will be accessed by future students and their parents as well as teachers, employers, anyone! Keep the information professional as you move toward a teaching career.

8. In your classroom site, create a Resource page that holds curriculum resources for your students/future students. Include at least three sections: one for search tools that are appropriate for the target population that you will be working with; one for curriculum links for your target population such as Math, or Science for the secondary teachers, and a variety for the elementary teachers such as Math, Science, Language Arts, Social Studies; and one for WebQuests that would be appropriate for your target population. Creating a collaborative page with your peers in your area of certification will reap additional great sites for all. Each of the sites should be annotated to let visitors (students, parents, other teachers) know what is found at the site.

References

Agosta, E., Graetz, J., Mastropieri, M., and Scruggs, T. (2004). Teacher-researcher partnership to improve social behavior through social stories. *Intervention in School and Clinic, 39*(5), pp. 276–287.

Albrecht, B., and Davis, P. (2000). Elemental, my dear Holmes, elemental. *Learning and Leading with Technology, 27*(8), pp. 22–27.

Alliance for Technology Access (2004). *Computer resources for people with disabilities.* Petaluma, CA: Alliance for Technology Access.

Anderson-Inman, L., Knox-Quinn, C., and Horney, M. (1996). Computer-based study strategies for students with learning disabilities: Individual differences associated with adoption level. *Journal of Learning Disabilities, 29*, pp. 461–484.

Anderson, K., and Anderson, C. (2001). Using software to help visualize mathematical processes. *Special Education Technology Practice, 3*(2), pp. 13–18.

Anderson, L. W., and Krathwohl, D. R. (2001). A taxonomy for learning, teaching, and assessing: A revision of Bloom's taxonomy of educational objectives. New York: Longman.

Anglin, G., Vaez, H., and Cunningham, K. (2004). Visual representations and learning: The role of static and animated graphics. In D. H. Jonassen (Ed.), *Handbook of research for educational communications and technology* (2nd ed.). Mahwah, NJ: Lawrence Erlbaum Associates.

Ausubel, D. (1963). *The psychology of meaningful verbal learning.* New York: Grune and Stratton.

Bangert-Drowns, R. (1993). The word processor as an instructional tool: A meta-analysis of word processing in writing instruction. *Review of Educational Research, 63*(1), pp. 69–93.

Barrett, H. (2000). *Electronic portfolios—multimedia development and portfolio development: The electronic portfolio development process.* Accessed in June 2005 from http://electronicportfolios.org/portfolios/EPDevProcess.html#stage3.

Barrett, H. (2005). *Researching electronic portfolios and learner engagement.* White Paper produced for TaskStream, Inc., as part of the REFLECT Initiative. Accessed July 7, 2009, from http://electronicportfolios.org/reflect/whitepaper.pdf.

Barry, N., and Shannon, D. (1997). Portfolios in teacher education: A matter of perspective. *The Educational Forum, 61*(4), pp. 320–328.

Bayraktar, S. (2001). A meta-analysis of the effectiveness of computer-assisted instruction in science education. *Journal of Research on Technology in Education, 34*, p. 173+.

Becker, H. (1994). How exemplary computer using teachers differ from other teachers: Implications for realizing the potential of computers in schools. *Journal of Research on Computing in Education, 26*(3), pp. 291–321.

Bitter, G., and Pierson, M. (2002). *Using technology in the classroom* (5th edition). Boston: Allyn & Bacon.

Blickensderfer, R. (1990). Learning chemical kinetics with spreadsheets. *Journal of Computers in Mathematics and Science Teaching, 9*(4), pp. 35–43.

Bottge, B., Heinrichs, M., and Chan, S. (2003). Effects of video-based and applied problems on the procedural math skills of average- and low-achieving adolescents. *Journal of Special Education Technology, 18*(2), pp. 5–22.

Brozo, W., and Puckett, K. (2009). *Supporting content area literacy with technology.* Boston: Allyn & Bacon.

Bulgren, J., Schumaker, J. B., and Deschler, D. D. (1988). Effectiveness of a concept teaching routine in enhancing the performance of LD students in secondary-level mainstream classes. *Learning Disability Quarterly, 11*(1), pp. 3–17.

Campbell, D. M., Melenyzer, B. J., Nettles, D. H., and Wyman, R. M. (2000). *Portfolios and performance assessment.* Boston: Allyn & Bacon.

Center for Applied Special Technology and LD OnLine (2007). *Accessible Textbooks: A Guide for Parents of Children with Learning Disabilities.* Accessed on May 14, 2009, from www.ldonline.org/article/16308.

Christmann, E., Lucking, R., and Badgett, J. (1997). The effectiveness of computer-assisted instruction on the academic achievement of secondary students: A meta-analysis comparison between urban, suburban, and rural educational settings. *Computers in the Schools, 13*(3/4), pp. 31–40.

Clark, R. (1985). Evidence for confounding in computer-based instruction studies: Analyzing the meta-analyses. *Educational Communications and Technology Journal, 33*(4), pp. 249–262.

Cognition and Technology Group at Vanderbilt. (1990). Anchored instruction and its relationship to situated cognition. *Educational Researcher, 19*(6), pp. 2–10.

Collis, B. (1990). *The best of research windows: Trends and issues in educational computing.* Eugene, OR: International Society for Technology in Education (ERIC document Reproduction No. ED 323 993).

Costantino, P., and De Lorenzo, M. (2002). *Developing a professional teaching portfolio: A guide for success.* Boston: Allyn & Bacon.

Council for Exceptional Children (2000). *Making assessment accommodations: A toolkit for teachers.* Alexandria, VA: Council for Exceptional Children.

Cuban, L. (2001). *Oversold and underused.* Boston: Harvard University Press.

Cullen, J., Richards, S. B., and Lawless-Frank, C. (2008). Using software to enhance the writing skills of students with special needs. *Journal of Special Education Technology, 23*(2), pp. 33–43.

Day, S. L., and Edwards, B. J. (1996). Assistive technology for postsecondary students with learning disabilities. *Journal of Learning Disabilities, 29,* pp. 486–492.

Dean, R. S., and Kulhavy, R. W. (1981). The influence of spatial organization in prose learning. *Journal of Educational Psychology, 73*(1), pp. 57–64.

Dewey, J. (1933). *How we think: A restatement of the relations of reflective thinking to the educative process* (2nd rev. ed.). Boston: D.C. Heath.

Duffy, P., and Bruns, A. (2006). The use of blogs, wikis and RSS in education: A conversation of possibilities. Proceedings of the Online Learning and Teaching Conference 2006, Brisbane: September 26. Retrieved July, 2008 from https://olt.qut.edu.au/udf/OLT2006/gen/static/papers/Duffy_OLT2006_paper.pdf.

Dye, G. A. (2000). Graphic organizers to the rescue? Help students link and remember information. *Teaching Exceptional Children, 32*(3), pp. 72–76.

Edwards, N., and Bitter, G. (1989). Teaching mathematics with technology: Changing variables using spreadsheet templates. *The Arithmetic Teacher, 37*(2), pp. 40–45.

Edyburn, D. (2000). Assistive technology and students with mild disabilities. *Focus on Exceptional Children, 32*(9): 1–23.

Edyburn, D. (2002). Cognitive-rescaling strategies: Interventions that alter the cognitive accessibility of text. *Closing the Gap, 21*(6), pp. 1, 10–11, 21.

Edyburn, D. (2003). Rethinking assistive technology. *Special Education Technology Practice, 5*(4), pp. 16–22.

Ehman, L., Glenn, A., Johnson, V., and White, C. (1992). Using computer databases in student problem solving: A study of eight social studies teachers' classrooms. *Theory and Research in Social Education, 20*(2), pp. 179–206.

Fletcher-Flinn, C., and Gravatt, B. (1995). The efficacy of computer-assisted instruction (CAI): A meta-analysis. *Journal of Educational Computing Research, 12*(3), pp. 219–241.

Frazier, M., and Bailey, G.D. (2004). *The technology coordinator's handbook.* Eugene, OR: International Society for Technology in Education.

Fry, E. B. (1977). Fry's readability graph: Clarifications, validity, and extensions to level 17. *Journal of Reading, 21,* pp. 242–252.

Fulton, W. (2005). *A few scanning tips.* Accessed on May 14, 2009, from www.scantips.com.

Gardill, M. C., and Jitendra, A. K. (1999). Advanced story map instruction: Effects on the reading comprehension of students with learning disabilities. *The Journal of Special Education, 33*(1), pp. 2–17.

Guillaume, A. M., and Yopp, H. K. (1995). Professional portfolios for student teachers. *Teacher Education Quarterly, 22*(1), pp. 93–101.

Hall, T., Strangman, N., and Meyer, A. (2003). *Differentiated instruction and implications for UDL implementation.* Wakefield, MA: National Center on Accessing the General Curriculum. Retrieved April 13, 2009, from www.cast.org/publications/ncac/ncac_diffinstructudl.html.

Hawisher, G. (1987). The effects of word processing on the revision strategies of college students. *Research in the Teaching of English, 21*(2), pp. 145–159.

Hawisher, G. (1989). Research and recommendations for computers and compositions. In G. Hawisher and C. Selfe (Eds.), *Critical perspectives on computers and composition instructions.* New York: Teachers College Press.

Heaviside, S., Riggins, T., and Farris, E. (1997). *Advanced telecommunications in U.S. public elementary and secondary schools, fall 1996* (NCES 97-944). U.S. Department of Education, National Center for Education Statistics. Washington, DC: U.S. Government Printing Office.

Hetzroni, O., and Shrieber, B. (2004). Word processing as an assistive technology tool for enhancing academic outcomes of students with writing disabilities in the general classroom. *Journal of Learning Disabilities, 37*(2), pp. 143–154.

Hollis, R. (1990). Database yearbooks in the second grade. *The Computing Teacher, 17*(6), pp. 14–15.

Horton, S. (2006). Access by design: A guide to universal usability for web designers. Berkeley, CA: New Riders.

House, J. D., Hurst, R. S., and Keeley, E. J. (1996). Relationship between learner attitudes, prior achievement, and performance in a general education course: A multiinstitutional study. *International Journal of Instructional Media, 12*(3), pp. 257–271.

Individuals with Disabilities Education Act Amendments of 2004, P.L. 108–446.

Inspiration (2002). *Achieving standards with Inspiration 7: Curriculum-aligned lessons for inspired learning.* Portland, OR: Inspiration Software.

Inspiration Software, Inc. (2006). *Visual thinking and learning.* Accessed May 14, 2009, from www.inspiration.com/Parents/Visual-Thinking-and-Learning.

Institute for the Advancement of Research in Education. (2003). *Graphic organizers: A review of scientifically based research.* Accessed May 14, 2009, from www.inspiration.com/sites/default/files/documents/Detailed-Summary.pdf.

Internet World Stats. (2008). *World Internet users and population statistics.* Available at www.internetworldstats.com/stats.htm.

ISTE. (2007). *National Education Technology Standards for Teachers: Preparing to use technology.* Eugene, OR: Author.

Jankowski, L. (1994). Getting started with databases. *The Computing Teacher, 21*(4), pp. 8–9.

Johnson, A. P. (2000). It's time for Madeline Hunter to go: A new look at lesson plan design. *Action in Teacher Education, 22*(1), pp. 72–78.

Jonassen, D. H. (1996). *Computers in the classroom: Mindtools for critical thinking.* Upper Saddle River, NJ: Prentice Hall.

Jonassen, D. H. (2000). *Computers as mindtools for schools: Engaging critical thinking* (2nd ed.). Upper Saddle River, NJ: Merrill.

Kelly, M. G. (Ed.). (2002). *National Education Technology Standards for Teachers. Preparing Teachers to Use Technology.* Eugene, OR: ISTE.

Kilbane, C., and Milman, N. (2003). *The digital teaching portfolio handbook: A how-to guide for educators.* Boston: Allyn & Bacon.

Kleiner, A., and Farris, E. (2002). *Internet access in U.S. public school and classrooms: 1994–2001* (NCES 2002-028). U.S. Department of Education, National Center for Education Statistics. Washington, DC: U.S. Government Printing Office.

Kukik, C., and Kukik, J. (1991). Effectiveness of computer-based instruction: An updated analysis. *Computers in Human Behavior, 7*(1–2), pp. 75–94.

Lake, D. (2004a). *Using Microsoft Word like a pro, part 1.* Accessed on September 28, 2008, from www.techlearning.com/story/showArticle.php?articleID=18902829.

Lake, D. (2004b). *Using Microsoft Word like a pro, part 6.* Accessed on September 28, 2008, from www.techlearning.com/story/showArticle.php?articleID=45400086.

Lamb, B. (2004c). Wide open spaces: Wikis, ready or not. *EDUCAUSE Review, 39*(5) (September/October), 36–48. Retrieved May 14, 2009, from www.educause.edu/EDUCAUSE+Review/EDUCAUSEReviewMagazineVolume39/WideOpenSpacesWikisReadyorNot/157925.

Lerman, J. (2006). *101 best web sites for teacher tools and professional development.* Eugene, OR: International Society for Technology in Education.

Levie, W. H., and Lentz, R. (1982). Effects of text illustrations: A review of research. *Educational Communications and Technology Journal, 30*(4), pp. 195–232.

Lewis, P. (2001). *Spreadsheet magic.* Eugene, OR: ISTE.

Lewis, P. (2002). Spreadsheet magic. *Learning and Leading with Technology, 30*(3), pp. 36–41.

Lewis, R. B. (1998). Assistive technology and learning disabilities: Today's realities and tomorrow's promises. *Journal of Learning Disabilities, 31,* pp. 16–26.

Lewis, R. B., Ashton, T., Haapa, B., Kieley, C., and Fielden, C. (1999). Improving the writing skills of students with learning disabilities: Are word processors with spelling and grammar checks useful? *Learning Disabilities: A Multidisciplinary Journal, 9,* pp. 87–98.

Lieberman, D. A., and Rueter, J. (1997). The electronically augmented teaching portfolio. In P. Selkin (Ed.), *The teaching portfolio: A practical guide for improved performance and promotion/tenure decisions* (2nd ed.) (pp. 47–57). Boston: Anker.

Lockard, J., and Abrams, P. (2003). *Computers for twenty-first century educators.* Boston: Allyn & Bacon.

Lynch, P., and Horton, S. (2009). *Web style guide: Basic design principles for creating web sites* (3rd ed.). New Haven: Yale University Press.

MacArthur, C. (1998). Word processing with speech synthesis and word prediction: Effects on the dialogue journal writing of students with learning disabilities. *Learning Disability Quarterly, 21*(2), pp. 151–166.

Mader, S. (2008). *The state of wikis in education.* Retrieved October, 2008 from www.ikiw.org/2008/04/10/interview-the-state-of-wikis-in-education.

Male, M. (2003). *Technology for inclusion: Meeting the special needs of all students.* Boston: Allyn & Bacon.

McBer, H. (June, 2000). Research into teacher effectiveness: A model of teacher effectiveness. In: Report by Hay McBer to the Department for Education and Employment. London. Available online www.teachernet.gov./uk/teacherinengland/detail.cfm?id:521.

Miller, M. (2002). *Using the Internet and the Web.* Indianapolis: Que.

Misovich, M., and Biasca, K. (1990). The power of spreadsheets in a mass and energy balance course. *Chemical Engineering Education, 24,* pp. 46–50.

Mittler, J., and Heiman, B. (2005). The Individuals with Disabilities Education Improvement Act of 2004 and assistive tech. *TAM Connector* (February–March), pp. 1–4.

Moore, M., Burton, J., & Myers, R. (2004). Multiple-channel communication: The theoretical and research foundations of multimedia. In D. Jonassen (Ed.) *Handbook of Research on Educational Communications and Technology* (2nd ed.) (pp. 536, 979–1005). Mahwah, NJ: Lawrence Erlbaum Associates, Inc.

Morrison, G., Ross, S., and Kemp, J. (2007). *Designing effective instruction* (5th ed.). Hoboken, NJ: Wiley/Jossey-Bass.

Moursund, D., and Bielefeldt, T. (1999). *Will new teachers be prepared to teach in the digital age: A national survey of information technology in teacher education.* Santa Monica, CA: Milken Exchange on Information Technology.

NCTI and CITEd (2007). *TECHMATRIX.* Accessed on September 16, 2008, from www.techmatrix.org/index.aspx.

National Center for Educational Statistics (2005). Internet access in U.S. public schools and classrooms: 1994–2003. Available at www.nces.ed.gov/pubsearch/pubsinfo.asp/pubid=2005015.

National Center for Educational Statistics (2008). Accessed on May 14, 2009 from http://nces.ed.gov.

National Center for Educational Statistics, U.S. Dept. of Education. (1999). *Teacher quality: A report on the preparation and qualifications of public school teachers.* Washington, DC. NCES 1999-80 (January). Retrieved January 18, 2004, from nces.ed.gov/pubs99/1999080.pdf.

National Center for Educational Statistics, U.S. Dept. of Education. (2001). Teacher preparation and professional development. Washington, DC. NCES 2001-088 (June). Retrieved January 18, 2004, from www.nces.ed.gov/pubs2001/2001088.pdf.

National Education Association and American Federation of Teachers. (2008). Access, adequacy, and equity in education technology: Results of a survey of America's teachers and support professionals on technology in public schools and classrooms. Washington, DC: Author.

National Instructional Materials Accessibility Standard (NIMAS) Report, version 1.0 (2005). Accessed June 23, 2005, from nimas.cast.org/about/report/index.html#2techpanelb.

National Library Service. (1996). Copyright law amendment, 1996: Public Law 104–197. National Library Service for the Blind and Physically Handicapped (NLS). www.loc.gov/nls/reference/factsheets/copyright.html.

Nolet, V., and McLaughlin, M. (2005). Accessing the general curriculum: Including students with disabilities in standards-based reform (2nd ed.). Thousand Oaks, CA: Corwin.

Owston, R. D., and Wideman, H. H. (1997). Word processing and children's writing in a high computer access setting. *Journal of Research on Computing in Education, 30*(2), pp. 202–220.

Panel on Educational Technology, President's Committee of Advisors on Science and Technology (1997). Report to the president on the use of technology to strengthen K–12 education in the United States. Accessed on May 14, 2009, from www.ostp.gov/cs/report_to_the_president_on_federal_energy_research_and_development.

Parker, J., and Widmer, C. (1991). Teaching mathematics with technology: How big is a million? *Arithmetic Teacher, 39*(1), pp. 38–41.

Parsad, B., and Jones, J. (2005). *Internet Access in U.S. Public Schools and Classrooms 1994–2003*. (NCES 2005–015). U.S. Department of Education, National Center for Education Statistics. Washington, DC: U.S. Government Printing Office.

Peeck, J. (1987). The role of illustrations in processing and remembering illustrated texts. In D. M. Willows and H. A. Houghton (Eds.), *The psychology of illustration: Volume 1, Basic Research* (pp. 114–151). New York: Springer-Verlag.

Pinter-Lucke, C. (1992) Rootfinding with a spreadsheet in pre-calculus. *Journal of Computers in Mathematics and Science Teaching, 11*(1), pp. 85–93.

Puckett, K., and Brozo, W. (2004). Using assistive technology to teach content area literacy for students with disabilities. *College Reading Association Yearbook, 26*, 462–479.

Rakow, S. J. (1999). Involving classroom teachers in the assessment of preservice intern portfolios. *Action in Teacher Education, 21*(1), pp. 108–115.

Rawitch, D. (1988). The effects of computer use and student work style on database analysis activities in the social studies. In *Improving the Use of Technology in Schools: What Are We Learning?* Research Bulletin #1. St. Paul, MN: MECC.

Richardson, W. (2006). Blogs, wikis, podcasts, and other powerful Web tools for classrooms. Thousand Oaks, CA: Corwin.

Rieber, L. P. (1990). Animation in computer-based instruction. *Educational Technology Research and Development, 38*(1), pp. 77–86.

Rieth, H., Bryant, D., and Kinzer, C. (2003). An analysis of the impact of anchored instruction on teaching and learning activities in two ninth-grade language arts classes. *Remedial and Special Education, 24*(3), pp. 173–184.

Roblyer, M. D. (2003). *Integrating technology into teaching* (3rd ed.). Columbus, OH: Merrill.

Rose, D. H., and Meyer, A. (2002). *Teaching every student in the digital age: Universal design for learning.* Alexandria, VA: Association for Supervisors of Curriculum Development. www.cast.org/teachingeverystudent.

Sandholtz, J. H., Ringstaff, C., and Dwyer, D. C. (1997). *Teaching with technology: Creating student-centered classrooms.* New York: Teachers College Press.

Sardo-Brown, D. S. (1988). Twelve middle-school teachers' planning. *The Elementary School Journal, 89*(1), pp. 69–87.

Schacter, J. (1999). The impact of educational technology on student achievement: What the most current research has to say. The Milken Foundation (Editors). Available at: www.mff.org/publications/publications.taf?page=161.

Sgroi, Richard J. (1992). Systematizing trial and error using spreadsheets. *Arithmetic Teacher, 39*(7), pp. 8–12.

Sharp, V. (2000). *Make it with Inspiration.* Eugene, OR: ISTE.

Shelly, G., Cashman, T., and Gunter, G. (2004). *Teachers discovering computers: Timeline 2004. Integrating technology in the classroom.* Boston: Thompson.

Sherman, T. M. (1988). A brief review of developments in problem solving. *Computers in the Schools, 4*(3–4), pp. 7–16.

Slater, J. (2002). A pictorial approach for improving literacy skills in students with disabilities: An exploratory research study. *Journal of Special Education Technology, 17*(3), pp. 58–62.

Smaldino, S. E., Lowther, D. L., and Russell, J. D. (2008). *Instructional technology and media for learning.* Upper Saddle Creek, NJ: Pearson Merrill/Prentice Hall.

Smith, G., and Throne, S. (2007). *Differentiating instruction with technology in K–5 classrooms.* Eugene, OR: ISTE.

Snyder, I. (1993). Writing with word processors: A research overview. *Educational Research, 35*(1), pp. 49–68.

Soloman, G., and Schrum, L. (2007). *Web. 2.0: New tools, new schools.* Eugene, OR: ISTE.

Stahl, S. (2004). *The promise of accessible textbooks: Increased achievement for all students.* National Center on Accessing the General Curriculum. Accessed June 9, 2005, from www.k8accesscenter.org/training_resources/udl/Accessible-textbooksHTML.asp.

Stragman, N., Hall, T., and Meyer, A. (2004). Background knowledge instruction and the implications for UDL implementation. National Center on Accessing the General Curriculum. Accessed June 7, 2005, from www.cast.org/publications/ncac/ncac_backknowledgeudl.html.

Tech Learning (n.d.). *How to: Cool tools.* Accessed on September 26, 2008, from www.techlearning.com/outlook/columns/howto.php.

Technology Counts. (2007). A digital decade, editorial projects in Education Research Center, *Education Week.*

Technology Counts State Reports (2009). Retrieved April 1, 2009, from www.edweek.org/ew/marketplace/products/tc2009-str.html.

Tomlinson, C. A. (2000). *Differentiation of instruction in the elementary grades.* (ERIC Document Reproduction service no. ED443572).

U.S. Department of Education. (1991). *America 2000: An educational strategy sourcebook.* Washington, DC.

Verderber, N. L. (1990). Spreadsheets and problem solving with AppleWorks in mathematics teaching. *Journal of Computers in Mathematics and Science Teaching, 30*(3), pp. 45–51.

Vockell, E., and van Deusen, R. M. (1989). *The computer and higher-order thinking skills.* Watsonville, CA: Mitchell Publishing, Inc.

Walser, P. (2004). Handheld computers in special education. *Closing the Gap, 23*(2), pp. 1–4.

Walsh, F. M. (1992). Planning behaviors of distinguished and award-winning high school teachers. Unpublished doctoral dissertation. Pullman, WA: Washington State University.

Wells, J., and Lewis, L. (2006). *Internet access in U.S. public schools and classrooms 1994–2005.* (NCES, 2007-020). U.S. Department of Education, National Center for Education Statistics. Washington, DC: U.S. Government Printing Office.

Whitmer, J. C. (1990). Modeling the Milky Way: Spreadsheet science. *Science Teacher, 57*(7), pp. 19–21.

Williams, R., and Tollett, J. (2006). *The non-designer's web book,* 3rd ed. Berkeley, CA: Peachpit.

Winn, W., and Holiday, W. (1982). Design principles for diagrams and charts. In D. Johnassen (Ed.), *The technology of text, Vol. 1* (pp. 277–299). Englewood Cliffs, NJ: Educational Technology Publications.

Wolcott, L. L. (1994). Understanding how teachers plan: Strategies for successful instructional partnerships. *School Library Media Quarterly, 22*(3), pp. 161–165.

Zabala, J. S. (1995). *The SETT framework: critical areas to consider when making informed assisitive technology decisions.* Houston, TX: Region IV Education Service Center (ERIC Document Reproduction service no. ED 381962).

Index

Page numbers followed by an f or t indicate a figure or a table.